D0401465

TV Finales
FAQ

TV Finales FAQ

All That's Left to Know About the Endings of Your Favorite TV Shows

Stephen Tropiano and Holly Van Buren

HARRISON
APR 2016
MEMORIAL
LIBRARY

APPLAUSE
THEATRE & CINEMA BOOKS

An Imprint of Hal Leonard Corporation

Copyright © 2015 by Stephen Tropiano and Holly Van Buren

All rights reserved. No part of this book may be reproduced in any form, without written permission, except by a newspaper or magazine reviewer who wishes to quote brief passages in connection with a review.

Published in 2015 by Applause Books
An Imprint of Hal Leonard Corporation
7777 West Bluemound Road
Milwaukee, WI 53213

Trade Book Division Editorial Offices
33 Plymouth St., Montclair, NJ 07042

The FAQ series was conceived by Robert Rodriguez and developed with Stuart Shea.

Printed in the United States of America

Book design by Snow Creative Services

Library of Congress Cataloging-in-Publication Data

Tropiano, Stephen.
    TV finales FAQ : all that's left to know about the endings of your favorite TV shows
/ Stephen Tropiano and Holly Van Buren.
      pages cm
    ISBN 978-1-4803-9144-4
  1. Television programs—United States—Miscellanea. I. Van Buren, Holly II. Title.
    PN1992.3.U5T725 2015
    791.45'75—dc23
                                                                          2015030432

www.applausebooks.com

HVB: For Michael and Sam, "I love you and I like you"
ST: For Steven, "Ditto"

Contents

Part 6: The Best TV Series Finales

Introduction

When *Entertainment Weekly* asked *Murphy Brown* creator Diane English to describe the process of writing a series finale, she simply said: "It's daunting." For years, television writers build an entire universe, putting each week together brick by brick in half-hour or hour installments. Fans grow to love their favorite television shows, welcoming their characters into their lives (and their living rooms). Even in the age of binge-watching—streaming episode after episode in rapid succession—avid television watchers can grow deeply attached to a series. When the end is near, fans (and critics alike) cling to the last remaining morsels of their favorite television show—savoring each moment before the final credits roll.

But for show runners like Diane English, however, the anticipation of a show's final moments can feel like a monumental task. After all, when you are applauded time and time again for surprising audiences with cleverly orchestrated plot twists, or for tugging at the heartstrings repeatedly, the expectations for the final episode can feel sky high. But for David Crane, co-creator (with Marta Kauffman) of *Friends*, it is the existence of those very expectations that tell you how meaningful your series has been. "If any show runner is complaining that people care too much, they're in the wrong business," Crane said. "'It's unfair how much they care about my show!' Oh that's a high-class problem!"

In this book we dissect those very "high-class" problems suffered by some of television's top writers. From the series finales that pleasantly surprised us, to those most notable for their head-scratching endings, this book provides insight into how a series finale came to be: from the beginning stages of the show's inception, to its success along the way, and then, lastly, to its final broadcast.

In part 1, "America Tunes In: The Most Watched TV Series Finales," we dissect the final episodes that grace the history books as ratings juggernauts. Beginning with what is arguably the first television series finale as we have come to know them (*The Fugitive*'s 1967 stunning "one-armed man" conclusion), and then counting down from the top spot (*M*A*S*H*'s 1983 swansong still remains tops after more than thirty years), this section aims to break down just what made these finales attract those record-breaking audiences, and how those same episodes stand up today.

In part 2, "WTF? Series Finales That Left Us Scratching Our Heads," we dig deeply into those finales that failed to meet our expectations—or simply left us breathless in their odd plot decisions. From *St. Elsewhere*'s snow globe ending, to *Roseanne*'s year in the basement, not to be outdone by David Chase's infamous cut to black on HBO's *The Sopranos*, this section attempts to piece together why these successful series opted to use their final moments to baffle their audience.

In part 3, "Flash Forward: Finales Jump to the Future," we focus on finales that take their characters to the future, sometimes to fulfill their destinies and other times out of mere necessity (namely those with actors desperately clinging to the title of "teen"). These finales, which were met with both praise and disappointment, utilize a frequently employed time-shifting device in order to hurry up and end the show. Each serves as an example of just how that device works when put to use, both good and bad.

In part 4, "All Talked Out: Daytime and Late Night Television," we include the final bows of television's most prolific contributors: those that grace our television screens every day and every night. From the soap operas that span decades, to the talk show hosts that just can't put down the microphone or step away from their desk, this section details how and why each of these series comes to a close. Spending that much time on air presents unique challenges in mustering up a goodbye—some even required multi-day affairs, such as Oprah Winfrey's three-day spectacular.

In part 5, "Saying Goodbye," we look at the series finales that presented their main characters with only one choice: close up shop and move on. From *Frasier*'s sign off to *The Office*'s documentary finally reaching the air, series finales can close the book definitively—offering fans the opportunity to have full and complete closure. In the case of *Sex and the City*, in which Carrie says goodbye to single life, sometimes the series finale that feels the most final can indeed find a second life.

In the final section, part 6, "The Best TV Series Finales," we examine those that made the greatest impression—almost immediately finding their place in television history. While perhaps not the highest rated in terms of audience, these finales rank highest in our minds in terms of satisfying fans and critics while also raising the bar for future series finales. Presented in this chapter in chronological order, these finales left indelible marks on television history, some departing nearly forty years ago, while others are just barely off the air. In addition, we have included an appendix that outlines additional series finales episodes that warrant a second look.

It almost goes without saying that this book is chock full of spoilers. Within each chapter we detail the events of the series finale, drawing back on episodes from each show's past to indicate important moments. If you are planning a marathon of any of these programs—hoping to maintain some level of surprise on how it all ends—we ask that you sit down, make some popcorn, binge watch the entire series, and then read on without any possibilities of spoilers. After all, we love television and the journey each series takes you on—we wrote a whole book about it!

For their guidance and patience with this project, we wish to thank our agent, June Clark, and, at Applause Books, Marybeth Keating; Jessica Burr, who first suggested a book on series finales; and Bernadette Malavarca for her expertise, patience, and support with this project. We'd also like to thank our friends, families, and colleagues for their support and love during the many hours spent at the computer, sifting through countless television reviews and episodes (even if that sometimes meant hanging with us on the couch as we did the exhausting research of watching the greatest television series of all time). We'd like to especially thank Steven Ginsberg, Faith Ginsberg, Michael and Sam Van Buren, Emil and Marilyn Pietromonaco, Linda, Rick and Elizabeth Van Buren, the Spirocostas and Mele families, Jenny Jediny, Adam Zax, Joe Fazzio, Jon Bassinger-Flores, Jackie Paul, and, of course, our beloved Rosie and Lottie.

Stephen Tropiano   Holly Van Buren
Los Angeles, California   New York, New York

This project was made possible in part by a James B. Pendleton Grant from the Roy H. Park School of Communications at Ithaca College.

Part 1
America Tunes In

The Most Watched
TV Series Finales

Tuesday, August 29, 1967

The Day *The Fugitive* Stopped Running

The Fugitive (ABC, 1963–1967)
Created by Roy Huggins
Premiere date: September 17, 1963
4 seasons / 120 Episodes
"The Judgment, Parts 1 and 2"
Airdates: August 22 and 29, 1967
Part 1: 37.2 rating • 56.7 percent share
Part 2: 45.9 rating • 72 percent share • 78 million viewers
Directed by Don Medford
Written by George Eckstein and Michael Zagor
Cast: David Janssen (Richard Kimble), Barry Morse (Lieutenant Gerard), Bill Raisch
  (Fred Johnson a.k.a. The One Armed Man), William Conrad (Narrator)
Guest Stars: Diane Baker (Jean Carlisle), J. D. Cannon (Lloyd Chandler), Diane
  Brewster (Helen Kimble) (uncredited), Jacqueline Scott (Donna Taft), Richard
  Anderson (Leonard Taft), Joseph Campanella (Captain Lee) (Part 1), Michael
  Constantine (Arthur Howe) (Part 1)

Themarked first TV series finale to be a major television event was the two-part conclusion of the ABC drama *The Fugitive*. A staggering 78 million viewers tuned in on August 29, 1967, making it the most watched episode to date in television history. The fact that so many people were still interested in the fate of Dr. Richard Kimble is surprising, considering that the show's ratings had dropped off significantly in its fourth and final season and there was a four-month gap between the last first-run episode of the season and the two-part finale.

In the show's pilot, Richard Kimble, wrongly convicted and sentenced to death for murdering his wife, is given a second chance to clear his name when the train transporting him to prison derails. Over the course of 118 episodes,

Kimble searches for the man he believes to be his wife's killer—a one-armed man he saw leaving the scene of the crime. At the same time, Lieutenant Gerard, the lead detective on the case, and Kimble's escort to prison when he escaped, hunts him down.

When *The Fugitive* debuted in the fall of 1963, ABC was the third most watched network behind CBS and NBC. Like its competitors, ABC's prime-time schedule was a mixture of westerns, situation comedies, variety shows, medical series, and legal dramas. Yet ABC was also willing to take risks with programming not seen on the other networks, such as the first prime-time animated series (*The Flintstones* [1960–1966]); youth-oriented shows (*The Patty Duke Show* [1963–1966], *Shindig!* [1964–1966], *Gidget* [1965–1966], and *Batman* [1966–1968]); and a detective series featuring TV's first female private eye (*Honey West* [1965–1966]).

The Fugitive was also unique because the entire series revolves around a single plotline: an innocent man on the run, sentenced to death for murder, must elude the authorities as he tries to clear his name. The premise was not entirely original. Director Alfred Hitchcock, the "Master of Suspense," repeatedly revisited the "wrong man" plot in films like *Young and Innocent* (1937), *Saboteur* (1942), *Spellbound* (1945), *Strangers on a Train* (1951), *The Wrong Man* (1956), and *North by Northwest* (1959). Still, *The Fugitive* was unlike any crime or legal drama on television because it poked some major holes in the American justice system which, up to that point, was portrayed on television as essentially infallible: police detectives always "got their man (or woman)," the accused received a fair trial, and only the guilty were convicted and punished.

Unfortunately, the justice system failed poor Dr. Kimble. Lt. Gerard testifies in court that he investigated Kimble's claim that he saw a one-armed man running from the crime scene. He even interviewed eighty-three men who fit that description, but none of them were anywhere near Kimble's house the night of the murder. So Kimble is arrested, tried, and sentenced to death for a crime he did not commit, while his wife's killer is still on the loose. Lt. Gerard may be dedicated, professional, and strictly by the book when it comes to the law, but his competency as a detective is questionable, considering it took four seasons to recapture Kimble despite the numerous times their paths crossed. In the show's finale, Lt. Gerard is only able to hunt down Helen Kimble's killer—Fred Johnson a.k.a. "the one-armed man"—with Kimble's help. By then, you would have expected Lt. Gerard to have been demoted to a desk job or forced to take an early retirement.

The Fugitive is a work of fiction, yet the parallels between the Kimble case and the highly publicized trial of Dr. Sam Sheppard, who was sentenced to life in prison in 1954 for murdering his pregnant wife, Marilyn Reese Sheppard, did not go unnoticed. In his post-season 1 appraisal of the series for the

New York Times, Paul Gardner observed how the circumstantial evidence that sent Kimble to jail is remarkably similar to the Sheppard murder trial. Throughout and after the trial, Dr. Sheppard claimed he was innocent. Twelve years later, due to the prejudicial publicity surrounding the case and

In his tireless pursuit of justice, Dr. Richard Kimble (David Janssen) gets closer to clearing his name in the series finale of *The Fugitive*.   *ABC/Photofest*

the court's failure to invoke procedures that would have guaranteed him a fair trial, Sheppard was retried and acquitted. Still, despite any similarities, *Fugitive* creator Roy Huggins flatly denied in a 1998 interview for the Archive of American Television that there was any connection between the Sheppard case and *The Fugitive*.

One source Huggins did draw from was Victor Hugo's 1862 novel, *Les Misérables*, the story of ex-convict Jean Valjean who is pursued for seventeen years by Javert, a by-the-book police inspector. In his autobiography, actor Barry Morse (Lt. Gerard) recalled his conversation with the show's producer, Quinn Martin, who acknowledged that *The Fugitive* was "loosely derived" from Hugo's novel, but added, "we're naturally not advertising that."

Actually, they did. A two-page ad in *Variety* on March 20, 1963, introducing *The Fugitive* as one of ABC's "Big New Shows Coming This Fall," describes Richard Kimble as "an underdog in the classic tradition of Jean Valjean. The Innocent Condemned." Perhaps the network marketing executive responsible for the ad read the original six-page treatment for the series (reprinted in Mel Proctor's *The Official Fan's Guide to* The Fugitive) in which Huggins states: "The story of Jean Valjean and his Javert has not remained a classic for insignificant reasons, and the best will be distilled from those reasons."

Huggins's treatment also explains in far greater detail his primary source of inspiration for the series—the western. According to Huggins, who also created the comedy-western *Maverick* (1957–1962) and was a writer/producer on *Cheyenne* (1955–1963) and *The Virginian* (1962–1971), *The Fugitive* aimed "to capture the essence of the western in a contemporary setting." Like the western hero, Kimble is "unregimented, apart from society, rootless, immune to permanent human commitment, and ever on the move." But in these "regimented and conformist times," Huggins adds, the audience "had to understand why this was so and to accept it with no uneasy sense of guilt; otherwise there would be a rejection of the protagonist and the concept."

Huggins's treatment also outlined the basic rules Kimble's character must follow. The doctor must: change his appearance and identity; keep moving to avoid being recognized, though he must stay in the country (so no passport is required); limit his employment to jobs that don't require a Social Security card or a background check; and engage only in short-term platonic and love relationships. Although the change in Kimble's appearance is minor (he blackens his hair), the show's writers adhere for the most part to Huggins's rules. Kimble always uses an alias (Bill Deane, author of *Following* The Fugitive, lists 113 names) and stays in one place for a single episode, except for an occasional two-part episode.

Huggins created *The Fugitive*, but his work on the show was limited to supervising the pilot, which was written by Stanford Whitmore, whose credits included *Adventures in Paradise* (1959–1962) and the detective series *Johnny Staccato* (1959–1960). But Huggins remained on the payroll throughout *The Fugitive*'s four-year run thanks to an agreement, which became known in Hollywood as "The Huggins Contract," that guaranteed he would be paid royalties and a fee whether or not he worked on the series. Huggins wisely sold only the television rights to United Artists Television and the show's producer, Quinn Martin. He held on to the film rights, which he later sold to Warner Bros. for the 1993 film version of *The Fugitive* starring Harrison Ford. Huggins received executive producer credit on the film, which scored $368.8 million dollars worldwide at the box-office.

The pilot episode of *The Fugitive* opens with the disembodied "Voice of God" narrator (William Conrad, who later starred on the television detective series, *Cannon* [1971–1976]), who sets the stage for Richard Kimble's escape:

> **Name:** Richard Kimble. Profession: Doctor of Medicine.
>
> **Destination:** Death Row, state prison. Richard Kimble has been tried and convicted for the murder of his wife. But laws are made by men, carried out by men. And men are imperfect. Richard Kimble is innocent. Proved guilty, what Richard Kimble could not prove was that moments before discovering his wife's body, he encountered a man running from the vicinity of his home. A man with one arm. A man who has not yet been found. Richard Kimble ponders his fate as he looks at the world for the last time and sees only darkness. But in that darkness, fate moves its huge hand.

The opening narration was shortened for the remainder of season 1 and rewritten for subsequent seasons to emphasize Dr. Richard Kimble's status as a fugitive in search of the one-armed man:

> **The Fugitive, a QM Production**—starring David Janssen as Dr. Richard Kimble: an innocent victim of blind justice, falsely convicted for the murder of his wife; reprieved by fate when a train wreck freed him en route to the death house; freed him to hide in lonely desperation, to change his identity, to toil at many jobs; freed him to search for a one-armed man he saw leave the scene of the crime; freed him to run before the relentless pursuit of the police lieutenant obsessed with his capture.

Surprisingly, the producers waited until the middle of season 1 to fill the audience in on Richard's backstory—his marriage to Helen, the events surrounding the night of her murder, and his trial and conviction. In episode 14 ("The Girl from Little Egypt"), Kimble is struck by a car and lands in the hospital with a concussion—one in a long list of injuries he sustains while on the run, including multiple gunshot and knife wounds, sprained ankles, and temporary blindness. While lying in the hospital, he has a series of flashbacks, during which we learn that Helen Kimble gave birth to a stillborn baby and, due to complications, she can no longer have children. Her strong opposition to adopting a child and excessive drinking is causing tension in their marriage. On the night of her murder, the couple has another fight. Richard leaves the house alone and goes for a drive. Upon returning home, he sees the one-armed man, who, illuminated by headlights, darts in front of his car and looks Kimble squarely in the eyes. Kimble then runs inside the house where he finds his wife dead.

Javert's hunt for ex-convict Jean Valjean in Victor Hugo's *Les Misérables* was the inspiration for Lt. Philip Gerard's (Barry Morse) (right) pursuit of Dr. Richard Kimble (David Janssen) (left) in *The Fugitive*.   *ABC/Photofest*

A typical episode of *The Fugitive* opens with Kimble arriving or already settled in at new location with a new identity and job. According to Bill Deane, his itinerary includes a mixture of real and fictional towns and cities in thirty-six states, plus Washington, D.C. and Mexico. The plot revolves around the constant threat Kimble faces of having his true identity exposed. The situation is further complicated by Kimble's penchant for playing Good Samaritan and helping strangers in need and becoming personally involved in their problems. In a touch of irony, Kimble even steps forward to clear the name of someone falsely accused of a crime. In the end, the guilty party is apprehended and justice is served. Once the people he helps learn his true identity, they usually return his kindness by helping him escape. Kimble occasionally even manages to find time for a little romance. When Kimble has particularly strong feelings for someone, he reveals his true identity to her—before running out the door.

The humanistic Dr. Kimble also upholds the Hippocratic Oath and offers medical assistance whenever necessary. In one episode ("Landscape with Running Figures, Parts 1 and 2"), he unknowingly gets on the same bus as Lt. Gerard's wife, Marie (Barbara Rush), and takes care of her when the bus crashes and she goes temporarily blind. In an earlier episode ("Nemesis"), Kimble inadvertently steals a car with Gerard's son, Phil Jr. (Kurt Russell), in the backseat. At one point, Phil Jr. gets his foot caught in a bear trap and Kimble stops to help him, which confuses the lad who has been led to believe by his father that Kimble is a bad man. Chance encounters and coincidences like these became one of the show's trademarks.

Over the course of four seasons, the show's ratings rose considerably and then sharply declined. *The Fugitive* ranked no. 28 in the Nielsen ratings at the end of season 1 (1963–1964) and by end of the season 2 (1964–1965) it climbed up to no. 5. The series ranked no. 34 at the end of season 3 (1965–1966) and dipped to no. 50 in its fourth and final season (1966–1967). When *The Fugitive* was canceled, the show's ratings were still passable (lower rated shows renewed for the 1967–1968 season included *Star Trek* [no. 52]; *The Wild, Wild West* [no. 53]; *Run for Your Life* [no. 60]; and *Voyage to the Bottom of the Sea* [no. 63]). *The Fugitive* was also immensely popular overseas, where it aired in sixty-nine countries, in fourteen languages. According to the *Chicago Tribune*'s Clay Gowran, the show was also profitable for ABC, grossing a total of $30 million dollars.

On April 3, 1967, the *New York Times* published a story on ABC's prime-time lineup for the upcoming fall television season. George Gent reported that *The Fugitive* was among the ten shows canceled to make way for eleven new series. Two weeks later, ABC started airing reruns, which made some fans very nervous. Was it possible that after four seasons and 118 episodes, viewers would never learn the fate of Richard Kimble? While the network may have pulled the plug, *Chicago Tribune* reporter Sheila Wolfe assured viewers that an ending to the series would air sometime before the start of the new television season in September. There was also some speculation as to why ABC decided it was time for Dr. Kimble to stop running, considering the show had won the Emmy for Outstanding Dramatic Series the previous year, beating out the no. 1 show of the 1965–1966 season, *Bonanza* (1959–1973), along with *I Spy* (1965–1968), *The Man from U.N.C.L.E.* (1964–1968), and the political drama *Slattery's People* (1964–1965).

The decision to end the show no doubt rested on the shoulders of its star, David Janssen, who told *TV Guide* reporter Dwight Whitney he turned down a lucrative contract for a fifth season: "They made me an offer. It would have been worth maybe half a million dollars to me. Then I decided against the fifth year. I think I would have fallen apart if I hadn't." But it's not surprising he walked away from the show because, in interview after interview, the actor openly shared how much of a toll the series he called "The Fuge" was taking on him, both physically and mentally. Arnold Hano's March 1967 profile of thirty-five-year-old Janssen for *TV Guide*, aptly titled "David's Drooping . . . Success Has Left Fugitive Janssen Tired, Tense, and Physically Ailing," paints Janssen as an overworked, physically tired actor who seems uncertain of how much longer he would be able to do the show. One month later, *The Fugitive* was officially canceled. When asked in an interview published in *The Hutchinson News* if he was sorry to see the series end, Janssen replied, "Not really. I think we had explored all the story possibilities. We stopped while we were ahead."

Unlike most television shows, *The Fugitive* was conceived with an ending in mind, which is spelled out in the final paragraph of Huggins's original treatment:

> An element that will be used in the series, but only in the most limited way, is the faint, almost unacknowledged hope in Richard Kimble that he might one day come face to face with the gaunt, red-haired man he had so briefly seen on the night of his wife's death. The reason for this is obvious. This will be brought to a planned conclusion, that conclusion being of course Richard Kimble's release from his predicament and the ultimate salvation of justice.

The finale follows Huggins's treatment on both accounts: Kimble does come face to face with the "gaunt, red-haired man" and justice is finally served when Kimble is a free man.

The two-part finale opens with Kimble abruptly quitting his job in Phoenix and heading to Los Angeles, where Fred Johnson, the one-armed man, was reportedly arrested for wrecking a bar. When Lt. Gerard travels to

Los Angeles to check out the story, Jean Carlisle, a court stenographer whose late father was a friend of Kimble's, recognizes him and contacts Kimble's sister, Donna. Jean manages to track Kimble down when he arrives in Los Angeles before anyone recognizes him and lets him hide out in her apartment. Meanwhile, Lt. Gerard interrogates Fred Johnson and discovers he was fired from his job in Indianapolis two weeks before the murder, which now makes him a suspect in Helen Kimble's murder. Gerard makes a public plea for Kimble to give himself up with a promise that he will investigate Johnson's story. Just when Kimble is about to surrender, Howe, a sleazy bail bondsman, gets Johnson out of jail thanks to a benefactor who wishes to remain anonymous. Howe proposes a scheme to Johnson to extort more money from his benefactor. Johnson confesses to Howe that he murdered Helen Kimble; Howe then gives him the name of his benefactor—Kimble's brother-in-law (Donna's husband), Leonard Taft. Now that he knows it was Taft, Johnson has no use for Howe and kills him. Meanwhile, Lt. Gerard grows suspicious of Jean, which leads him to Kimble, who surrenders and is escorted back to his home town of Stanford, Indiana.

Part 2 of "The Judgment" is set in Stanford, where Kimble is reunited with his sister, Donna, and her husband, Leonard. Lt. Gerard grants Kimble fifteen more hours to prove his innocence (and spend time with Jean, who arrives in town). After ruling out that Leonard posted Johnson's bail, Kimble and Gerard eventually figure out that the anonymous benefactor was Kimble's neighbor, city planner Lloyd Chandler, who meets up with Johnson, who blackmails him for fifty-thousand dollars. Chandler confesses to his wife that he was in the Kimble house on the night in question, comforting a distraught Helen when the one-armed man broke in and killed her. Instead of coming to the rescue, Lloyd froze and never came forward, believing the murderer would be found and to save his reputation as a war hero and his wife from a scandal. Meanwhile, an armed Lloyd is off to meet Johnson at the drop-off point, an abandoned amusement park. Kimble and Lt. Gerard interrupt Johnson and Lloyd as they shoot it out. Lloyd is disarmed and wounded. Kimble chases the one-armed man to a tower at the top of one of the park's rides. Kimble gets Johnson to confess, but when the one-armed man pulls a gun on him, Lt. Gerard shoots Johnson, who falls to his death. As Johnson's confession will not hold up in court, Lloyd agrees to testify.

In the "Epilogue," Kimble walks out of courthouse a free man with his family and Jean. He and Jean walk by Lt. Gerard, who nods and shakes Kimble's hand. No words are exchanged. A police car pulls up, causing Kimble to tense up. Jean says, "Hey," to remind him that it's okay. He replies, "Hey," and the two continue walking.

Narrator: "Tuesday, August 29th—the day the running stopped."

The network's bold, unprecedented decision to delay the finale for four months paid off. It seemed as if all of America was watching. *Variety* reported the reactions of viewers around the country. Radio disc jockeys gave listeners updates. One police department sent a call out to all patrol cars: "Stop looking for Richard Kimble—the one-armed man did it." WJZ-TV in Baltimore preempted an Orioles game for the finale. In Tulsa, Oklahoma, the transmission at KTUL-TV broke down during the running of part 1. Fortunately, an engineer was smart enough to tape the show so the station could run it later that evening. Some residents in Glenview, Illinois, were not so lucky when a power outage during the last half hour of part 2 prevented them from seeing the final shootout in the amusement park. As a courtesy, the *Chicago Tribune* published the ending the following day.

But the ratings for the final episode were the real story. The finale, seen by 78 million viewers, had a 45.9 rating (the percentage of households with a television set that watched *The Fugitive*) and a 72 percent share (the percentage of television sets in use at the time that were tuned in to *The Fugitive*). *The Fugitive* held on to that record for thirteen years, until Friday, November 21,

In the series finale of *The Fugitive*, Dr. Richard Kimble (David Janssen) confronts the "One-Armed Man" (Bill Raisch), who murdered Kimble's wife.   *ABC/Photofest*

1980, when *Dallas* answered the question, "Who shot J. R.?" (Answer: Kristin Shepard [Mary Crosby], J. R.'s ex-mistress and sister-in-law). The episode, entitled "Who Done It," scored a 53.3 rating and a 76 percent share and was watched by an estimated 83 million people.

The finale received mixed reviews from critics around the country. "No TV series has ever died with such as crescendo," remarked *Arizona Republic* critic Stewart Allen. "It's pleasant to find that TV, a medium prone to forget its audience, actually ended something. And ended it well." Cynthia Lowry, television-radio critic for the Associated Press, acknowledged, "[T]he conclusion was hard to pull together," so she wasn't surprised "the final chapter wasn't up to the standards of the rest of the long-running series." She felt the revelation (that there was an eye-witness to Helen Kimble's murder) wasn't dramatic enough, and the chase through the amusement park and the final fight between Johnson and Kimble to be "a familiar pair of end-of-show television clichés." Lowry also revealed that ABC considered having the one-armed man arrested and tried for murder. His defense attorney would be Clinton Judd, the title character of ABC's new legal drama, *Judd for the Defense* (1967–1969) starring Carl Betz. Fortunately for everyone involved, it didn't work out. Dean Gysel, a writer for the *Chicago Daily News*, not only thought having "that socially disadvantaged, culturally deprived, one-armed gentleman" be the murderer was "an enormous letdown," but having "war hero-city planner" Lloyd Chandler be a witness "was a slur against all city planners."

Variety was more impressed with the first half of part 2 because "it maintained the pace of the series," while the climactic scene in the amusement park was "not particularly believable, with the climax so stagey it was a poor man's Hitchcock." The climax, in which Johnson and Kimble face off, was shot in Pacific Ocean Park (nicknamed Pea-O-Pea) in Santa Monica, California, at the top of the tower of the "Mahi Mahi" Ride (the tower had three arms, at the end of which was an eight-passenger car that rose in the air and spun around). Built to compete with Disneyland, Pacific Ocean Park opened its doors in 1959, but fires and financial problems led to its closure in the fall of 1967, a few months after the finale was shot. Noting that Janssen played Kimble with a lack of emotion throughout the episode (even after the killer was caught and he's exonerated), *Variety* speculated that perhaps it was "because the series had been guillotined."

In his autobiography, Barry Morse shares with his readers some anecdotes regarding the final episode. He and Janssen jokingly suggested that the show should end with Kimble waking up in bed with his wife Helen and crying out, "Oh! Oh, honey! Oh thank God—I've just had the most terrible nightmare!" Morse was amused by the fact that variations of their proposed ending turned up on television many years later on the season 9 (1985–1986) finale of *Dallas*, in which the late Bobby Ewing, who was killed off in the season 8 finale, appears in his wife Pam's shower, thereby making all of season 9 a bad dream for both Pam and the audience; and, more notably, in the finale of *Newhart* (see chapter 24). Morse also revealed that the final non-verbal exchange between Kimble and Lt. Gerard originally included "overly sentimental dialogue" in which Gerard apologizes to Kimble, and says, "No hard feelings." To point out the absurdity of the dialogue, on the first take the two actors threw their arms around each other and kissed each other on the mouth. Apparently the producers got the message and the scene was rewritten.

On the evening the second part of "The Judgment" was broadcast, Janssen was on location making *The Green Berets* in Columbus, Georgia, where, according to *Variety* columnist Army Archerd, he watched part 1 in his hotel room with his co-star, John Wayne. After part 2 aired, Janssen was interviewed through the use of a split screen on *The Joey Bishop Show* (1967–1969), a late night talk show that aired on ABC from 11:30 p.m. to 1 a.m. As Bishop's show would not air until after *The Fugitive*, Janssen confirmed for Bishop, albeit a bit reluctantly, that the one-armed man killed Helen Kimble. *Variety* reported that Janssen's appearance paid off for Bishop, whose talk show received its highest rating to date in New York City (even beating *The Tonight Show Starring Johnny Carson*). Bishop also posed the question to Janssen about how he felt about the show's ending. "My feeling was not one of remorse," Janssen explained, "and it was not one of melancholy when the show was over. . . . It was a positive ending rather than a negative one."

Soon afterwards, *The Fugitive* finale aired in overseas markets in England, Ireland, Mexico, Japan, Finland, and Spain. *Variety* reported that West German fans were told they had to wait until October to see it due to "dubbing difficulties." Fearing that the ending could not be contained until then, the station was besieged with complaints. In Spain, two journalists, identified as "J. A. Plaza" and "Yale," managed to break what they considered the biggest investigative news story of the year when they were given the chance to interview two of the major players in the series finale—J. D. Cannon (Lloyd Chandler) and Diane Baker (Jean Carlisle)—who happen to be in Spain shooting the feature film, *Krakatoa: East of Java* (1969). Although the actors were able to resist the questions from the local press, they gave in to the "unrelenting questioning" of the two reporters and revealed two key elements of the finale.

One month later, *Variety* reported that six Spanish writers wished there had been more of a "surprise" ending; they even shared how they would have rewritten the finale. Their suggestions ranged from making Dr. Kimble the killer "but with a comical treatment," to introducing another murder and suspect, to the police killing Dr. Kimble before he had the chance to clear his name. Writer/actor Alvaro de la Iglesia, who thought the finale was disappointing, suspected "the Spaniards had been duped with an ending different from the one seen in America."

The Fugitive can be credited for spawning a new television genre about a man on the move. The reason the show's protagonist can't—or won't—stay in one place varies from show to show:

- Inspired by his own show, Huggins created another man-on-the-move series, *Run for Your Life* (NBC, 1965–1968), starring Ben Gazzara as Paul Bryan, a lawyer who is told he has between nine and eighteen months to live (the series lasted longer than his prognosis) and decides to cram thirty years of living into two. Unlike *The Fugitive*, the series never had a proper ending. The last time viewers saw Paul Bryan he was very much alive.

- *Run, Buddy, Run* (CBS, 1966–1967) is a comic twist on *The Fugitive.* Buddy Overstreet (Jack Sheldon) is an ordinary guy who overhears a crime syndicate boss, Mr. D (Bruce Gordon), making plans to knock off one of his associates (using the code phrase, "Chicken Little"). Now Buddy is also on Mr. D's hit list and so, like Richard Kimble, he must keep moving from town to town and job to job. Buddy' journey was cut short by CBS, which pulled the plug on the show. By the thirteenth and final episode, the identity of "Chicken Little" is revealed and Mr. D, who is in hot water with the IRS, calls off the hit.

- *Branded* (NBC, 1965–1966) focuses on Jason McCord (Chuck Connors), a former U.S. Cavalry captain unjustly kicked out of the military for cowardice and desertion (the only survivor of the Bitter Creek massacre, he was under the command of an unstable general). With plenty of free time on his hands, he roams the Old West trying to prove to those who are aware of his reputation that he is no coward.

- Larry Cohen, creator of *Branded*, conceived another man-on-the-move series around the same time for CBS. *Coronet Blue* (1967) was a mystery series starring Frank Converse as a man who is drugged and dumped into a river by three people who unsuccessfully try to kill him. Suffering from amnesia, the man, who adopts the name Michael Alden, remembers only two words: "Coronet Blue." He tries to piece his life together as he continues to run from the people who are still out to kill him. *Coronet Blue* was produced for the 1965–1966 season, but CBS put the show on hiatus when they decided to renew the political drama *Slattery's People* (1964–1965). Consequently, production was halted after thirteen episodes. CBS decided to air the episodes in the summer of 1967, yet they never expected anyone would be watching. *Variety* reported that

Coronet Blue debuted strong and continued to do well in the ratings. Unfortunately, even if CBS wanted to revive the series, it wasn't possible as Converse was set to star in a new ABC police series, *N.Y.P.D.* (1967–1969). Unfortunately, a final episode was never produced, so all of the questions regarding Alden's real identity and the meaning of "Coronet Blue" were left unanswered. In a *New York Times* story about the show's popularity, an unidentified CBS executive admitted to reporter George Gent, "I certainly don't know how it would have ended. I doubt the author does." Cohen did, but he wasn't talking because he was then negotiating with *TV Guide* to publish an article revealing the ending (unless another network decided to revive the series). He did reveal that *The Fugitive* was the inspiration for the series and the lead role was written with an older actor in mind (Converse was twenty-nine years old). Thirty years later, Cohen revealed to his biographer that Converse's character was not an American, but a Russian spy trained to be an American, who belonged to a unit called "Coronet Blue." He decided to defect, which is why Soviet agents were after him.

- In 1966, Val Adams reported in the *New York Times* that ABC had a man-on-the-run western in development. In *The Long Hunt of April Savage*, a gunfighter travels around the world in search of the eight men responsible for his wife's death. The network planned to run the show, to be produced by *Star Trek* creator Gene Roddenberry and Desilu, for either forty-eight or sixty-four weeks, with the gunfighter catching up with one of the eight men every six or eight episodes. The pilot of the show aired in 1967.

America hadn't seen the last of Richard Kimble. After the success of the 1993 big screen version of *The Fugitive*, CBS revived the show in 2000 with Tim Daly as Kimble. In addition to running from Lt. Gerard (Mykelti Williamson) and looking for the one-armed man (Stephen Lang), Kimble also had to contend with bounty hunters hired by his father-in-law. The ratings were low and the show, canceled after one season, ended with a major cliffhanger: Special FBI Agent Gagomiros (Dennis Boutsikaris), who has inexplicably shot Lt. Gerard, finds Kimble and the one-armed man in an abandoned building. He aims and fires his gun at Kimble. The end—his fate never to be revealed, which is ironic considering the number of people who tuned in on Tuesday, August 29, 1967, to see *The Fugitive* stop running.

2

Cease Fire

M*A*S*H 4077th Goes Out of Business

M*A*S*H (CBS, 1972–1983)
Developed for television by Larry Gelbart
Premiere date: September 17, 1972
11 seasons / 256 episodes
"Goodbye, Farewell, and Amen"
Airdate: February 28, 1983
60.2 rating • 77 percent share • 105.9 million viewers
Directed by Alan Alda
Written by Alan Alda, Karen Hall, Burt Metcalfe, John Rappaport, Thad Mumford,
    Dan Wilcox, David Pollock, and Elias Davis
Cast: Alan Alda (Captain Benjamin Franklin "Hawkeye" Pierce), Mike Farrell
    (Captain B. J. Hunnicutt), Harry Morgan (Colonel Sherman T. Potter), Loretta
    Swit (Major Margaret "Hot Lips" Houlihan), David Ogden Stiers (Major
    Charles Emerson Winchester III), Jamie Farr (Sergeant Maxwell Q. Klinger),
    William Christopher (Father Francis Mulcahy), Allan Arbus (Major Sidney
    Freedman) (recurring). Kellye Nakahara (Lieutenant Kellye Yamato), Jeff
    Maxwell (Igor Straminsky)

In the early 1970s, CBS ushered in a renaissance in television comedy with three popular sitcoms that modernized and revitalized the genre: *The Mary Tyler Moore Show* (1970–1977), *All in the Family* (1971–1979), and *M*A*S*H* (1972–1983). Although their subject matter and comic tones were very different, the quality of both the writing and directing of all three series were consistently high. In fact, in the 1970s the trio dominated the comedy writing and directing categories for the Emmys and the Writers Guild of America and Directors Guild of America Awards. Their characters, comedic plots, and, in the case of *All in the Family* and *M*A*S*H*, their treatment of topical and/or universal themes, were infused with something that had been missing from the rural and fantasy sitcoms of the 1960s—realism.

The cast of *M*A*S*H*: Jamie Farr (seated); (middle row, left to right) Mike Farrell, Alan Alda, Loretta Swit, Harry Morgan; (back row, left to right) David Ogden Stiers, William Christopher.   *Authors' collection*

M*A*S*H is based on the 1970 comedy directed by Robert Altman and written by Ring Lardner Jr., whose Academy Award-winning screenplay was adapted from the 1968 best-seller, *MASH: A Novel About Three Army Doctors*, written by H. Richard Hornberger (under the pseudonym Richard Hooker). Hornberger's semi-autobiographical novel is based on the author's experiences as an army surgeon at a Mobile Army Surgical Hospital (MASH) during the Korean War. The film, released by Twentieth Century Fox, was the third highest grossing film of 1970 and won the Palme d'Or at the Cannes Film Festival.

The film is a satirical black comedy about army doctors at a MASH unit who act like a pack of juvenile pranksters as they try to stay sane amidst the chaos and bloodshed, which the audience witnesses in a series of harrowing, graphic scenes set in the operating room. The parallels between Korea and Vietnam were obvious to a 1970 audience and the growing unpopularity of America's involvement in Vietnam no doubt contributed to the film's success at the box office. According to Joseph Carroll, a Gallup Poll conducted in January of 1970, when *MASH* opened in theatres in New York, reported that 57 percent of Americans believed it had been a mistake to send troops to Vietnam. Over the course of the year, the percentage would dip down to 51 percent (April 1970), and then rise to a record 60 percent in January of 1971. In an interview with critic David Thompson, Altman admitted, "Although the book and script were set in Korea, to me it was Vietnam. I wanted to mix it up and have people thinking of a contemporary story—that is, 1969, 1970. All the political attitudes in the film were about Nixon and Vietnam."

William Self, a television executive at Twentieth Century Fox, had the idea of adapting *MASH* to the small screen. In the 1960s, Self was responsible for turning his studio into a major supplier of television series, including several successful series based on feature films, such as *Peyton Place* (1964–1969), *Twelve O'Clock High* (1964–1967), and *Voyage to the Bottom of the Sea* (1964–1968). He hired producer Gene Reynolds, who, in turn, hired writer Larry Gelbart to pen the series pilot, which included several characters featured in the film that were eventually phased out. As in the film, the series focused on two surgeons, Captain Benjamin "Hawkeye" Pierce (Alan Alda) and Captain "Trapper" John McIntyre (Wayne Rogers), although Hawkeye eventually became the show's focal point (Wayne Rogers departed after season 3). Like Hawkeye and Trapper, the commander of the 4077th, Lieutenant Colonel Henry Blake (McLean Stevenson), is not "regular army," which puts him at odds with Major Frank Burns (Larry Linville) and Head Nurse Major Margaret "Hotlips" Houlihan (Loretta Swit), both of whom thought Lt. Colonel Blake incompetent; they repeatedly tried (and failed) to undermine his command. The supporting characters include the efficient company clerk, Corporal Walter "Radar" O'Reilly (Gary Burghoff, who originated the role in the Altman film); the resident chaplain, Father Francis John Patrick Mulcahy (William Christopher); and Corporal Maxwell Klinger (Jamie Farr).

When *M*A*S*H* debuted on September 17, 1972, as part of CBS's new Sunday night lineup, it was scheduled at 8 p.m., between two family-oriented half-hour comedies: *Anna and the King* (1972), a non-musical version of *The King and I* with Yul Brynner reprising his Oscar and Tony-winning role, and *The Sandy Duncan Show* (1972), a revamped version of the perky actress's show from the previous season, *Funny Face* (1971). In its fourth week, *M*A*S*H* tied 53rd in the ratings, and there was no significant change when Brynner's show was replaced mid-season by *The New Dick Van Dyke Show* (1971–1974). At the end of the 1972–1973 season, *M*A*S*H* ranked no. 46 in the Nielsen ratings, making it an unlikely candidate for renewal, yet, as *Variety* television reporter Bob Knight recalled in 1983, the show remained on the schedule because it was "the darling of CBS execs."

Based on what Knight heard from "show's insiders," *M*A*S*H* found its voice in the seventeenth episode of season 1. In "Sometimes You Hear the Bullet," Hawkeye's best friend since grammar school, Cpl. Tommy Gillis (James Callahan), pays a surprise visit. Like Hawkeye, he's a prankster and also a journalist who enlisted in the Army so he could write a firsthand account of the life of a soldier during wartime. At the end of the episode, Tommy returns as one of the wounded. Hawkeye can't save his friend, marking the first time someone identifiable dies on the operating table. When Hawkeye cries for the first time since he's been in Korea, Colonel Blake consoles him by saying, "There are certain rules about a war. And rule no. 1 is young men die. And rule no. 2 is doctors can't change rule no. 1."

In an interview for the Archive of American Television (AAT), Gene Reynolds recalled how the network found the episode too depressing for a comedy, yet for the producers it marked a creative turning point for the show. As Larry Gelbart explained in his autobiography, *Laughing Matters*, the episode was "the first indication that a mixture of laughter and tragedy might be possible, without any heavy-handed manipulation of the audience's emotions." CBS wisely renewed the series for a second season (1973–1974), and gave *M*A*S*H* a choice slot on the Saturday night lineup between two comedies that were also geared for older audiences, *All in the Family* (the no. 1 rated show for the 1972–1973 season) and *The Mary Tyler Moore Show* (no. 7). At the end of season 2, *M*A*S*H* ranked no. 4 in the ratings and would remain in the Top 10 for eight of its next nine seasons.

In the television industry, *M*A*S*H* is what is known today as a *dramedy*, a term popularized in the late 1980s to classify such shows as *The Days and Nights of Molly Dodd* (1987–1991), *Hooperman* (1987–1989), *Doogie Howser,*

M.D. (1989–1993), and the critically acclaimed, yet short-lived *Frank's Place* (1987–1988). A dramedy is a comedy-drama hybrid, usually a half hour in length, shot with one camera and utilizes no laugh track. But in the early 1970s, a show like *M*A*S*H* was considered a comedy-drama. The order in which the words "comedy" and "drama" appear in relation to the hyphen is significant because it indicates that CBS classified *M*A*S*H* as a comedy with dramatic overtones. Consequently, CBS demanded that the producers include a laugh track, which was perfectly fine for shows like *All in the Family* and *The Mary Tyler Moore Show*, which were shot with three cameras in front of a live audience. But it made no sense for a one-camera comedy shot on a studio soundstage without a live audience.

This was not unprecedented. Prior to *M*A*S*H*, Gene Reynolds produced *Room 222*, a half-hour comedy-drama about a high school in Los Angeles that was shot on film with a single camera. The show, which dealt with topical issues such as race relations, the Vietnam War, women's rights, and homophobia, also had a laugh track. Still, *M*A*S*H*'s laugh track was a point of contention between the producers and the network. The laugh track was not used in the operating room scenes (except maybe at the end to punctuate a joke) and not in all episodes. In *They'll Never Put That on the Air*, Gene Reynolds explained to author Allan Neuwirth that they used a "discreet" laugh track: "We made the damn joke *earn* the laugh. Some sitcoms, you see 'em and Jesus, that laugh comes in there *whappo*, whether it earns it or not." In an interview for the AAT, Gelbart admitted that he saw no value in using mechanical laughter, which he felt "cheapened the show" and was completely "out of character." When *M*A*S*H* first aired in Britain, the laugh track was not used; the recently released DVDs include a menu that gives the viewer the option of turning on or off the laugh track.

Over time, *M*A*S*H* lost four of its original cast members. McLean Stevenson left at the end of season 3 because, as the actor explained to Associated Press reporter Bob Thomas, he was tired of playing "second banana" for five years (three seasons on *M*A*S*H* and two seasons on *The Doris Day Show* [1968–1973]). In the final episode of season 3, entitled "Abyssinia, Henry," Lt. Colonel Blake is discharged from the Army ("Abyssinia" was the name of the country now known as Ethiopia, but in the 1920s and 1930s, it was a slang pun for "I'll be seeing you."). Written by Jim Fritzell and Everett Greenbaum, the episode revolves around Henry's send-off as he prepares for his long-awaited return to civilian life. In an emotional moment, Radar, who is hit the hardest by the commander's departure, salutes Henry as he is about to board the helicopter. Col. Blake salutes him back and gives him a hug.

But it was the final scene that caught everyone off guard. In one of the most memorable television moments of the 1970s, a visibly shaken Radar appears in the operating room and reads a message that serves as a powerful, painful reminder of the tragic toll of war: "Lieutenant Colonel Henry Blake's plane was shot down over the Sea of Japan. It spun in. There were no survivors." Cut to commercial. Larry Gelbart revealed in his AAT interview that with the exception of Alda, the cast was told about Henry's fate right before the scene was shot because they didn't want their knowledge of the ending to affect their performances during Blake's send-off. "Abyssinia, Henry" was also Rogers's last episode. In the one-hour season 4 opener, Hawkeye returns from a week of R and R (via a rickshaw) and discovers that Trapper left a few hours before his arrival. The episode also marks the arrival of Captain B. J. Hunnicutt (Mike Farrell) and the 4077th's new commanding officer, Colonel Potter (Harry Morgan).

At the end of season 5, Larry Linville chose not to renew his contract when it expired (Frank Burns is replaced by Boston-bred Major Charles Emerson Winchester III, played by David Ogden Stiers) and Burghoff's Radar says goodbye in a two-part episode in season 8. While the departure or replacement of one or more main characters can often cause a show's ratings to plummet, the introduction of new characters like Hunnicutt, Potter, and Winchester seemed to have had the reverse effect. If all the original characters had remained, it's questionable whether the show would have stayed on the air for eleven seasons.

Halfway through season 10, UPI Hollywood correspondent Vernon Scott reported that *M*A*S*H* would end its run the following season with sixteen new episodes, including a two-hour series finale to air in February 1983. While the cast and many of the people behind the scenes felt it was time to move on, it's unlikely that Fox and CBS were eager to end a series which, as *Variety*'s John Dempsey reported, was garnering high ratings in syndication and on its way to grossing $1 million dollars for each of the show's 255 episodes. The show also won a total of fourteen Emmy Awards with Alda, a major creative force behind the show, becoming the first (and only) person to win Emmys in the comedy category for acting (three in all) and one each for writing ("Inga") and directing ("Dear Sigmund"). Swit won two and Burghoff and Morgan each won one, not to mention the seven Directors Guild Awards (Alda won three) and seven Writers Guild Awards.

M*A*S*H ran for eleven seasons, while the Korean War lasted three years, one month, and two days (June 25, 1950–July 27, 1953). In some episodes, the exact year and, in some instances, the month or even the exact date is stated or conveyed through references to actual historical events. But the writers apparently didn't feel there was a problem if an episode set in 1952 was followed by one set in 1951. In their exhaustive analysis of the series down to the smallest details, Ed Solomonson and Mark O'Neil, authors of *TV's M*A*S*H: The Ultimate Guidebook*, reveal how the writers played fast and loose with dates, which sometimes resulted in anachronisms. Certain props used by the characters had not yet been manufactured and the dialogue often contained references to future events and popular culture, resulting in the occasional anachronism, such as Hawkeye singing the beginning of the theme song to *The Mickey Mouse Club* ("The Colonel's Horse"), which did not debut on television until 1955, or B. J.'s reference to the 1957 musical *The Music Man* ("War of Nerves"). But even more problematic were references to specific events in the war. According to Solomonson and O'Neil, in "Major Ego," an episode from season 7, a wounded G. I. says he was wounded at the Battle of Pork Chop Hill, which occurred in the spring and summer of 1953. In season 9, a "year in the life" episode chronicling various events at the MASH unit from winter through fall, opens with the 4077th ringing in 1952.

One date that is used with historical accuracy is July 27, 1953. On that morning, a cease-fire and armistice was made official with the signing of the Armistice Agreement by U.S. Army Lieutenant General William Harrison Jr., who represented the United Nations Command, and General Nam II, who signed on behalf of the North Korean People's Army and the Chinese People's Volunteer Army.

M*A*S*H's two-and-a-half-hour finale, "Goodbye, Farewell, and Amen," takes place before and after the signing of the Armistice Agreement. The first hour crosscuts between the 4077th, where everyone is cautiously optimistic as the end of the war draws near, and a mental hospital where Hawkeye is being treated by psychiatrist Dr. Sidney Freedman (Allan Arbus). At first, Hawkeye (and the viewers) are not exactly sure what he's doing there, though we soon learn that he had a nervous breakdown and tried to operate on a patient without an anesthetic, accused the anesthetist of trying to smother the patient with the mask, and, later, drove a Jeep through the Officers' Club.

Over the course of his sessions with Dr. Freedman, Hawkeye has a break-through when he recalls, through a series of flashbacks, what happened on a bus that was transporting members of the 4077th back from a day of R and R at a beach at Inchon. Along the way they pick up some refugees and then some wounded soldiers, who warn them about an enemy patrol coming down the road. As a safety precaution they must hide the bus in some bushes. Hawkeye gets angry when a refugee seated in the back of the bus can't keep the chicken she's holding quiet. She starts squeezing the chicken until it stops cackling. Hawkeye, in the present, then begins to cry uncontrollably when he remembers it was not a chicken the woman was holding, but a baby, which she strangled to death.

Hawkeye, still reeling from his nervous breakdown, returns to the 4077th, where everyone is preoccupied with his or her own personal issues: Klinger is helping a Korean woman named Soon-Lee (Rosalind Chao) look for her parents; Margaret is planning her future (with some help from her father); Charles is nervously waiting to see if he will be hired as the new chief of surgery at Boston General; and Father Mulcahy is in denial that a shell blast has left him deaf in one ear. B. J. is discharged early, but his efforts to get back to the U.S. in time for his daughter Erin's second birthday are futile when his orders are rescinded (later in the episode, the 4077th throws Erin Hunnicutt a birthday party, with a two-year-old orphan as a stand-in).

Meanwhile, the 4077th is under mortar attack by the North Koreans because there is an abandoned tank in the middle of their compound. When the shelling increases, Hawkeye decides something must be done and gets in the tank and drives it into the camp garbage dump (knocking over the latrine on the way). Later that night, incendiary bombs spark a wildfire in the nearby forest, forcing the camp to "bug out" (evacuate) and move to a new site. This plot point was added to the finale script when *M*A*S*H*'s outdoor sets at Malibu State Park were completely destroyed on October 9, 1982, by the Dayton Canyon Fire, which claimed ninety-seven homes and 54,000 acres of land. The final draft of the script for "Goodbye, Farewell and Amen" is dated September 16, 1982, and the additional scenes pertaining to the fire and its aftermath are dated October 15, 1982, six days after the fire. Two of the actors—Harry Morgan and Kellye Nakahara—returned to Malibu State Park to shoot a short scene in which their respective characters survey the ruins of the still-smoldering compound.

The end of the war is officially declared via Armed Forces Radio by the voice of Robert Pierpoint, a correspondent for CBS news who reported on the war on Edward R. Murrow's newsmagazine show, *See It Now* (1951–1958). Eight hours before the ceasefire, Pierpoint provides some startling statistics of the cost of war in dollars ($22 billion for the United States) and lives (2 million people on both sides), not to mention the number of casualties and men and women missing in action.

When the cease-fire comes, the doctors are busy in the operating room, working on the wounded. Pierpoint, who recorded his voice-overs specifically for this episode, signals the official ending of the Korean War: "It's one minute before 10:00 p.m. We can still hear the sound of nearby artillery. At some point in the next few seconds the guns should go silent as the cease-fire officially goes into effect."

The firing stops, the operating room grows silent, and everyone stops what they are doing.

Pierpoint continues: "There it is, that's the sound of peace."

The doctors and nurses resume working on the wounded.

The two-and-a-half-hour running time allows ample time for the viewer to see how the war has affected each of the characters as he or she looks toward the future.

- Corporal Klinger and Soon-Lee, who spend most of the episode looking for her parents, fall in love. He proposes, and she accepts. Ironically, Klinger, who used to wear dresses in hopes of getting discharged on a Section 8, is staying in Korea to help his bride continue her search. At the end of the episode, Klinger and Soon-Lee are married.
- Major Charles Winchester fears his application to be the new chief of thoracic surgery at Boston Mercy will be turned down, so Major Houlihan puts a good word in for him with her "Uncle Bob," who is the head of the hospital. He gets the job, but he's angry with Margaret for interfering. She accuses him of being ungrateful and having no regard for other people. Meanwhile, Winchester finds some solace conducting five North Korean musicians who are being held as prisoners at the 4077th. The POWs are transferred to a relocation center, only to be killed en route. Winchester is shaken and, realizing he was unkind to Major Houlihan, he makes amends by giving her back a book of poetry he once lent her. (David Ogden Stiers, an underrated actor and underutilized member of the cast, is terrific in his scenes, particularly his reaction to the death of the North Korean musicians. He goes into his tent, begins to listen to a few bars of classical music on his record player, takes the record off the machine, and smashes it to pieces.)
- Major Houlihan decides it is time to take charge of her own life and not let her father, Colonel Alvin "Howitzer Al" Houlihan, make her decisions for her. She turns down the job he set up for her at NATO in Belgium, and decides to pursue her dream of being a hospital nurse in the States.
- Colonel Potter is looking forward to returning home to his wife, Mildred, and becoming a semi-retired country doctor.
- Hawkeye opens up to B. J. and admits how much he cares about him, yet fears they will never see each other again. Hawkeye teases B. J. that this means "goodbye," which is the message B. J. spells out in rocks for his friend to see when his helicopter takes off.

The goodbyes exchanged at the very end between the main characters are emotional because you feel the actors are really saying goodbye to one another.

The *M*A*S*H* finale was a bona fide media event, thanks to CBS's publicity machine. There were no preview screenings and no scripts were made available to the press, so critics could only speculate what was going to happen. Jerry Buck, from the Associated Press, reported that a tabloid claimed to have a copy of the script and although it wasn't known at the time, what they reported was actually accurate: Hawkeye has a breakdown, Klinger marries a Korean woman, and Father Mulcahy suffers a hearing impairment. Buck reported that CBS would be earning $450,000 for each thirty-second commercial. He also made an accurate prediction: "The end of *M*A*S*H* has generated such attention that the final show could set a viewing record."

He was correct. A record number of viewers *did* tune in. According to Robert Johnston's detailed analysis of the ratings for *M*A*S*H*'s finale posted on MASH4077TV.com, "Goodbye, Farewell, and Amen" received a 60.2 rating and a 77 percent share. The 60.2 rating translated into an estimated 50.15 million homes. In other words, more than half of all the television households in the United States were watching *M*A*S*H* and 77 percent of all televisions in use from 8:30 p.m. to 11:00 p.m. were tuned to CBS. In regards to the total number of viewers, there are actually two figures that should be taken into account: the total audience (121.6 million), which is the number of people who watched all or as few as six minutes of the finale, and the average number

B. J. Hunnicutt's (Mike Farrell) final message for Hawkeye (Alan Alda) in the series finale for *M*A*S*H*.   *Authors' collection*

of viewers (105.9 million) who watched the two-and-a half-hour finale in its entirety.

M*A*S*H did break the previous record held by the "Who shot J. R.?" episode of *Dallas* on November 21, 1980, which averaged a 53.3 rating and a 76 percent share. In addition, "Goodbye, Farewell, and Amen" set the record for the most television households to watch a single program, the largest number of viewers, and the largest total audience. One record it did *not* beat was the "largest share of the audience to watch a single program," which was held by the 42nd Academy Awards in 1970, which drew a 78 percent share.

Of course, not everyone watching the *M*A*S*H* finale did so alone. Private and public viewing parties were held around the country. Associated Press writer Scott Kraft reported that Tony Packo's Café—home of the Hungarian hot dog—located in Jamie Farr/Corporal Klinger's hometown of Toledo, Ohio—was sponsoring a party featuring a life-size statue of Klinger. At Fordham University, a farewell bash was held in a dormitory in Suite E-6, which had been occupied some twenty-seven years earlier by then-undergraduate Alan Alda. Saloons in countless cities were holding Hawkeye, Klinger, and "Hot Lips" lookalike contests. The Nugget Casino in Nevada was serving "Hawkeye martinis" during the broadcast. The day of the broadcast was declared "Loretta Swit Day" in the actress's hometown of Passaic, New Jersey.

When a show is on for eleven years and is seen daily in syndication, it does not fade from view so quickly. There was a spinoff, *AfterMASH* featuring Harry Morgan, William Christopher, Jamie Farr, and Rosalind Chao recreating their roles. The show was set at the General Pershing Veterans Administration Hospital in River Bend, Missouri, where Colonel Potter was chief of staff, Klinger his administrative assistant, and Father Mulcahy the hospital chaplain. Loyal viewers finally got the chance to meet Colonel Potter's beloved wife, Mildred (Anne Pitoniak), for the very first time. The show ranked no. 15 in the 1983–1984 season ratings, but viewership fell off significantly during season 2 and it was canceled in December of 1984. Another potential spinoff, *W*A*L*T*E*R*, starred Gary Burghoff reprising his role as Radar O'Reilly. The pilot had Radar selling the family farm and losing his wife to another man. He moves to St. Louis, Missouri, and with his cousin's help, gets a job on the police force. The pilot was not picked up by CBS, but it did air on July 17, 1984, as a "CBS Special Presentation."

Three years later, there was an unofficial *M*A*S*H* reunion when Burghoff, Linville, Rogers, Swit, Morgan, and Christopher appeared together in a television commercial for IBM's new personal computer, the PS 2. It's odd to see the actors out of their fatigues and dressed like executives. Alda also appeared along his former co-stars (and solo) in commercials for the IBM Application System/400.

In 1997, a "deactivation ceremony" was held to mark the closing of the 43rd Mobile Army Surgical Hospital in Camp Humphreys, South Korea, which was the basis for the 4077th. Present at this ceremony was *M*A*S*H*'s head writer, Larry Gelbart, and cast members Loretta Swit, Larry Linville, and David Ogden Stiers. It was a worthy tribute to the brave doctors and nurses who served their country by providing aid and comfort to their fellow soldiers.

3

"Where Everybody Knows Your Name"

Diane Returns to *Cheers*

Cheers (NBC, 1982–1993)
Created by James Burrows, Glen Charles, and Les Charles
Premiere date: September 30, 1982
11 seasons / 270 episodes
"One for the Road"
Airdate: May 20, 1993
45.5 percent rating • 64 percent share • 84.4 million viewers
Directed by James Burrows
Written by Glen and Les Charles
Cast: Ted Danson (Sam Malone), Kirstie Alley (Rebecca Howe), Rhea Perlman
(Carla Tortelli), John Ratzenberger (Cliff Clavin), Woody Harrelson (Woody
Boyd), George Wendt (Norm Peterson), Kelsey Grammer (Dr. Frasier Crane)
Guest Stars: Shelley Long (Diane Chambers), Tom Berenger (Don Santry), Jackie
Swanson (Kelly Boyd) (recurring), Tim Cunningham (Tim) (recurring), Steve
Giannelli (Steve) (recurring), Alan Koss (Alan) (recurring), Anthony Heald
(Kevin), Paul Willson (Paul Krapence), Mark Harelik (Reed Manchester), Kim
Alexis (herself), Mike Ditka (himself)

elcome to Cheers—the Boston bar and the long-running NBC
sitcom that debuted in September of 1982 as part of the network's new "Must See TV" Thursday-night lineup. *Cheers*, along
with other "Must See TV" comedies, including *The Cosby Show* (1984–1992),
Family Ties (1982–1989), and *A Different World* (1987–1993), played a major
role in NBC's meteoric rise in the mid-1980s from third place (behind no. 2
ABC and no. 1 CBS) to America's most-watched network. Early in its run,
Cheers earned consistently high marks from television critics, yet it would take
three seasons and two consecutive Emmy wins for Best Comedy Series (1983,
1984) for the sitcom to qualify as a hit. *Cheers* took some time to find an

"Where everybody knows your name": The cast of *Cheers*: (clockwise from top left) Shelley Long, Ted Danson, Woody Harrelson, John Ratzenberger, George Wendt; (center) Rhea Perlman.

Authors' collection

audience because prime-time comedy in the 1980s was dominated by family-oriented sitcoms. But unlike *Cosby, Family Ties,* and other high-rated shows like CBS's *Kate & Allie* (1984–1989) and ABC's *Who's the Boss?* (1984–1992) and *Growing Pains* (1985–1992), the setting of *Cheers* was strictly a "no-kids zone"—a neighborhood bar owned and operated by a handsome, womanizing, ex-Boston Red Sox relief pitcher (and recovering alcoholic) named Sam "Mayday" Malone (Ted Danson).

During the show's first five seasons, Sam is involved with a pretty, blonde waitress named Diane Chambers (Shelley Long), who is everything he's not—intelligent, educated, and cultured. Diane also has some negative qualities: she's opinionated, pretentious, very insecure, and slightly annoying. Director James Burrows, who co-created the show with brothers Glen and Les Charles, told *New York Times* reporter Peter Kerr that Diane and Sam were modeled after Katharine Hepburn and Spencer Tracy in the "battle-of-the-sexes" romantic comedies of the 1940s and 1950s, such as *Woman of the Year* (1942), *Adam's Rib* (1949), *Pat and Mike* (1952), and *Desk Set* (1957). During the first season, before Diane and Sam are officially a couple, their relationship is fraught with sexual tension. Like the romantic comedies made after 1934, when the Production Code prohibited sex before marriage, Sam and Diane's sexual energy is channeled through what she might call "witty repartee and banter." When the bartender and the waitress finally hit the sheets at the start of season 2 ("Power Play"), their relationship grows even more dysfunctional.

In the series' pilot ("Give Me a Ring Sometime"), Diane walks into Cheers with her professor, Sumner Sloan (Michael McGuire), before getting on a plane to Barbados, where they plan to get married the following day. But before they leave town, Sumner insists on retrieving his mother's wedding ring from his first wife, Barbara, to give to Diane. While waiting at Cheers, Diane meets an odd assortment of characters: Carla Tortelli (Rhea Perlman), a tart-tongued waitress and divorced mother of four; Ernie "Coach" Pantusso (Nicholas Colasanto), a befuddled bartender and Sam's former coach; and the bar's most loyal patrons, mailman Cliff Clavin (John Ratzenberger) and accountant Norm Peterson (George Wendt). According to *Cheers* writer/ producer Ken Levine, there was another regular in the original pilot, an elderly woman named Mrs. Littlefield, who can be seen in a wheelchair in the background of many shots, yet she never speaks or is acknowledged. Mrs. Littlefield, who Levine describes as "an opinionated old broad from the D. A. R. [Daughters of the American Revolution]," was written out of the series. *Variety* critic Tony Scott, who must have seen an early cut of the pilot, mentions in his review a "wheelchair patron" (played by Margaret Wheeler) and her "nasty nurse" (played by Elsa Raven). Levine explains that "politics just didn't fit with the mix," so her part was cut from the pilot and the series.

After waiting for hours, Diane is relieved when Sumner returns. He admits he couldn't take the ring and how when he was with Barbara "something stirred" inside of him. Barbara calls Sumner at Cheers and insists he come back to get the ring, leaving poor Diane alone again. When Diane expresses her fears that she may be losing him, Sam is honest and tells her "that goofy professor" is leaving her for his ex-wife. When Diane later calls the airlines to change her plane reservations, she finds out that Sam was right—Sumner and Barbara are on their way to Barbados. Knowing Diane can't go back to working for Sumner, Sam offers her a job as a waitress. Diane admits she's not qualified to do anything, but scoffs at the idea of working at Cheers, preferring to wait to find a job for which she's perfect. But when Diane is able to recall verbatim a long drink order Carla gives Sam, she realizes she's found it.

The show's setting was based on a real Boston bar, the Bull & Finch Pub, located on the Boston Common at 84 Beacon Street. Despite the bar's location, it is not a historic landmark (the pub opened its doors in 1969). Loosely modeled on the bar's interiors, the *Cheers* set was designed by two-time Oscar-winning Hollywood production designer Richard Sylbert (*Who's Afraid of Virginia Woolf* [1966], *Dick Tracy* [1990]). In a profile of Sylbert, Sylvia Townsend reveals that the designer received a $12,500 fee plus a $500 royalty for each episode. But what put the Bull & Finch on the map was a shot of the bar's exterior, which doubled as the exterior of Cheers. According to *TV Guide* reporter Deborah Starr Seibel, at the time the show's finale aired in 1993, the Bull & Finch was pulling in around $7 million annually, half from merchandising alone. In 2001, Bull & Finch opened Cheers Faneuil Hall, a replica of the Cheers bar. The following year, the Bull & Finch Pub was officially renamed Cheers Beacon Hill, which the Travel Channel ranks no. 5 in its list of Boston's Top Five Attractions (following the Freedom Trail, Faneuil Hall Marketplace, Fenway Park, and Cambridge).

The *Cheers* pilot is required viewing for anyone pursuing a career as a television comedy writer. The dialogue is sharp and funny, the seed is firmly planted for Sam and Diane's relationship, and we also learn just enough about the four supporting characters: Carla is tough and crass, Coach is a tad confused, Cliff is a know-it-all, and Norm prefers sitting on a bar stool to being at home with his wife, Vera. The critics agreed that *Cheers* was the best new show on the fall schedule. Associated Press critic Fred Rothenberg predicted the sitcom would be a "warm and wacky companion of a television show, a delightful place to spend idle times, a five-star watering hole." In his review for the *Washington Post*, Tom Shales dubbed *Cheers* "the best new series of the season . . . a comedy series with the potential to enter the ranks of the all-time greats." *New York Times* critic John J. O'Connor agreed that *Cheers* "looks as if it could be the best new situation comedy of the season. . . . Five minutes into the show, it is apparent that this is one of those projects that rapidly clicks into place." Levine remembers the big viewing party for the show's premiere hosted by the Charles Brothers and James Burrows at Chasen's, a Hollywood hotspot, where the invited audience erupted into "enthusiastic applause." "Tonight we were part of the best show on television," Levine recalls, "Tomorrow we'd be part of the lowest rated show on the lowest rated network."

Levine was not exaggerating. The ratings were so low that *Variety*'s Tom Bierbaim was questioning the future of "NBC's heralded Thursday lineup." But, to be fair, *Cheers* and *Taxi*, for which the Charles Brothers and Burrows won Emmys, were up against the second half of a two-hour *Magnum, P.I.* (on CBS) and an hour season opener of *Too Close for Comfort* (on ABC). The show (and NBC) continued to struggle in the ratings, yet the network believed in it enough to put a thirteen-episode order in for season 2, despite the fact it landed no. 74 out of 77 in the Nielsen ratings for the 1982–1983 television season.

In an interview with *Variety*'s Dave Kaufman, Shelley Long was optimistic about the show's future: "The order for 13 scripts is encouraging. We have a very loyal following. Our ratings have improved. We haven't reached our peak. It's a matter of time and I am confident we will do better; I feel we will get the chance." *Cheers* also scored major points for NBC when the 35th annual Emmy Awards were handed out two weeks prior to the start of season 2. The sitcom was nominated for thirteen Emmys and won five categories: Outstanding Comedy Series, Outstanding Writing (Glen and Les Charles, for the pilot episode), Directing (James Burrows, for "Showdown, Part 2"), Lead Actress (Long) and Outstanding Individual Achievement in Graphic Design and Title Sequences. During its eleven seasons on the air, *Cheers* received 117 Emmy nominations, winning 28 statues, including three for Outstanding Comedy Series.

Cheers' ranking in the ratings improved from season 2 (no. 35) to season 3 (no. 12). For its next seven seasons (4–10), *Cheers* ranked in the top five shows until it dropped down to no. 8 in its eleventh and final season. Eleven seasons is a long run for a situation comedy, especially for a show that lost two major cast members during the first five years: supporting actor Nicholas Colasanto, who we were told died offscreen at the start of season 4 (Colasanto died of heart attack in 1985), and Shelley Long (Diane), who surprised everyone when she chose not to renew her five-year contract.

Cheers is an ensemble comedy, yet Sam and Diane's relationship is the focus of the show's first five seasons, though they are officially a couple for only one and a half seasons (season 2 and the second half of season 5). In the two-part finale of season 2 ("I'll Be Seeing You, Parts 1 and 2"), Sam and Diane call it quits and she walks out of Cheers for what we are supposed to believe is the very last time. Season 3 focuses on the aftermath of the breakup: Sam turns back to the bottle and Diane lands in a psychiatric hospital, where she falls in love with her psychiatrist, Dr. Frasier Crane (Kelsey Grammer). To help Sam stay sober, Diane returns to Cheers and finds herself in the middle of triangle between Sam and the erudite Dr. Crane, who is left at the altar by Diane when she decides to once again return to Cheers. In the middle of season 5, Diane accepts Sam's marriage proposal ("Chambers vs. Malone"), but when her ex-fiancé Sumner Sloan appears to inform her a publisher is interested in her manuscript, she asks Sam to delay their wedding for six months so she can finish her book ("I Do, Adieu"). When she leaves, Sam knows that, this time, she won't be back.

Shelley Long's departure presented some challenges for the show's writers. At the end of season 5, *Cheers* ranked no. 3 in the season ratings behind its lead-ins, *The Cosby Show* (no. 1) and *Family Ties* (no. 2). At the same time, it would have been a challenge to have Sam and Diane continue their tumultuous relationship for much longer. After Long's departure, the writers added a new female character, Rebecca Howe (Kirstie Alley), and engaged in a little role reversal by making her Cheers' new manager (and Sam's boss) when he sells the bar to the Lillian Corporation. Rebecca thinks of herself as an astute businesswoman, but underneath her steely exterior she's a hot, neurotic mess, especially in her failed attempts to land a rich husband. The Lillian Corporation eventually sells Sam his bar back for .85 cents as a way of thanking him for turning in Rebecca's boyfriend Robin (Roger Rees), who was only using her to break into the Lillian Corporation's corporate accounts.

The absence of the Sam and Diane storyline also allowed the writers to devote more time developing the characters' personal lives. Woody Boyd (Woody Harrelson), who took Coach's place behind the bar at the start of season 4, pursues an acting career and marries Kelly Gaines (Jackie Swanson), whose millionaire father is vice-president of the Lillian Corporation. They have a child together and Woody runs for a seat on the Boston City Council. Carla, who starts the series with four children, adds four more. Five of her kids were fathered by her now ex-husband, Nick Tortelli (played by Dan Hedaya, who starred in the short-lived *Cheers* spinoff, *The Tortellis* [1987]). Baby no. 6 was with Frasier's mentor, Dr. Bennett Ludlow (James Karen), and her baby twin boys were with her husband, Eddie LeBec (Jay Thomas), a goalie for the Boston Bruins. Unfortunately, Eddie gets cut from the team and is forced to take a job playing a penguin in a traveling ice show, where he's accidentally run over by a Zamboni machine.

Frasier manages to fall in love and marry Dr. Lilith Sternin (Bebe Neuwirth), who is his intellectual equal (and equally neurotic), and together they have a son, Frederick. Lilith admits to having an affair, which sends Frasier over the edge. She leaves (to go live in an eco-pod), comes back, and the couple reconciles. Meanwhile, by comparison, Cliff and Norm's lives are far less dramatic, though Norm does lose several jobs and temporarily splits with his wife, Vera.

When it was time to write the ending to *Cheers*, Les and Glen Charles, who had been away since writing the introduction of Rebecca in the season 6 opener, planned to pen a half-hour finale and then agreed with the network on an hour. In their interview with the Archive of American Television (AAT), the Charles brothers revealed how the finale was expanded to ninety minutes because President Bill Clinton wanted to make an appearance on the *Cheers* finale. His five-minute scene was written, but the president had to attend a summit, prompting a rewrite of the script. In his AAT interview, James Burrows, who directed the finale and had a cameo (he's the guy who appears at the door and is told by Sam that they're closed), admitted that the finale was too long and a bit "hokey" (he also cited the last episode of *Mary Tyler Moore* as the best series finale he had seen [see chapter 23]). Actually, there is one thing the *Cheers* finale has in common with the *MTM* finale—irony. Just as everyone in the WJM-TV newsroom is fired except the incompetent anchor Ted Baxter, there are some touches of irony in regards to what the future has in store for the gang at *Cheers*.

Rebecca Howe, who devoted most of her time trying to land a rich husband, falls for a nice, very handsome, though certainly not rich, plumber named Don Santry (Tom Berenger). She's excited he's going to pop the question, but when he asks her to marry him, she can't bring herself to say "yes" (and she can't understand why). Meanwhile, sweet, naïve, and dim-witted Woody is sworn in as District 3's new city councilman despite his complete lack of qualifications. Woody's victory is the result of Frasier's bet with the gang at Cheers that he can get anyone 10 percent of the vote. But Woody's genuine naiveté, along with Kelly's announcement during a televised debate that she's pregnant, charms the voters, who elect the bartender into office. Woody then uses his newfound influence to get unemployed Norm an accounting job down at City Hall, which means Woody is now technically his boss.

The biggest surprise (though considering the amount of advanced publicity, not much of a surprise at all) was the return of Diane Chambers (and Shelley Long). Diane is first seen, much to the surprise of the patrons of Cheers, on television accepting a writing award for her television movie, *The Heart Held Hostage.* She later reveals that the story of a hardworking mother raising six children alone is based on Carla's life (in the end, the character goes berserk and takes out a few people with an Uzi). Sam manages to track Diane down and they catch up over the phone, each lying to the other that they are happily married with kids.

When Diane arrives unexpectedly at Cheers with her "husband" Reed (Mark Harelik), Sam is forced to pass Rebecca, who is a physical and emotional wreck over losing Don, off as his wife. In something straight out of a sitcom playbook, their lies are exposed when Reed's male lover appears and accuses Reed of cheating on him, followed by Don who enters to propose to Rebecca one last time (she accepts). Sam and Diane, who are clearly still hot for each other, announce to everyone that they are once again a couple and he is moving with her to California. He gets no support from the Cheers gang, who accuse him of deserting them. Sam lashes out at them, telling them to get a life; he's not their mother, he says angrily, and Cheers is not their home. While waiting for their plane to take off, Sam and Diane get a chance to rethink their plan with some help from the plane's PA system which, in addition to giving them updates on the delay, dispenses to each of them individual and very personal relationship advice. They both decide, amiably, that this is not going to work.

The most satisfying part of the finale begins with Sam's return to Cheers, where he (and the viewer) are led to believe that he is getting the cold shoulder from everyone. But Sam (and the viewer) are relieved that it's only a prank and they are glad to have him back. They say goodbye to Rebecca, who

After a six-year absence, Shelley Long returned for the series finale of *Cheers*. *Authors' collection*

still can't believe she's marrying a plumber, and spend the remainder of the episode sitting around, smoking cigars, and waxing philosophical about the meaning of life. Sam admits that by telling his friends they don't have a life, he was really talking about himself ("Irony!" they chant). The final exchange between Norm and Sam is quite touching. Norm admits that he knew Sam would come back because "you can never be unfaithful to your one true love. You always come back to her." It takes a moment before Sam realizes he means the bar. Alone, he then admits to himself, "Boy, I tell you, I'm the luckiest son-of-a bitch on earth."

The end of *Cheers* was a major entertainment news story, so television critics and reporters from around the country traveled to the West Coast in

January, four months before the finale, to get the cast and crew's reactions to the show's impending conclusion. Paramount Studios, where *Cheers* was filmed in front of a live audience, opened Stage 25 so journalists would have some brews with the cast and talk about the show's legacy.

There was brief period a few months into season 11 when Danson was considering returning for one more season. Although the show's ratings had gone down, *Cheers* was still a top-rated show that consistently won its time-slot. *Variety*'s Brian Lowry reported in November 1992 that Danson (who was by then making $400,000 an episode) and Charles/Burrows/Charles were in "active negotiations" with NBC. One month later, with a *Variety* headline reading "*Cheers* is Toast: NBC Pulls Plug," Lowry reported that the longest-running comedy on prime-time television, which had earned more Emmy nominations than any other prime-time series, would not be returning the following season. According to sources, the decision was made by the cast and crew and didn't stem from the show's licensing fee (the amount NBC paid Paramount Television to license the show, which was over $2 million per episode due to the cast's high salaries). *Variety* printed a correction the following day, stating that the headline to the story was "incorrect" and clarified that "the decision to halt production on the show after the eleventh season was made by the cast and crew of the show" as opposed to NBC, which is what the headline implied. Some NBC executive most likely feared he or she would be held responsible for "pulling the plug" on *Cheers*.

In one of the many newspaper and magazine stories about the show's finale, *Los Angeles Times* reporter Susan King asked Ted Danson how he was feeling about the decision to call it quits after eleven seasons. "I feel very certain about the decision to move, to stop," Danson admitted. "All the feelings (about leaving) I am sure will come flooding in once I indeed stop. There will be sadness, regret, fear, exhilaration. There will be lots of stuff—lots of feelings."

Nineteen years later, in Brian Raftery's *GQ* article commemorating *Cheers*'s thirtieth anniversary, George Wendt explained that the cast did ask each other at the end of season 7 and onward if they wanted to continue, yet "it was always on Ted, ultimately." In the same article, Danson admitted that at the time he decided to leave the show, he was going through changes in his life (a separation from his wife and an affair) that "were all very messy and public. It felt like I really wanted to rock my boat and make changes in my life, and who I am and how I am, that would also mean moving on from *Cheers*. I don't think it was an emotionally mature decision. I brought the house down around my ears, lit it on fire, and then went 'I have to go.'"

At least *Cheers* went out in a blaze of glory. In terms of viewers, "One for the Road" was seen by over 84 million people, making it the second-most-watched television finale, behind *M*A*S*H*. The finale received favorable reviews, yet the critics were in agreement that the one major issue was its length (the ninety-minute finale was preceded by a half-hour retrospective, Cheers: *Last Call!* hosted by Bob Costas). "There is a good reason why sitcoms are only a half-hour long," observed *Variety* critic Tony Scott, who praised the writing, direction, and the cast, all of which were in "top form." *Washington Post* critic Tom Shales appreciated how *Cheers* "went out . . . with a lot of class." He found the final scene in which the characters sat around, smoked cigars, and talked about life not as emotional as the *Mary Tyler Moore* finale, "but it has its own piquant poignancy" (of course no one just got fired or was saying goodbye). *New York Times* critic John J. O'Connor found the finale "overall long and uncharacteristically labored," reserving most of his praise for Danson's work ("the show's one essential ingredient") and appreciated the realization his character made in the final few episodes that he was a sex addict, getting older, and not happy.

While it's to be expected that NBC would pull out all the stops to promote (and cash in) on the finale of one of its most popular series, the network decided to make it an all-day affair. The festivities began earlier that day with a visit by some cast members to the State House in Boston, where Governor William Weld declared May 20, 1993, "*Cheers* Day." Outside the Bull & Finch in Boston, bleachers and a video screen were set up for a public viewing of the finale. The *Cheers* cast (minus Bebe Neuwirth, who didn't appear in the finale, Shelley Long, and Kirstie Alley, who appeared via satellite) watched from inside the Bull & Finch. After the 11:00 p.m. news, *The Tonight Show with Jay Leno* was broadcast live from inside the bar, where Leno interviewed the series regulars, most of whom were too inebriated to carry on an intelligent conversation. In a 2013 piece for *Vulture*, Ken Levine, who was in the bar that historic evening, recalled the chaotic scene: "They [the *Cheers* cast] were so drunk they need designated walkers. They giggled like schoolgirls over nothing, fired spitballs into each other's mouths, squirted water guns, Woody Harrelson implied he gave oral sex to both Ted Danson and Oliver Stone, and Kirstie Alley sang a song where the only lyric was 'dick, dick, dick'." Poor Jay Leno, who had only been the permanent host of *The Tonight Show* for a year, didn't quite know how to respond to the lack of cooperation he was getting from his guests. A week later, the *Los Angeles Times* printed a Reuters story in which Leno admitted it was a "huge mistake": "But I guess you have to expect people to show up totally drunk when you do a live show from a real bar." Leno added that Ted Danson sent flowers the next day to apologize, "and Norm called."

The gang at *Cheers* has not reunited for a special or a made-for-television movie, though we did get an update not too long after the show ended when several *Cheers* regulars appeared on its spinoff, *Frasier*. Sam Malone paid his friend Dr. Crane a visit in Seattle in a 1995 episode of *Frasier* ("The Show Where Sam Shows Up"). A self-identified recovering sex-addict, Sam has been engaged for six months to a fellow sex addict, Sheila (Téa Leoni), whom Frasier realizes he slept with two months earlier. Sam comes clean and admits that he "slipped" and slept with someone the night he and Sheila got engaged. Sheila names two men who hang out at Cheers whom she's slept with: Paul, who is short and bald, and Cliff Clavin (Frasier is relieved she doesn't reveal their secret). But Cliff is the deal breaker for Sam, and the engagement is called off. Sam also gives Frasier an update on the Cheers gang: ironically, Rebecca's husband, Don, dumped her after he struck it rich inventing some "toilet thing," Woody and Kelly have a son who is smarter than his parents, Norm is still a steady customer, and Cliff hasn't been seen in a while because he won't leave his mother's house after reading about flesh-eating bacteria.

In Jefferson Graham's official companion to *Frasier*, Kelsey Grammer admitted he wasn't happy with the episode with Sam because there was no conflict between Frasier and Sam, an element that would have led to "a new understanding about each other." But that's exactly what happens the following season when Diane visits Seattle where her play is being produced ("The One Where Diane Shows Up"). She seems happy—until the truth comes out. She has lost her beach house, her boyfriend, and her job writing on *Dr. Quinn, Medicine Woman* (she accidentally set actress Jane Seymour's hair on fire). Diane asks for his help, and Frasier, who puts all his animosity behind him, obliges. But once he sees a rehearsal of her "feminist odyssey" based on her experiences working at Cheers, and realizes Diane is dating one of the actors, Frasier goes berserk and denounces her as the devil. Diane, in turn, apologizes for the way she has treated Frasier over the years.

In later episodes, Woody pays a visit to Frasier ("The One Where Woody Shows Up") and after one evening, they grow bored of each other but are ashamed to admit it. In season 9, Frasier returns to Boston and drags his brother, Niles (David Hyde Pierce), his father (John Mahoney), and his father's caregiver, Daphne (Jane Leeves), to Cliff's retirement party and is reunited with Carla, Cliff, Norm, and some other members of the Cheers gang.

And—no surprise—everyone seems exactly how we left them.

4

The Finale About Something

Seinfeld on Trial

Seinfeld (NBC, 1989–1998)
Created by Jerry Seinfeld and Larry David
Premiere date: July 5, 1989
9 seasons / 180 episodes
"The Finale, Parts 1 and 2"
Airdate: May 14, 1998
41.3 rating • 58 percent share • 76.3 million viewers
Directed by Andy Ackerman
Written by Larry David
Cast: Jerry Seinfeld (Jerry Seinfeld), Jason Alexander (George Costanza), Julia
 Louis-Dreyfus (Elaine Benes), Michael Richards (Cosmo Kramer), Wayne
 Knight (Newman), Jerry Stiller (Frank Costanza), Estelle Harris (Estelle
 Costanza), Liz Sheridan (Helen Seinfeld), Barney Martin (Morty Seinfeld)

On Christmas day 1997, Jerry Seinfeld announced that his series *Seinfeld*—then the most popular show on television—would complete its run at the end of its current ninth season. While the show had routinely given its millions of fans immense joy, this news—especially given its timing—felt like a lump of coal. For nine years the series had graced the airwaves with its own particular style, wit, and charm—famously a show about "nothing," it certainly felt like "something" to its dedicated viewers. For Jerry Seinfeld, the reasoning was simple, as he told the *New York Times*: "I wanted to end the show on the same kind of peak we've been doing it on for years. . . . I wanted the end to be from a point of strength. I wanted the end to be graceful." The series star and executive producer went on to say that as a comedian his "sense of timing is everything," and, for him, the time was right. Despite NBC's attempts to throw more money at him than a sitcom star had ever been given (reportedly $5 million per episode), Seinfeld would not budge. Two weeks later, his face would grace the cover of *Time* magazine with the headline: "That's All, Folks." NBC had just five months to prepare to say goodbye to their ratings juggernaut, a series that had come to define the modern sitcom. Speculation on how it would all end ran rampant, but the exit of Jerry, Elaine, George, and Kramer would remain a well-kept secret until its broadcast in May 1998.

Seinfeld was created by Jerry Seinfeld and Larry David. Seinfeld, a working standup comic, regularly appeared on *The Tonight Show Starring Johnny Carson* (first appearance in 1981), while David briefly worked as a writer on *Saturday Night Live* (1984–1985), and as a writer/performer on *SNL*'s Friday counterpart, NBC's *Fridays* (1980–1982). Their series was born out of their own friendship, mostly from their endless conversations. Jerry Seinfeld explained: "Our conversations were always funny explorations of the smallest, most arcane subjects, matters of such small importance they came to govern all of life." Together, the pair wrote the first episode of what was then called *The Seinfeld Chronicles*, which NBC agreed to air on July 5, 1989, billing it as a "sitcom-comedy special." The episode starred Jerry Seinfeld playing a version of himself, Jason Alexander as the neurotic Larry David stand-in George Costanza, and Michael Richards as wacky next-door neighbor Kessler. An additional part of the ensemble, Claire the waitress (played by Lee Garlington), also appeared in the first episode. The episode pulled in moderate ratings, coming in second in its given timeslot—but NBC bigwigs were not convinced. While NBC executive Warren Littlefield believed the show was "something different" (in a good way), his then-boss Brandon Tartikoff famously dismissed the show (in not such a good way) as "too New York, too Jewish." The test audience, then polled by telephone after being sent the network's pilot, agreed with Tartikoff. NBC's research department report included the following assessments: "No segment of the audience was eager to watch the show again"; "None of the [supporting characters] were particularly liked"; and, to add to Tartikoff's feelings, "Many did not identify with the things with which Jerry was involved." Given this feedback, the show was likely to never see the light of day again—a fact made only more evident by its absence from NBC's 1989–90 prime-time lineup.

Just as the show was looking to become a footnote in NBC's history, Rick Ludwin, an NBC executive in the late night/specials department, pressed for a second chance for *The Seinfeld Chronicles*. Ludwin sent the following memo to NBC execs on September 14, 1989: "Would you please contact Castle Rock Entertainment [producer of the show] to structure a deal for four half-hour episodes of *The Seinfeld Chronicles* which will be bookkept as specials and run in the spring of 1990. Jerry Seinfeld as the star is of the essence." Ludwin would finance four additional half-hour episodes of *The Seinfeld Chronicles* by reducing his specials by two one-hour spots—garnering him the nickname of "patron saint of NBC" by fellow exec Warren Littlefield. NBC gave the greenlight to the four episodes (often noted to be the smallest television order ever), with one stipulation: a female character must be added to the main ensemble.

The minor character of Claire the waitress was tossed out and replaced with Elaine Benes, characterized as Jerry's former girlfriend turned platonic friend. Many actresses read for the role of Elaine, including future sitcom stars Megan Mullally (Karen on *Will & Grace* [1998–2006]) and Patricia Heaton (Debra on *Everybody Loves Raymond* [1996–2005] and Frankie on *The Middle* [2009–present]), but the part eventually went to Julia Louis-Dreyfus, who had previously worked with Larry David on his one season at *Saturday Night Live*. With Julia's Elaine now on board (and Michael Richards's Kessler renamed Kramer), David and Seinfeld went to work on their short order of four episodes. The episodes would air beginning May 31, 1990, nearly a year after the original broadcast of *The Seinfeld Chronicles*. Renamed simply *Seinfeld*, the show grabbed the Thursday 9:30 p.m. timeslot, airing immediately after *Cheers* summer reruns. Billed as the "hot summer hit soon to be a series," the show did well enough to warrant a second season and thus NBC made it official by ordering thirteen more episodes to begin airing in January of 1991. *Seinfeld*, advertised as "one part sitcom, one part standup," had wriggled its way onto the airwaves, despite the initial unlikely odds. What was Rick Ludwin's gamble became NBC's greatest boon, as the show would go on to earn the network more than $1 billion dollars.

The series was not an immediate hit, taking its time to find its footing. With a dedicated fan base and praise from critics—Howard Rosenberg of the *Los Angeles Times* called it "a winner"—the ratings remained steady. The show aired on Wednesdays at 9:00 p.m. (opposite ABC's popular *Home Improvement*, starring Tim Allen) until the middle of its fourth season when it moved to the coveted Thursday after-*Cheers* 9:30 p.m. spot. Within four weeks, *Seinfeld* increased its audience by more than 50 percent and went from the no. 40 most-watched show on television to no. 5. The show had gone from little-seen gem to bona fide hit, even surpassing *Cheers* (ranked no. 7), which at the time was airing its farewell season. The show went on to snag the Emmy for Outstanding Comedy Series for that same season, besting both *Cheers* and former competitor *Home Improvement*.

By the time the series hit syndication in 1995, it became a cultural sensation. Episodes like season 4's "The Contest"—which was about resisting the urge to masturbate (although that word was never used)—ushered the phrase "Master of my domain!" into the national lexicon. Episodes frankly spoke of male "shrinkage," and Elaine's measure of a man's sexual worth (which she deemed "sponge worthy"), as well as hitting on the then-culturally touchy subject of homosexuality after Jerry and George are mistaken as a gay couple—"not that there's anything wrong with that." The show created new categories for how to describe its gaggle of side characters—whether they are "low-talkers," "close-talkers," or have the misfortune of being a woman with "man-hands." George's father, Frank, played by comedy legend Jerry Stiller, created (and thus popularized) a new holiday called Festivus (not Christmas or Hanukkah but a holiday "for the rest of us"), and lived by the mantra "Serenity now!" George played a tense game of Trivial Pursuit with the so-called Bubble Boy, while Elaine confronted (and bested) the "Soup Nazi." Episodes referenced (and parodied) other notable pop-culture entities, including Superman's Bizarro-Earth concept ("The Bizarro-Jerry"), the Zapruder film of the JFK assassination ("The Boyfriend"), and Harold Pinter's play *The Betrayal*, which presents its entire story backwards, starting at the end ("The Betrayal"). Nearly every episode of the show created a "water-cooler" moment, as the English language struggled to keep up with all of *Seinfeld*'s new additions to its vocabulary.

As the show neared the end of its run, NBC ramped up its promotion of the finale episode to hysteria-level proportions. The end of the show had become, as Caryn James of the *New York Times* noted, a "communal experience." She continued: "*Seinfeld* mania reveals a longing for community that highlights television's unifying social role. . . . Knowing a *Seinfeld* catch phrase like 'master of your domain' makes you an insider, even if you're one of millions." NBC counted on this "communal experience" to be a record-breaking event, bumping up advertising rates for the finale to Super Bowl–sized proportions (a reported $1.7 million for a 30-second spot). Though an air of secrecy surrounded the finale, Larry David, who had left the series in season 7 but returned to pen the finale, promised that the last episode "would have finality . . . the weight of a finale . . . it ties up all the knots." The finale episode was preceded by an hour-long clip show, including moments from the show's most famous episodes, as well as bloopers and backstage moments, with the final montage set to Green Day's then-recent hit "Good Riddance (Time of Your Life)." The final shot shows the four leads taking their final bow on the set of Jerry's apartment.

The two-part hour-long finale (aptly titled "The Finale") opens with Jerry doing a standup routine, a convention of the show that had been abandoned in recent seasons. Jerry and George soon find out that their television show *Jerry* (originally introduced as "the show about nothing" in season 4) has been resurrected at NBC, with a thirteen-episode commitment. As Jerry and George prepare to move to Los Angeles, they are informed by the top brass at NBC that a private jet will be at their disposal to take them anywhere they would like. Taking full advantage of this luxury, Jerry and George, along with Kramer and Elaine, decide to head to Paris for one last adventure together. While on the private plane, Kramer, having complained about water left in his ear after a trip to the beach, jumps up and down trying to get the water out. He clumsily falls into the cockpit and the plane begins to descend rapidly. The gang, believing they are all about the die, confess their darkest sins, including George who admits to having cheated in "The Contest," and Elaine who manages to get out "Jerry, I've always loved—" before the plane levels out (the implication is that the end of the sentence would have been "you"). The plane is temporarily grounded after the mishap, setting down in the small town of Latham, Massachusetts. The gang heads into town to kill some time, and while they are there they witness a carjacking, which Kramer records on his video camera. They make fun of the carjacking victim (John Pinette), who happens to be overweight, as the victim looks to them for help. After the carjacker gets away in his vehicle, the victim calls over a police officer, who then approaches the gang to tell them they are under arrest. They have violated "Article 223-7 of the Latham County penal code," a recently enacted law that "requires you to help or assist anyone in danger as long as it is reasonable to do so" (also known as "The Good Samaritan Law"). The four friends are carted off to jail, learning that breaking this law could mean up to five years in prison. They are encouraged to get a good lawyer, which in the *Seinfeld* universe means the return of Johnny Cochran caricature Jackie Chiles (Phil Morris).

Upon hearing that the gang has hired the reputable publicity hound, the prosecution sets out to dig up as much dirt on the gang as possible, making "character" the main point of attack. Geraldo Rivera (appearing as himself) covers the trial, joining in on the media circus surrounding "the New York Four" as Jerry, George, Elaine, and Kramer are now being called. Many of the series' most memorable characters are seen heading to Massachusetts for the trial, including Jerry's parents (Liz Sheridan and Barney Martin), George's parents (Estelle Harris and Jerry Stiller), Newman (Wayne Knight), Puddy (Patrick Warburton), J. Peterman (John O'Hurley), Mickey (Danny Woodburn), Bania (Steve Hytner), Uncle Leo (Len Lesser), Susan's parents Mr. and Mrs. Ross (Warren Frost and Grace Zabriskie), Keith Hernandez (as himself), and George Steinbrenner (played by Lee Bear). At the trial, the district attorney goes on the attack, promising to prove that there is a history of "selfishness, self-absorption, immaturity and greed" within the group, continuing that "everyone that has come into contact with these four individuals has been abused, wronged, deceived, and betrayed." What proceeds is a parade of witnesses who can attest to the questionable character of "the New York Four," which allows the show to bring back every memorable victim

The gang stands trial, led by defense attorney Jackie Chiles: (left to right) Jackie (Phil Morris), Jerry (Jerry Seinfeld), Elaine (Julia Louis-Dreyfus), George (Jason Alexander), and Kramer (Michael Richards).   *NBC/Photofest*

of the *Seinfeld* wrath. This includes series favorites (The Soup Nazi, Bubble Boy, Mr. Pitt, Babu), former girlfriends (Marla the virgin, Sidra "they're real" Holland, Leslie the Low-Talker), and many others that have been wronged and seek revenge. By the end of the trial, Geraldo reports that "the jury has been in deliberation for four hours," but the outlook is not good. When the verdict is read, the gang is found guilty and sentenced to one year in prison, or as the judge puts it "one year removed from society." The final scene follows the gang as they slowly walk to their jail cell, contemplating how they will spend their year behind bars. Over the credits, Jerry, wearing his prison orange jumpsuit, performs a standup routine for his fellow prisoners, as Kramer cracks up in the crowd, while the rest of the prisoners boo him.

Ratings for the episode were tremendous—reaching 76.3 million viewers nationwide, with nearly 58 percent of all households in America tuning in to the finale. Cable's TVLand even joined in on the viewing, suspending their own programming and instead running an hour-long message that read: "We're TV fans so . . . we're watching the last episode of *Seinfeld*. Will return at 10:00 p.m. ET, 7:00 p.m. PT" (a tactic used again by IFC, Sundance, WE tv, and BBC America during *Mad Men*'s 2015 finale, see appendix). Even the Department of Water and Power in Los Angeles measured the viewing audience, citing that water usage spiked 10–15 percent during the episode's commercial breaks, and 35 percent when the show ended. In a pre-DVR

The *Seinfeld* gang ends up sentenced to a year behind bars.   *Authors' collection*

television world, NBC agreed to broadcast an encore of the finale the following week (only to add even more to that whopping 76.3 million).

While viewership hit record-breaking highs, the viewers themselves were conflicted on the content of the finale. Many criticized Larry David's choice to suddenly judge his own characters, punishing them for the same characteristics fans had come to love. Ken Tucker of *Entertainment Weekly* agreed: "This crew led miserable lives, and we relished their exceptional pettiness. That they should be punished for all the vicarious fun we had at their expense is David's way of saying we never should have made these cruel losers Must See-worthy." Caryn James of the *New York Times* disagreed, calling the finale "*Seinfeld* at its best: mordant, unsentimental . . . wildly self-referential and slightly surreal," continuing, "the final episode revels in petty details, turns clichés on their heads and reveals why *Seinfeld* worked so well." Larry David defended his choice of sending the four off to jail, citing that he "wanted to leave open the possibility that they could come back, that they could emerge from somewhere. Not that they would come back and do the series, but just to, perhaps, give people some hope. You never know." David would eventually make good on this statement, bringing the characters back in a staged reunion as part of the seventh season (2009) of his own series, HBO's *Curb Your Enthusiasm*—a move that many cited as a "do-over" on the actual *Seinfeld* finale. Jerry Seinfeld, who decided to cut the cord on the show when he did, would not put the series finale "into the category of fun." In a moment of self-reflection, Seinfeld admitted:

After nine years, how do you say goodbye to the experience, the people, the accomplishments? It was one of those major life transitions, like birth or death, where there's so much going on it becomes a little overwhelming. Human beings aren't designed to handle things so big. Emotionally, I just hoped not to get crushed, yet all the while I knew I would.

The series finale's ratings cemented the show as one of the top-five most-watched finales of all time—a fitting way to wrap up a show that had continuously outperformed everyone's expectations.

In a December 2014 interview with popular podcaster (and editor-in-chief of Grantland.com) Bill Simmons, Larry David admitted that the final episode resulted in him receiving "so much grief" from fans, elaborating that "people hated it." David concluded that as a result of these passionate responses, he would never attempt to write another series finale for any show he worked on—which signaled that his current show *Curb Your Enthusiasm*, having wrapped production in 2011 without any formal finale, would potentially never again grace our television screens. David's decision was predicated on the fact that inevitably viewer opinion is skewed no matter how you slice it. He said:

> I think the thing about finales is that everybody writes their own finale in their head. Whereas if they just tune in during the week to a normal show, they're surprised by what's going on. They haven't written it beforehand. They don't know what the show is. But for a finale, they go "oh, this should happen to George. And Jerry and Elaine should get together." And all that. And so they've already written it and often they're disappointed, because it's not what they wrote.

Lucky for Larry David, Bill Simmons admitted that over time his disappointment in the *Seinfeld* finale turned into admiration, a feeling that has been shared by many of the series' viewers. Since its finale, *Seinfeld* has been ranked in the Top 10 of nearly every list of "Television's Greatest Series," landing the top spot on *TV Guide*'s 2002 list. The show has never truly left the airwaves, having enjoyed multi-billion-dollar syndication profits since its sixth season. Jerry Seinfeld and Larry David continue to collect a yearly salary based on the show's continually renewed syndication contracts. Even the owner of Tom's Restaurant, the exterior of which stood in for *Seinfeld*'s Monk's Diner, accounts that 5 to 10 percent of his customers patronize his diner because of the show. To attempt to account for all of the lasting impact of the series would be too long a story to tell, so it's best to evoke one of the series' most famous catchphrases and just say the show's success cannot be understated, yada, yada, yada, keep watching.

The One Where It's All Over

TV's Favorite *Friends*

Friends (NBC, 1994–2004)
Created by Marta Kauffman and David Crane
Premiere date: September 22, 1994
10 seasons / 236 episodes
"The Last One, Parts 1 and 2"
Airdate: May 6, 2004
29.8 rating • 43 percent share • 52.46 million viewers
Directed by Kevin S. Bright
Written by Marta Kauffman and David Crane
Cast: Jennifer Aniston (Rachel Green), Courteney Cox Arquette (Monica Geller-
   Bing), Lisa Kudrow (Phoebe Buffay), Matt LeBlanc (Joey Tribbiani), Matthew
   Perry (Chandler Bing), David Schwimmer (Ross Geller)
Guest Stars: Anna Faris (Erica), James Michael Tyler (Gunther), Paul Rudd (Mike
   Hannigan)

In March of 1994, the *New York Times* began a series of four articles following the development of a television series from its infancy (or pitch), to its casting, and finally its eventual pickup and broadcast. When writer Elizabeth Kolbert selected a new twenty-something Generation X sitcom written by Marta Kauffman and David Crane (then best known for creating HBO's *Dream On* [1990–1996]), there was no way of knowing that the show would someday become the mega sensation (and ratings giant) *Friends*. At the time of the first article's publication, the show was titled "Friends Like Us," and was only one of three potential pilots Kauffman and Crane had on the front burner (one, which they considered more promising, was a high school drama/comedy with musical numbers—fifteen years before Ryan Murphy's *Glee*). With each subsequent article, their show progressed and changed: the title became "Six of One," veteran television giant James Burrows signed on to direct, and again the title changed, this time simply to *Friends*. While the articles focused on the ins and outs of the television business, what also emerged was the faith and confidence that Kauffman and Crane, along with producing partner Kevin Bright, had in their show. Kauffman proclaimed: "We didn't want to make it like every other sitcom." Les Moonves, then the president of Warner Bros. Television, was charged with the task of selling *Friends* to NBC. He called it "a very hip show," but worried initially that it was a "little bit edgy." Moonves thought that by overselling the "hipness" of the show, he would paint the series as too different and "different is harder to sell." Luckily for all involved, including the very lucky Elizabeth Kolbert, out of the nearly 100 hopeful television shows, *Friends* made the cut.

Ordered initially for just twelve episodes (in addition to the first episode, or "pilot"), NBC had taken a chance on the ensemble sitcom, which included a cast of virtual unknowns. Perhaps the only known entity on the show was Courteney Cox. Her biggest claim to fame at the time of the *New York Times* articles was as "Michael J. Fox's old flame from *Family Ties*" (she was also recognizable as Jerry's pretend wife, who helps him get a dry cleaning discount, on an episode of *Seinfeld*, and the girl Bruce Springsteen picks from the audience to dance with him onstage in the "Dancing in the Dark" video). Cox was cast as the neurotic, yet likeable, chef Monica Geller, a character who in its inception was, according to co-creator David Crane, thought to be "darker and edgier and snarkier," a Janeane Garofalo type. But Cox brought something new to the table and the creators shaped the character around her energy. Also cast was David Schwimmer as the romantic and nerdy Ross Geller (Monica's brother). Schwimmer, whose credits were then only small roles on *The Wonder Years*, *LA Law*, and *NYPD Blue*, had previously auditioned for Kauffman and Crane for a failed project, and his presence resonated with the creative duo. Matt LeBlanc won the role of Joey Tribbiani, a character whose casting was detailed in the second of the four-part series in the *New York Times* ("Finding the Absolutely Perfect Actor: The High-Stress Business of Casting"). Kauffman and Crane were looking for a "handsome, smug, macho guy in his 20s," and eventually found LeBlanc, a former model who had scraped by with odd jobs in New York before landing a failed spinoff of *Married . . . with Children* called *Vinnie & Bobby* (1992). For the part of Rachel Green, the creators, with casting director Ellie Kanner, found Jennifer Aniston, then best known for taking on Jennifer Grey's part in the television adaptation of John Hughes's 1986 hit *Ferris Bueller's Day Off* (and, of course, for being the daughter of soap opera legend John Aniston, the actor who portrays Victor Kiriakis on NBC's *Days of Our Lives*). In an interview with Oprah Winfrey in 2011, Aniston, seated alongside her *Just Go with It* co-star and *Saturday Night Live* vet

The cast of *Friends* (left to right): Matthew Perry, Jennifer Aniston, David Schwimmer, Courteney Cox, Matt LeBlanc, and Lisa Kudrow.   *Authors' collection*

Adam Sandler, admitted that in choosing *Friends* she turned down the opportunity to audition for *SNL*. Finally, for the roles of Chandler Bing and Phoebe Buffay, two characters that Kauffman and Crane initially viewed as secondary to the previous four (providing those snappy one-liners at most), the creators found Matthew Perry and Lisa Kudrow. Perry was initially unavailable as he was cast in a Fox pilot called *LAX 2194*, a show about airport baggage handlers in the future (really)—but he was eventually released and free to take on the cynical funnyman role. The character of Phoebe, initially described as a "New Age waif," went to Kudrow, who appeared at the time in a small, but memorable, part on the network's other hit comedy *Mad About You* (the character, clueless waitress Ursula, would reappear on *Friends* as Phoebe's twin sister). When the six players came to the table to perform the first read-through of the pilot script, Kauffman remembered there was a feeling of magic. She recalled: "The first day we went to a run-through, and the six of them were together for the first time, onstage in the coffee shop, I remember the atmosphere being electric. A chill ran down my spine." Crane agreed: "There was not a weak link." The chemistry of the cast made the series come alive, and ultimately, it would be this same electricity that would catapult the series to become one of television's greatest hits.

When *Friends* was officially put on the NBC schedule in the fall of 1994, the network showed their confidence in the show, and its virtually unknown cast, by giving the freshman series a plum spot in their coveted Thursday night lineup. Sandwiched between *Mad About You* (then in its third season) and *Seinfeld* (in its sixth season), *Friends* premiered on September 22, 1994, at 8:30 p.m. NBC's famed Thursday night lineup that once included *Family Ties* (1982–1989), *Cheers* (1982–1993), and *The Cosby Show* (1984–1992) was now populated by three shows set in New York City: *Mad About You*, covering the married angle; *Seinfeld*, exploring the eccentric/neurotic side; and *Friends*, which delivered the post-college, twenty-something experience. The advantageous spot on the fall lineup led *Friends* to pull in an admirable 22 million viewers in its first episode—a number certainly helped by its lead-in and follower, as well as the series of articles in the *New York Times*. Critics were cautiously optimistic about the premiere. *Variety*'s Tony Scott found the actors to be "resourceful" with "sharp sitcom skills," but touted: "[The] spirited ensemble, directly aptly by James Burrows, should help the show through its early days, but if the series is to have legs, funnier writing is needed." Howard Rosenberg of the *Los Angeles Times* went out on a limb by calling it "the best comedy series of the new season," but noted: "It has the burden of sorting out the major characters in this communal comedy, six singles in their 20s who spend much of their time slouching around . . . talking about being single. It sounds vacuous, and it is, sort of, but wittily vacuous, with crisply written dialogue adroitly executed by the show's strong ensemble cast." After viewing the first few episodes, *Entertainment Weekly*'s Ken Tucker declared that *Friends* had a "momentum and charm that win you over even if you're not laughing." He concluded: "It's just another sitcom, but even so, *Friends* is pretty irresistible." Fans agreed with Tucker. *Friends* had become the runaway hit of the season, marking its territory as a new major player on Thursday nights.

At the start of the second season, the show had become part of everyday pop culture conversation. Jennifer Aniston's layered coif—envied and imitated by many—became "The Rachel" haircut. The Rembrandts' theme song for the show "I'll Be There for You" was a chart-topping radio hit. Fans gathered at local coffee shops, drinking lattes from Central Perk–sized mugs. By midseason, NBC was ready to bet all their chips on their Gen X–defining show—airing it after their broadcast of Super Bowl XXX. While the game pitted the Dallas Cowboys against the Pittsburgh Steelers (Dallas won), the episode, aptly titled "The One After the Super Bowl," pitted Rachel against Monica for the attention of movie star Jean-Claude Van Damme (playing himself). Joey is pursued by crazed soap-fan Brooke Shields (Shields's comedic chops proved her worthy of her own sitcom, *Suddenly Susan* [1996–2000], the following season). Meanwhile, Phoebe is romanced by singer Chris Isaak, and Ross and Chandler are reunited with old friends (Ross with his pet monkey Marcel, and Chandler with old flame Julia Roberts). The never-ending parade of guest stars may not have made for the best episode of *Friends* (critics panned it for being "overstuffed" and not all that funny), but the ratings exploded. Pulling in almost 53 million viewers (the most for the show in its history—but more on that later), *Friends* emerged as the true winner of the Super Bowl (sorry, Cowboys), and from there, it was nothing but up.

Realizing their worth in this now mega-profitable show, the actors famously banded together in several well-publicized salary negotiations. Agreeing to stand as one, and asking for equal pay per episode (a move that went on to inspire similar negotiating tactics for the stars of *The Big Bang Theory* and *Modern Family*), the six stars negotiated their way from $40,000 per episode in season 1 to $750,000 by the end of season 6. By the eighth season, the stars each raked in a *Seinfeld*-level salary of $1 million per episode. As the ninth season began in the fall of 2002, talk of negotiations with the cast resurfaced, only this time for a very different reason. Previously, it was believed that the ninth season would indeed be the series' last. Jennifer Aniston, then married to mega-movie star Brad Pitt, was becoming a movie star in her own right (the summer's indie sleeper *The Good Girl* was generating awards buzz), and her fellow cast members followed suit—Cox continuing with her role in the *Scream* franchise, and Perry and Kudrow in mob comedies *The Whole Nine Yards* and *Analyze This*, respectively. NBC ran promos for the upcoming ninth season, urging viewers to "Cherish every episode." As the writing staff prepared to pour one last cup of java at Central Perk, hope emerged in December of 2002, when the cast seemed amenable to a contract extension—for the right price. NBC was all too eager to accept their terms, which included a shortened season (only eighteen episodes versus the usual twenty-four), while maintaining their seven-figure salary. Since the network had failed to launch an heir apparent to the series (*Inside Schwartz* [2001–2002] and *Leap of Faith* [2002]) and the future of their Thursday night "Must See TV" brand depended on it, contracts were signed without missing a beat. Kauffman, Crane, Bright, and their writing staff restructured their ninth-season plans, building the show's conclusion out far enough to include another season.

Leading up to the finale, NBC knew they needed to capitalize on the end of their hit series. As the ninth season wrapped in May 2003, entertainment news sources reported that NBC was already setting the rates for commercials during the following season's finale. After agreeing to the salary demands of the cast, and settling the usual production costs, an episode of *Friends* in its final season was set to cost approximately $10 million. Thus, an 18-episode season would result in a hefty $180 million tab (for context, NBC's *ER*, with its cast twice the size of *Friends* and its running time clocking in at an hour, cost nearly the same amount). With those numbers firmly in place, NBC sought out Super Bowl–sized ad rates for the final episode: roughly $2 million for a 30-second spot—and, luckily for the network, brands were all too eager to get in on the game. The finale would go on to feature ads from Super Bowl perennials Budweiser and Coors Light, Gen X favorite The Gap, and insurance brand Allstate, who shot their commercial on a set redolent of *Friends*' famous Greenwich Village spot.

As fans emotionally prepared to say farewell to the six New Yorkers they had grown to love, the stars themselves, appearing in countless interviews to promote the big finale, grappled with the reality of the show's conclusion. Jennifer Aniston called the cast "delicate china . . . speeding toward a brick wall." Matthew Perry found the emotions surrounding the final episode "impossible to ignore," admitting that during shooting he "had this huge headache. It was this moment before you're supposed to start weeping, and I just stayed there for the whole night . . . it was the end of something significant." In the week leading up to the finale, NBC featured a *Dateline* special on the series, as well as an hour-long retrospective immediately preceding the finale. The sentiment among the cast was unanimous—they would all miss one another the most. How appropriate that one of the potential titles for the series was "Six of One"—as these six actors had truly become one unstoppable force of nature. In the final days leading up to the finale, co-creator David Crane made a clear promise to the show's dedicated fans: "Everybody ends up in a place where you can feel satisfied . . . [but] there are some surprises." Marta Kauffman added: "What we hope is that people feel good about saying goodbye to them, and that they're all going to be OK." Reassured and ready to move on, the cast, crew, and fans braced for the rapidly approaching finale episode.

When the tenth season began, the friends are still in Barbados attending Ross's paleontology conference. At the previous season's end, Ross and Charlie (Joey's girlfriend, played by Aisha Tyler) have kissed and unbeknownst to them, Joey saw it all unfold. Emboldened by Ross's betrayal, Joey feels he is now free to finally tell Rachel how he feels about her—having harbored feelings for her since season 8. As Rachel opens her hotel door, she is met with a kiss from Joey. Both new couples decide that it would be for the best if they discussed the recent developments, and in a call back to the infamous "We were on a break" episode of season 3 ("The One With the Morning After") and the post-Emily wedding episode of season 5 ("The One with all the Kips"), Chandler, Monica, and Phoebe listen through the wall to both conversations. Later, as the group heads back to New York, Ross comes clean to Joey, but Joey is unable to break the news about Rachel—but Ross finds out anyway. The remainder of the season deals with the aftermath of these decisions, with Joey and Rachel eventually agreeing to be just friends (much to the delight of fans), and Ross and Charlie split after she returns to an old flame. Monica and Chandler's season-long storyline follows them as they go through the adoption process, finally finding a birth mother in the sweet, naïve Erica (Anna Faris). The Bings decide along the way to move out of the city in favor of the suburbs, which is not a popular choice among the friends, particularly Joey. Phoebe, who reunited with ex-boyfriend Mike (played by Paul Rudd) in the final episodes of season 9, finally ties the knot with her sweet beau, in a wedding planned, unsurprisingly, by Monica ("The One with Phoebe's Wedding"). Rachel, still working at Ralph Lauren, takes a meeting with Gucci for a potential job, only to have her current boss find out and fire her ("The One with Princess Consuela"). Down on her luck, Rachel bumps into former colleague Mark (Steven Eckholdt)—the same Mark that came between her and Ross in season 3—who tells her about a potential opening with Louis Vuitton. There's just one catch—the job is in Paris. When Rachel scores that all-too-precious job, Ross panics, fearing that he may lose the mother of his daughter, and the love of his life. When the gang gets together to give Rachel a grand send-off, Ross is upset when Rachel barely acknowledges him. When he finally decides to confront her, the two kiss. On the eve of the finale, the Ross and Rachel will-they-or-won't-they tension that simmered for most of the ten seasons of *Friends* had finally hit its boiling point.

The series finale, titled "The Last One," aired in two parts, both broadcast on Thursday, May 6, 2004. The episode was written by series creators Kauffman and Crane, and directed by executive producer Kevin Bright. The episode finds Monica and Chandler at the hospital as Erica goes into labor with their child—only to discover she was carrying twins. Ross and Rachel, after having spent the night together, are no closer to a resolution. Ross wants Rachel to stay, and Rachel views their latest tryst as the "perfect way to say goodbye." As Rachel heads to the airport, Ross, encouraged by Joey and Phoebe, decides to follow her in hopes of stopping her from leaving—Ross's line "I'm gonna go after her!" is followed by long, excited audience applause. When Ross finally makes it to the airport and reaches Rachel, she is overwhelmed by the moment and decides to board the plane. Dejected, Ross returns to his own place, opting not to rejoin the gang at Monica and Chandler's, and checks his answering machine. On it, he hears a message from Rachel, who confesses that she loves him. He then overhears her attempts to get off the plane. As the message cuts off, Ross screams, "Did she get off the plane?" only to look up and see Rachel in the doorway as she says, "I got off the plane." The audience goes wild, and the two are finally back together, and this time it's for good. Ross and Rachel return to Monica and Chandler's apartment, which is now fully packed up in preparation for their move. Looking out into the empty apartment, each of the six friends ceremoniously return their own key and decide to go for one last cup of coffee. They each exit, as the last shot of the series lingers on the apartment door, closed behind them.

Over 52 million viewers tuned in to the finale, but it's still the second-most watched episode of the series (just barely edged out by the Super Bowl bonanza). Fans gathered to watch the final scenes of their beloved *Friends* in their living rooms, in college dorms, at coffee shops, and even on huge screens in New York's Times Square and Los Angeles's Universal City Walk. Advertisers who had poured in millions to appear with the show got their money's worth. Critics liked the finale, but couldn't resist giving it to NBC for the overdone hype machine that propelled viewers towards the final show. Robert Bianco of *USA Today* called it "satisfying," noting: "It may have been impossible for any one episode to live up to the hype and expectations built up around the *Friends* finale, but this hour probably came as close as fans could have reasonably hoped." Frazier Moore, of the Associated Press, joked that "NBC took a break from promoting the *Friends*

Television's favorite friends take their final bow after taping the finale.   *Authors' collection*

finale to air it Thursday night." Tom Shales of the *Washington Post* called it a "predictable excess of hugs, kisses and warm fuzzy moments" which "probably satisfied longtime fans of the show." Following the broadcast of the show, Jay Leno hosted *The Tonight Show* from the *Friends* set, interviewing the cast about those final moments. Matt LeBlanc summed it up best: "It was overwhelming, it was fulfilling, it was satisfying, funny and sad. . . . It was too much to process." Luckily for fans, the acceptance process for the finale never meant having to say goodbye to their favorite friends—wide, and hugely profitable, syndication would keep the lights on at Central Perk for a very long time to come.

Aside from scoring a spot in television history books as one of the most watched series finales, the legacy of *Friends* cannot be understated. Following the show's epic rise, every network scurried to find their version of the winning formula—and more than twenty years after its debut, the search continues. For fans looking to hold on to the *Friends* magic, Matt LeBlanc took his beloved dim bulb Joey Tribbiani out west to Los Angeles for NBC's spinoff *Joey*, premiering just four months after the *Friends* finale. After a solid debut, ratings slumped and fans fled—the spinoff, with hopes to become the network's next *Cheers* to *Frasier* transition, was cut short midway through its second season. The failure of *Joey*, however, did not put a ding in the legacy of *Friends*. When including the show on its 2007 list of the all-time 100 best TV shows, *Time* magazine described its lasting appeal:

> It wasn't just the sharp writing or the comic rapport that made *Friends* great. Its Gen-X characters were the children of divorce, suicide and cross-dressing, trying to grow up without any clear models of how to do it. They built ersatz families and had kids by adoption, surrogacy, out of wedlock or with their gay ex-wives. The show never pretended to be about anything weightier than "We were on a break." But the well-hidden secret of this show was that it called itself *Friends*, and was really about family.

You can now visit that family any night of the week on TBS, TVLand, or Nickelodeon. A simple tour on the Warner Bros. studio lot allows fans to enter Stage 24, the longtime home of the series, and take a seat on Central Perk's famous rust-colored couch. For its twentieth anniversary in 2014, a pop-up shop filled with *Friends* memorabilia and decorated to look like the show's beloved Central Perk—going as far as to actually sell coffee!—opened in New York City's SoHo neighborhood for a two-month stay. While each mention of a reunion is widely quashed by the six stars, multiple cross-overs have kept the friends together. Jennifer Aniston and Matthew Perry guest starred on Courteney Cox's sitcom *Cougar Town* (2009–2015). Cox, Perry, David Schwimmer, and Matt LeBlanc all appeared on Lisa Kudrow's online-to-HBO show *Web Therapy* (2011–present). Even late night talk show host Jimmy Kimmel staged the closest thing to a reunion when he brought Aniston, Cox, and Kudrow on board to play out his own "fan fiction" version of the series. The three stars, with Kimmel (as Ross), appeared on a replica of the famous apartment set (the clip went on to get over 18 million hits and counting on Kimmel's YouTube channel). While *Friends* lives in the history books, with no return to Central Perk in sight, Monica, Rachel, Chandler, Ross, Joey, and Phoebe have never seemed very far from reach.

One Final Case

Aloha, *Magnum, P. I.*

Magnum, P. I. (CBS, 1980–1988)

Created by Donald P. Bellisario and Glen A. Larson

Premiere date: December 11, 1980

8 seasons / 162 episodes

"Resolutions, Parts 1 and 2"

Airdate: May 1, 1988

30.3 rating • 45 percent share • 50.7 million viewers

Directed by Burt Brinckerhoff

Written by Stephen A. Miller and Chris Abbott

Cast: Tom Selleck (Magnum), John Hillerman (Higgins), Roger E. Mosley (Theodore "TC" Calvin), Larry Manetti (Orville "Rick" Wright)

Guest Stars: Brandon Call (Billy), Julie Cobb (Karen), Elisha Cook Jr. (Francis "Ice Pick" Hofstetler), Phyllis Davis (Cleo Mitchell), Gillian Dobb (Agatha Chumley), Howard Duff (Captain Thomas Sullivan Magnum I), Fay Hauser (Tina Calvin), Kathleen Lloyd (Carol Baldwin), Patrice Martinez (Linda Lee Ellison), Joe Regalbuto (Don Eddie Rice), Shavar Ross (Bryant Calvin), Joe Santos (Police Lieutenant Nolan Page), Jean Bruce Scott (Lieutenant Commander Maggie Poole, USN), Gwen Verdon (Katherine Peterson), Hal Williams (Dave), Amy Yasbeck (Diana), Peter Elbling (Emile), Jay Ingram (Captain Brackett, USN), Tim Rossovich (Hank), Lily Catherine (Kristen Carreira)

 agnum, P. I. is the brainchild of writer/producers Donald P. Bellisario and Glen A. Larson, who set the new detective series in Hawaii, home to a production facility owned by CBS that would soon be vacated by *Hawaii Five-0*, which was ending its twelve-season run at the end of the 1979–1980 television season. Larson, a former singer turned television producer (he was a member of the 1950s singing group The Four Preps) whose credits included the original *Battlestar Galactica* (1978–1979), *Switch* (1975–1978), and *Quincy, M. E.* (1976–1983), offered Bellisario the opportunity to direct a television pilot for an action series entitled *Magnum*, starring

Tom Selleck. In her detailed history of the show, writer Sylvia Stoddard described the Magnum character in the original script as an ex-CIA agent turned "James Bond private eye" who lives with a killer Doberman pinscher in a guesthouse on the private estate of an author named Robin Masters. Like Agent 007, Magnum has "a roomful of fantastic gadgets" at his disposal, including a hand glider that doubles as a machine gun.

In an interview for the Archive of American Television (AAT), Bellisario described the original *Magnum* pilot as "not the best script I ever read." Selleck, who was also not a fan of the script, told Bellisario he was tired of playing the handsome leading man and wanted to do a series with some humor. Selleck liked Bellisario's writing as he had read his script for a proposed series entitled *Gypsy Warriors* (1978) in which Selleck and James Whitmore Jr., played a pair of World War II espionage agents posing as gypsies in France and Germany. The pilot to *Gypsy Warriors* was one of several failed attempts to get a series for Selleck off the ground. In *Bunco* (1977), he and Robert Urich (*Vega$* [1978–1981] and *Spenser: For Hire* [1985–1988]) co-starred as detectives who are part of a special police squad that goes after swindlers and scam artists. In an interview with David Gritten for *People* magazine, Selleck revealed that the network didn't greenlight the show because, ironically, those in charge didn't think he and Urich had "enough presence . . . to carry a series." Stephen J. Cannell, who produced *Gypsy Warriors*, once again paired Selleck with James Whitmore Jr., in *Boston and Kilbride* (1979). Boston (Selleck), a military commando, and Kilbride (Whitmore), a computer whiz, are a pair of detectives hired for impossible missions, like retrieving a stolen airline company's prototype for a new jet. In a potential spinoff of *The Rockford Files* (1974–1980), Selleck played Lance White, a handsome, suave, and incompetent private eye.

A few years back, Bellisario had written a script entitled "H. H. Flynn" about three Vietnam vets: Rick, a club owner, who idolizes Humphrey Bogart; TC, a helicopter pilot; and Magnum, a private investigator who lives in guest house on a Bel Air estate owned by the "florist to the stars." Bellisario rewrote "H. H. Flynn" as *Magnum, P. I.*, changing the setting in the process from Los Angeles to Hawaii. There was one slight problem—Bellisario had never been to Hawaii, so he had to rely on a Fodor's travel book from 1955. When he did go to Hawaii to scout locations, he was stunned by how different the island look compared to the pictures in the travel book. Instead of rewriting the pilot for contemporary Hawaii, he decided the islands should look the way they did before World War II. So Magnum's Hawaii had no condos, telephone poles, and four-lane roads—only empty beaches, palm trees, and narrow roads through sugar fields.

In the pilot episode, we are introduced to Thomas Sullivan Magnum IV, private investigator, a likable, laid back guy, who doesn't have the confidence and oversized male ego one expects from a television detective, especially one who is so strikingly handsome. Magnum has a self-effacing sense of humor and when it comes to his work, he's no James Bond. In fact, he's known to make an occasional mistake. In an interview with Stephen Dark for *Primetime* magazine, Bellisario admits *Magnum* is not an easy show for writers, who fall into the trap of making the lead character either too macho or merely foolish. "Magnum is vulnerable. Magnum makes mistakes," Bellisario explains, "right up to where

The coolest guy on TV in the 1980s: Tom Selleck as Thomas Sullivan Magnum IV, private investigator.   *Authors' collection*

it really counts. When it really counts he's very macho, he's very good at what he does." But it's when it doesn't count that he makes the same mistakes we all do. "He works on a locked door to pick the lock," Bellisario adds, "and then realizes that it was open all the time." While his skills might be questionable, his morals are not. Magnum is also always on the right side of the law, though he's not above breaking the rules or into someone's office when he's working on a case and needs a little information.

Magnum is also a war hero—a graduate of the U.S. Naval Academy who served three tours of duty in Vietnam with the VMO-2 Da Nang unit, along with his friends Rick (Larry Manetti) and TC (Roger E. Mosley), a helicopter pilot in the Marine Corp. The recipient of the Golden Cross and the Purple Heart, he spent three harrowing months with TC in a prisoner of war camp. Magnum has since soured on the navy. When he's asked why he quit, he gives a simple reason: "One day I woke up age thirty-three and realized I had never been twenty-three." As civilians, Magnum, Rick, and TC are still the best of friends. Rick manages the King Kamehameha Club, a private club that doubles as Magnum's office. Rick's contacts with the underworld are often a valuable source of information for Magnum when he's working on a case. TC, who now manages his own helicopter charter business, gives Magnum the occasional lift into the air.

While Magnum may appear to be living the Bond lifestyle, driving around the island in a Ferrari and sunning himself on the grounds of a posh ocean-front estate, he is always strapped for cash. His Ferrari and the estate, known as Robin's Nest, are both the property of his employer, pulp novelist Robin Masters, who is never seen (Orson Welles supplies his voice early in the show's run). Magnum oversees the security for the estate under the supervision of the majordomo, Jonathan Quayle Higgins III (John Hillerman) and two doberman pinschers, Apollo and Zeus, whose dislike for Magnum is a running joke. Having served for thirty-seven years as a regimental major in the British Army during World War II, Higgins, like Magnum, has a military background. But that's where the similarities end. Higgins is a gentleman in the traditional sense of the word. He is highly educated (he holds a doctorate in mathematics from Cambridge), very formal, and a tad rigid in his thinking. Consequently, Magnum's laid-back attitude presses all of Higgins's buttons and they sometimes bicker like an old married couple. Still, there's a great deal of admiration and respect between them. Magnum also suspects that Higgins is actually Robin Masters and, in the series finale, he admits that he is—only to later tell him he lied. It's difficult to believe, but Hillerman is not British, but a native of Denison, Texas.

The location used for Robin's Nest in the series is the Anderson Estate, the home of Eve Glover Anderson, stepdaughter of the richest woman in

Hawaii, the late Barbara Cox Anthony, daughter of the founder of Cox Enterprises. In March of 2015, the *New York Times* reported that Marty Nesbitt, a Chicago businessman and close friend of President Barack Obama, purchased the estate, where the Obama family has spent their winter holidays in recent years.

One device Bellisario incorporated into the series—voice-over narration—is straight out of a 1940s film noir (in a black-and-white, fantasy episode, "Murder by Night," Magnum is a P. I. in 1940s San Francisco). Sounding as if they were ripped from the pages of a Dashiell Hammett novel, Magnum speaks to the audience, sometimes filling them in on his latest client, like an old friend he met back in Vietnam: "Kate had been a wire service reporter working out of Saigon, where she came to do a story on our team. She was an idealist; not naïve, but an idealist" ("The Jororo Kill"). Sometimes he would wax philosophical ("Fate has a nasty way of popping up and waving its long, bony finger under your nose" ["The Eighth Part of the Village"]) or poetic, particularly his observations of the beauty of Hawaii ("Hawaiian sunsets are among the most breathtakingly beautiful in the world" ["I Witness"]). Another technique used to engage the audience is the breaking of the fourth wall (the invisible wall that separates the characters from the audience). Magnum and the other characters occasionally react to what someone said or did by reacting into the camera, or even speaking directly to the audience. In fact, after the credits roll, the series finale ends in a highly reflexive moment. The image of Magnum and his daughter walking on the beach freezes and the camera pulls out to reveal the image on a television set, followed by the Universal Studios logo. Magnum then walks to the set and shuts it off. He then turns to the camera, says "Good night," points the clicker toward the camera and clicks. The image cuts to a black screen—as if Magnum has turned off his audience and their television sets.

Although Magnum lives in the present, his days in Vietnam are not entirely forgotten. Flashbacks are incorporated into several episodes and tied to the current day storylines, beginning with the pilot episode. In "Don't Eat the Snow in Hawaii, Parts 1 and 2," Magnum must clear the name of his former navy buddy and childhood friend, Lt. Dan Cook, who dies from a drug overdose when the packets of cocaine in his stomach break open. Magnum doesn't believe that Cook, a former U.S. Navy Seal who served alongside Magnum, TC, and Rick on Special Op missions in Vietnam, would be smuggling drugs. With help from Cook's sister, Alice (Pamela Susan Shoop), Magnum uncovers the truth about how the U.S. military was transporting gold illegally to Hawaii and that the island's gold kingpin, known as La Bull, is Philippe Trusseau (Robert Loggia), a former French paratrooper who served alongside Magnum and Cook in Vietnam and was believed to be dead after being left behind on a mission.

Magnum's days in a P.O.W. camp are the focus of a memorable two-part episode entitled "Did You See the Sun Rise?" which opens with Magnum watching *Stalag 17*, a 1953 film starring William Holden about a group of American airmen in a German World War II prison camp. The *Magnum* episode revolves around a visit from a Vietnam veteran named Nuzzo (James Whitmore Jr.), who was in the same POW camp as Magnum and TC. He arrives on the island to warn them that their camp's commander, a sadistic, racist Russian named Ivan (Bo Svenson), is on the island. When Magnum's car blows up, killing his friend Lt. "Mac" McReynolds (Jeff MacKay), he seeks revenge on Ivan. But Nuzzo is actually working with Ivan, who, in one of those plots that stretches the imagination, brainwashed TC back in Vietnam to be a killer he is now going to "activate" to kill a Japanese prince. Their plan is foiled. The last scene of the episode is shocking and disturbing. Magnum confronts Ivan, who tells Magnum he is incapable of killing an unarmed man because of his "sense of honor and fair play." Recalling the last thing Mac said to Magnum before the explosion ("Hey, what do you say we drive up to Poli Lookout and see the sunrise? It ought to be beautiful!") Magnum asks Ivan, "Did you see the sunrise this morning?" Ivan says, "Yes, why?" Without missing a beat, Magnum turns around and shoots him point-blank (the last image is a freeze frame of Magnum firing his gun).

Magnum P. I.'s perspective on the military and war, specifically Vietnam, was unusual for American television. A former U.S. Navy Seal and an officer in the Office of Naval Intelligence, Magnum distrusts authority figures, particularly high-ranking officers like Col. Buck Green (Lance LeGault). Magnum's strongest allies are officers lower in the chain of command who share his sense of honor and justice, like Lt. Maggie Poole (Jean Bruce Scott), who, after Lt. McReynolds's death, provides Magnum with classified information. More importantly, Magnum, Rick, and TC shattered the stereotype of the Vietnam veteran in films and on television as shell-shocked or deranged loose cannons. They are a "band of brothers" whose time in Vietnam is not forgotten. Bellisario admitted that CBS was not thrilled when he used Vietnam as part of the storyline; the network claimed people were tired of it (because of heralded films like *The Deer Hunter* [1978] and *Apocalypse Now* [1979]). He told journalist Stephen Dark the letters he's received from Vietnam veterans are positive, thanking him for *Magnum*'s portrayal of Vietnam veterans who are in no way mentally disturbed: "I get a lot of letters saying that it's terrific to see a Vietnam vet who's just portrayed as a kind of regular guy, rather than somebody who's in deep trauma or somebody who's a crazed killer—not functioning properly."

At the end of its freshman season (1980–1981), *Magnum, P. I.* ranked no. 14, and at the peak of its popularity, when it aired on Thursday nights, 8:00 p.m. to 9:00 p.m., the show ranked no. 4 (season 3, 1982–1983) and no. 5 (season 4, 1983–1984). Around the same time, *Magnum, P. I.* was sold into syndication and, according to *Variety* reporter John Dempsey, turned a hefty profit, grossing a record $70 million dollars for its distributor, MCA Television, which is part of Universal Studios. The ratings began to decline when *Magnum* was up against the no. 1 and no. 2 shows on television, *The Cosby Show* and *Family Ties*. Selleck took the competition with Bill Cosby in stride and lived up to his reputation as a gentleman. According to David Bianculli, a reporter for Knight-Rider Newspapers, Selleck sent Cosby a fan letter before his show premiered wishing him luck and later accepted Cosby's invitation to attend the taping of the season finale of his show. In one episode, Cosby acknowledged Selleck by wearing a *Magnum, P. I.* hat.

Meanwhile, the competition with *The Cosby Show* prompted CBS to move Selleck's show to Wednesday nights at 9:00–10:00 p.m., where it ranked no. 34 for season 7 (1986–1987) against *Dynasty* (no. 25), and no. 40 for its eighth and final season (1987–1988).

Initially, the season 7 finale of *Magnum, P. I.* was intended to be the series finale. The episode, entitled "Limbo," opens with a gun battle in which three guys are chasing Magnum in a warehouse. Two of the men shoot the P. I. and leave him for dead. Critically wounded, Magnum lies in a hospital in a coma on a respirator. Higgins and Magnum's buddies are in shock. His mother (Gwen Verdon) flies in to see him. Meanwhile, Magnum is walking on a beach where he runs into his late friend, McReynolds, who turns out to be his angelic guide to heaven. The men who shot at Magnum are actually after his ex-wife, a French woman named Michelle, whom he met while serving in Vietnam. Presumably killed during the fall of Saigon, Michelle resurfaced ten years later and revealed that she, along with her husband, a North Vietnamese general, are both double agents working against the Communist Government. When they were reunited several years before, Magnum and Michelle slept together and she became pregnant with their child, Lily. Magnum doesn't meet his daughter until she's five years old ("Little Girl Who"). So Michelle is back again with Lily, only Magnum is now fighting for his life in the hospital. With some guidance from McReynolds, he visits each of his friends and also manages to save Michelle's life by guiding her (she seems to be able to hear him and follow his directions) during a car chase. At the end of the episode, Magnum flat lines and the private investigator is last seen walking towards heaven as we hear John Denver singing "Looking for Space."

Apparently CBS, Universal, and the show's fan base were not pleased with the idea that Magnum had died. Selleck was signed on to do more episodes (no doubt to add to their lucrative syndication package). In the season opener, Magnum makes a miraculous recovery and it's not before long he returns to work. As they never intended to continue the show after season 7, it's possible the writers were short on ideas for episodes, which might explain why several were more gimmicky than usual. In "Pleasure Principle," Magnum and Higgins appear to have swapped demeanors, wardrobe, and lifestyles when the latter falls in love. Then it's Magnum's turn to fall in love with a Hawaiian princess—who died in a fire in 1901 ("Forever in Time"). "Legend of the Lost Art" is an extended joke referring back to when Selleck was Steven

The cast of *Magnum, P.I.*: (clockwise from top) John Hillerman, Roger E. Mosley, Tom Selleck, and Larry Manetti.   *Authors' collection*

Spielberg's first choice to play Indiana Jones in *Raiders of the Lost Ark*, only to lose the role when the writers' strike delayed production on *Magnum*.

In the two-part series finale, "Resolutions," Magnum travels back home, but he's in no mood for his Naval Academy reunion, his surprise birthday party, meeting his elusive paternal grandfather, nor entertaining an invitation to return to the navy and command his own ship. He has read a letter from his late wife, Michelle, passed on to him by Maggie Poole, confirming that he is Lily's father. He cuts his trip short when Higgins calls to tell him that someone tried to kill his former girlfriend, Linda Lee Ellison (Patrice Martinez), who has been working on a story about organized crime. Magnum and Linda rekindle their affair, but he has to cut it short when he becomes preoccupied with finding out if his daughter Lily is actually alive. In a previous episode, his nemesis Quang Ki, in retaliation for Magnum killing his brother, sent him a videotape in which Michelle and Lily are apparently killed in a car explosion. Magnum resigns from his job to look for his daughter. In the middle of all this, his grandfather visits him in Hawaii, and Rick is getting married. Thankfully, Magnum's daughter is very much alive, and she and her father are reunited. As a bonus, Magnum manages to catch Linda's stalker. The wedding is on—and Magnum, dressed in his naval whites (he's returning to active duty), finally arrives with Lily, who is serving as the flower girl.

The two-hour series finale of *Magnum* was the no. 1 rated show for the week of April 25–May 1, with a 30.3 rating (percentage of all televisions) and a 45 percent share (percentage of televisions in use). A whopping 50.7 million viewers tuned in, placing it at no. 6 in the list of most watched series finales. While the ending is certainly more emotionally satisfying than the show's first series finale at the end of season 7 ("Limbo"), the problem with "Resolutions" is that there is simply too much going on. It almost seems as if the cast and crew were shooting three episodes simultaneously and poor Tom Selleck appears to be dashing from one plotline to the next. Unfortunately, the threads of the individual stories don't quite fit together, particularly the one involving Linda's stalker, which felt like it was leftover from a previously unaired episode. While it is certainly in Magnum's character to hop on a plane to help a friend in need, the story itself seemed extraneous. *New York Post* critic David Bianculli agreed, finding the episode "too busy, too disconnected," and, for *Magnum, P. I.*, "oddly unfunny."

The second finale to *Magnum, P. I.* definitely left the door open for a made-for-TV movie sequel, which, surprisingly (considering the ratings generated by the power-packed windup episode) never materialized. Selleck has never stopped working, though he has found more success in television than in films. His post-*Magnum, P. I.* work has included sitcoms (*The Closer* [1998–1999], and the role of Courteney Cox's much older love interest on

Friends), made-for-TV movies (as detective Jesse Stone), and his most recent series, *Blue Bloods* (2010–present), in which he plays the police commissioner of the New York Police Department and the patriarch of an Irish-American family of police officers.

But whenever you see Tom Selleck on the screen, it's difficult not to think about that guy with a mustache in a Hawaiian shirt driving a Ferrari and flashing that smile.

One Last Dance

The Cosby Show Waltzes off the Air

The Cosby Show (NBC, 1984–1992)
Created by Ed. Weinberger, Michael Leeson, and William Cosby Jr., Ed. D.
Premiere date: September 20, 1984
8 seasons / 202 episodes
"And So We Commence, Parts 1 and 2"
Airdate: April 30, 1992
28 rating • 45 percent share • 44.4 million viewers
Directed by Jay Sandrich
Written by Janet Leahy, Gordon Gartrelle, Courtney Flavin, and Hugh O'Neill
Cast: Bill Cosby (Heathcliff "Cliff" Huxtable), Phylicia Rashad (Clair Hanks
     Huxtable), Sabrina Le Beauf (Sondra Huxtable Tibideaux), Geoffrey Owens
     (Elvin Tibideaux), Malcolm-Jamal Warner (Theodore "Theo" Huxtable),
     Tempestt Bledsoe (Vanessa Huxtable), Keshia Knight Pulliam (Rudy Huxtable),
     Raven-Symoné (Olivia Kendall), Erika Alexander (Pam Tucker)
Guest Stars: Earle Hyman (Russell Huxtable), Clarice Taylor (Anna Huxtable),
     William Thomas Jr. (Dabnis Brickey), Ethel Ayler (Carrie Hanks), Joe Williams
     (Al Hanks), Deon Richmond (Kenny), Allen Payne (Lance Rodman), Karen
     Malina White (Charmaine Brown), Gary Gray (Nelson Tibideaux), Jessica Ann
     Vaughn (Winnie Tibideaux)

By 1984, the sitcom was largely considered "over." The comedies of producer Norman Lear that dominated the airwaves in the 1970s—*All in the Family* (1971–1979), *Maude* (1972–1978), *Sanford and Son* (1972–1977), and *Good Times* (1974–1979)—had run their course, with only the *The Jeffersons* (1975–1985) remaining for an impressive total of eleven seasons. Television programming had gone the way of prime-time soaps about the super-rich, like *Dallas* (1978–1991) and *Dynasty* (1981–1989), and action-adventure series like *The Dukes of Hazzard* (1979–1985), *T. J. Hooker* (1982–1986), *Magnum, P. I.* (1980–1988), and *The A-Team* (1983–1987). The comedies that remained on the prime-time schedule lagged behind in the ratings. The world inhabited by sitcom characters seemed confined and stagnant compared to stories about large families feuding over oil, power, and big money, or crime fighters who were always up for a good car chase and played by their own rules. It would take a compelling series to steal the attention away from the over-the-top flash and sparkle of early '80s television. Enter *The Cosby Show*.

Built on the standup comedy of Bill Cosby, best known for his multi-Emmy-winning streak on NBC's 1960s spy adventure *I Spy* (1965–1968), *The Cosby Show* was a fairly standard rendering of a family sitcom. A simple story, well told: a family led by two working parents tackles the day-to-day problems of the typical 1980s household. Children learn about death through the passing of their goldfish, and a son rebels against his parents by flunking school and piercing his ear. Daughters fight over the bathroom, while Mom and Dad sneak away to have a moment of peace. On paper, this would all read as too tidy a concept, but in the case of *The Cosby Show* there was one important detail: the family was African American. Never before portrayed in this light, the Huxtable family represented the African-American upper-class experience by making their race seem invisible—the problems, triumphs, and funny moments they shared transcended the label of "black" or "white." Gone were the days of Lear's *Good Times* where African-American families were portrayed as fighting their way to the top, scraping by on what they had with high hopes for the future. The Huxtables had already made it—Cliff (played by Cosby), the patriarch, a private practice doctor, and matriarch Clair (Phylicia Rashad), a high-powered attorney. Their children attended prestigious colleges like Princeton and New York University, and themselves became teachers, doctors, lawyers, and humanitarians. The series portrayed the Huxtables as an entirely relatable family, one that could stand in for any American family, regardless of race and class. The Huxtable crew featured straight arrow Sondra (Sabrina Le Beauf), fashionista rebel Denise (Lisa Bonet), smart aleck Theo (Malcolm-Jamal Warner), brainy Vanessa (Tempestt Bledsoe), and sassy Rudy (Keshia Knight Pulliam). They argued over usage of the phone (in the pre-cell phone days of the '80s), jockeyed for car privileges, raided the fridge, and begged their parents to indulge in the materialistic 1980s culture (Theo's season 1 desire for the fictional $95 Gordon Gartrelle shirt ["A Shirt Story"] is a particular highlight). Folded into the series, however, were also high-art touchstones of the African-American cultural experience, including Cliff's preference to fill the house with the jazz of Art Blakey, Dizzy Gillespie, and B. B. King, and Clair's investment of thousands of dollars into the purchase of an original Ellis Wilson painting, *Funeral Procession*, which hung over the living room mantle for seven of the series' eight seasons. The series was set in New York, with the Huxtables inhabiting a coveted brownstone in the

The Huxtable family (left to right): Sondra (Sabrina Le Beauf), Vanessa (Tempestt Bledsoe), Denise (Lisa Bonet), Cliff (Bill Cosby), Rudy (Keshia Knight Pulliam), Theo (Malcolm-Jamal Warner), and Clair (Phylicia Rashad).   *Photofest*

Brooklyn Heights section of Brooklyn. The series was even shot in New York, originally at Brooklyn Studios (formerly a silent era hub for Vitagraph) and then migrating to the Kaufman Astoria Studios in Queens.

By the end of the first season, NBC had a mega hit on their hands. *The Cosby Show* had resonated with audiences and elevated the sitcom beyond the confines previously outlined by 1970s pioneers like Lear and Grant Tinker (*The Mary Tyler Moore Show* [1970–1977], *Rhoda* [1974–1978], *The Bob Newhart Show* [1972–1978]). Within its first year of broadcast, the series became the number one most watched show on television, and remained tops for five consecutive seasons. The show's popularity pulled its fellow sitcoms from the ratings doldrums, breathing life into NBC's existing lineup of *Family Ties* (1982–1989), *Cheers* (1982–1993), and *Night Court* (1984–1992), which respectively became the number two, three, and seventh highest rated shows. Other networks even benefitted from the *Cosby* bump, as ABC's Tuesday night lineup of family sitcoms, *Who's the Boss?* (1984–1992) and *Growing Pains* (1985–1992), rounded out the Top 10. Beyond its format, *The Cosby Show* also fostered an environment that reinvigorated Lear's decade of television series that meshed comedy and purpose, tackling tough issues peppered within the laughs—adapting this model to fit within the new reality of the Reagan era, which found both parents in the workplace and teenagers with even more cultural power (both economically and socially). Cosby's series also left behind the necessity of goofy gimmicks or catch phrases to produce the laughs, instead favoring situational moments that rang true with audiences. The television landscape ushered in by Bill Cosby's new sitcom breed would continue on well past the show's lifespan, setting the stage for other NBC must-see comedies to come, such as *Seinfeld* (1989–1998), *Friends* (1994–2004), and *Will & Grace* (1998–2006).

By the show's eighth season, Cosby had taken the Huxtables as far as he wanted to go, telling *The Today Show*'s Jane Pauley, "I've run out of everything I have to say with the Huxtables." Cliff and Clair had become grandparents to Sondra's twins Winnie and Nelson (named after the Mandelas), while the show's kids grew into adulthood. Denise, back from her detour on series spinoff *A Different World* (1987–1993), was married with a stepdaughter, while Theo pursued a career in teaching, and Vanessa was now away at college. With teenager Rudy the only remaining original Huxtable left in the Brooklyn Heights household, the show attempted to recapture the flavor of earlier seasons by promoting Denise's precocious stepdaughter, Olivia (Raven-Symoné), to be a regular cast member—but even she started to outgrow the mold. With the children grown (and mostly out of the household), it was time for Cliff and Clair Huxtable to enjoy their sunset years off-camera. The series set its final broadcast for Thursday, April 30, 1992.

As the finale episode approached, race relations in the United States had become a hot button issue. In March 1991, just a year earlier, Rodney King had been badly beaten by Los Angeles police officers following a high-speed chase. The beating was videotaped by a nearby witness who sent the footage to the local news station. The brutality of the altercation catapulted the nation into a frenzy, as the African-American community demanded justice. The policemen involved in the beating were put on trial, charged with assault and use of excessive force, only to be acquitted on Wednesday, April 29, 1992—just the day before *The Cosby Show* was to take its final bow. Riots erupted in Los Angeles, as fires raged in South Central through the night and into the next day. The National Guard was called in to keep order, while the city's mayor, Tom Bradley, instituted a mandatory curfew, urging his constituents to stay safe and at home and watch *The Cosby Show* finale. Cosby pre-taped two messages for the local Los Angeles NBC affiliate (KNBC) to run in the event that his finale aired or if it were pre-empted due to news coverage. KNBC decided to go forward with airing the finale, stating live on air:

> Today Mayor Bradley urged us to stay home, stay off the streets and watch *The Cosby Show*. We believe we need this time as a cooling off period . . . to remember what our Thursday nights were like before this all began. If major events dictate, be assured that we will return immediately.

The *Los Angeles Times*' Rob DuBrow debated whether this move was motivated by the high stakes May sweeps period on television, or by the message the show may send to its many African-American viewers. DuBrow considered the possibility of the latter: "The broadcast about a beloved black TV family—headed by the nation's favorite father—might indeed have a positive effect, at least to the extent of giving a sense of breathing room amid chaos." Viewers had the option to stay on NBC to watch the final moments of their beloved sitcom, or switch over to the number of other channels embroiled in wall-to-wall riot coverage. Former NBC chairman Grant Tinker decried the decision to move forward with the broadcast as "crass commercialism," adding: "Bill and everybody else should be mightily embarrassed, doing this frivolous thing while the town is burning." However, DuBrow cited that during the finale broadcast KNBC received almost 200 calls praising the station for airing *The Cosby Show*. The episode was capped with Cosby's pre-taped message, in which he implored his audience to "pray that everyone from the top of the government down to the people in the streets would all have good sense . . . and let us pray for a better tomorrow, which starts today." The uplifting storyline and heartfelt farewell to the Huxtables was certainly a good place to start.

The finale episode, titled "And So We Commence," begins in a familiar place, finding Cliff on a ladder attempting to fix that darn doorbell while

Clair looks on disapprovingly. Theo, excited for his upcoming graduation from New York University checks in with his parents regarding how many people will be attending the commencement ceremony. Theo presses his father to cap the invitations, as seats are limited, but Cliff, in his excitement, insists that everyone that has ever known Theo be in attendance. His pride in his son's accomplishment has overtaken his own reason and logic, as he prepares to bring lawn chairs with him as a backup (a move he similarly pulled when Sondra put on her cap and gown at Princeton). As the family gathers at the Huxtable residence, they reflect on how far Theo has come, overcoming his dyslexia and general lack of enthusiasm for school to graduate with honors in psychology, with plans to become a teacher. Denise, now in Singapore with husband Martin, calls in to wish Theo well, making the announcement that she is pregnant—the Huxtables, filling the kitchen to the brim, erupt in cheers. At the commencement ceremony, Cliff recalls a conversation he had with Theo many years back, allowing for the show to flashback to its first episode, featuring Cliff's famous "economics lesson." In the lesson, Cliff uses Monopoly money to illustrate Theo's financial situation should he decide to forgo college and get a "regular" job, slowly pulling bills out of his hand. Theo then gives an impassioned speech, begging for acceptance, telling his father he would not love him any less if he weren't a doctor but instead a "regular" person. As the audience applauds, Cliff pauses and, in only the way he can, delivers the series' defining monologue:

> Theo . . . that is the dumbest thing I have ever heard in my life! No wonder you get Ds in everything! Now you are afraid to try because you are afraid that your brain is going to explode and it's going to ooze out of your ear. Now I'm telling you, you are going to try as hard as you can and you are going to do it because I said so. I am your father—I brought you in this world and I'll take you out.

In a more serious vein, he tells his son he just wants him to do the best that he can, and the two embrace in a sweet moment. The episode flashes back to the graduation ceremony, and Cliff and Clair watch as their son gets his degree. Back at the house, Theo bids goodnight to his parents, heading off to graduation parties, as Cliff begs Clair to try out the new doorbell. Clair refuses, having been zapped in the past, so Cliff heads off to press the button. As he presses the button, Frank Loesser's "If I Were a Bell" (performed by the Miles Davis Quintet) plays and the two begin to dance, literally dancing off the set. Breaking the fourth wall, Bill Cosby and Phylicia Rashad walk off the set and in front of the studio audience to thunderous applause, waving goodbye along the way. Following this final moment, a three-minute "thank you" to the fans plays over images and scenes from the series' eight seasons. The message reads:

To our loyal viewers on NBC:

1983: "Television situation comedy is dead" — TV Expert. Now unemployed.

In no time at all . . . a television show charmed an entire nation,

The show that everyone watched on Thursday and talked about on Friday.

As the audience grew . . . the Cosby kids grew too!

America's favorite father became a grandfather.

In a house filled with love . . . there's always room for more.

For joining us for 8 years of magic . . . we say "Thank You"

This "thank you" note reached a record-breaking audience, as more than 44 million viewers tuned in to say goodbye to the Huxtables, making the episode the most watched series finale in NBC's history (a record that would be eclipsed by *Cheers* just one year later).

Critics celebrated the show's achievements throughout its run, but felt the finale lingered in the sentimental. *Entertainment Weekly*'s Lisa Schwarzbaum called it "a little wistful and soft of punch," but acknowledged that it seemed fitting for the show, as given the current television climate this ending was more in keeping with the show's content as opposed to trying to match the comedy on hits like *The Simpsons* (1989–present) and *Married . . . with Children* (1987–1997). John J. O'Connor of the *New York Times* called it "a vintage Bill Cosby moment: no fuss, unassuming and brilliantly calculated." While ratings had slumped in recent years, bringing the once dominant program from the top spot to number twenty, the finale had proven the consistent quality of *The Cosby Show*, never forgoing its quiet charm for ratings gimmicks or flash.

As quietly as Bill Cosby and Phylicia Rashad danced off the set, the finale of *The Cosby Show* gently glided into the night, finding its final resting place in the hall of television history, both for its record-breaking ratings, and its indelible cultural impact.

Part 2
WTF?

Series Finales That Left Us Scratching Our Heads

In the Mind of Tommy Westphall

St. Elsewhere's Fantastical Twist

St. Elsewhere (NBC, 1982–1988)
Created by Joshua Brand and John Falsey
Developed by Mark Tinker and John Masius
Premiere date: October 26, 1982
6 seasons / 137 episodes
"The Last One"
Airdate: May 25, 1988
17 rating • 29 percent share • 22.5 million viewers
Directed by Mark Tinker
Story by Tom Fontana, John Tinker, Channing Gibson
Teleplay by Bruce Paltrow and Mark Tinker
Cast: William Daniels (Dr. Mark Craig), Norman Lloyd (Dr. Daniel Auschlander),
    Ed Flanders (Dr. Donald Westphall), Ronny Cox (Dr. John Gideon), Bonnie
    Bartlett (Ellen Craig), Ed Begley Jr. (Dr. Victor Ehrlich), Stephen Furst (Dr.
    Elliot Axelrod), Bruce Greenwood (Dr. Seth Griffin), Eric Laneuville (Luther
    Hawkins), Howie Mandel (Dr. Wayne Fiscus), David Morse (Dr. Jack Morrison),
    France Nuyen (Dr. Paulette Kiem), Cindy Pickett (Dr. Carol Novino), Christina
    Pickles (Nurse Helen Rosenthal), Jennifer Savidge (Nurse Lucy Papandrao),
    Denzel Washington (Dr. Philip Chandler)
Recurring: Chad Allen (Tommy Westphall), Byron Stewart (Warren Coolidge),
    Christina Kokubo (Paramedic Faith Yee)
Guest Stars: Nestor Serrano (Mr. Pierson), John Short (Dr. Brandon Falsey), Craig
    Reed (Mr. Mirkin), Ealynn Voss (Brigitta Swensen), Arthur Gerunda (Neil
    Dubin), Christopher and Joseph Michael (Pete Morrison)

n the 1970s, Mary Tyler Moore's production company, MTM
Enterprises, produced several successful sitcoms, including her own
series, *The Mary Tyler Moore Show* (1970–1977) and its spinoff *Rhoda*

Quality TV at its best—the large ensemble cast of *St. Elsewhere*: (bottom row, left to right) Cynthia Sikes, William Daniels, Ed Flanders, David Birney; (middle row, left to right) Denzel Washington, Kim Miyori, Ed Begley Jr., David Morse, Ellen Bry, Norman Lloyd; (top row, left to right) Kavi Raz, Christina Pickles, G.W. Bailey, Barbara Whinnery, Howie Mandel, and Terence Knox.

NBC/Photofest

(1974–1978); *The Bob Newhart Show* (1972–1978); and *WKRP in Cincinnati* (1978–1982). Toward the end of the decade, MTM's production roster was dominated by several critically acclaimed dramatic series set in such varied locations as a fictional Los Angeles daily newspaper (another *Mary Tyler Moore* spinoff, *Lou Grant* [1977–1982]), a high school in South Central Los Angeles (*The White Shadow* [1978–1981]), a rundown Boston hospital (*St. Elsewhere* [1982–1988]), and a police station in a crime-ridden neighborhood (*Hill Street Blues* [1981–1987]).

When the police drama *Hill Street Blues* debuted in January of 1981, it was hailed by critics as ground-breaking television. Critic Todd Gitlin described *Hill Street* "at its best a mature and even brilliant show that violated many conventions, pleased critics, caught the undertow of cultural change, and ran away with the Emmys." Each episode focused on "a day in the life" of the officers, detectives, and captain of Hill Street Station, located in an unnamed American city. Steven Bochco, who co-created the show with Michael Kozoll, told *Chicago Tribune* reporters Ellen Warren and James Warren that he conceived the show's setting as an amalgam of Buffalo, New York; Pittsburgh, Pennsylvania; and Chicago, Illinois, where the Maxwell Street Precinct, the station house seen in exterior shots, is located. *Hill Street* was also unlike any police drama on television. The show had a large ensemble cast of thirteen main characters and multiple storylines that were not all necessarily resolved in a single episode. The series also introduced a documentary style of shooting to prime-time through the use of a handheld camera that puts the viewer right smack in the middle of the chaos of the overcrowded station house. *Hill Street Blues* was a hit with the critics, but not with viewers. At the end of season 1 (1981–1982), the show ranked no. 87 in the Nielsen ratings, yet NBC still renewed the series. It was the right decision because season 1 of *Hill Street* received a record twenty-one Emmy nominations and won eight, including its first of four consecutive Emmys for Outstanding Drama Series.

Hill Street Blues is often cited as the show that inspired another groundbreaking series, the medical drama *St. Elsewhere*, which is the nickname of St. Eligius, a rundown, Catholic hospital in Boston. In his autobiography, *Tinker in Television*, MTM president (and future CEO and chairman of NBC) Grant Tinker recalled pitching the idea of *St. Elsewhere* to NBC programming executive Brandon Tartikoff as "*Hill Street Blues* in a hospital." But Robert C. Thompson, author of *Television's Second Golden Age*, contends that the "notion that *St. Elsewhere* evolved out of *Hill Street Blues* is an oversimplified one." Prior to *Hill Street*, Steven Bochco and Bruce Paltrow, creator of *The White Shadow* (and father of Gwyneth), collaborated on a one-hour unsold pilot for MTM Enterprises and NBC entitled *Operating Room* (1978). Like *St. Elsewhere*, *Operating Room* approached the medical profession more realistically than previous hospital dramas. When the medical drama wasn't picked up, Bochco went on to co-create *Hill Street Blues* with Kozoll. Paltrow was hired by MTM to oversee *St. Elsewhere*, created by Joshua Brand and John Falsey, with *White Shadow* writer John Masius and producer Mark Tinker credited for developing the series. During season 1, Brand and Falsey received story credit for all but one episode and then moved on to create the 1986 mini-series and series *A Year in the Life* (1987–1988), and the critically acclaimed *Northern Exposure* (1990–1995) and *I'll Fly Away* (1991–1993).

Hill Street Blues and *St. Elsewhere* marked the beginning of a new era in American television history dubbed by media scholar Thompson as the "Second Golden Age of Television." The first "Golden Age" was in the late 1940s through the 1950s—a period best remembered for anthology shows like *Playhouse 90* (1956–1960), *Studio One* (1948–1958), and *Kraft Television Theatre* (1947–1958) that presented original and adapted television dramas penned by talented writers (Paddy Chayefsky, Horton Foote, William Gibson,

Abby Mann, and Rod Serling, etc.) and performed live by A-list and up-and-coming actors (Helen Hayes, Jack Lemmon, Charles Laughton, Maximilian Schell, Claude Rains, Piper Laurie, and Sal Mineo, etc.) working under such notable directors as John Frankenheimer, Sidney Lumet, Robert Mulligan, Arthur Hiller, and George Roy Hill.

In his book *Television's Second Golden Age*, Thompson singled out the 1980s as a time when "a new type of programming was emerging that they thought was better, more sophisticated, and more artistic than the usual network fare." Thompson applied a term used by critics—"Quality Television"—to distinguish certain programs that share some or all of the following attributes: complex writing; a large ensemble cast of characters; multiple storylines; experimentation, to varying degrees, with traditional television genres (police/detective, medical, etc.) to create a whole new genre; a realistic approach from a liberal humanist perspective toward subject matter, including controversial and even taboo topics (AIDS, homosexuality, abortion, racism, religion, etc.); and memory of their own history in regards to past events and characters, which may have an impact on a current storyline. In addition to *Hill Street Blues* and *St. Elsewhere*, Thompson's list of Quality TV shows includes *Cagney & Lacey* (1982–1988), *Picket Fences* (1992–1996), *China Beach* (1988–1991), *Northern Exposure* (1990–1995), *Moonlighting* (1985–1989), *thirtysomething* (1987–1991), and *Twin Peaks* (1990–1991).

There are other similarities in regards to their reception. Quality shows generally appeal to the demographic advertisers most desire—young, upscale, college-educated urbanites. Still, many such programs never achieved high ratings during their run. During its four-seasons on CBS, for example, David E. Kelley's *Picket Fences*, a quirky drama about small-town life, which was considered the kinder, gentler version of David Lynch's *Twin Peaks*, never ranked higher in the ratings than no. 61 in the end-of-the-season tally. Still, the network brass kept in on the air because, like many quality shows, it won awards. Over the course of four seasons, *Picket Fences* won fourteen Emmy Awards including Best Dramatic Series twice, in 1993 and 1994. This was not unusual for a Quality Television series, which "cleaned up" during award season, winning Emmys, Golden Globes, Writers Guild and Directors Guild Awards, Peabody Awards, and Humanitas Prizes. There was even an award for Quality Television (the "Q") given by Viewers for Quality Television (VQT), a non-profit grassroots organization under the leadership of Dorothy Swanson. In the 1980s, Swanson led successful campaigns to get CBS to keep *Cagney & Lacey* on CBS and the same network to return *Designing Women* (1986–1993) to its Monday night time slot after the network moved it to Thursday, where its ratings plummeted to the point that the show was on the brink of cancellation.

As a Quality Show, *St. Elsewhere* experimented with the basic elements of the medical/hospital drama, a genre popularized in the 1960s by long-running series like *Ben Casey* (1961–1966) and *Dr. Kildare* (1961–1966) and in the 1970s with *Medical Center* (1969–1976) and *Marcus Welby, M.D.* (1969–1976). At the center of all four series was a pair of doctors—a young, handsome physician (or surgeon) and his older, wiser mentor and father figure: Dr. Casey (Vince Edwards)/Dr. Zorba (Sam Jaffe), Dr. Kildare (Richard Chamberlain)/Dr. Gillespie (Raymond Massey), Dr. Gannon (Chad Everett)/Dr. Lochner (James Daly), and Dr. Kiley (James Brolin)/Dr. Welby (Robert Young). Another long-running medical series, the pseudo-*M*A*S*H* (1972–1983) spinoff, *Trapper John, M.D.* (1979–1986), also paired a young surgeon, Dr. Gates (Gregory Harrison), with chief of surgery Dr. "Trapper" John McIntyre (Pernell Roberts), who, unlike his counterparts on previous medical series, didn't always follow hospital procedures if it was in his patient's best interest. The supporting characters on medical dramas consisted of other hospital personnel (doctors, nurses, hospital administrators) and a lead character's supportive wife or girlfriend.

While police/detective series of the 1950s through the 1970s assured American audiences that criminals would be apprehended, and legal dramas of the same period guaranteed that justice would always prevail, medical dramas painted an overwhelmingly positive picture of the health profession and the American health care system. On medical shows, doctors are heroic, infallible figures who are able to treat any ailment, illness, or disease. They take a personal interest in each of their patients, all of whom receive quality hospital care from the doctors, nurses, and staff. There was never a question that television doctors like Kildare, Gannon, and Welby had the medical know-how to treat their patients, who, even if they had a life-threatening illness, would never die on camera.

Unlike previous medical dramas, *St. Elsewhere* mixed realism with absurd, oftentimes silly humor—a creative strategy that provided the writers the opportunity to challenge the genre's traditional representation of doctors, nurses, patients, and the inner workings of a hospital. In an interview with journalist Sally Bedell, Bruce Paltrow cited the 1971 satire *The Hospital* as the inspiration for *St. Elsewhere*. Written by Paddy Chayefsky and directed by Arthur Hiller, the black comedy stars George C. Scott as the suicidal chief of medicine at a New York Hospital plagued by an incompetent staff that results in the death of patients. Also contributing to the death toll is a murderer running loose in the hospital, a plot *St. Elsewhere* loosely borrowed with a storyline involving a ski-masked rapist terrorizing the hospital (the culprit turned out to be one of the physicians, Dr. Peter White, played by Terence Knox). But the one important difference was that, unlike the old-fashioned medical shows, patients and doctors died on *St. Elsewhere*. In fact, St. Eligius had the highest mortality rate of any hospital on television.

Although it varied from season to season, the ensemble cast was comprised of eleven to sixteen characters, three of whom were longtime veterans of St. Eligius who served as the hospital's (and the series') resident patriarchs: Dr. Donald Westphall (Ed Flanders), the amiable, soft-spoken director of medicine; Dr. Daniel Auschlander (Norman Lloyd), St. Eligius's beloved chief of services, who has been diagnosed with metastatic liver cancer; and Dr. Mark Craig (William Daniels), a brilliant surgeon, who is also an arrogant, narrow-minded bully. Craig's tolerance for the rest of the human race is exceedingly low, particularly his undisciplined protégé, Dr. Victor Ehrlich (Ed Begley Jr.), who is the target of his continuous stream of verbal abuse. The main cast also included Nurse Helen Rosenthal (Christina Pickles), who has been working at St. Eligius since 1965, and an assortment of doctors, residents, and staff, with characters exiting the hospital (and the series) without explanation. The show was also a springboard for the careers of two unknowns: standup comedian Howie Mandel, whose character, Dr. Wayne Fiscus, provided the comic relief, and future two-time Oscar winner Denzel Washington as mild-mannered Dr. Philip Chandler.

When it came to practicing medicine, *St. Elsewhere* wasn't afraid of pushing the envelope. The writers didn't shy away from doctors and patients talking about symptoms and ailments that are usually discussed in private, behind a doctor's closed door, like infertility, hemorrhoids, constipation, impotence, and foreskin restoration. *St. Elsewhere* also tackled AIDS— the disease, and the fear, ignorance, and homophobia surrounding it. "AIDS and Comfort," which aired in December of 1983, was the first prime-time scripted episode about AIDS to air on American television. The story focused on a popular, up-and-coming Boston city councilman, Tony Gifford (Michael Brandon), who is diagnosed with AIDS. The doctors are puzzled as to how Gifford could have contracted it, given that he's heterosexual and married, not an IV drug user, and has never received a blood transfusion. He finally admits to having anonymous sex with men and agrees to go public about his condition. The episode also addresses how, at the time, the public at large, including many in the health care profession, believed they could contract the disease through casual contact or by donating blood. At the end of the episode, the sage of St. Eligius, Dr. Auschlander, has the final word. He reminds his colleagues that as medical professionals their job is to care for the sick, not pass moral judgment: "And I tell you something: I don't give a damn for all this talk about morality and vengeful gods and all that. If you have AIDS, you're sick, you need help."

St. *Elsewhere's* treatment of AIDS was not limited to a single episode. Later in the show's run, handsome plastic surgeon Dr. Bobby Caldwell (Mark Harmon), the Don Juan of St. Eligius, became the first regular character of a television series to have AIDS when he discovers a Kaposi's sarcoma lesion on his hand and tests positive for what were then called the HTLV-III antibodies ("Family Feud"). He comes close to committing suicide, but ends up moving to the West Coast at the end of season 4 to work at an AIDS hospice. In an example of how Quality TV shows remember past characters and events, when word reaches the hospital in the middle of season 6 that Caldwell has died, a memorial service is held. Another AIDS-related story involves a homophobic doctor, Seth Griffin (Bruce Greenwood), who thinks he is HIV positive after he accidentally pricks himself when drawing blood from a gay AIDS patient ("Night of the Living Bed"). Griffin struggles with his own mortality and becomes a Born Again Christian. In the series finale, he finally sees the result of his HIV test, which is negative.

What kept people tuned in to *St. Elsewhere* was the fact that the show didn't play by the rules, nor did it stick with the long-established conventions of the television medical drama. In a statement that first appeared in the Viewers for Quality Television's newsletter in February 1988 (and reprinted in Swanson's history of VQT), writer/producer Tom Fontana elaborated on the general philosophy behind the show's use of humor in relation to its serious treatment of death and dying:

> We decided to take more chances—to go much further with the comedy in order to balance out the specter of death. And we only killed people whom the audience had gotten to know and care about, so when they died, the viewers felt something. The truth is, we thought we were going to be canceled and realized we had nothing to lose, and this sense of imminent cancellation, of "kamikaze" television, has remained with us ever since.

Although *Variety* reported, on May 8, 1987, that *St. Elsewhere* would be back for a sixth season, anyone who watched the season 5 finale ("Last Dance at the Wrecker's Ball") a few weeks later may have thought this was the end of St. Eligius (and *St. Elsewhere*). The hospital is bankrupt and everyone has cleared out, except for a very ill Dr. Auschlander, who is wandering the halls in a hospital gown as a wrecking ball is about to demolish the hospital. Monica Collins reported in *USA Today* that when Arthur Price, head of MTM Enterprises, read the script, he immediately wanted some assurance that they had a way out of this.

They did—and it gave the writers the opportunity to tackle another controversial issue: the corporate takeover of American hospitals. In her historical overview of medicine and health in the 1980s, Joan Laxson demonstrates how, from 1980 through 1989, national health expenditures rose by 142 percent. During that time, the average cost of a hospital room increased by 99 percent. In 1985, the average daily cost to the hospital for a semi-private room was double the charge to the patient. The solution was to have corporations, experts in cutting costs and corners, take over hospitals and treat health care like a business. Consequently, corporate-owned hospitals were accused of specializing in services based on profitability, and pushing patients out too early to ensure quicker turnover so doctors can increase profits by performing more surgeries and procedures.

In season 6, St. Eligius is under the ownership of Ecumena, a for-profit hospital chain based in in the Midwest that manages an artificial heart program. Apparently the fictional company hit too close to home for Humana, Inc., a hospital chain based in Louisville, Kentucky, which specializes in taking over and modernizing hospitals that are in the red. Humana is also home to the only permanent artificial heart program in the United States. Mark Potts reported in the *Washington Post* that Humana filed a lawsuit against NBC-TV for copyright infringement, claiming the names are too similar. *St. Elsewhere* writer John Tinker contends they were not thinking of Humana when they came up with the name Ecumena, which is a play on the word "Ecumenical" (a term that refers to "a number of different Christian churches" as opposed to only one). A federal district judge refused to block the showing of an episode ("A Moon for the Misbegotten"), which Humana may or may not have known was particularly critical of Ecumena's corporate control of St. Eligius. Dr. Westphall, who was pushed out as head of the hospital and replaced by Dr. Gideon (Ronny Cox), is fired for continuing to put pressure on the corporation to agree to an AIDS hospice at the hospital, even if it is paid for through outside funding. At the end of the episode, Dr. Gideon offers to try to get Dr. Westphall his job back (as long as he is less critical of the company's policies and agrees to compromise a little). Westphall responds, "Well, it's a very interesting offer, John. Let me try to tell you in terms I think you're going to understand." Westphall drops his pants, turns his back to Gideon, and says, "You can kiss my ass, pal." Fade to black, followed by a disclaimer that NBC agreed to air: "ECUMENA is a fictional company that does not represent any actual company or corporation." Maybe it was or wasn't intentional, but one can't help think that Westphall's response was also directed at Humana.

According to Thompson, another attribute of Quality Television are references to popular culture. For example, in one of the rare episodes set outside of the hospital ("Their Town"), Mark and his wife, Ellen (Bonnie Bartlett), Dr. Westphall's daughter, Lizzie (Dana Short), and his former girlfriend, Dr. Novino (Cindy Pickett), travel to New Hampshire to celebrate Dr. Westphall's birthday. The writers borrowed a device used in Thornton Wilder's play *Our*

Town and have Westphall, like the Stage Manager in the play, serve as the episode's narrator and break the "fourth wall" by speaking directly into the camera. In an even more surreal episode, Dr. Fiscus is shot, flatlines, and visits heaven, hell, and purgatory, where he runs into Dr. White, the ski-mask rapist. But as Thompson discusses at length in his book, *Television's Second Golden Age*, most of the allusions and references in *St. Elsewhere* pertain to television, and in some instances their production company, MTM. One example is a storyline involving a psychiatric patient, John Doe no. 6 (Oliver Clark), who, at one point (in the episode "Close Encounters"), thinks he's Mary Richards (Mary Tyler Moore's character on her eponymous 1970s sitcom). While he's in the psych ward, he meets another patient, this one named Mr. Carlin, portrayed by Jack Riley, the same actor who played Elliot Carlin, a regular patient of psychologist Bob Hartley on another 1970s MTM production, *The Bob Newhart Show*. When John Doe walks through the halls of St. Eligius, he runs into Captain Gloria Neal (Betty White), whom he mistakes for White's character, the "Happy Homemaker" Sue Ann Nivens, on *The Mary Tyler Moore Show*. At one point in the psych ward, someone is turning the channel and another MTM show, *The White Shadow*, is seen on the television screen. A character from that show, Carver High School basketball player Warren Coolidge (Byron Stewart), is now working as a hospital orderly at St. Eligius. Coolidge mistakes guest star Timothy Van Patten, who played Mario "Salami" Pettrino on *The White Shadow*, for his former teammate. There was also a literal crossover with another NBC series when Drs. Craig, Westphall, and Auschlander stop into Cheers for a drink.

Finally, the show whose cast always felt they were on the brink of cancellation came to an end. The aptly entitled finale, "The Last One," maintains the show's well-established tone with just the right mixture of emotionally charged moments and comically absurd antics. There are two major plot developments: Ecumena, which has changed its name to Weigert, decides to sell St. Eligius back to the Catholic Archdiocese, and Gideon, who is moving to California, asks Dr. Westphall, at Dr. Auschlander's request, to take over the hospital. Dr. Westphall is interested and decides to talk to Dr. Auschlander—except the doctor had passed away suddenly at his desk earlier that day. Several doctors are also moving on: Dr. Fiscus, who is preparing to leave for Nicaragua, is feeling nostalgic on the last day of his residency; Dr. Craig, who has reconciled with his wife, decides to move with her to Cleveland, where she's taken a new job; and Dr. Ehrlich, who went off to do some surfing and soul searching, returns to his wife, Nurse Lucy Papandrao (Jennifer Savidge). Then there's Dr. Jack "Boomer" Morrison (David Morse), a character who endured more personal tragedies than all the other characters combined. Over the course of six seasons, he lost his wife in a freak bathroom accident, becoming a single dad to his infant son, Pete; he had to go back to medical school when legal questions were raised about his medical degree from a Mexican school; he was raped by a male inmate during a prison riot; and his son was kidnapped from the hospital (fortunately, the police found him on the street). In the final episode, Jack and Pete move to Seattle to be with Jack's second wife, Joanne (Patricia Wettig).

There are also the usual self-referential jokes, including nods to two of the most famous series finales: *The Fugitive* (1963–1967) (Dr. Kimble's patient, a one-armed amputee named Mr. Mirkin, is missing and being hunted down in the hospital), and *The Mary Tyler Moore Show* (when they say goodbye, Boomer's friends, who are crying and locked in a group hug, shuffle over to get some tissues and Fiscus says, "Maybe we should sing 'It's a Long Way to Tipperary.'") The first patient treated at the top of the hour is "General Sarnoff," who is warned by Fiscus to rest his optic nerves and cut down on the time he spends watching television. (General Sarnoff is a reference to David Sarnoff, a television and radio pioneer and general manager of RCA, as well as the founder of NBC.) A new first-year resident, Brandon Falsey (John Short), named after the show's creators, Joshua Brand and John Falsey, prescribes the incorrect dosage of a drug. One of Fiscus's last patients is a female opera singer, Brigitta Swenson, who has lost her voice the day of a final dress rehearsal. She is dressed as the Valkyrie Brünnhilde, from *Götterdämmerung*, the last part of Richard Wagner's opera cycle, *Der Ring des Nibelungen*, in which she sings a twenty-minute aria before throwing herself into the fire and Valhalla, as the gods are engulfed in flames. Towards the end of the episode, Dr. Gideon tells Dr. Fiscus, who appears to be lingering on his last day, to go home—his residency is over. "It ain't over until the fat lady sings," he responds. Suddenly, from behind a curtain, the "fat lady," Brigitta, played by opera singer Ealynn Voss, begins to sing. This aria becomes the background music in what one expects to be the final scene, in which a teary-eyed Dr. Westphall sits in Dr. Auschlander's office, while his autistic son Tommy looks outside the window at the snow. There is an exterior shot of St. Eliguis, which would logically be the show's final shot.

But it's not.

We suddenly find ourselves in an unfamiliar place—inside an apartment where we see Tommy Westphall sitting on the floor with a glass globe in his hands. Dr. Auschlander is sitting in a chair nearby, reading a newspaper. Wearing a hard hat, Dr. Westphall enters and addresses Auschlander as "Pop," who asks how his day was "up on the building?" Westphall remarks that they finally topped off the 22nd story. He then asks about Tommy, who "Pop" says has been sitting there all day since he left this morning.

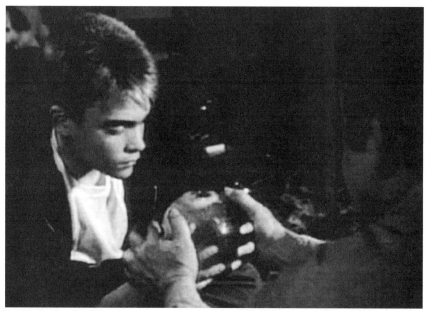

In the finale of *St. Elsewhere*, viewers are shocked to learn the entire series only existed in the mind of an autistic boy, Tommy Westphall (Chad Allen).   *Authors' collection*

"I don't understand this autism thing, Pop," Westphall says. "He's my son. I talk to him. I don't even know if he can hear me. He sits there all day long—in his own world. Staring at that toy. What's he thinking about?"

Tommy shakes the globe. Westphall takes it away from him and helps him up from the floor and the two go into the other room. The camera zooms in on the snow globe, which contains the model of a building that looks like St. Eligius.

Viewers were certainly shocked by this ending, which suggested that the entire series was actually the product of an autistic child's imagination. Bruce Paltrow revealed to Associated Press television writer Kathryn Baker that the producers had actually conceived the ending a few years earlier. He then elaborated on their intentions: "We were looking for the metaphor for all of us to have created this fiction. To place the entire six years into the imagination of a boy who could not communicate with the outside world, but had this staggeringly exciting inner life was, we thought, an excitingly existential end to the series." The problem is this so-called "metaphor" seems to have been created by the writers for themselves rather than their audience. That's how critic Gene Seymour interpreted the sequence—"something that existed separate and apart from the show; a comment by the writer-producers on what it means to imagine and create a whole, living, breathing universe from the impassive and the intangible." In an interview with the Archive of American Television, Tom Fontana, who co-wrote the teleplay with Bruce Paltrow and co-wrote the story with John Tinker and Channing Gibson, recalled how people were divided over the twist at the end. "People loved it," Fontana explains, "but the ones who hated it just wanted us eviscerated." When asked why he thought people didn't like it, he suggested that loyal viewers felt betrayed by the ending:

> I think because it said, this was all make-believe. When people are pas-
> sionate about a series, they actually want to believe that it's happening.
> They want to believe that it's true. They want to believe that these char-
> acters that they've invested this time and passion in are real people and
> real friends of theirs and so I think they felt betrayed by the fact that we
> had actually taken away the curtain and revealed the fact that it was just
> pretend.

In his review of the finale, *New York Times* critic John J. O'Connor followed the producers' instructions and did not give away the ending. He did predict that scene, which he characterized as "a touch too flip, too arrogant," would "leave devoted fans reeling." And, "In a sense," O'Connor adds, "the scene is characteristic of the underlying contempt for itself and the audience that I sensed developing earlier in the series."

In a 2012 cast reunion for *Entertainment Weekly*, the actors had mixed reactions when asked by reporter Dan Snierson how they felt then and now about the show's surprise ending. Norman Lloyd said he feels the same way now as he did back when they were shooting the scene: "For me, it was a cheat. But for others, it was a stroke of inspiration. . . . I thought it was a letdown. . . . I felt it wasn't serious." William Daniels admitted he was "shocked" by the show's "provocative ending" and recalled "a lot of the cast didn't care for it at all." One cast member who thought it was a "terrible ending" was Daniels's wife, Bonnie Bartlett, who played his onscreen wife, Ellen Craig. She thinks the producers did it because they wanted "to kill the show" so they wouldn't have a reunion episode. Ed Begley Jr., felt that it kept with the spirit of the show: "They tried to really think outside the box—the box in this case being that little television box of the '80s—and they did something so different. . . . It was highly unpredictable, just like every episode."

The enigmatic ending has not been forgotten. In the series finale of *30 Rock* (see chapter 20), Kenneth the Page (Jack McBrayer), who is now running NBC, holds a snow globe while listening to Liz Lemon's granddaughter pitching a show based on her grandmother's experiences working at 30 Rock, suggesting the entire series was actually in the mind of man-child Kenneth. In an ending that channeled both *St. Elsewhere* and *Newhart* (1982–1990), talk show host Craig Ferguson ended his late night show as Mr. Wick, the character he played on *The Drew Carey Show* (1995–2004). He wakes up in bed with Drew, who now hosts *The Price Is Right* (1972–present) and tells him he had a dream in which Drew was a game show host and he was a late night talk show host who was stuck in a "cheap, dimly lit studio with a robot skeleton and a fake horse" for ten years. They go back to sleep and we see a snow globe on Craig's nightstand containing images of Craig, the horse, and the skeleton inside.

The snow globe seems to have overshadowed the real contribution *St. Elsewhere* made to prime-time television. As Robert Thompson observes, *St. Elsewhere* "crowded the screen with a large ensemble cast, padded the script with a bewildering number of ongoing stories and introduced human flaws to a breed of professionals that television had presumed to be super-human." Its legacy is the "quality" and the edge it brought to the genre with shows like *ER* (1994–2009), *House* (2004–2012), and *Grey's Anatomy* (2005–present).

Since St. Eligius opened its doors, the medical drama has never been the same.

Meanwhile, in the Basement . . .

Roseanne Is Writing Her Novel

Roseanne (ABC, 1988–1997)

Created by Matt Williams
Based on a character created by Roseanne Barr
Premiere date: October 18, 1988
9 seasons / 222 episodes
"Into That Good Night, Parts 1 and 2"
Airdate: May 20, 1997
11.6 rating • 19 percent share • 16.6 million viewers
Directed by Gary Halvorson
Part 1 written by Jessica Pentland and Jennifer Pentland, story by Roseanne Barr
Part 2 written by Roseanne Barr and Allan Stephan
Cast: Roseanne Barr (Roseanne Conner), John Goodman (Dan Conner), Laurie
 Metcalf (Jackie Harris), Sarah Chalke (Becky Conner-Healy), Sara Gilbert
 (Darlene Conner-Healy), Michael Fishman (D. J. Conner), Johnny Galecki
 (David Healy), Glenn Quinn (Mark Healy), Estelle Parsons (Beverly Harris),
 Martin Mull (Leon Carp), Fred Willard (Scott), Sandra Bernhard (Nancy
 Bartlett), Lecy Goranson (Becky no. 1) (clip only)

O n August 23, 1985, thirty-three-year-old nasal-voiced comedian
Roseanne Barr performed on *The Tonight Show Starring Johnny
Carson.* A self-professed housewife who prefers to be called a
"domestic goddess," Barr cracked jokes about the suburbs, watching *Donahue,*
Barbra Streisand, why fat people give the best directions, and the advantages
of having a fat vs. a skinny mom. America had neither seen (nor heard) a
comedian like Barr in a long time. Although her delivery was not polished
and her jokes were a string of non sequiturs, Barr's self-deprecating humor
was in the comic tradition of such comediennes as Totie Fields, Phyllis Diller,
and Joan Rivers.

Among those tuning in that night were Marcy Carsey and Tom Werner, executive producers of the no. 1 comedy on television, *The Cosby Show*. Impressed with Barr's performance, they decided to star her in a series based on her standup material. In an interview with the Archive of American Television, Carsey recalled that at the time there was no situation comedy on television focusing on "the absurdity and the prevalence of the phenomenon of the working mom in America." In 1988, the year *Roseanne* debuted, the only bona fide blue-collar family on television were The Bundys on FOX's *Married . . . with Children* (1987–1997). But while Peg Bundy (Katey Sagal) is a do-nothing, stay-at-home-mom with an aversion to housework, Barr's character, Roseanne Conner, is a do-everything, working mom who, after her factory shift, spends her remaining waking hours doing the housework and taking care of her husband, Dan (John Goodman), and their three kids: Becky (Lecy Goranson, 1988–1992, 1995–1996; Sarah Chalke, 1993–1997), Darlene (Sara Gilbert), and D. J. (Michael Fishman). But unlike most television moms, she is not happy about it—and she lets everyone know it. That's why, Carsey explains, they needed "a loud, and interesting and unique and in your face kind of presence to take it [the role] to the more outrageous end of the spectrum." She definitely fit the bill, though it was not always clear where Roseanne Barr ended and her TV alter ego Roseanne Conner began.

The Carsey-Werner Company hired *Cosby Show* writer Matt Williams to adapt Barr's standup routine into a half-hour sitcom. The pilot, entitled "Life and Stuff," introduced America to the Conners, a working-class family living in Lanford, a small town in Illinois. The first episode is a-day-in-the-busy-life of Roseanne Conner, who gets her three rambunctious kids off to school in the morning, works the day shift at Wellman Plastics, and returns home to do the housework and make dinner. In between, she meets with Darlene's snooty history teacher Miss Crane (Judy Prescott), who insinuates that Darlene's behavioral problem (she barks in class) is due to Roseanne's failure to spend "quality time" with her daughter. Roseanne scoffs at the suggestion and later solves the problem by simply telling Darlene to "cut it out." Back at home, a weary Roseanne goes off on Dan, a freelance contractor, for spending the day at his friend's house instead of fixing the clogged sink like he promised. Their fight is interrupted by Darlene, who cuts her finger. One Band-Aid later, the bleeding has stopped, order is restored, and everything in the Conner house is back to normal.

The pilot established that the Conners occupied a very different universe than most television families. In terms of both their demeanor and physical appearance, Roseanne and Dan Conner are not your typical TV mom and dad. The same goes for their smart-mouthed kids who talk back to their parents, especially Roseanne, who makes equally snide and sarcastic comments right back at them. We know she loves her kids, even though after Darlene and her brother leave for school she tells Dan, "Quick they're gone, change the lock." The pilot also begins to establish that the Conners are struggling to make ends meet, which would be one of the sitcom's major themes in the first five seasons.

Prior to starring in her own series, Roseanne Barr had no previous acting experience, which is why Carsey-Werner cast two respected, yet relatively unknown, character actors—Goodman and Laurie Metcalf—to play Dan and Roseanne's sister, Jackie. Goodman's film credits included supporting roles in *Sweet Dreams* (1985), *The Big Easy* (1986), and *Raising Arizona* (1987). He also played Huck Finn's father on Broadway in the musical *Big River* (1985). Metcalf was a member of the Chicago-based Steppenwolf Theatre Company and appeared in two films directed by Susan Seidelman, *Desperately Seeking Susan* (1985) and *Making Mr. Right* (1987). The cast would later add a pair of Academy Award–winning actresses: Estelle Parsons (*Bonnie and Clyde* [1967]) as Roseanne and Jackie's overly critical, annoying mother, Beverly Harris; and Shelley Winters (*The Diary of Anne Frank* [1959], *A Patch of Blue* [1965]) as the Conners's free-spirited, outspoken grandmother, Nana Mary.

The Conners—one big happy dysfunctional family: (seated, left to right) D. J. (Michael Fishman); Roseanne (Roseanne Barr); Dan (John Goodman); (back row, left to right) Darlene (Sara Gilbert); Becky (Lecy Goranson); and Jackie (Laurie Metcalf).   *Authors' collection*

"I want to do real revolutionary TV," Roseanne told *New York Times* journalist Joy Horowitz. "I want to do a show for the '90s. I want to do a show that reflects how people really live." Horowitz believes Roseanne succeeds, in part, because Roseanne Conner is a "flawed" television mom who doesn't have "cover-girl looks": "In short, she is real. And smart. And self-confident. And sexual. And not so wonderful to her kids all the time. Roseanne says what most of us think but repress. She is a true TV anomaly."

The critics who embraced the show were entertained by the comedian's biting, sardonic wit and impressed by the show's authentic portrayal of domestic life. In his review of the show's pilot, *Winnipeg Free Press* critic Brad Oswald found the show "so darned refreshing" and Roseanne Conner to be "the closest thing TV's had to a real-life mom in a long, long time. Like ever, maybe." Bob Niedt, a critic for the *Syracuse Herald-Journal*, described the sitcom as a "saga of a family unit built on love, but the little imperfections are faced head-on, and not glossed over for a just-right, all-questions-answered TV ending." *Los Angeles Times*' Howard Rosenberg dubbed *Roseanne* "Mother Insults Best" and praised the pilot as a "rip-roaring romp in which boisterous Roseanne and Dan are as often hilarious and likable as they are loud." The East Coast critics agreed. After seeing the pilot, *New York Times* critic John J. O'Connor thought the show was "off to a terrifically hilarious start." *Washington Post* critic Tom Shales agreed: "*Roseanne* is really different and very funny . . . the first fresh domestic sitcom since the arrival of *The Cosby Show*."

Some critics were concerned about the show's comic tone, which *Chicago Tribune* critic Clifford Terry described as "snippy." *Variety* critic Timothy Gray warned the show's creative team to "be careful *Roseanne* doesn't become merely 30 minutes of insults—a clear danger given the preponderance of wisecracks and putdowns in the premiere episode as well as the mocking attitude of the title character." At the same time, Gray also praised Barr for her "expert timing and a dry, whiny, nasal delivery that is unique" and acknowledged that her "strong personality . . . could put off a lot of people, but will probably attract even more." A negative review (to put it mildly) of the pilot by Daniel Ruth, a critic for the *Chicago Sun-Times*, created a critical firestorm—but it wasn't simply because he found "ABC's meager attempt to copy the successful formula of the Fox Network's *Married . . . with Children*" to be "stupid." Ruth made several disparaging remarks about the show's "250-pound heroine": "If she were the last woman on Earth and you were the last man," he wrote, "she would make celibacy the preferred lifestyle." In December of 1988, Ruth choose *Roseanne* for the worst series of 1988 and called its star "a tub of lard (Roseanne Barr) with a voice like a braying alley cat in heat." (In all fairness, other critics did describe Barr as "pudgy" [Niedt, Oswald] and a "strange dumpling of a person" [Rosenberg].) In response to the complaints he received, Ruth justified his remarks by claiming there was a double standard because he received no mail regarding his reference to John Goodman's character as Roseanne's "lard-o-mondo husband." Ruth contended that Barr uses her looks "as a reference point for her comedy, so her looks are fair game for critical comment with respect to her performance," and the "appearance of an actor or actress is a vital aspect in casting a particular part." In his response, Ruth also reminded his readers that he had been in the "critic business" all his life, yet apparently along the way nobody explained the difference between criticism and childish name-calling.

Ruth's prediction that *Roseanne* would fail was also dead wrong. In fact, in its first season, Roseanne ranked no. 2 in the season ratings behind *The Cosby Show*, which it tied for first place in season 2 (1989–1990) and then surpassed in season 3, ranking no. 3 behind *Cheers* and *60 Minutes*. For seasons 1–7, Roseanne was in the Top 10 and then fell to no. 16 in season 8 (1995–1996) and no. 35 in its final season (1996–1997).

In an effort to keep the show authentic early in its run, the episodes revolved around the Conner family's struggle to make ends meet, which is complicated by Dan's bike shop going under and Roseanne getting a series of jobs before becoming co-owner of the Lanford Lunch Box with Jackie, their friend Nancy (Sandra Bernhard), and Roseanne's former boss, Leon (Martin Mull). There was also plenty of dysfunction and conflict within the Conner family, which grew in size with the addition of the Healy brothers—Becky's boyfriend/husband Mark (Glenn Quinn), and Darlene's boyfriend/husband David (Johnny Galecki).

Roseanne is also credited for dealing with taboo subject matters that most family situation comedies wouldn't touch, like menstruation (Darlene gets her first period in "Nightmare on Oak Street"), flatulence (Becky farts while giving a speech in school in "Inherit the Wind"), obesity (Roseanne and Dan try to lose weight in "I'm Hungry"), masturbation (D. J. spends too much time locked in a bathroom in "Homeward Bound"), birth control (Becky wants to go on the pill in "A Bitter Pill to Swallow"), and child abuse (David prefers to live with the Conners rather than his abusive mother in "It's a Boy"). Then there's a hilarious episode (and a definite first for a family sitcom) in which Roseanne and Dan find an old bag of pot in Darlene's room and proceed to get high with Jackie ("A Stash from the Past"). A scene in which the three stoned adults are hiding out in the bathroom is one of the series' highlights. One audience member who wasn't laughing was Senator Orrin Hatch (R-Utah). Dennis Wharton reported in *Variety* that Hatch cited the episode on the Senate floor in a speech attacking the entertainment industry as a whole and the writers of *Roseanne* in particular for encouraging drug use and positively reinforcing "a truly negative message."

Later that same season, another controversial episode ("Don't Ask, Don't Tell") featured guest star Mariel Hemingway as Nancy's new girlfriend, who plants a kiss on an unsuspecting Roseanne when she and Jackie go out to a gay bar. Greg Braxton reported in the *Los Angeles Times* that ABC, fearing a loss of advertising revenue, intended not to air the episode because the subject matter was not appropriate for an 8:00 p.m. show. But ABC went ahead and aired it, albeit with a parental advisory. Apparently the media-generated controversy paid off because the March 1, 1994, broadcast beat CBS's live telecast of the Grammy Awards in the ratings. As Brian Lowry reported in *Variety*, despite the parental warning, the *Roseanne* episode attracted a 33 percent share among children. Before *Ellen* (1994–1998) and *Will & Grace* (1998–2006), *Roseanne* was the gay/lesbian/bisexual-friendliest comedy on television, winning the Gay and Lesbian Alliance Against Defamation (GLAAD) award for Best Comedy Series in 1992, 1993, and 1995.

Throughout its nine-season run, there was controversy offscreen as well due to what the press reported as Roseanne's constant clashing with the show's writers, beginning with the series' creator, Matt Williams, who Roseanne demanded be fired after thirteen episodes. In his first interview after his exit, Williams told *Los Angeles Times* reporter Nikki Finke that his conflict with Roseanne was over creative control of the series. When a show is a hit, the star trumps the writer, even if he or she is the show's creator. Williams did go on to create another hit series for ABC, *Home Improvement* (1991–1999), while a steady stream of writers and producers entered and exited through the revolving door of the *Roseanne* "writers' room." The distinguished list of Roseanne writers included writer/director Joss Whedon, creator of *Buffy the Vampire Slayer* and director/co-writer of *The Avengers* (2012); Amy Sherman-Palladino, creator of *Gilmore Girls*; Chuck Lorre, creator of *Grace Under Fire* and *Cybill,* and co-creator of *Dharma & Greg, Two and a Half Men, The Big Bang Theory,* and *Mom*; and future *Saturday Night Live* cast member Norm Macdonald.

The Conners' financial woes were ongoing as was the never-ending family drama, which, as the kids got older, focused on the "life choices" regarding careers, men, and babies made by Becky and Darlene and Roseanne's little sister, Jackie. The Conner family also expanded with the birth of Jackie's baby, Andy; Roseanne and Dan's fourth child, Jerry Garcia Conner; and Darlene and David's daughter, Harris Conner-Healy. In the midst of all the family drama, *Roseanne* started to take itself a little less seriously (in a good way), particularly in the final moment of some episodes (known as the "Tag"), when we see Nancy's annoying husband, Arnie (Tom Arnold), being abducted by aliens ("Aliens"); *General Hospital*'s Luke and Laura Spencer (Tony Geary and Genie Francis) sharing their marital problems with Roseanne and Dan

("Suck Up or Shut Up"); and recent Emmy winner Laurie Metcalf on the set of the show polishing her first of three statues ("The Dark Ages"), which Roseanne and John Goodman try to steal. The latter self-reflexive moment is one of several instances when the show would break "the fourth wall" and acknowledge that it was, in fact, a television show. At the end of one episode ("Single Married Female"), in which the show's title character hardly appears, a pregnant Roseanne (the star) explained to the audience her absence was due to doctor's orders that she stay in bed.

There are also entire episodes that acknowledge, in a playfully post-modern way, the show's status as a television sitcom by tipping its hat to television history with tributes to black-and-white sitcoms ("The Fifties Show"); *Gilligan's Island* (1964–1967) and its creator, Sherwood Schwartz ("Sherwood Schwartz: A Loving Tribute"); and famous TV sitcom couples ("Call Waiting"). Roseanne's most "hyper-conscious" episode ("All About Rosey") blurred the lines between reality and fiction when Roseanne (the actress, not the character), alone on the show's soundstage, walks onto the set of the Conner kitchen and finds five famous sitcom moms cleaning: June Cleaver (Barbara Billingsley, from *Leave It to Beaver* [1957–1963] / *The New Leave It to Beaver* [1983–1989]), Joan Nash (Patricia Crowley, from *Please Don't Eat the Daisies* [1965–1967]), Ruth Martin (June Lockhart, from *Lassie* [1958–1964]), Norma Arnold (Alley Mills, from *The Wonder Years* [1988–1993]), and Louise Jefferson (Isabel Sanford, from *The Jeffersons* [1975–1985]). Roseanne begins to recall some of the things that have happened on her show, which shocks the television moms, who also can't believe they named the show after the mom character.

Roseanne took a dramatic turn at the end of season 8 ("Heart and Soul") when Dan suffers a near-fatal heart attack at Darlene and David's wedding right after he has reconciled with his pregnant daughter and walked her down the aisle. Dan survives, but when he goes against doctor's orders and won't stick to his diet, Roseanne walks out on him and their marriage ("Fights and Stuff"). But their fight is not just about Dan's lack of willpower, but how he and Roseanne both failed as parents for letting their daughters marry so young, which is really about the regrets they both have concerning their own lives.

By the time the final episode of season 8 aired, *Roseanne* had been renewed for a ninth season. Although the show's ratings declined in season 8, it still ranked no. 16 among the key demographic (adults 18–49), which is why, according to *Variety*'s Brian Lowry, ABC renewed the show, though the licensing fee (the amount the network pays to air the show, which doesn't cover the entire budget) was reduced from an estimated $3.25 million to roughly $2 million per episode. Goodman, who intended to leave the show, appears in twelve episodes in season 9, including the two-part series finale.

Season 9 of *Roseanne* is an uneven blend of family melodrama and sitcom fantasy. Last season's cliffhanger is resolved in the season opener ("Call Waiting") in which Roseanne realizes she and Dan are meant to be together, like other famous sitcom couples from television. Roseanne dreams she and Dan are Ann and Don from *That Girl* (1966–1971), Jeannie and Major Nelson from *I Dream of Jeannie* (1965–1970), and Mary and Mr. Grant from *The Mary Tyler Moore Show* (1970–1977). But most of season 9 revolves around another "fantasy" that begins with Jackie and Roseanne winning $108 million dollars, the biggest prize in Illinois lottery history. A family that had been struggling for eight seasons was suddenly filthy rich, which opens a sitcom portal for Roseanne and Jackie, complete with wacky adventures and absurd plotlines: Jackie is courted by Prince Carlos Charmaine of Moldavia (Jim Varney) ("Someday My Prince Will Come"), who later jilts her ("Say It Ain't So"); Roseanne meets Hillary Clinton and fights terrorists on a train ("Roseambo"); and the Conners rub elbows with an uptight rich family on Martha's Vineyard and teaches them how to loosen up ("Hoi Polloi Meets Hoiti Toiti"). Roseanne also pays it forward to the unemployed of Lanford when she buys a stake in Wellman Plastics so the factory, where she and Jackie worked in season 1, can reopen.

The remaining episodes of the season revolve around Dan's departure and return from California, where he was visiting his institutionalized mother and falling in love with her nurse. Roseanne becomes severely depressed, but they eventually reconcile in time to deal with a bigger crisis—the premature birth of Darlene and David's baby girl, Harris Conner-Healy. In the series finale, the Conners welcome Darlene, David, and their healthy baby back into the home, where they agree to stay indefinitely.

The finale is a kinder, gentler episode of *Roseanne*. There's less shouting and the wisecracks are overshadowed by more serious moments, most of which involve reflecting on the past. D. J. is forced to give up his room upstairs and move down into the basement, which he and Roseanne recall (in flashback) that her family once fixed up as an office as a birthday present for Roseanne, so she can write the novel she always dreamed of writing. The Conners also reflect on how their lives have changed since winning the lottery and how living the high life just wasn't for them. "It's been a very weird year," remarks Jackie, which might be their way of saying to the audience "Yes, we know. It's been a very weird season." They eat take-out pizza, but not before Roseanne insists they say grace to express their gratitude that baby Harris is alive and they are all together.

Part 2 is more of the same as the Conners are joined by great-grandmother Bev, Nancy, and Leon and his partner, Scott (Fred Willard), who announce that they are adopting a baby from Romania (Becky and Mark are also expecting, but they decide to keep it a secret). The most poignant moment of the episode is an exchange between Roseanne and Darlene, who have always had a special, though oftentimes contentious, mother-daughter relationship because they are so much alike. Darlene thinks Roseanne only wants her new family to stay for a limited amount of time. Grandmother Roseanne assures her that she is thrilled they are living there and that they can stay as long as they like.

When the preview tape of the *Roseanne* finale was sent out to critics, who would typically pre-screen the episode and publish their review the day it airs, the last fifteen minutes were omitted. According to *Chicago Sun-Times* critic Lon Grahnke, the tape was accompanied by a press release from Eileen Kurtz, director of ABC media relations, stating, "At the request of Roseanne and the producers, the final 15 minutes of the program [are] not included on the tape. It is their wish that everyone see the conclusion of the episode for the first time on May 20th." This was certainly a bold move on the part of the producers and the network as a series finale for a long-running show is treated as a series event that can garner high ratings during "Sweeps Week."

In the final scene, while everyone is sitting around the table eating Chinese food, Roseanne's interior monologue begins—and it is revealed that the entire series (or at least the majority of it) is the product of Roseanne Conner's imagination. She explains that her characters were inspired by her actual family and friends, though she had to take some artistic license, explaining that Darlene and Mark are a couple, but she thought David, who is with Becky, was better suited for Darlene; her sister (like Roseanne's in real life) is a lesbian, but she made Bev a lesbian because she had grown up in a time when women were submissive, and she wanted her to have some sense of herself as a woman. But the real shocker was to learn that Dan had died from a heart attack at Darlene's wedding and the Conners never won the lottery. When we see Roseanne leave her office in the basement and go upstairs, the house looks similar (though not entirely) like it did prior to winning the lottery. Roseanne sits, alone and forlorn, on her couch. The following quotation appears on the screen from T. E. Lawrence, also known as "Lawrence of Arabia":

> Those who dream by night, in the dusty recesses of their minds wake in the day to find that all was vanity; but the dreamers of the day are dangerous men, for they may act their dream with open eyes, and make it possible.

The quotation, which leaves out the first sentence "All men dream: but not equally" is from Lawrence's 1922 autobiography, in which he recounts his experiences during the Arab Revolt of 1916–1918 when he was serving in the British Forces of North Africa.

In the series finale of *Roseanne*, the audience learns Roseanne Conner (Roseanne) lost her beloved husband, Dan (John Goodman), to a heart attack.   *Authors' collection*

As Roseanne and the producers requested, Dan's death was not revealed to the audience (including the critics) until the show aired. Perhaps if the "twist" had been publicized, *Roseanne* would have pulled in higher numbers for its final telecast. The finale competed with the arrival of Jamie and Paul Buchman's daughter on the season 6 finale of NBC's *Mad About You*. According to the Nielsen ratings, 25.7 million viewers tuned in to watch the birth of Mabel Buchman, which was the highest rated show of the week. By comparison, the series finale of *Roseanne* was viewed by 16.6 million people and ranked no. 14 for the week. As Ray Richmond noted in *Variety*, Roseanne's series finale ratings were still above the season 9 average, but still surprisingly low for a series that had been a Top 10 show for seven seasons. But the show was not able to recover from the viewers they lost at the start of season 9, when the show plummeted to no. 35 in the overall ratings. For this, television critics blame the lottery storyline. Perhaps the audience preferred seeing the Conners counting their pennies instead of rolling in dough.

Letting Go

Lost Comes Full Circle (Sort of)

Lost (ABC, 2004–2010)
Created by Jeffrey Lieber, J. J. Abrams, and Damon Lindelof
Premiere date: September 22, 2004
6 seasons / 121 episodes
"The End"
Airdate: May 23, 2010
7.5 rating • 13 percent share • 13.5 million viewers
Directed by Jack Bender
Written by Damon Lindelof and Carton Cuse
Cast: Matthew Fox (Jack Shephard), Evangeline Lilly (Kate Austen), Jorge Garcia (Hugo "Hurley" Reyes), Josh Holloway (James "Sawyer" Ford), Henry Ian Cusick (Desmond Hume), Michael Emerson (Ben Linus), Terry O'Quinn (John Locke), Emilie de Ravin (Claire Littleton), Daniel Dae Kim (Jin Kwon), Yunjin Kim (Sun Kwon), Naveen Andrews (Sayid Jarrah), Dominic Monaghan (Charlie Pace), Elizabeth Mitchell (Juliet Burke), John Terry (Christian Shephard)

Like any great puzzle, ABC's hit mystery thriller *Lost* found fans enthralled, mystified, and frustrated as they followed its labyrinth of twists and turns. Desperately trying to solve the show's central mystery—one that seemed to continuously evolve with each season—fans grasped at any clues, hanging onto the most minute details. *Lost* engaged its audience like no other television series had before—watching the show was part entertainment, part obsession. "Losties," as die-hard fans were called, despaired when the show neared its end, but reveled in the possibility of finally having the answers they craved. Having endured six seasons of smoke monsters, hidden hatches, and time-travel (which barely scratches the surface of the *Lost* universe), Losties knew anything was possible within the world of the show—after all, as Mark A. Perigard of the *Boston Herald* so eloquently put it, the series had been "a jungle adventure, a thriller, a conspiracy story, a sci-fi mind-bender and sometimes, surprisingly, a lush romance." Hitting all of these notes in the finale seemed unlikely, but executive producers Damon Lindelof and Carlton Cuse—collectively responsible for writing a third of the series 121 episodes, including each season's finale—had known since May 2007 that the series would come to a close at the end of its sixth season, allowing them to fully flesh out the series' mysteries. Going into the finale, Lindelof and Cuse remained tight-lipped on any clues, and promised to remain so even after the finale aired, citing the "interpretive element" of the show—the enthusiastic fan communities that shared countless conspiracy theories following each episode—as the main factor in their decision. For Lindelof, this desire to analyze every detail of the series was "the bread and butter of the show." He admitted, "The more we talk about what our intention was [for the finale], the more we take it away from the audience. And we have no interest in doing that, ever." Loyal to their Losties until the very end, Cuse and Lindelof attempted to satisfy the lofty hopes for the finale, while remaining true to their desire to shock and subvert the viewers' own expectations—a task that proved to be a very difficult one.

The origins of the series appropriately mirror its twisty narrative. ABC, trailing the other major networks in a distant fourth place, was desperate to inject energy into its programming. Tom Hanks had recently been nominated for an Oscar for his turn in Robert Zemeckis's *Cast Away* (2000), a film that followed a man who survives a plane crash, only to find himself stranded, alone, on a remote island. Hanks lost to Russell Crowe for his performance in *Gladiator*, but Hanks's performance stuck with the executives at ABC, particularly Lloyd Braun, then-chairman of ABC Entertainment. Braun put out the call for a television version of *Cast Away*, hoping that his team would find a way to make it work. Many dismissed the idea out of hand—too expensive, too lofty, too reminiscent of the coconut phones and wacky adventures of *Gilligan's Island*. Some, however, saw possibility. At the same time, CBS's reality show *Survivor* was the biggest hit on television. Marrying these two concepts—Hanks's *Cast Away* with a voted off-the-island *Survivor* appeal—seemed possible. In a 2007 interview with David Bernstein for *Chicago* magazine, writer Jeffrey Lieber, who was hired to flesh out the concept, admitted that he imagined "something like *Lord of the Flies* . . . a realistic show about a society putting itself back together after a catastrophe." Lieber created the world and pitched the show to ABC in 2003, getting an almost immediate greenlight to proceed with the pilot. After positive feedback and more work on the script, Lieber found out that his services were no longer required. ABC had hired J. J. Abrams—with whom they had worked on the spy thriller *Alias* (2001–2006)—and Damon Lindelof (then an unknown writer) to carry the project through. Abrams and Lindelof had expanded on Lieber's universe, taking his *Lord of the Flies* meets *Survivor* concept and adding in sci-fi elements and the possibility that supernatural forces were at play on the island (Lieber called this "more *Lord of the Rings* than *Lord of the Flies*"). ABC agreed to produce Abrams and Lindelof's pilot for a record-breaking $12 million—leaving Lieber in the dust. After an appeal to the Writers Guild of America, the agency that determines the appropriate credits for its unionized members, Lieber won the right to be named as one of the series' creators. While Abrams and Lindelof would carry the series through its six seasons—creating and

The original castaways: (left to right) Jack Shephard (Matthew Fox); Kate Austen (Evangeline Lilly); and Sawyer Ford (Josh Holloway).   *Authors' collection*

lexpanding upon the universe that Lieber outlined—Lieber's name would appear alongside (and above) theirs in the opening credits, as well as on the yearly payroll.

When the show did eventually premiere on ABC in September of 2004, critical praise was swift and passionate. Matthew Gilbert of the *Boston Globe* called it "one of the best new series of the fall," while *Newsweek*'s Marc Peyser added that "any show with this kind of imagination deserves to be seen." Tim Goodman of the *San Francisco Chronicle* concluded: "*Lost* has a stellar, varied cast, it is shot beautifully and it surprises more often than it makes you wince or wheeze," continuing, "it's no guilty pleasure—it's great, no-apologies television." The premiere drew a huge audience, raking in more than 18 million viewers and winning its timeslot, making it the highest rated premiere for a drama series on any network in four years. ABC had successfully found the injection of energy it was hoping for in *Lost*, only to one-up themselves with the series premiere of the much-buzzed about soap *Desperate Housewives* just two weeks later (which brought in a record 21 million viewers), and the midseason entry of Shonda Rhimes's *Grey's Anatomy* (also a ratings giant, with 16.25 million tuning in for the first episode). By the end of the 2004–2005 television season, ABC emerged in second place, barely trailing behind FOX's *American Idol*–fueled ratings juggernaut. *Lost* was renewed for a second season and went on to win six statues at the 2005 Emmys, including the coveted prize for Outstanding Drama Series.

As early as season 2, series creator Damon Lindelof warned fans to keep in mind that the series had a rapidly approaching expiration date, stating: "I felt at the beginning, and still feel [the lifespan of the series], is about 100 episodes." Lindelof attributed this to the nature of the show, which he called:

> A show about people who are metaphorically lost in their lives . . . and crash in an airplane and become physically lost on the planet Earth. Once they are able to metaphorically find themselves in their lives again, they will be able to physically find themselves in the world again. When you look at the entire show when it finally ends, that is what it will look like, and that's what it has always been about.

Lindelof's prediction came to fruition when, in May of 2007, ABC announced that the series would end in the 2009–2010 television season, giving the show just three more seasons (for a total of six) to wrap up the stories of the survivors of Oceanic Flight 815. ABC Entertainment exec Steve McPherson, speaking on behalf of the network, told *Variety*: "In considering the powerful storytelling of *Lost*, we felt this was the only way to give it a proper creative conclusion . . . due to the unique nature of the series, we knew it would require an end date to keep the integrity and strength of the show consistent throughout, and to give the audience the payoff they deserve."

J. J. Abrams, now pursuing a lucrative deal with Warner Bros. and Paramount to continue developing television and films (including his *Star Trek* movie franchise reboot), had turned over the executive producer reigns to staff writer Carlton Cuse, and together with Lindelof, Cuse thanked ABC for the "bold and unprecedented move" of announcing the conclusion of a series so far in advance. He then added:

> I think for story-based shows like *Lost*, as opposed to franchise-based shows like *ER* or *CSI*, the audience wants to know when the story is going to be over. When J. K. Rowling announced that there would be seven *Harry Potter* books, it gave the readers a clear sense of exactly what their investment would be. We want our audience to do the same. In making this deal, Damon and I had two priorities: defining an end point for the show and keeping the quality bar high.

Variety noted that ABC's strategy with *Lost* marked new ground for a hit television series. Typically, a series as popular as *Lost* would hit the 100-episode mark and begin to pursue lucrative syndication deals, set to begin before the series had come to its conclusion. This "traditional syndie business model," as *Variety* called it, would no longer work for heavily serialized shows like *Lost*—syndication was simply not in the cards. Instead, ABC focused on the digital downloads, and the possibility of the show to live on through streaming opportunities—after all, the nature of the show's plot fit perfectly within the burgeoning Netflix and iTunes binge-viewing model. ABC's decision to announce *Lost*'s end date with adequate lead time also allowed the network to rev up the hype machine leading up to the series finale—and for *Lost* no amount of hype would ever be enough.

The series finale of *Lost* would occupy ABC's entire prime-time lineup on the night of May 23, 2010. A two-hour retrospective titled *Lost: The Final Journey* would air from 7:00 p.m. to 9:00 p.m., providing fans with both a refresher and a celebration of the series' six seasons. The two-part finale titled "The End" would run for a supersized two-and-a-half hours from 9:00 p.m. to 11:30 p.m., only to be followed by a special edition of late night's *Jimmy Kimmel Live!* called "Aloha to *Lost*," featuring an hour-long post-show interview with the series' stars. Speculation of how the mythologized series would end dominated headlines, while fans gathered together for finale-watching parties. In the many interviews Cuse and Lindelof gave in promotion of the finale event, they remained, as promised, tight-lipped when it came to any hints. Cuse did offer one spoiler in terms of how *Lost* would measure up to television's most famous series finales, telling the *Washington Post*'s Jen Chaney: "We feel like *Lost* deserved a real resolution, not a snow globe, waking up in bed, it's all been a dream, cut to black kind of ending" (referencing *St. Elsewhere*, *Newhart*, and *The Sopranos* all in one fell swoop). As the series began its final descent

Jack's (Matthew Fox) final moments on the island . . . we think.   *ABC/Photofest*

into television history, fans braced for just about anything—the series had long taught them to manage their expectations.

"The End" is grounded in two different realities: the world of the island, and the sideways reality that puts its characters back in Los Angeles, having their time on the island buried deep within their own psyches. The story on the island follows Jack (Matthew Fox), Kate (Evangeline Lilly), and Hurley (Jorge Garcia) as they make their way to the "light" at the heart of the island, as instructed by Jacob, who had turned over protection of the "light" to Jack in the previous episode. Without the "light," death is imminent for all inhabitants of the island. Meanwhile, Sawyer (Josh Holloway) breaks off from the group to seek out Desmond (Henry Ian Cusick), who has become trapped in a well, thanks to Ben (Michael Emerson) and John Locke (Terry O'Quinn), whose body has been taken over by an evil force. As Sawyer approaches the well, Ben points a gun at him, as Locke watches on. When Sawyer discovers that Desmond is no longer in the well, he rightly assumes that Locke and Ben are hunting Desmond down in order to destroy the island (which Locke confirms). Sawyer manages to steal Ben's gun and leaves, as Locke eventually comes upon Desmond and kidnaps him. Locke, with Ben and Desmond in tow, runs into Jack and his crew as they all head toward the heart of the island. Terse words are exchanged, as Jack promises to kill Locke before he can go through with his plan to destroy the island, using Desmond as his primary weapon against Locke. When everyone reaches the cave that houses the heart of the island, only Jack, Locke, and Desmond proceed inside. Inside the cave, Desmond reaches a pool of light and is hurt by its pulsing electromagnetic energy. Now in the pool, Desmond struggles to reach the center stone to remove it, and, as he does, the light goes out and the pool dries up. Desmond, long believed to be a weapon for good, has instead become a weapon for evil, putting out the "light" that is so crucial to the island's survival. An earthquake rocks the island, and as Jack chases Locke out of the cave, he lands a punch and Locke bleeds, disproving the notion that he cannot be injured. Locke then renders Jack unconscious. The rest of the gang—thanks to Ben and Locke's boat—heads to Hydra Beach where a plane awaits them, ready to whisk them away from the impending doom of the island. Locke, also heading for the boat, has one last showdown with Jack, who has miraculously regained consciousness. During the fight, Locke stabs Jack, only to be shot in the back by Kate when she emerges. Locke then falls to his death—thus killing the evil of the island. Jack, fatally wounded, begs Kate and Sawyer to go to the plane, as he will stay behind to reverse Desmond's actions. Hurley, with Ben, returns to the heart of the island with Jack, who heads back into the cave, entrusting the continued protection of the island to Hurley. In the cave, Jack rescues Desmond and revives the light, only to awaken in a familiar spot—the bamboo forest first seen in the pilot episode.

In the sideways universe in Los Angeles (where anyone who has died has been brought back to life), Desmond, parked outside of a church, signs for the recently delivered casket of Jack's father, while Jack prepares to perform surgery on Locke. Kate accompanies Desmond to a benefit concert featuring Charlie's (Dominic Monaghan) band. Hurley and Sayid (Naveen Andrews) also head to the concert. Back at the hospital, Juliet (Elizabeth Mitchell) performs an ultra-sound on Sun (Yunjin Kim) while Jin (Daniel Dae Kim) remains by her side. Jack promises to "fix" the currently paralyzed Locke, and the two joke as Locke heads into surgery. Back at the concert, a still-pregnant Claire goes into labor, and as she gives birth to baby Aaron, triggering memories of the island for herself, Kate, and Charlie, both of whom assist with her delivery. Following Locke's surgery (which is a success), Jack and Locke also have flashes of the island, while Sawyer's visit to Sun and Jin leads him to bump into Juliet, an event which also helps him remember. When Jack sees Kate at the concert, he vaguely remembers her, as she cryptically asks him to come with her if he wants to understand. The gang reassembles at the church where Jack's father's body has been delivered. Outside the church, Ben begs for Locke's forgiveness (which he receives), and says goodbye to Hurley, as Ben refuses to enter the church. Jack and Kate enter the church, as Jack tells her that this is the location where he planned to hold his father's funeral.

Kate alerts Jack that this is precisely why they are there and that they will all be waiting for him inside once he is ready. When Jack asks Kate, "Ready for what?" she responds, "To leave." When Jack eventually enters the church, he is flooded with memories of the island. He finds the casket empty, and instead sees his father (aptly named Christian Shephard) alive in the church. A confused Jack asks how his father is able to be there, to which Christian replies, "How are *you* here?" Jack starts to realize that this church may ultimately be his fate—that perhaps he, also, is dead. Wondering if the rest of the crew attending the church service are dead as well, Christian replies: "Everyone dies sometime, kiddo. Some before you, some long after you." Jack asks how, then, is everyone assembled together now, to which Christian answers, "There is no *now* . . . here." Jack enters the church, where Locke greets him warmly ("We've been waiting for you"). Seated in the church pews, he sees the former inhabitants of the island—all happy, all together. His father heads towards the back of the church, opening the doors to reveal a warm white light. This final moment is cut together with Jack, stumbling through the bamboo forest on the island, finally falling on his back, looking up to the sky. As Jack slowly dies, Vincent the dog joins him, lying next to him. The final shot is a close-up of Jack's face, as Michael Giacchino's moving score swells in the background. The series' final moment, in which Jack's eyes close, corresponds with the first episode's opening scene where Jack's eyes open—bringing the series full circle. Over the credits, images of the plane-crash site fill the screen, as the waves gently wash onto the beach.

Famously in the series, Charlie asks, "Where are we?" and by the end of the series, at the moment of Jack's death and ultimate reunion with the survivors of Oceanic Flight 815, the answer remains unclear. Cuse and Lindelof had promised to fill in the blanks for fans, finishing up their time-traveling series by merging the past, the present, and the future—only to leave fans and critics alike scratching their heads. Are they all dead? Have they *always* been dead? Was the island even real, or was it just a prolonged purgatory that would host the "survivors" until they were ready to "let go" and pass on? *Los Angeles Times* critic Mary McNamara began her review of the finale by simply stating: "Well, it could have been worse. It could have all been a dream." She continued, disappointedly:

> Six seasons of polar bears, bachelor-pad hatches, landlocked ships, personal submarines and a fleet of fallen airplanes and it was all, apparently, some sort of shared afterlife experience. In the end *Lost* was not, despite all that blogging to the contrary, a modern allegory of good vs. evil or faith vs. science. *Lost*, it turns out, was nothing more or less than a love story, the 2½ hours of its finale tilted much more toward lovers' reunions than the final battle between Jack and John Locke.

While many critics agreed with McNamara's assessment, some believed the finale lived up to the hype, including *USA Today*'s Robert Bianco who called it "an emotional feast of a finale . . . one that can stand with the best any series has produced." Fans retreated to message boards, unpacking every image and symbol, grasping to their own theories—but also expressing disappointment. Cuse and Lindelof were prepared for that reaction, and Cuse later told *Entertainment Weekly*: "We found ourselves trying to do all these narrative backflips. There was no way to sustain a mystery show for 121 episodes of television and tie up every loose end." An estimated 13.5 million viewers had tuned in, hoping to see as many threads tied up as possible—by no means a record-breaking audience, but consistent with the season-long average viewership.

In October of 2013, three years after *Lost*'s castaways had walked into the light, show creator Damon Lindelof was asked by *The Hollywood Reporter* to write about the impending series finale of *Breaking Bad*, a television show with an energetic fan base akin to that of *Lost*. As he sat down to pen his farewell to Vince Gilligan's series, he realized that his motivation for writing the piece was two-fold: the first reason being that he counted himself as a fan, and the second because he found himself "deeply and unhealthily obsessed with finding ways to revisit the *Lost* finale and the maddening hurricane of shit that has followed it." Morphing his review into an open letter to the legions of disappointment fans of his ground-breaking series, Lindelof begged the question: "If it's unpleasant and exhausting for me to keep defending the *Lost* finale, aren't you getting tired of hating it?" He proposed a solution: he would stop talking about the finale, if the fans acknowledge that he knows how they feel about the ending. He then promised, "I will think about your dissatisfaction always and forever." Lindelof's cheeky piece ended with one final proclamation: "I stand by the finale. It's the story we wanted to tell, and we told it. No excuses. No apologies."

We'll take his word for it.

In the Dark

The Sopranos' Last Supper

The Sopranos (HBO, 1999–2007)

Created by David Chase

Premiere date: January 10, 1999

6 seasons / 86 episodes

"Made in America"

Airdate: June 10, 2007

11.9 million viewers

Written and Directed by David Chase

Cast: James Gandolfini (Tony Soprano), Edie Falco (Carmela Soprano), Lorraine Bracco (Dr. Jennifer Melfi, credit only), Michael Imperioli (Christopher Moltisanti, credit only), Dominic Chianese (Junior Soprano), Steven Van Zandt (Silvio Dante), Tony Sirico (Paulie "Walnuts" Gualtieri), Robert Iler (A. J. Soprano), Jamie-Lynn Sigler (Meadow Soprano), Aida Turturro (Janice Soprano Baccalieri), Frank Vincent (Phil Leotardo), Ray Abruzzo (Carmine Lupertazzi Jr.), Dan Grimaldi (Patsy Parisi), Sharon Angela (Rosalie Aprile), Maureen Van Zandt (Gabriella Dante)

Guest Stars/Recurring: Matt Servitto (Agent Dwight Harris), Carl Capotorto (Little Paulie Germani), Max Casella (Benny Fazio), Donna Pescow (Donna Parisi), Jenna Stern (Dr. Doherty), David Margulies (Neil Mink), Arthur Nascarella (Carlo Gervasi), Gregory Antonacci (Butch DeConcini), John "Cha Cha" Ciarcia (Albie Cianflone), Frank John Hughes (Walden Belfiore), John Cenatiempo (Anthony Maffei), Michael Kelly (Agent Ron Goddard), Daniel Sauli (Patrick Parisi), Joe Perrino (Jason Gervasi), Geraldine LiBrandi (Patty Leotardo), Emily Wickersham (Rhiannon Flammer), Michael Drayer (Jason Parisi), Michele DeCesare (Hunter Scangarelo), Anthony J. Ribustello (Dante Greco), Rick Aiello (Ray-Ray D'Abaldo), Frank Albanese (Uncle Pat), Peter Mele (George Pagilieri), Melanie Minichino (Tara Zincone), Paolo Colandrea (Man in Members Only Jacket)

I n the fifth episode of HBO's ground-breaking series *The Sopranos*, Tony Soprano (James Gandolfini) is on a road trip with his daughter Meadow (Jamie-Lynn Sigler) to look at colleges in Maine. She takes advantage of their time alone to pose the inevitable question every mobster knows his child will one day ask: "Are you in the mafia?"

At first he denies it, claiming he is in the "waste management business." He continues to protest: "Everybody immediately assumes you're mobbed up. It's a stereotype, and it's offensive. And you're the last person I would want to perpetuate it. . . . There is no mafia." She points out that the police have shown up at their front door with warrants at 3:00 a.m. and reminds him of the time she and her brother, A. J. (Robert Iler), found $50,000 in Krugerrands (South African gold coins) and a .45 automatic when hunting for Easter eggs. He admits that some of his money comes from illegal gambling, but fails to mention that he is a member of the DiMeo crime family. She appreciates the fact that he doesn't deny it like her mother and adds that the kids at school "think it's actually kind of neat" (because they've seen Martin Scorsese's Las Vegas mob film, *Casino*).

The cast of *The Sopranos*: (left to right) Lorraine Bracco, Tony Sirico, Steven Van Zandt, James Gandolfini, Edie Falco, Michael Imperioli, Jamie-Lynn Sigler, Robert Iler, Dominic Chianese, Aida Turturro, and Steve Schirripa.   *Authors' collection*

When they stop to fill their car with gas, Tony spots Fabian "Febby" Petrulio (Tony Ray Rossi), a "made" member of the DiMeo family, who ratted out family members when he was busted for selling drugs. Petrulio was in the witness protection program, from which he was booted for reasons unknown, and now he's living in Waterville, Maine, under a different name, working as a travel agent and peddling drugs. Tony starts stalking Febby, who, once he realizes Tony is in town, tries and fails to get one of his drug customers to kill him. When Febby steps out of his office, Tony comes up from behind and strangles him with a piece of piano wire. Later, Meadow, noticing her father is acting strangely, becomes suspicious when he arrives late to pick her up and notices that his hand is bleeding. Tony denies anything happened, but she isn't entirely convinced.

While Meadow is in her interview at Bowdoin College, Tony sits outside the admissions office up and reads a quotation on the wall from the school's most famous alumnus, Nathaniel Hawthorne: "No man can wear one face to himself and another to the multitude without finally getting bewildered as to which may be true." The Hawthorne quotation encapsulates the premise of creator David Chase's modern-day mob tale. Anthony John "Tony" Soprano is a man divided: he's a suburban husband and father living in a McMansion in the affluent suburb of North Caldwell, New Jersey, and a high-ranking member (and future head) of a New Jersey crime family. His difficulty in reconciling the "two Tonys" results in panic attacks and, in the pilot episode, lands him in the office of a psychiatrist, Dr. Jennifer Melfi (Lorraine Bracco), who writes him a prescription for Prozac. In his therapy sessions he discusses his relationship with his wife, Carmela (Edie Falco), who experiences the occasional pangs of guilt for condoning her husband's illegal activities so she and her kids can have a better life, and his monster of a mother, Livia (Nancy Marchand), a manipulative woman with an undiagnosed borderline personality disorder, who convinces her brother-in-law Junior (Dominic Chianese), the current head of the DiMeo crime family, to put a hit on her own son because he wants to move her into a nursing home. *The Sopranos* creator, writer/director David Chase, has spoken candidly about how the heinous Livia was inspired by his own mother, whom he described to *New York Times* reporter Alex Witchel as a "complete original. . . . She had this incredible thing where she was very easily offended, yet there was never a person on earth who censored herself less. . . . As she got older, she started insulting more and more people, taking umbrage at things they said and cutting herself off from the world."

"College," which ranks no. 2 in *TV Guide*'s 2009 list of the best television episodes of all time, shocked viewers. It makes perfect narrative sense why Tony has to kill: in the mob world, Febby is a "rat" because he informed on his family, so he must be "whacked" (murdered). But American audiences are not accustomed to seeing the protagonist on a television series brutally strangle someone to death with a piece of piano wire. In his interview for the Archive of American Television (AAT), Chase recalled how he responded to the network when the issue was raised: "I said, 'This guy is a mob boss in New Jersey. If he doesn't kill this guy, he's worthless as a mob boss. He's worthless as a TV gangster.' And I knew I was right about that." The one (and only) concession Chase ever made to HBO, which he now regrets doing, was to include a short scene in which Febby tries to convince a junkie to kill Tony, which suggests that, despite all appearances, the guy is not on the straight and narrow.

Febby is not the last man Tony will kill or have killed. He will be responsible for three of the show's most shocking deaths: DiMeo crime family member Salvatore "Big Pussy" Bonpensiero (Vincent Pastore), whom Tony, Silvio (Steven Van Zandt), and Paulie (Tony Sirico) take for a one-way boat ride and riddle with bullets for being an FBI informant to escape a thirty-year prison sentence ("Funhouse"); Adriana (Drea de Matteo), girlfriend of Tony's nephew and DiMeo family member, Christopher Moltisanti (Michael Imperioli), who is also forced into being an FBI informant and, in one of the show's most harrowing scenes, taken for a ride and executed by Silvio; and Christopher, a loose cannon whose drug habit results in a near-fatal car crash with Tony, who then decides it's time to say goodbye to his protégé and suffocates him.

The critics showered *The Sopranos* with praise: "The best thing to hit TV this season. . . . It has sharp, subtle writing, artful direction, vivid acting, and a nonpandering point of view" (David Wild, *Rolling Stone*); "Elevates pulp fiction to art" (Howard Rosenberg, *Los Angeles Times*); "The most unusual series to play on TV. So bizarre you can't take it very seriously at first—until you're inevitably drawn into it. I was enthralled by *The Sopranos*" (Monica Collins, *The Boston Herald*); "Achieves a fresh tone to match its irresistibly winning concept" (Caryn James, *New York Times*). The critics and reporters at the *New York Times* were so taken with *The Sopranos* they published the articles and interviews that appeared in the paper in book form. In January of 2000, *Saturday Night Live* even did a commercial parody poking fun at the overhyped critical responses to the show with fake pull quotes like "*The Sopranos* will one day replace oxygen as the thing we breathe in order to stay alive" and "*The Sopranos* is so good that I'm afraid to look away from the screen while it is on, for fear that it will disappear and I'll be forced to kill myself." Maybe critics didn't go that far, but there was no shortage of superlatives in declaring *The Sopranos* "the richest achievement in the history of television" (David Remnick, *The New Yorker*); "perhaps the greatest pop-culture masterpiece of its day" (Peter Biskind, *Vanity Fair*); and "the top television series of the decade" (Barry Garron, *The Hollywood Reporter*). In 2013, the Writers Guild of America (East and West) voted *The Sopranos* the "Best Written TV Series of All Time."

Summarizing what happens on *The Sopranos* over the course of seven seasons can fill an entire book, so heavily plotted was the series. In addition to the main cast of characters, which consists of Tony and the members of his two "families" that matter the most to him (and of course, Dr. Melfi), there are dozens more, most of them with Italian last names and/or nick-names, e.g., "Big Pussy," Phillip "Philly Spoons" Parisi (Dan Grimaldi), Robert "Bobby Bacala" Baccalieri (Steve Schirripa), and Dominic "Fat Dom" Gamiello (Tony Cucci), all of whom are six feet under by the series finale.

The final season of *The Sopranos*, which was divided into two parts (March–June 2006 and April–June 2007), focused on the struggles within and between the major crime families as the FBI continued to close in. The show also ventured into some new territory, even taking a surreal turn when a comatose Tony, who was accidentally shot by Uncle Junior, dreams that he is an optics salesman staying in a hotel in Costa Mesa, California ("Join the Club"). Christopher co-writes and produces a Mafia-themed slasher film *Cleaver*, in which the killer, played by actor Daniel Baldwin, resembles Tony ("Stage 5"). The series also moved out of its New Jersey setting when Tony travels to Las Vegas, where he has a fling with a stripper and does peyote ("Kennedy and Heidi"). There's also a subplot that follows Vito Spatafore (Joseph R. Gannascoli), a closeted gay member of the DiMeo Crime Family who, fearing he will be "outed," hides out in New Hampshire, where he has a brief affair with a short order cook ("Moe 'n' Joe"). He eventu-ally returns home and tries to buy his way back into the family, only to be wacked by homophobic Phil Leotardo (Frank Vincent), the acting boss of the Lupertazzi family, whose cousin is married to Vito. A series of subsequent events leads to a war between the New Jersey DiMeos and the New York Lupertazzi families, which escalates in the penultimate episode ("My Blue Comet") in which Leotardo decides it's time to take out the DiMeo family. Tony is warned by FBI Agent Harris that he and his crew are in danger, but Tony isn't able to warn two of his family members in time: Bobby Baccalieri, who is gunned down in a toy train store, and Silvio, who is critically wounded while leaving the Bada Bing Club.

In the series finale, Tony is in hiding, planning his next move. He con-soles Bobby's widow (his sister Janice) and convinces Paulie to take over as capo (captain) of one of the crews. He reluctantly accepts, but expresses his concern that all the crew's former capos have had bad luck. Tony's son A. J., who is being treated for his depression after his suicide attempt, decides he wants to go into the military, but Carmela manages to get him a low-level job at the film company owned by Christopher's former producing partner. Tony visits his friend Silvio, who is in a coma, and a demented Uncle Junior, a prisoner in a government mental hospital, who barely recognizes Tony. In one of the show's most gruesome moments, Leotardo, who has been in hiding, pulls up to a gas station in his SUV in the company of his wife and infant granddaughters. One of Tony's men, Walden, puts a few bullets in him and he falls to the ground. His wife gets out of the SUV, which happens to be in drive, and the vehicle starts to move—and rolls right over Leotardo's head, crushing it. Meanwhile, hanging over Tony's head is the news from his lawyer that someone is testifying against him at a grand jury and he will most likely be indicted.

It's clear that all of the viewers' questions will not be answered when there is only seven minutes left and the scene cuts to Holsten's, a restaurant where Tony and Carmela are meeting their kids for dinner. Tony sits at a booth and puts a coin in the jukebox and selects Journey's "Don't Stop Believin'." Carmela enters and sits down. Tony tells Carmela the bad news his lawyer shared with him about the possible indictment. A. J. walks in behind a man who is wearing a Members Only jacket. Through the course of their conversation, A. J. quotes something Tony once told him, "Focus on the good times." Tony mistakenly thinks his son is being sarcastic. While they sit there eating onion rings, various individuals walk in. At one point, the man in the Members Only jacket appears to be looking in the direction of their table. He then gets up and goes into the men's room. Meanwhile, outside, Meadow is having trouble parallel parking her car. She finally manages to do so, exits the vehicle, and runs to the entrance of Holsten's. We hear the entrance bell-ring and cut to a close-up of Tony. Cut to a silent, black screen for ten seconds. Following this, the final credits roll, completely devoid of music. (Chase told Brett Martin, author of The Sopranos: *The Complete Book*, that he didn't want any credits at all, but "the black screen to go the length of the credits—all the way to the HBO *whoosh* sound." But the Directors Guild of America wouldn't give them a waiver.)

Many members of the viewing audience, which totaled approximately 11.9 million people, were in a state of shock. For a moment, some people even thought their cable had gone out. The enigmatic ending opened the critical floodgates for anyone with a keyboard to begin speculating what exactly just happened and what, if anything, it all meant. The following day, television critics around the country offered their readers some perspective on what everyone saw (or didn't seen) in that final scene. On one hand, some critics interpreted the ending as Chase's hostile gesture toward his audience. "While it is one thing to flout the conventions of television," wrote *Los Angeles*

Tony Soprano (James Gandolfini) shares a tender moment with his daughter, Meadow (Jamie-Lynn Sigler).   *Authors' collection*

Times critic Mary McNamara, "it is another to flip dramatic tradition, not to mention your audience, the bird." *New York Times* critic Alessandra Stanley had a similar reaction: "The abrupt finale last night was almost like a prank, a mischievous dig at viewers who had agonized over how television's most addictive series would come to a close. . . . Mr. Chase's last joke was on his audience, not his characters." "So this is how it ends," lamented *Tampa Bay Times* critics Eric Deggans, "with a big raised middle finger aimed straight at the TV audience." Hollywood insider Nikki Finke reported in *Deadline Hollywood* that angry fans crashed the HBO website—but she couldn't blame them. She accused Chase of being lazy and not caring about *Sopranos* fans: "Instead he crapped in their faces. Those many minutes of tension-building cutaways where we only find out that Meadow can't parallel-park are exactly why American hates Hollywood: arrogance masquerading as art." (Ms. Finke got it all wrong. The reason why America hates Hollywood is because it produces *crap* that masquerades as art.)

    Sopranos fans were also part of the story as newspapers reported on how viewers reacted to the ending. *Washington Post* reporter Philip Rucker gave local fans a forum to express their disappointment ("I was waiting for a big huge climax, and it didn't happen, so I was let down"), disbelief ("Me and my buddy were like, 'Tony's gonna get it, he's gonna get it,' and all of a sudden it was like, 'bam!' Nothing."), and resentment toward the writer ("It was really David Chase's joke on all of us . . . you can imagine [him] sitting at home tonight chuckling.").

While it's understandable that fans were surprised and even disappointed by the ending, why would viewers, along with some critics, think that David Chase (or the writer/producer of *any* television series) harbored ill feelings for the people who watched his show faithfully for the past six seasons? In The Sopranos: *The Complete Book*, Chase directly addressed this issue:

> I saw some items in the press that said, "This was a huge 'fuck you' to the audience." That we were shitting in the audience's faces. Why would we do that? Why would we entertain people for eight years only to give them the finger? We don't have contempt for the audience. In fact, I think *The Sopranos* is the only show that gave the audience credit for having some intelligence and attention span.

Some critics felt that the unconventional ending perfectly suited the show. *Denver Post* TV critic Joanne Ostrow found the final scene to be, like the whole series, "unpredictable, unsettling and oddly satisfying." Jill Vejnoska, critic for the *Atlanta Journal-Constitution*, wrote, "It was one of the best endings to a TV series ever, period." Vejnoska also challenged accusations that Chase was "thumbing his nose at us," suggesting that Chase's "nonending ending" was a reward to his audience—"a completely unexpected twist at a time when—thanks to the instant, on-demand informational era we now live in—we thought nothing could possibly take us by surprise anymore."

But the majority of critics and fans were more interested in making sense of the final scene and figuring out what, if anything, Chase was trying to say. In response to the flood of e-mails the *Los Angeles Times* received in less than twenty-four hours, Mary McNamara reported on June 13 that "the black screen . . . has become the monolith in *2001*, the Rorschach blot, Stonehenge, and *Ulysses* all rolled in to one." According to McNamara, the most popular interpretation of the black screen was that it signified Tony's death because it was how he described death to Bobby (who would, in fact, soon die) in an earlier episode. Suddenly, every little detail about the scene was called into question. Who was the guy in the Members Only jacket (and wait, wasn't the title of the season 6 opener, in which Uncle Junior accidentally shot Tony, "Members Only"?) And why did he glance over at Tony and his family? Why did he go into the men's room? To go to the bathroom? Or was it to retrieve a gun? (Like Michael Corleone did in *The Godfather* to kill Virgil Sollozzo?) And what is the significance of Journey's "Don't Stop Believin'"? Why did the song cut off at the words "don't stop" at the exact moment the screen went black? (Although it has nothing to do with the finale, another question still on everyone's list is the fate of the Russian, Valery [Vitali Baganov], who disappeared somewhere in the Pine Barrens back in season 3.)

When the finale aired, the man with all the answers, David Chase, was vacationing in France and reportedly not available for interviews. But Chase did an exclusive interview with Alan Sepinwall, then television critic for the Newark-based *Star-Ledger* in the Sopranos' home state of New Jersey. In regards to the finale, Chase said,

> I have no interest in explaining, defending, reinterpreting, or adding to what is there. No one was trying to be audacious, honest to God. We did what we thought we had to do. No one was trying to blow people's minds, or thinking, "Wow, this'll (tick) them off." People get the impression that you're trying to (mess) with them and it's not true. You're trying to entertain them. Anybody who wants to watch it, it's all there.

Sepinwall also asked, as some fans have suggested, if the ending was purposely ambiguous to leave open the possibility of a movie. Chase said, "I don't think about [a movie] much. I never say never. An idea could pop into my head where I would go, 'Wow, that would make a great movie,' but I doubt it." The only information he offered was in regards to the choice of "Don't Stop Believin'," which he chose and then played to members of the crew to get their opinion. Their initial reaction was negative, but eventually they came around. In an interview for the Archive of American Television (AAT), Chase added that he realized how much he liked the song when his nephew gave him a compilation CD. He also chose it because he thought it was a song that Tony Soprano would have played on the jukebox.

While Chase didn't offer his interpretation of the final scene, he did share some tidbits of information about the show's ending season. One decision that upset fans was the large gap of time between the season 5 finale ("All Due Respect"), which aired on June 6, 2004, and the season 6 premiere ("Members Only"), which aired twenty-one months later, on March 12, 2006. Chase explained that he was given that "long break" to think of a conclusion for the series. The final episode was originally slated to air in 2006, but HBO ordered additional episodes, which is why season 6 was divided into two parts, with the second part airing from April 8, 2007, through the series finale on June 10, 2007.

When asked about the final episode in his interview for the AAT, Chase explained, "There's not a lot of mysteries there. It was all so fun to a certain extent. All those crazy explanations. . . . It just reminded me of all that 'Walrus is Paul' [the line in the Beatles' song 'Glass Onion,' which was part of the urban legend that Paul McCartney was dead and replaced by a lookalike] . . . . It was insane. It was really fun. God, you imagine, just to have that much attention be put to what you do? It was spectacular."

In a lengthy blog entitled "*The Sopranos*: Definitive Explanation of 'The END,'" the anonymous author conducted a painstakingly detailed shot-by-shot analysis of the final sequence and interprets Chase's use of symbolism, claiming that it is "the definitive explanation as to why Tony died in Holsten's in the final scene of *The Sopranos*." The author goes as far as to interpret Chase's initial comment ("If you look at the final episode really carefully, it's all there") to imply "since there is essentially no reason to look at the final scene 'really carefully' if Tony lived as he is clearly alive the last time we saw him."

The question regarding the fate of the Tony Soprano was also posed to the actors a few nights later when cast members, including the four Sopranos— Gandolfini, Falco, Sigler, and Iler—attended a fundraising cruise around Manhattan which benefitted St. Jude Children's Research Hospital. The actors all seemed to like the ending, even if they didn't necessarily understand it. Sigler admitted to *New York Daily News* reporter Denis Hamil that she had no idea why Meadow was having so much trouble parallel parking at the end: "It was on the page, and like always, I played what was written. But I loved the ending. I can't think of a single better way to have ended the show." Falco agreed that she thought the ending was "great." "Yes, I was at that table," she added, "but I have no idea what happened after the screen went blank." Gandolfini had a similar response: "The ending was exactly what it should have been. Don't look at me, I don't have an answer. All I know is that it's over." Steven Van Zandt (Silvio), who hosts a radio show on Sirius, observed how public opinion about the ending seemed to be shifting across the country: "It started out fifty-fifty, and by last night, it was eighty-twenty in favor of the ending." Van Zandt, best known as a guitarist and an original member of Bruce Springsteen's E Street Band, debunked the rumor that David Chase shot more than one ending. "He knew what he wanted," Van Zandt said, "and it was great. Just like the show."

Journalists simply wouldn't let the subject go. In 2012, in an interview with the Associated Press about his new film, *Not Fade Away*, Chase was asked once again about the ending. Jake Coyle published Chase's explanation in the *Huffington Post*, in which he reiterates some of his previous comments (he was proud of the ending, never intended to make a fool of the audience, etc.), but elaborates on his intentions:

> To me the question is not whether Tony lived or died, and that's all people wanted to know. . . . There was something else I was saying that was more important. . . . About the fragility of all of it. . . . Tony was dealing with mortality every day. He was dishing out life and death. And he was not happy. He was getting everything he wanted, that guy, but he wasn't happy. All I wanted to do was present the idea of how short life is and how precious it is.

The Associated Press reporter then states Chase's point: "The meaning of the show didn't have to be there in that final moment. It was there all along."

But the controversy was still not laid to rest. On August 27, 2014, critic Martha P. Nochimson published an interview for *Vox* with David Chase, who was asked, "Is Tony dead?" Nochimson wrote, "Chase startled me by turning toward me and saying with sudden, explosive anger, 'Why are we talking about this?' I answered, 'I'm just curious.'"

The article features the last image of Tony looking directly at the camera, followed by a black rectangle (representing the now-famous black screen) with the following words printed over them, like a "pull quote" highlighted in a magazine article: "Just the fact and no interpretation. He shook his head 'no.' And he said simply, 'No he isn't.' That was all."

Within twenty-four hours of Nochimson's piece being published, *Vox* issued a statement from Chase through his publicist:

> A journalist for *Vox* misconstrued what David Chase said in their interview. To simply quote David as saying, "Tony Soprano is not dead," is inaccurate. There is a much larger context for that statement and, as such, it is not true. As David Chase has said numerous times on the record, "Whether Tony Soprano is alive or dead is not the point." To continue to search for this answer is fruitless. The final scene of 'The Sopranos' raises a spiritual question that has no right or wrong answer.

In his response, Todd VanDerWerff, cultural editor of *Vox*, states that they, along with other publications, boiled Nochimson's story down to Chase's answer to her question "despite the presence of an entire piece discussing Chase's background, his influences, and our lack of comfort with ambiguity in storytelling." The latter point is key: Chase does not subscribe to the conventions of American television in regards to storytelling. His sensibility is not in the classical Hollywood tradition, but a more modernist, European style of storytelling with an ending that is ambiguous or "open ended"—something that makes some American audience members confused and even angry.

Based on his response, one would assume that Chase would no longer be interested in fielding any more questions about the series finale and the final scene. But he surprised *Sopranos* fans, especially the ones still losing sleep over the identity of the man in the Members Only jacket, the reason Meadow can't parallel park, and the symbolic meaning behind the sudden cut to black, by publishing a shot-by-shot commentary of the finale scene in an article by James Greenberg for The Directors Guild magazine, *The DGA Quarterly.* Chase discusses the *mise-en-scène* and offers some insight into certain details, such as the choice of songs on the jukebox ("[I]t's almost like the soundtrack of his life. . . . I wanted it to be a song that would have been from Tony's high school

"Don't Stop Believin'": The enigmatic final scene of *The Sopranos* with Tony (James Gandolfini, left), Carmela (Edie Falco), and A. J. (Robert Iler).   *Authors' collection*

years, or his youth"), the timing of the lyrics of "Don't Stop Believin'" with certain images (for example, Carmela is a "small town girl," Tony is a "city boy," and the "streetlights" illuminate the street outside). Chase demonstrates how he created tension with the presence of the Members Only guy (he admits the scene from *The Godfather* in which Michael kills Sollozzo did occur to him), and cross-cutting between inside Holsten's and Meadow trying to park her car.

As for the final shot of Tony, the black screen, and what it may or may not mean, Chase states that he "thought the possibility would go through a lot of people's minds or maybe everybody's mind that he was killed. He might have gotten shot three years ago in that situation. But he didn't. Whether this is the end here, or not, it's going to come at some point for the rest of us." As for the cut to a black screen, Chase states, "I thought it would be somewhat jarring, sure. But not to the extent that it was, and not a subject of such discussion. I really had no idea about that. I never considered the black a shot. I just thought what we see is black." But his own reading of its significance is actually quite simple: "The ceiling I was going for at that point, the biggest feeling I was going for, honestly, was don't stop believing. It was very simple and much more on the nose than people think. That's what I wanted people to believe. That life ends and death comes, but don't stop believing."

In other words, the ending is not only about the fate of an Italian mobster named Tony Soprano. It's really about all of us.

Alive and Still Creepy

Dexter Makes a Major Career Change

Dexter (Showtime, 2006–2013)
Developed by James Manos Jr.
Based on *Darkly Dreaming Dexter* by Jeff Lindsay
Premiere date: October 1, 2006
8 seasons / 96 episodes
"Remember the Monsters?"
Airdate: September 22, 2013
2.8 million viewers
Directed by Steve Shill
Written by Scott Buck and Manny Coto
Cast: Michael C. Hall (Dexter Morgan), Jennifer Carpenter (Debra Morgan), James
    Remar (Harry Morgan, credit only), David Zayas (Angel Batista), Desmond
    Harrington (Joey Quinn), C. S. Lee (Vince Masuka), Aimee Garcia (Jamie
    Batista), Geoff Pierson (Tom Matthews)
Guest Stars: Yvonne Strahovski (Hannah McKay), Sean Patrick Flanery (Jacob
    Elway), Darri Ingolfsson (Oliver Saxon), Jadon Wells (Harrison Morgan)

hile the early 2000s brought with it a glut of hit reality shows, audiences also found themselves gravitating to cops in lab coats—more specifically, procedurals featuring forensic analysts. At the end of 2006, Nielsen Media Research revealed its top television shows of the year, listing CBS's hit *CSI: Crime Scene Investigation* as the only non-reality show within the Top 5 (top spots went to FOX's *American Idol* and ABC's *Dancing with the Stars*). Audiences loved following detectives as they used modern technology to uncover the minutia of forensic data—a far cry from the crime-solving techniques of TV's past (sorry, *Dragnet*). The original incarnation of *CSI*, set in Las Vegas, spawned divisions (or spinoffs) in Miami, New York, and most recently Quantico, Virginia. Add into the mix CBS's *Cold Case* (2003–2010), *Without a Trace* (2002–2009), and *The Mentalist* (2008–2015), and it was clear that CBS was rebranding itself as, what the *Chicago Sun-Times* called, "The Crime Broadcasting System.'" *CSI*'s influence extended well beyond its record-breaking ratings bonanza on CBS's prime-time schedule—eventually reaching its recently acquired cable sister station Showtime. Long thought to be the lesser station when compared to original programming giant HBO, Showtime, now under the leadership of CBS President and *CSI* shepherd Les Moonves, was ready to make itself a contender. Moonves was determined to elevate the programming on Showtime beyond what he deemed "a little too much of an off-Broadway play" (likely referring to *Queer as Folk* [2000–2005], *The L Word* [2004–2009], and *Soul Food* [2000–2004]). In an effort to move toward more commercially salable programming, in June of 2005 Showtime greenlit an adaptation of Jeff Lindsay's 2004 book *Darkly Dreaming Dexter*, helmed by James Manos Jr., a former producer and writer for HBO's *The Sopranos*. Lindsay's book follows the life of Dexter Morgan, a blood splatter expert working for Miami's homicide squad. The hook: this forensics expert just happens to moonlight as a serial killer, one who meticulously and ritually knocks off every deserving bad guy. Simply called *Dexter*, the success of the series would be completely dependent on viewers—already roped in by the *CSI* level fancy forensics—rooting for the bad guy. The key was finding just the right bad guy.

Michael C. Hall had just wrapped five seasons of HBO's hit drama *Six Feet Under* (2001–2005). He starred as the uptight David Fisher, co-owner of Fisher & Sons Funeral Home. The series chronicled the lives of the entire Fisher family—a family whose profession and circumstances kept them surrounded by the lingering effects of death. Following the end of *Six Feet Under*, the former Broadway performer had no expectations to return to another television series. In an interview with David Bauder of the Associated Press, Hall claimed: "When *Six Feet Under* ended, I imagined I would never do another television series, just because I thought it would be impossible that I would be so lucky that I would find something as successful." Luckily for *Dexter* fans, Hall learned "never to say never." Signing on to the Showtime series meant that the network's high expectations rested firmly on Hall's shoulders—a burden that also included having to distinctly differentiate Dexter from his previous pay-cable role. In the eyes of television fans, David Fisher would need to move on from the funeral home and on to the street, or as Matthew Gilbert of the *Boston Globe* noted: "David tended to already dead bodies; Dexter, alas, is more of a supplier." Hall agreed on the comparison, adding: "Dexter's a great deal more proactive."

The series premiered on October 1, 2006, pulling in just over a million viewers, and high praise from television critics. Hall's performance was cited as the most compelling aspect of the series, with the show's darkly comedic

America's favorite serial killer, Dexter Morgan (Michael C. Hall), subdues an unsuspecting victim.
Authors' collection

tone (highlighted by Dexter's deadpan narration) and stylish cinematography also contributing. Alessandra Stanley of the *New York Times* called it "impossible to resist" and named the character of Dexter a "smart, wittily self-aware homicidal maniac in the tradition of Richard III and Hannibal Lecter." And as for Dexter's vigilantism? Stanley called it "*Death Wish* for the Quentin Tarantino generation." *Los Angeles Times* critic Paul Brownfield also likened Hall's Dexter to other pop culture psychopaths, namely Matt Damon's Tom Ripley of *The Talented Mr. Ripley* (1999), Christian Bale's Patrick Batemen of *American Psycho* (2000), and even having the "too-wide-eyed Norman Bates gaze." John Maynard of the *Washington Post* admitted that the show was "far-fetched, perhaps, but the concept works," continuing that "at times it can be graphic, but there's nothing here you wouldn't see on a 'sweeps' episode of CBS's *CSI*." Maureen Ryan of the *Chicago Tribune* also commented on the gory nature of the show: "To deny yourself the engrossing *Dexter* based on its subject matter would be to miss out on one of television's most fiendishly intelligent new dramas." As buzz grew and more praise piled in, Michael C.

Hall pinned down the ultimate appeal of the show: "We live in a world in which many people feel more and more out of control. And Dexter is someone who, in his little corner of it, is taking control." As for Showtime's foray into buzzworthy original programming—*Dexter* most certainly was in control. By November 3, 2006—just six episodes into the first season—the series was officially renewed for a second season. Robert Greenblatt, then Showtime's entertainment president, called the show "a homerun for us, both critically and in popularity."

While the first season remained true to Lindsay's book, following Dexter as he hunts down, and eventually murders, the infamous "Ice Truck Killer" (revealed to be his long lost biological brother Brian), subsequent seasons were wholly created by the writing staff of the show. Storylines primarily focused on Dexter navigating the waters between being a regular Joe working for Miami Metro PD (bringing doughnuts in to win over the staff), and following his father Harry's "code"—outlining the rules for his kills, bringing order to his disorderly underworld as an unstoppable, and tidy, vigilante. Flashbacks would reveal how and why Dexter became a serial killer (a result of witnessing his own mother's death by chainsaw), as well as outlining how his adopted father, respected cop Harry Morgan (James Remar), wrangled in Dexter's murderous urges by creating an unbreakable code Dexter could rely on to remain undetected. Dexter's relationships with his coworkers factored in prominently with the continued appearance of "normalcy" in his life—joking around with horndog forensic tech Vince Masuka (C. S. Lee), sharing theories with tough but sensitive Detective Angel Batista (David Zayas), and proving to be a good solider to his superiors Lieutenant Maria LaGuerta (Lauren Velez) and Captain Tom Matthews (Geoff Pierson). Some relationships were fraught with more tension than others, as both Sergeant James Doakes (Erik King) and Detective Joey Quinn (Desmond Harrington) proved their sharp skills as cops, sniffing out something odd about Dexter from the get go. Dexter's personal relationships were also explored on the show, beginning with his girlfriend-turned-wife-turned-mother-of-his-child Rita (*Buffy* alum Julie Benz), and venturing into darkness with lovers like season 2's sociopath Lila (Jaime Murray), season 5's kidnap-victim-turned-vigilante Lumen (Julia Stiles), and eventually fellow serial killer Hannah McKay (Yvonne Strahovski) in seasons 7 and 8. But no relationship on the show trumped that of Dexter and his adopted sister, Debra Morgan (Jennifer Carpenter). Deb, a foul-mouthed but up-and-coming detective for Miami Metro PD, regularly confided in Dexter, both about her personal life (and dating disasters) as well as airing out her suspicions and leads on Miami Metro's darkest cases. Although the siblings appear very close (perhaps a bit *too* close in Debra's incestuous season 6 dreams), Dexter conceals his true identity from her, manufacturing lie after lie to maintain their relationship—a relationship that remains a pivotal plot point in every season (and especially the finale).

As for Dexter's victims, each episode explored his kills, as well as his season-long hunts for fellow serial killers. Headline-making murderers like "The Skinner" (season 3), "The Barrel Girl Killers" (season 5), "The Doomsday Killer" (season 6), "The Phantom Arsonist" (season 7), and "The Brain Surgeon" (season 8) were all taken out by Dexter's handiwork. In season 2, Dexter outsmarts FBI Special Agent Frank Lundy (Keith Carradine) in the pursuit of the infamous "Bay Harbor Butcher"—a serial murderer who leaves his victims cut to pieces, tied up neatly in a black garbage bag tossed in the bay (spoiler: it was Dexter). Season 4's Arthur Mitchell, better known as "The Trinity Killer" (expertly played by John Lithgow, the series' only recipient of an acting Emmy) hits Dexter close to home by killing his sweet (but long suffering) wife, Rita, leaving Dexter alone to raise their son, Harrison. With each season, Dexter's adherence to Harry's code becomes more muddled as he justifies kills through his own growing set of rules. As each season approached its big reveal, whether it be the true identity of the killer, or Dexter's last stab, viewers were pulled more and more into Dexter's life. Showtime's ratings rose with Dexter's body count—breaking its own records with each season. In April 2013, on the heels of the eighth season's June 30th premiere, Showtime announced that Dexter would have to pack up his knives and go. Each season had added cracks to Dexter's steely veneer, leaving viewers and critics alike to wonder how season 8 would wrap up Dexter's dark tale, and, ultimately, if the series' last kill would leave their favorite serial killer six feet under.

As the final season began, fans were still reeling over the previous season's end. Deb, having already discovered Dexter's "Dark Passenger" at the end of season 6, finds him standing over the tranquilized body of their colleague Maria LaGuerta. LaGuerta had spent the majority of the season in search of the true "Bay Harbor Butcher," eventually leading her to suspect Dexter. As LaGuerta regains consciousness, she pleads with Debra to take Dexter out, screaming "Put him down!" In season 7's final twist, Deb turns and shoots LaGuerta, shocking even Dexter with her loyalty. This development leads the eighth and final season to focus on the aftermath of Deb's decision—a decision that has left her broken, too destroyed to continue with the force. Meanwhile, Dexter, and the crew of Miami Metro, hunt "The Brain Surgeon," a killer whose victims are discovered to be missing the same part of their brain (removed postmortem). Dr. Evelyn Vogel (Charlotte Rampling), a therapist who specializes in a particular breed of sociopath, is brought in to assist Miami Metro with the case. Vogel soon reveals to Dexter that she helped Harry create his code, thus, joining the very short list of people privy to

Dexter's secret life. Vogel pleads with Dexter to bring "The Brain Surgeon" to justice, believing that it is one of her former patients. During Dexter's season-long investigation, fellow serial killer Hannah McKay resurfaces, having escaped from prison. Dexter harbors Hannah (much to Deb's distaste), and the two realize they are indeed in love, leading Dexter to decide to run away with her and his son, Harrison. Deb, who returns to Miami Metro after a brief stint as a private investigator (and with the help of some Dr. Vogel counseling), helps Dexter hunt down their prime suspect: Oliver Saxon (Darri Ingolfsson). Saxon, in addition to being a psychopath, is also revealed to be Dr. Vogel's long-believed lost son. Saxon's connection to Vogel puts her in jeopardy, and Dexter's worst fears are realized when she turns up dead. Saxon offers Dexter a way out—a mutual decision to leave each other alone. Dexter, preparing to skip town with Hannah, should take this deal, but decides instead to end Saxon before he leaves. When Dexter finally has him caught, he decides not to put the final knife in him, suggesting that his Dark Passenger has been liberated through his relationship with Hannah. Instead, Dexter calls Deb to let her arrest him the legal way. After Dexter leaves, Saxon comes to, and just as Deb has him caught, he shoots her, leaving her for dead.

The series finale, titled "Remember the Monsters?," aired on Sunday, September 22, 2013—curiously opposite the broadcast of the sixty-fifth Prime-time Emmys, where *Dexter* net zero nominations. Fans and critics alike wondered if the final episode would leave Dexter (or Deb) in a body bag care of "The Brain Surgeon." Previous seasons' finales included the unexpected deaths of Doakes, Rita, and LaGuerta, thereby setting up the notion that anything goes in Dexter's world—no one was ever truly safe. Going into the last episode, ratings soared and Showtime anticipated that the series finale would be another record breaker. As Dexter made breakfast one last time—the ritual gruesomely portrayed in the brilliant opening credits—fans awaited his fate.

The finale finds Deb in the hospital, clinging to life. Dexter, believing he secured Saxon's fate by calling in Deb, is at the airport ready to leave the country with Hannah and Harrison. An incoming hurricane prevents Dexter from taking off, thus leaving him available to receive the dreaded news about Deb. Rushing to her side, Dexter finds that her prognosis is good, and when he visits her she encourages him to leave. Dexter feels immense guilt, admitting to his sister, "I screwed up your life." Deb pleads with him to leave: "I don't want you to feel guilty about anything," and finally: "The next word I want to hear you say is goodbye." Dexter leaves her side, calling Hannah to tell her to flee as soon as possible with Harrison, promising to join them as soon as he finishes his business (read: ends Saxon's life). Saxon reappears in the hospital, presumably to exact revenge and finish the job on Deb (though his motives for going to the hospital are not abundantly clear). Dexter spots

Throughout the series, Dexter (Michael C. Hall) puts a lot of effort into his relationship with his sister, Deb (Jennifer Carpenter).   *Authors' collection*

Saxon in the hallway, and rushes to be with Deb in fear of Saxon's plan. When he arrives at Deb's room, he finds Saxon—this is their moment. Before they can hash it out one last time, Batista swoops in, gun to Saxon's head. Saxon is arrested and removed from the hospital. Dexter enters Deb's room to find that she has been moved—she has suffered a major stroke and is now in a vegetative state. Dexter is stunned. Saxon is brought in to Miami Metro where Detectives Batista and Quinn hammer him with questions. Dexter arrives, forensic kit in hand, and despite no longer being employed by Miami Metro (he had quit to run off with Hannah), insists on administering the test. When Dexter is alone with Saxon, he threatens him, only to have Saxon stab him in the shoulder with a pen. Dexter deals the fatal blow, pulling the pen out and using it to brutally kill Saxon. Batista and Quinn agree that it was self-defense, and Dexter leaves. With hurricane evacuations underway, Dexter returns to Deb in the hospital, arriving on the choppy waters thanks to his trusty boat "Slice of Life." After apologizing several times, Dexter tells a brain-dead Deb: "I can't leave you like this. I'm your big brother." With that, he unplugs her, and somehow goes undetected while wheeling her out of the hospital and onto his boat (conveniently parked right outside the waterfront hospital). Managing to steer his boat through the punishing waters, he buries Deb at sea—his first victim to hit the water still perfectly intact. He calls Hannah (who still expects him to join her) and delivers an ominous goodbye to his son, finally tossing his cell phone into the ocean, as we hear Dexter's voiceover: "I destroy everyone I love. I can't let that happen to Hannah, to Harrison. I have to protect them from me." Dexter then puts his boat in high gear, driving directly into the eye of the storm.

A shocked audience sees a piece of the boat floating in the waters, as the hurricane dies down. Batista learns of Deb and Dexter's disappearances, as does Hannah, who is now comfortably settled with Harrison in Argentina. The episode then fades to black, and just as audiences believe their favorite serial killer was beaten by a storm, it fades back in. We are no longer in Miami (or Argentina) but decidedly in the cloudy, logging headquarters of the Pacific Northwest. We find Dexter, now bearded, walking away from a logging job site. He walks into an apartment, quietly sits at an empty table gazing out the nearby window. As the camera moves in, he closes his eyes and opens them slowly, blankly staring straight ahead.

Fans were stunned. Within minutes of the final shot, an online firestorm brewed. The episode net 2.8 million viewers—another record breaker for Showtime—and most were not shy about their disappointment. Moments after the final scene, *BuzzFeed* posted an article titled: "The *Dexter* Series Finale was Unbelievably Awful." Blogs immediately fanned the flames. Becca Day-Preston of the *Guardian*'s TV and radio blog wrote: "It all fell apart completely in the last few minutes, with Dexter making two boneheaded, un-Dexter like decisions that wearily knocked the final nails into the coffin that season 8 built." Frazier Moore of the Associated Press called it "the lamest series finale since *Seinfeld*," proclaiming that "Dexter deserved better. So did *Dexter* fans." Many online critics, including both actual critics and fans chiming in on social media, believed the show had already been in decline for some time. Recalling better days, overwhelmingly fans agreed that the show had failed to hit the heights of the spectacular season 4—featuring John Lithgow's Trinity Killer—and had never truly recovered. *Variety*'s Brian Lowry echoed the sentiment: "*Dexter* had been running on creative fumes for the past few seasons and Sunday night's series finale—despite its emotional flourishes—merely underscored that this was a series well past its expiration date. Some of the sloppiness in the finish was perhaps the biggest surprise, given how meticulous its serial-killer leading man usually is." Despite this trend among the series' most vocal fans (and critics), expectations were still high going into the finale. Perhaps fans believed the show could recapture its past glory—a final Hail-Mary pass for their favorite serial killer. Instead, disappointment was the outcome, with anger trailing close behind.

Comparisons between *Dexter* and AMC's *Breaking Bad* ran rampant. *Breaking Bad* aired its penultimate episode ("Granite State") opposite the *Dexter* finale. Coming off a spectacular week with the previous episode "Ozymandias" (eventual Emmy winner for Best Writing for a Drama Series), fans of *Breaking Bad* were overwhelmingly pleased with the direction the show was taking as it approached its finale. Unfortunately, the same could not be said for *Dexter*. Despite their differences (and duration on the air), *Dexter* and *Breaking Bad* were likely bedfellows. Both followed a morally questionable anti-hero whose actions were unquestionably despicable, but somehow garnered respect from fans—rooting for Dexter and *Breaking Bad*'s Walter White seemed wrong, but felt so right. When *Breaking Bad* wrapped the following week, fans were elated (see chapter 28 for a complete description). Their beloved Walter White had gone out in a blaze of glory, avenging his enemies, and ensuring the freedom of his longtime partner Jesse Pinkman. Walter White's death was inevitable—it was only a matter of time before everything he had done caught up to him. Likewise, fans of Dexter desired the same sense of justified closure. Seeing Dexter continuing to live his life—a life now in total solitude—felt incomplete. Does he still kill? Does he follow the code? Will he ever resurface? Would Dexter really rather fake his own death and live a miserable life in seclusion than go out on his own terms? *Breaking Bad*'s finale only added more fuel to the burning fire of disappointment still harbored by *Dexter* fans. A week after the finale aired, *Dexter* producer John Goldwyn—appearing at the New York Film Festival for his film *The Secret Life of Walter Mitty*—spoke out regarding the choice to keep Dexter alive. Goldwyn pointed the finger at *Dexter*'s most loyal champion—Showtime:

> They won't let us kill him. . . . Showtime was very clear about that. When we told them the arc for the last season, they just said, "Just to be clear, he's going to live." There were a lot of endings discussed because it was a very interesting problem to solve, to bring it to a close. People have a relationship with *Dexter*, even if it doesn't have the size and ferocity of the fan base for *Breaking Bad*. But it has a very core loyal following.

Would the series have been better off with Dexter dying in the hurricane-ravaged waters? Should Dexter have had a happy ending with Hannah and Harrison in Argentina? For Scott Buck, series executive producer (and co-writer of the finale episode), the final decision to have Dexter survive and restart his life was "the most humane thing he ever did in the series." Unfortunately, this same sense of humanity did not ring true for *Dexter*'s most loyal fans.

In May of 2014, nearly eight months after the airing of the finale, the show's star Michael C. Hall spoke out. In an interview with the *Daily Beast*, he confessed to never having watched the finale, but that he believed it was "narratively satisfying—but not so savory." Hall confessed:

> I think the show had lost a certain amount of torque. Just inherently because of how long we'd done it, because of the storytelling capital we'd spent, because our writers may have been gassed. Maybe some people wanted a more satisfying—maybe they wanted a happy ending for him, either a happy ending or a more definitive sense of closure. They wanted him to die or something, but I think the fact that he's sort of exiled in a prison of his own making is, for my money, pretty fitting.

In what seemed like an apology, or perhaps a final stab at the writers' expense, Hall's comments resonated with fans. Perhaps their "darkly dreaming" Dexter had simply run out of steam. Their record-breaking viewership pushed Showtime to extend the series again and again. As Dexter's body count ticked up and up, storylines became stretched to their capacity. While not an easy pill to swallow, the overall unhappiness with Dexter's final moments—the baffling and bizarre detour to the Pacific Northwest lumberyards—may have simply stemmed from the story well running dry. Perhaps if Walter White had gone to eight seasons, he, too, would have joined Dexter in his unlikely final place in television history—the land of disappointment.

Despite the unpopular and improbable ending of *Dexter*, the series' legacy remains somewhat intact. Ushered in by earlier anti-heroes like *The Sopranos*' Tony Soprano and *The Shield*'s Vic Mackey, the success of a character like Dexter Morgan—an unapologetic "monster" who follows a regular killing ritual—paved the way for even more complex characters on television. This includes prisoner-of-war-turned-terrorist Nicholas Brody of Showtime's *Homeland*, bootlegging mobster Nucky Thompson of HBO's *Boardwalk Empire*, as well as Kevin Spacey's political deviant Frank Underwood in Netflix's *House of Cards*. Bryan Cranston's beloved Walter White might not have existed had Hall's Dexter Morgan not been such a hit with fans. Being bad was good—and networks were willing to take their chances on questionable protagonists. After all, if audiences could get behind a vigilante serial killer who ruthlessly stalks, taunts, and chops up his victims, there was little to be squeamish about. The resurgence of quality and compelling programming in the last decade—often deemed the new "Golden Age of Television" — is largely due to writers, producers, and executives taking risks on characters and scenarios that push boundaries once believed unreachable. *Mad Men*'s Don Draper, *Game of Thrones*' Cersei Lannister, and *The Blacklist*'s Raymond Reddington all owe a debt to Dexter and his "Dark Passenger." Even though Dexter may not have gone out with a bang (a whimper seems more apt), his legacy—and trail of bloody footprints—outshines his final moments on the small screen.

Part 3
Flash Forward

Finales Jump to the Future

All Grown Up

The Teens of *Dawson's Creek* and *Gossip Girl* Come of Age

Dawson's Creek (The WB, 1998–2003)

Created by Kevin Williamson
Premiere date: January 20, 1998
6 seasons / 128 episodes
"All Good Things . . ." and " . . .Must Come to an End"
Airdate: May 14, 2003
4.8 rating • 7 percent share • 7.3 million viewers
Directed by James Whitmore Jr. ("All Good Things . . .") and Greg Prange
     (". . . Must Come to an End")
Written by Kevin Williamson and Maggie Friedman
Cast: James Van Der Beek (Dawson Leery), Katie Holmes (Joey Potter), Michelle
     Williams (Jen Lindley) Joshua Jackson (Pacey Witter), Kerr Smith (Jack
     McPhee), Mary Beth Peil (Evelyn "Grams" Ryan), Busy Philipps (Audrey Liddell,
     credit only)
Guest Stars: Meredith Monroe (Andie McPhee), Virginia Madsen (Maddie Allen),
     Nina Repeta (Bessie Potter), Mary-Margaret Humes (Gail Leery), Dylan
     Neal (Doug Witter), Kyle Searles (Colby), Sam Doumit (Sam), Jeremy Sisto
     (Christopher)

Gossip Girl (The CW, 2007–2012)

Developed by Josh Schwartz and Stephanie Savage
Based on the book series by Cecily von Ziegesar
Premiere date: September 19, 2007
6 seasons / 121 episodes
"New York, I Love You XOXO"
Airdate: December 17, 2012
0.8 percent rating • 2 percent share • 1.5 million viewers
Directed by Mark Piznarski

Written by Stephanie Savage

Cast: Blake Lively (Serena van der Woodsen), Leighton Meester (Blair Waldorf), Penn Badgley (Dan Humphrey), Chace Crawford (Nate Archibald), Ed Westwick (Chuck Bass), Kaylee DeFer (Ivy Dickens), Kelly Rutherford (Lily Bass), Matthew Settle (Rufus Humphrey)

Guest Stars: Michelle Trachtenberg (Georgina Sparks), William Baldwin (William van der Woodsen), Desmond Harrington (Jack Bass), Taylor Momsen (Jenny Humphrey), Connor Paolo (Eric van der Woodsen), Margaret Colin (Eleanor Waldorf), Wallace Shawn (Cyrus Rose), Sofia Black-D'elia (Sage Spence), Zuzanna Szadkowski (Dorota Kishlovsky), Jessica Szohr (Vanessa Abrams), Ella Rae Peck (Lola Rhodes), Katie Cassidy (Juliet Sharp), Willa Holland (Agnes Andrews), Rachel Bilson (Herself), Kristen Bell (Herself/Voice of Gossip Girl)

While the inhabitants of *Dawson's* sleepy New England town Capeside and *Gossip Girl*'s swanky Upper East Side may not seem likely bedfellows, their finales share a common bond found frequently in soapy teen dramas—their actors simply got too old to play convincing teens. Aging out of a role is certainly not an uncommon occurrence among teen stars: veterans of *Beverly Hills 90210* (1990–2000) had all moved on from their high school days, morphing the show into something more akin to *Melrose Place* (1992–1999) as opposed to *Saved by the Bell* (1989–1993). If *Dawson's Creek* and *Gossip Girl* were to continue, both series would have to take the logical steps of advancing their teens to college—a route they both eventually did take. But even the college years have an expiration date. Both series became hits with teen audiences, becoming the ideal image of the teenage experience for their fans. But as the final episode approached, with high school and college graduation long behind them, it was time for the alumni of Capeside High and Constance Billard-St. Jude's Private School to start to "act their age"—requiring the finale episode to flash forward in time.

Dawson's Creek followed the life of fifteen-year-old movie super fan Dawson Leery (James Van Der Beek) as he navigated the increasingly choppy waters of his teenaged life. By his side was his best friend, Joey Potter (Katie Holmes), the tomboy-girl-next-door who was slowly evolving from just-one-of-the-guys to a complicated (and gorgeous) teenage girl. Also beside Dawson was sex-crazed slacker Pacey Witter (Joshua Jackson), whose only focus in life was scoring the Van Halen "Hot for Teacher" fantasy. Finally, new to the quiet town of Capeside was Jennifer "Jen" Lindley (Michelle Williams), Dawson's next-door neighbor whose mysterious appearance in their sleepy New England town was only rivaled by her simple beauty.

Proving that teen dramas operate from the same playbook, *Gossip Girl*'s roster of teens felt very similar to Capeside's crew. "It" girl Serena van der Woodsen (Blake Lively) returned to the scene of the Upper East Side after a mysterious (and rushed) disappearance the previous year. *New York Magazine* even likened Serena to *Dawson's* Jen Lindley, calling both the "reformed courtesan," continuing: "Essentially wise and good of heart, she tries to make up for past mistakes, but her efforts are often greeted with suspicion and distrust." Joining Serena was her best friend, and at-times foe, Blair Waldorf (Leighton Meester), a stereotypical Queen Bee. Wanna-be author and self-confessed outsider (and Brooklynite!) Dan Humphrey (Penn Badgley) pined for Serena's attention, while filthy rich Nate Archibald (Chace Crawford) felt torn between Blair and Serena. Rounding out the cast was Chuck Bass (Ed Westwick), a smooth-operating troubled rich boy—less goofy than *Dawson's* Pacey, but fulfilling the role of the series' bad boy nonetheless. Each series dealt with typical teenage problems—the very same found in any John Hughes 1980s teen movie classic. This included: sexuality and virginity, underage drinking and drug use, class warfare, and, of course, parents that "just don't understand."

While both series borrowed from the same teen archetype playbook, *Dawson's Creek* and *Gossip Girl* each respectively revived the teen soap genre in their own decades. *Dawson*'s capitalized on the idealized version of late 1990s teen-dom as represented by popular mall shops Abercrombie & Fitch and American Eagle (the latter eventually signing on to costume the actors in the series). Creator Kevin Williamson, best known for his teen-horror franchises *Scream* (1996) and *I Know What You Did Last Summer* (1997), tapped into what was quintessentially the late-'90s teen—smart, savvy creatures, with enormous buying power, itching for edgy content designed just for them. In *Dawson's Creek*, teen viewers found attractive, fashionable friends, with an Ivy League–level command of the English language—a characteristic enviable among its SAT-obsessed audience. Likewise, Josh Schwartz, creator of yet another teen series, *The O.C.* (2003–2007), courted the newly minted millennial teen fan base with his adaptation of Cecily von Ziegesar's popular *Gossip Girl* book series. The teens of *Gossip Girl* were glued to their phones and computers, constantly being updated on the recent entries into the rumor mill. Like *Dawson's*, these teens spoke of topics far beyond their grade-level, taking *Dawson's* frank talk of teenage sexuality one step further by adding in immeasurable wealth, privilege, and casual drug use (all topics *Dawson's* skimmed the surface of as well). Both series premiered on networks specifically aimed at a teen audience: *Dawson's* on *Buffy*'s home channel The WB, and *Gossip Girl* on The CW—a network born from the 2006 merger of The WB and UPN, home of *Veronica Mars*, and *America's Next Top Model*.

The baby-faced teens of *Dawson's Creek*: (left to right) Joey Potter (Katie Holmes), Dawson Leery (James Van Der Beek), Jen Lindley (Michelle Williams), and Pacey Witter (Joshua Jackson).
Authors' collection

Dawson's Creek arrived on January 20, 1998, after a long promotional tour, that critic Matthew Gilbert of the *Boston Globe* referred to as a "huge wave of hype." Much was touted about series creator Kevin Williamson, still riding his own wave of success after re-launching the slasher film with teenage meta-horror blockbuster *Scream*. Williamson's foray into television with *Dawson's Creek*—a series he based on his own upbringing in a small all-American coastal town—would prove once and for all if he was indeed the teenage cultural whisperer of the moment. Shot in Wilmington, North Carolina, standing in for a near-Boston town on the cape, the production quality of the series immediately differentiated it from its lesser predecessors. Jon Corman of the *San Francisco Chronicle* called the show's look "downright luxuriant," with "its teenagers [inhabiting] a sun-dappled, seaside world of sparkling water, spacious green lawns and ample white houses adorned with shutters." Matching its beautiful setting, the show's dialogue resonated with many critics—both favorably and unfavorably. The fast-paced, sophisticated dialogue—well-beyond the typical teenager's capacity—had cast members uttering such lines as: "Repressing our desire can only make it more powerful," and, "Our raging hormones are destined to alter our relationship, and I'm trying to limit the fallout." Using this particular line as an example, Ray Richmond of *Variety* called the show "the teenage equivalent of a Woody Allen movie—a kind of *Deconstructing Puberty*." Richmond continued: "Despite the utter precociousness of their pop-culture '90s speak, their show proves an addictive drama with considerable heart." The premiere episode netted more than 5 million viewers—firmly cementing it as a hit for the network, and officially crowning it the flagship show of The WB. The stars each graced their own cover of *TV Guide* in March of 1998, with the magazine calling it "the show of the moment, the can't-miss series destined to launch thousands of CD soundtrack sales, teen-magazine covers and frenzied shopping-mall appearances."

Gossip Girl premiered on September 19, 2007, raking in just 3.5 million viewers—not a record-breaking number by any account, but significant in just how it reached viewers. The pilot was released on iTunes five days before its initial broadcast, scoring a spot in the streaming service's Top 10 most-downloaded series—proving that the young Internet-savvy audience was indeed being reached. Comparisons to other teen shows and films ran rampant in initial reviews. Brian Lowry of *Variety* called it "teenage *Dynasty*," while *Entertainment Weekly*'s Jessica Shaw described it as "*Sex and the City* meets *Mean Girls*." Even literary figures were evoked, as *Los Angeles Times* critic Mary McNamara declared: "If J. D. Salinger and Jackie Collins had a love child, she would be writing for *Gossip Girl*." McNamara furthered her analogy, calling the show: "*A Separate Peace* on pheromones for the Information Age." In addition to the endless comparisons to previous versions of pop culture's world of teenagers, critics uniformly admitted that the show possessed a type of addictive "guilty pleasure" quality. Like the over-the-top dialogue of *Dawson's Creek*, acceptance of the outrageous scenarios and equally outrageous wealth and excess was part of *Gossip Girl*'s appeal. But for John Maynard of the *Washington Post* any criticism of the show's content for going "overboard" was missing the point. "Overboard is exactly where *Gossip Girl* wants to be—and what viewers must embrace when taking the guilty plunge." The CW was ready to take the plunge with its much-talked-about new series, renewing it for a second season by March of 2008—more than two months before the first season was set to end, and just a month before *New York Magazine* named *Gossip Girl* "the greatest teen drama of all time."

While both shows capitalized on the teenage zeitgeist of their respective moment, they also shared a common foe: The Parents Television Council (PTC). In its first season, *Dawson's Creek* was named the number-one worst show by The PTC, calling it "the crudest of the network shows aimed at kids." Complaints by The PTC included "an almost obsessive focus on pre-marital sexual activity," and "references to topics of pornography and condoms are commonplace." Not to be outdone, the freshman season of *Gossip Girl* also landed itself a top spot with The PTC, most notably for the seventh episode, "Victor, Victrola." The PTC named the episode—one that featured drug addiction and Internet porn in its storyline—"the worst TV show of the week," adding that "the depictions of teenage behavior in this episode were mind-blowingly inappropriate on any network at any time." While The PTC recommendations may have made an impact on certain circles of viewers, The CW embraced the show's criticism as a type of badge of honor. To prove this, The CW ran a series of ads for *Gossip Girl*'s second season that included The PTC's quote in the section of the ad where it was commonplace for a rave review. Splashed across huge billboards plastered in

Blair (Leighton Meester) and Chuck (Ed Westwick) tie the knot in dramatic fashion in the *Gossip Girl* series finale.   *Authors' collection*

every major city in the country were photos of shirtless teens in bed together with the quote "Mind-blowingly inappropriate" topping the image. The PTC was not amused at the shock tactic, stating: "It reeks of desperation, if they have to position themselves as so edgy and so controversial that they've been called out by us." Whether the ads truly were desperate, or simply devilishly clever, one fact remained for *Gossip Girl*, as it did for its predecessor *Dawson's Creek*: fans were undeterred by warnings of questionable content—the edgy, no holds-barred style of both shows was exactly what led viewers to watch in the first place.

As each series matured into its own sense of adulthood, it became clear that the initial appeal of the show—teens navigating unfamiliar territory in beautiful, idyllic locations—began to wane. Each show had taken its characters through high school, now finding them in increasingly complicated and tangled webs while making it through college. For the teens of *Dawson's Creek*, initially this spread the cast between Los Angeles, where Dawson attends film school, and Boston, where Joey enrolls in an Ivy League college, Jack (Kerr Smith) and Jen become roommates in their own apartment, and Pacey (literally) drops his anchor. The challenge of getting the cast back in the same town resulted in the dramatic death of Dawson's father, bringing the main character back for good.

Likewise, *Gossip Girl* faced the challenge of transitioning to college while maintaining the central NYC location of its characters. Blair and Dan find themselves at New York University, Nate at Columbia University, while Serena forgoes her plans to attend Brown University in Rhode Island to stay in New York. *Gossip Girl* had long been touted as a love letter to Manhattan, and though it toyed with the idea of skipping town for L.A. or Europe, the central location of its main cast would be a key factor in maintaining the drama within the series, and the development of any future storylines.

Both series faced growing pains as their characters grew into their adult selves, mirrored only more so by the aging actors portraying those same characters. When *Dawson's Creek* began, series lead James Van Der Beek was already twenty years old, and co-stars Joshua Jackson and Katie Holmes were nineteen and eighteen, respectively. Michelle Williams's portrayal of fifteen-year-old Jen was closest to her real age of seventeen, while Kerr Smith's portrayal of season two's new guy in town, sixteen-year-old Jack McPhee, subtracted ten years from his actual age. Five years into the series, the characters were only just entering college, while their actual ages would have had them in caps and gowns. For *Gossip Girl*, the same rang true, as all of the series' leads were pushing twenty-six as their characters only just broke into their twenties. Costuming and styling were crucial to maintaining the illusion of their teenaged characters, though *Gossip Girl* ditched their girly (and iconic) headbands as prep school came to a close. For both shows, by season 5 it was evident that teenage drama may no longer fit the bill for their stars—tackling adult situations for their young characters seemed completely apropos. When each series announced that its sixth season would indeed be its last, the timing was apt. The expiration date on their teen world was rapidly approaching.

The series finales for *Dawson's Creek* and *Gossip Girl* both flash forward to the future. *Dawson's* chose to spend the entirety of its two-part finale five years in the future, while *Gossip Girl* only just glimpsed the future in a final five-minute speed-ahead. *Dawson's Creek* creator Kevin Williamson told *Entertainment Weekly* that he intended to end the series with Joey jet setting to Paris to live out her dream of being an artist, but the network suggested fast-tracking five years to see how the friends ended up. Williamson embraced this idea, realizing that it now allowed him to "tell a new story." The same could be said of *Gossip Girl*, as the finale's big reveal—the identity of the long-sought-after "Gossip Girl"—begged the creators to flash to the future to see the fallout of the earth-shattering revelation. Each series included weddings in their finales—a logical next step for their now-grown teens—as well as deaths of main characters, using the device as a means to reconnect the once-tight gang. However, just as Capeside could never be Manhattan's ultra-chic Upper East Side, that's where the similarities end, and where these genre-redefining, decade-specific shows close out their final chapters in their own way.

For *Dawson's Creek*, as creator Kevin Williamson attested, the final chapter of the series had already been written. Joey left for Paris, while Jen and Jack transferred to New York University and began their New York adventure. Dawson's faith in his future as a film director is renewed by the help of his friends who pull him from the brink of despair. Easily, the series could have ended on this hopeful note—the kids of Capeside had made good. But as Williamson explained, when the opportunity arose to continue that story, the series took a turn to a new chapter—five years in the future. The two-part finale, titled "All Good Things . . ." and ". . . Must Come to an End" begins with Dawson working as a successful showrunner of a hit television show conveniently titled *The Creek*. Clearly autobiographical, Dawson's characters of Colby, Sam, and Petey—three friends locked in a love triangle with no exit—act as stand-ins for himself, Joey, and Pacey, allowing Dawson to recreate his past as he wished it would have happened. Dawson heads back to Capeside to attend his mother's wedding, reuniting with Jack (now a high school teacher), and Pacey (owner and head chef of The Ice House). Joey, now a successful literary editor, leaves her boyfriend Christopher (Jeremy Sisto) in New York to attend the nuptials, while Jen also returns to Capeside, with new baby Amy in tow. Although the flash forward has afforded the gang more time from their high school pasts, the same issues reappear: Pacey gets into a fight over the older, very-married woman he is dating; Jack argues with boyfriend Doug (Dylan Neal) about Doug's fear of being outed; Jen builds more mystery around herself by acting erratically and popping pain pills; and Joey, confused about her relationship with her boyfriend, seeks solace in a familiar place—Dawson's bedroom. Their issues, however, come to a halt when Jen collapses at the wedding. At the hospital, the gang discovers (through Jen's beloved Gram) that Jen has an existing heart condition, and while the initial prognosis is good, things take a turn for the worse. The news sets Joey on edge; she seeks comfort in Dawson, even though, previous to Jen's incident, Joey had begun to warm to Pacey again. Dawson, Joey, Pacey, and Jack each visit Jen to say their goodbyes, and upon her death, reconsider the direction of their lives—Jack now commits to raising Amy, and Joey makes the Dawson-Pacey decision once and for all. Dawson, who has been struggling with writing the season finale of *The Creek*, talks it out with Joey, who asks that he make the ending a happy one. In a tender moment, they realize what they have goes, as Dawson puts it, "beyond friendship" and their connection will last forever. In the final scene, Joey, back in her New York apartment, watches the season finale of *The Creek*, which results in Colby (Dawson) kissing Sam (Joey), the pair promising themselves to each other. As the episode on her television ends, Joey declares the show to be "perfect," only to reveal that all along Pacey has been watching the show beside her. The two kiss and she picks up the phone to call Dawson to congratulate him. Dawson, now back in Los Angeles, tells his friends that he has a meeting with his idol Steven Spielberg, and on this happy news the audience sees a high school photo of the original Capeside crew—Joey, Dawson, Pacey, and Jen—perched on Dawson's desk, as key scenes from the series play over a touching song with the lyrics "say goodnight, not goodbye."

As the sun set on *Dawson's Creek*, with old friends reconnected and living out their own happy endings (with the exception of Jen, of course), the series' flash forward served as the final word on the characters stories. For *Gossip Girl*'s series finale, this literally meant the final word for the title character—the ever-elusive Gossip Girl would finally be revealed. The series finale, titled "New York, I Love You XOXO," began on the heels of the shocking death of Chuck's ruthless father, Bart Bass (Robert John Burke). Fighting with Chuck on a building rooftop, Bart stumbles, hanging onto the edge of the building, begging for Chuck's help. Instead, Chuck, with Blair by his side, watches as his father loses his grip, falling to his death (note: this was Bart's second death of the series, having returned in season 5 after a faked season 2 death by car accident). Georgina (Michelle Trachtenberg) is called in to help hide Blair and Chuck from the eventual police investigation—a job she succeeds at easily. Dan holds off on submitting the final chapter of his book to *Vanity Fair*, hoping that Serena discovers the copy he's left for her in her luggage—the very luggage brought onto the private plane about to sweep her away to Los Angeles for good. Serena discovers the chapter and, after reading it, decides to stay in New York to hash things out with her former flame, Dan, who eventually opens up to her about how difficult it was for him to assimilate into the Constance-St. Jude's crowd. Meanwhile, Blair and Chuck decide to marry quickly to avoid Blair having to testify against Chuck—a marriage that is borne of convenience and necessity, but ultimately rooted in their deep affection for each other. The wedding is hastily arranged (thanks to Georgina) and the crew gathers in Central Park to finalize the nuptials. Dan, on his way to the ceremony, overhears a conversation between Blair and Serena—one in which Blair restates her firm belief that Dan will never truly be worthy of Serena's love or friendship. Upon hearing this, Dan is compelled to give his final chapter to Nate, who, since the death of Bart Bass, is head of the New York newspaper *The Spectator*, free and clear. Nate sends his assistant off with the chapter, instructing her to post it immediately. As police sirens roar towards the wedding, Blair's stepfather Cyrus (Wallace Shawn) officiates the world's quickest wedding. Just as the couple seals the deal with a kiss, the police descend, scurrying the newly married couple away. Just as Blair and Chuck exit, the sound of text messages fill the air—texts that suggest Gossip Girl is already reporting the quickie marriage. Without missing a beat, Nate announces that the texts are not from Gossip Girl, but instead, from *The Spectator*. The camera then pans to Dan, who looks nervously ahead.

What follows is a flurry of shots bringing back old characters (a treat for loyal fans) who react to the news of Gossip Girl's big reveal (also included are then-NYC mayor Michael Bloomberg and longtime voice of Gossip Girl, Kristen Bell). In voice-over, Dan reveals himself to be Gossip Girl, having created the rumor mill maven as a means to break into the Upper East Side social scene, admitting: "If I wasn't born into this world, maybe I could write myself into it." The gang, awaiting the return of newlyweds Chuck and Blair from police custody, confront Dan about his revelation, mostly admitting how duped they feel—only to have Serena, Gossip Girl's number-one target, defend him. Newlyweds Chuck and Blair return triumphantly, as the police admit to having no evidence against them. Blair is unable to hide her contempt for Dan, convinced that he is responsible for ruining their lives. The gang seems unaffected and Serena eventually calls Gossip Girl's writing a "love letter" that made her realize where she belongs (logic that even the most diehard fans find troublesome). As Dan announces Gossip Girl's death, the episode flashes forward five years, finding the gang gathered at Blair and

Five years after revealing himself to be "Gossip Girl," Dan (Penn Badgley) marries his longtime love Serena (Blake Lively).   *Authors' collection*

Chuck's townhouse for a special occasion. The camera focuses on Serena, descending the stairs in a white and gold designer gown; it then pulls back to reveal Dan, awaiting his bride. In the series' final moments, the two are married as the camera pulls out to the street, as a whole new group of high school students pass by. The voice of Gossip Girl announces: "You may be rid of Dan Humphrey, but you'll never be rid of me. There will always be someone on the outside wanting to get in. Who am I now? That's one secret I'll never tell. XOXO, Gossip Girl."

Ratings wise, both shows fared well in their final bows, with *Dawson's Creek* scoring 7.3 million viewers (its best since its inaugural 1998 season), and *Gossip Girl* ending on a season high of 1.5 million viewers, providing the struggling CW with its best numbers in a year. *Entertainment Weekly* called *Gossip Girl*'s final entry "a perfect balance of nostalgia, mythology, wit, trickery and closure," while *The Hollywood Reporter* concluded that the series finale "reminded viewers what *Gossip Girl* ultimately is and should be remembered as: a soapy, cheeky, guilty pleasure." For *Dawson's Creek*, critics remained focused on the ratings boost in their reviews. Looking back on his finale, Kevin Williamson admitted that the finale was "kind of safe," and among fans the resolution of the Joey-Dawson-Pacey triangle remains "extremely

polarizing." Ultimately, he felt that the storyline was "the last bit of growth that pushed [the characters] into adulthood."

Dawson's Creek and *Gossip Girl*'s flash-forwarded entries into the teen drama history books embraced just that—respecting their actors' own transition into adulthood, honoring their authenticity and, ultimately, completing their stories without forcing them to stay forever young.

Prime-Time Soulmates

Will & Grace, Jack & Karen, and Ben & Laila

Will & Grace (NBC, 1998–2006)

Created by David Kohan and Max Mutchnick

Premiere date: September 21, 1998

8 seasons / 184 episodes

"The Finale"

Airdate: May 18, 2006

11.7 rating • 18 percent share • 18.4 million viewers

Directed by James Burrows

Written by David Kohan and Max Mutchnick

Cast: Eric McCormack (Will Truman), Debra Messing (Grace Adler), Sean Hayes (Jack McFarland), Megan Mullally (Karen Walker), Shelley Morrison (Rosario Salazar)

Guest Stars: Kevin Bacon (Himself), Harry Connick Jr. (Marvin "Leo" Markus), Bobby Cannavale (Vince D'Angelo), Leslie Jordan (Beverley Leslie), Maria Thayer (Lila), Ben Newmark (Ben), Jere Burns (Man in Cast)

On May 6, 2012, the host of *Meet the Press* asked Vice President Joe Biden about the Obama administration's position on same-sex marriage. Vice President Biden replied that while the President sets the policy, he, personally, is "absolutely comfortable with the fact that men marrying men, women marrying women and heterosexual men and women marrying one another are entitled to the same exact rights, all the civil rights, all the civil liberties." Biden attributed the changes in the American public's attitudes toward same-sex marriage to changes in the "social culture" and one television show in particular: "I think *Will & Grace* probably did more to educate the American public than most anything anybody's ever done so far. And I think people fear that which is different. Now they're beginning to understand."

On the following day, David Kohan, co-creator of *Will & Grace* with Max Mutchnick, told *Variety* senior editor Ted Johnson that to hear the vice president credit their show for changing public attitudes was "thrilling and surprising and humbling." Mutchnick agreed, explaining that while they "never made the show to have a political and social impact," he considered Biden's remarks "the dot on the exclamation." Kohan and Mutchnick thanked the vice president by sending him the complete series on DVD.

Mutchnick, who is gay and a President Barack Obama supporter, added that he personally found Obama's claim that his views on same-sex marriage were "evolving" to be "wholly offensive." He believed the president "knows better," but in an election year the incumbent needed to gain the support of LGBT (lesbian, gay, bisexual, and transgender) voters, yet, at the same time, prevent key swing states from swinging in the wrong direction. Two days later, Mutchnick's criticism became moot when, in an interview with ABC News anchor Robin Roberts, President Obama publicly stated, for the first time, "I think same-sex couples should be able to get married."

Vice President Biden's praise of *Will & Grace* is not entirely surprising. The popular, long-running sitcom about the friendship between a gay man and a heterosexual woman, was a critical and ratings hit. During the show's eight-season run, *Will & Grace* received eighty-three Emmy nominations and won sixteen, including Best Comedy Series in 2000. The show made stars out of its four cast members—Eric McCormack (Will), Debra Messing (Grace), Sean Hayes (Jack), and Megan Mullally (Karen). All four of them won one or more Emmys, a feat achieved by the entire casts of only two other sitcoms, *All in the Family* (1971–1979) and *The Golden Girls* (1985–1992). In addition to Kohan and Mutchnick, credit for the show's success must also be paid to veteran television director James Burrows, who helmed all 184 episodes of *Will & Grace* (something rare in television) and served as one of the show's executive producers.

Will & Grace ranked no. 40 in the Nielsen ratings at the end of its first season, but it soared to no. 9 in season 2 when it joined NBC's Thursday night prime-time lineup, better known as "Must See TV," a programming block comprised of two half-hour situation comedies and, in the third hour, the hospital drama *ER* (1994–2009). The list of Must See comedies has included such highly rated series as *Seinfeld* (1989–1998) and *Friends* (1994–2004), long-running shows like *Frasier* (1993–2004), *Just Shoot Me!* (1997–2003), and *Scrubs* (2001–2010), and shows that lasted anywhere from two seasons (*The Single Guy* [1995–1997], *Jesse* [1998–2000]) to four episodes (the awful U.S. version of the very funny British sitcom *Coupling* [2003]). The majority of the

Will & Grace's fabulous foursome: (front) Will (Eric McCormack) and Grace (Debra Messing); (back) Karen (Megan Mullally) and Jack (Sean Hayes). *Authors' collection*

Must See comedies were both about and aimed at the same demographic coveted by advertisers: white, affluent urbanites, between the ages of eighteen to forty-nine.

When *Will & Grace* premiered in the fall of 1998, the show became the first network situation comedy with an out and proud gay male lead character. Up to that point, gay men were primarily supporting or recurring characters within an ensemble cast, including Jodie Dallas (Billy Crystal) on *Soap* (1977–1981), and, more recently, Leon Carp (Martin Mull) and his partner, Scott (Fred Willard), on *Roseanne*, and Carter Heywood (Michael Boatman) on *Spin City* (1996–2002). The closest television came to a gay male lead was designer Dennis Sinclair on Dudley Moore's short-lived CBS sitcom *Daddy's*

Girls (1994). Dennis was played by gay actor/playwright Harvey Fierstein, who earned a place in television history as the first openly gay man playing a gay character on a network television show.

There's no question that the landmark coming out of Ellen DeGeneres and her television alter ego, Ellen Morgan, on *Ellen* (1994–1998) also paved the way for *Will & Grace*. Unfortunately, ABC pulled the plug on *Ellen* one year later due to low ratings. But as DeGeneres revealed to Jess Cagle for an *Entertainment Weekly* cover story (with the headline, "Yep, She's Too Gay"), *Ellen*'s post-coming out season was its last because ABC failed to promote the show and bowed to pressure groups by tacking on an unnecessary advisory ("Due to adult content, parental discretion is advised"). While *Will & Grace* was conceived before DeGeneres's coming out made national headlines, NBC's support of *Will & Grace* demonstrated that at least one of the four major commercial broadcast networks recognized that America's attitudes toward LGBT people were changing. As Warren Littlefield, former president of NBC Entertainment, recalls in his interview with the Archive of American Television, Mutchnick and Kohan, who were under contract with NBC Studios, pitched an ensemble comedy that included a "Will & Grace relationship." He suggested making the gay man and his straight, female friend the center of the show. Littlefield admitted there was some fear that advertisers would "run from it," but fortunately they recognized that it was a "wonderful character comedy relationship like all the other ones you do on NBC—and so, controversy was overcome by quality."

Will & Grace is a sitcom about two soul mates, Will Pierce Truman and Grace Elizabeth Adler, created by a pair of writers, Kohan and Mutchnick, who have been friends since they were students at Beverly Hills High School. In Will & Grace: *Fabulously Uncensored*, Jim Colucci reveals that the inspiration for the character of Grace Adler was their mutual friend, Janet Eisenberg, whom Kohan met back in the third grade and who dated Mutchnick in high school. After college, Mutchnick and Eisenberg lived in New York in a "Will-and-Grace-like existence" until he moved to Los Angeles. When he came out to her, she got angry, and stopped speaking to him for a year, which is what happens when Will comes out to his girlfriend, Grace, while they are in college ("Lows in the Mid 80s"). Convincing the viewing audience that two sitcom characters are longtime friends can be challenging for the actors, who must have a special kind of comical chemistry so viewers will believe one knows what the other is thinking and that they can finish each other's sentences. Fortunately, that's exactly the kind of chemistry that actors Eric McCormack and Debra Messing had from the very beginning.

The unlikely pairing of Will and Grace is also in the tradition of the Hollywood screwball comedies of the 1930s, which inspired a long list of mismatched sitcom couples, from Lucy and Desi on *I Love Lucy* (1951–1957), to Sam and Diane on *Cheers* (1982–1993), to Marge and Homer on *The Simpsons* (1989–present). Although Will and Grace's relationship is strictly platonic, the central myth of the romantic comedy prevailed: opposites attract and, despite their differences, love triumphs—or, in the case of Will and Grace, a gay man and a heterosexual woman can be soul mates for life.

Will is a handsome, sensitive, intelligent Manhattan attorney from a WASP-ish Connecticut family. He is pragmatic, yet his behavior borders on compulsive, particularly when it comes to keeping things, especially his apartment, neat and tidy. But Will is not always in touch with his emotions or, at the very least, able or willing to express them. He is also insecure (we're told he was fat as a child), which contributes, along with the restrictions imposed by NBC, to his lack of a romantic life until midway through the show's run.

In too many ways, Grace is Will's polar opposite. Born in Schenectady, New York, to a middle-class Jewish family, she is an interior designer who, compared to Will, is impulsive, spontaneous, and outspoken. At times, she is insecure about her talent as a designer and her relationship with Will. In one episode ("William, Tell") she mistakenly thinks Will is keeping a major secret from her; and, in another ("Grace, Replaced") she is certain she is losing her spot as Will's best friend to their kooky neighbor. Grace can be fiercely competitive, especially when she teams up with Will against their friends on game night ("Alley Cats"), or when she and Will are on opposite sides and vying for the attention of their cute new neighbor ("Yours, Mine & Ours"), running for the presidency of their building's tenant board ("Election"), or playing poker ("Poker? I Don't Even Like Her"). Grace is a fiercely loyal friend, but she lacks self-discipline (especially when food is involved) and has a selfish side. She forces a miserable Will to spend his birthday at an ice skating show ("Will on Ice"), sleeps with Will's brother ("Big Brother is Coming, Parts I and II"), and takes advantage of Will's good nature by convincing him to date a creep (Miguel Ferrer) to help her get and hold on to a major design job ("Saving Grace").

As Kohan and several of the show's writers explained in 2005 to *Variety*'s Anna Stewart, Will's character did pose some challenges. "We tried to embody the whole spectrum of being a gay man in America in Will," Kohan explained, "and he became a very schizophrenic character. So we split him in half and made Jack. The more competent, together, controlling qualities remained with Will." At the same time, they also felt it was important that as the only gay leading man on a situation comedy, Will not be portrayed as neurotic (that was Grace's department). Yet over time, adds producer Tracy Poust, Will and Grace "switched places," so she had a chance to grow and become "a little more laissez-faire" while he is "the one who's been having crisis after crisis."

While they may have some neurotic tendencies, Will and Grace are adults compared to the duo who occupy way too much of their time and attention: self-absorbed, hyper-gay Jack McFarland and boozy, shallow socialite Karen Walker. Jack and Karen are id personified—pleasure seekers totally wrapped up in themselves; they remain either oblivious or completely incapable and unwilling to attend to life's little details. They are also both gold diggers: Karen married her obese, off-screen husband, Stanley Walker, for his money (though she claims she really does love him), and Jack hangs out with Karen because she has money (though Will also bails him out). Karen and Jack are also the ones who are having all the fun and get all the good zingers.

The first two seasons of *Will & Grace* consist of mostly stand-alone episodes, while story arcs (plots that continue over multiple episodes), which often involve the introduction of new characters, are more prominent for the remainder of the show's run. Over the course of the series, Jack has several careers (cabaret "star" [of *Just Jack!* and *Jack 2000*], actor, nursing student, back-up dancer, and television executive and host on OutTV); marries Karen's loyal, wise-cracking maid Rosario (series regular Shelley Morrison) to keep her in the country; meets and bonds with his teenage son, Elliot (Michael Angarano), who became a recurring character in seasons 3–8; and has a five-episode relationship with inventor Stuart Lamarack (Dave Foley).

Karen's too self-involved for a story arc, except when it comes to her husband, who serves time in jail for tax evasion and cheats on her. When she begins divorce proceedings, he dies unexpectedly—but actually he faked his death—only to resurface and reconcile with her. In the final season, Karen learns that Stan is broke, leaving her penniless.

One of the criticisms leveled against *Will & Grace* from the beginning is the lack of romance and sex in Will's life. It's difficult to believe that a smart, attractive, gay lawyer living in New York City would be essentially date-less episode after episode. In the pilot, Will had recently ended a seven-year relationship with someone named Michael, who broke poor Will's heart. Michael (Chris Potter) is introduced in the middle of season 2 ("Hey La, Hey La, My Ex-Boyfriend's Back") when he hires Grace to decorate his new townhouse (we're told it's been two years since the breakup). Will mistakenly thinks he and Michael will be getting back together, only to be devastated when he discovers his ex is already living with someone else. In season 3, Will pretends he likes sports to impress Matthew (Patrick Dempsey), an aspiring sportscaster, who catches on pretty quickly that Will is no athlete ("Crazy in Love"). But their romance comes to a screeching halt when Matthew introduces Will as his brother ("Brothers, A Love Story"). Will falls harder for his Canadian boyfriend James (Taye Diggs) in season 8. Grace agrees to a green card wedding to keep him in the country ("The Definition of Marriage"), though Will has the marriage annulled when he finds out that James is an insensitive creep ("Grace Expectations"). The show's obvious lack of physical contact between two males was addressed in a self-reflexive season 2 episode ("Acting Out") in which Will, Grace, and Jack tune in to a fictional NBC sitcom entitled *Along Came You* to see what will be the first "guy-guy lip action" on network television. Jack is outraged when the camera cuts away. Will is not surprised because, as he explains to Jack, "Clearly, nobody wants to see two men kissing on television. Not the network, not the viewers, not the advertisers." Grace convinces Will to go down to NBC's headquarters to support Jack, but when an assistant tells them they will never see two gay men kissing on television, they seize an opportunity and kiss live on the air during the *The Today Snow*.

Grace has a series of boyfriends (played by Woody Harrelson, Edward Burns, and Eric Stoltz), though most of them only stick around for a few episodes. Then, finally, Will and Grace both meet the men of their dreams: Grace falls for a Jewish doctor, Leo Markus (Harry Connick Jr.), while the love of Will's life is an Italian New York City cop named Vince D'Angelo (Bobby Cannavale).

Grace marries Dr. Leo in season 5, but their marriage doesn't last. They spend time apart when he volunteers for Doctors Without Borders. When he admits that he has slept with another woman (season 6), Grace divorces him despite the fact that she still loves him. Leo reappears in season 7 and they almost reconcile, but she just can't go through with it ("FYI: I Hurt Too"). Grace's relationship with her ex-husband takes an unexpected turn in season 8 ("Love is in the Airplane") when Will and Grace run into Leo on a plane bound for England (Will is determined not to go to his grave without seeing *Billy Elliot: The Musical*, then playing on London's West End). Grace and Leo enter The Mile-High Club and, nine episodes later, she finds out that she is pregnant. At first Grace decides to tell Leo ("Grace Expectations"), but changes her mind when she discovers that he's engaged. Thus, Will and Grace will raise the baby together as they planned to do back in season 4. While the introduction of Leo interrupted their original plan, the return of Vince D'Angelo complicates matters as well. Will is forced to choose between spending his life with Vince or Grace. Another complication presents itself when Grace learns that Leo has broken off his engagement. She is hopeful that he will come back, which angers Will, who, only an hour before, broke up with Vince to be with Grace.

The Leo and Vince storylines occurred over the course of seasons 6–8, during which the show's ranking fell from no. 16 (season 6) to no. 44 (season 7) to no. 61 (season 8). At least part of the reason for the declining ratings was the loss of its highly rated lead-in, *Friends*, which, in its final two seasons ranked no. 2 (2002–2003) and no. 5 (2003–2004). During the show's final three seasons, the storylines, particularly those involving Will and Grace, became more serious, with the comic relief provided by Jack and Karen. The finale was designed to resolve the tension between Will and Grace and gives us an idea of what the future holds for all four characters. Still, parts of the finale, written by creators Kohan and Mutchnick, who had left the show after season 4, seemed more like the end of a drama than a situation comedy. "I think everyone will be satisfied," Max Mutchnick reassured Rob Owen, a reporter for the *Telegraph-Journal* in New Brunswick. The finale was shot on Stage 17 at CBS Studio Center in Studio City, California, on April 10, 11, and 13, 2006, before a live audience.

The major themes of the *Will & Grace* finale are fate and destiny. It was fate that brought Will and Grace together when they met as freshmen in college and lived across the hall from one another. By the end of the finale, fate would bring them back together again because they are destined to be friends for life. The story picks up from the end of the previous episode with a look into the future to see what life is like for Will and Grace if they stayed together to raise her son. Everyone is miserable: Will is bald, Grace is fat, and her teenage son is a brat. Jack and Karen stop by for a visit. Jack and Kevin Bacon were recently married and Karen hasn't aged a day. Fortunately, this glimpse into the future is only Grace's dream (or rather, her nightmare). We soon realize that this is not the way everything is going to turn out when Leo suddenly appears out of nowhere and tells Grace that he loves her—and discovers that he is about to be a father.

At this point, *Will & Grace* takes its first in a series of time jumps. Two years later, Will and Vince are the proud parents of a baby boy named Ben, and Grace and Leo are raising their baby daughter, Lila, in Brooklyn. But the two have not spoken because Will is still angry that Grace ditched him and he has never returned her "hundreds" of apologetic phone messages. Unfortunately, the big scene in which Grace tells Will she is choosing Leo over him is played off-screen. So it's up to Karen and Jack to get Will and Grace in the same hospital room, where they agree to have a piece of "cafeteria cake" in celebration of Will's birthday. Once again, their conversation takes place off-screen, though Grace calls Will out on his residual anger when they are joined by Karen and Jack. It seems that Will and Grace are back together, though as friends who are now leading their own lives often do, saying they are going to call each other and somehow never getting around to it. When Grace says goodbye, she looks around Will and Vince's apartment and realizes that she doesn't live there anymore. Later, they each tell their respective spouses how at one time they believed that they were destined to meet and be together—but now, as Grace observes, "It just feels like a closed chapter."

Life is about to get complicated for Grace (Debra Messing) when her rendezvous on a plane with ex-husband Leo (Harry Connick Jr.) leaves her pregnant in the final season of *Will & Grace.*
Authors' collection

"People come into your life randomly," Will tells Vince, "and they leave randomly. You can't force it. That's just how things happen."

"Destiny," Grace laments to Leo, "is just something for young people to believe in."

Here comes the part that many of the show's die-hard fans may have found difficult to accept. We are supposed to believe that two best friends living in the same city who spent the majority of their adult lives together don't see each other (and presumably don't talk to one another) for over *fifteen years.* Perhaps deep down they were just waiting for fate, which is exactly what happens when Lila (Maria Thayer) and Ben (Ben Newmark) meet while moving across the hall from each other into their respective dorm rooms and go off to have coffee together—just like Will and Grace, who are then reunited as they help their children move in and walk off-screen and talk. The episode later makes another leap in time as Will and Grace are chatting on the phone about Lila and Ben's upcoming wedding. While it is certainly a nice twist, it's also a shame we didn't get a chance to spend a little more time with Lila and Ben, who, based on their short exchange in the hallway when they first meet, seem to have inherited their parents' neurotic tendencies. The same goes for

Will and Grace—we would have liked to have listened in on their conversation over a piece of cafeteria cake. If only Kohan and Mutchnick had allowed the scenes die-hard fans were likely to care about the most to be played out.

Jack and Karen's storyline begins with her discovery that she is flat broke because everything Stan had was borrowed, so her divorce settlement is worthless. The only way she can go back to the life to which she is accustomed is to force Jack to accept her arch rival Beverley Leslie's (Leslie Jordan) offer to be his new "business associate" in exchange for his millions, which Jack inherits when the Lilliputian closet case falls to his death after being lifted by a heavy wind over the balcony of his penthouse. Later, Jack and Karen, living the high life once again in her penthouse apartment, interrupt their quiet evening at home with a duet of Nat King Cole's "Unforgettable," with Jack at the piano. It's a sweet, albeit self-indulgent, moment that feels as if it was included to please Mullally and Hayes more than the audience. Then again, perhaps the two talented performers had earned this moment in the spotlight. As Jack complains to Karen, "It's like all people see when they look at us are the supporting players in the Will and Grace show."

Will & Grace comes full circle in the final moment when the foursome has a drink at the same bar from the pilot episode (after Grace ditched her fiancé Danny at the altar, she, in her wedding dress, and Will, in a tuxedo, are mistaken by the patrons for a newly married couple). Will proposes a toast—"To family. Family that loves you and accepts you for exactly who you are"—and observes, "We haven't changed a bit." With a clink of their glasses, their older selves turn back into their younger as we hear a rather on-the-nose song choice: Queen's "You're My Best Friend."

Although *Will & Grace* was not the ratings juggernaut it had been, NBC heavily promoted the finale, which aired during the May 2006 sweeps week. The finale was preceded by an hour-long retrospective, *Will & Grace: Say Goodnight Gracie*, featuring clips, bloopers, cast interviews, and behind-the-scenes footage. According to *Variety*'s Rick Kissell, 18.43 million viewers tuned in to watch the finale—the sitcom's largest audience since April 2004. Although CBS's *CSI: Crime Scene Investigation* won the hour, the *Will & Grace* finale attracted more viewers in the coveted demographic of viewers aged eighteen to forty-nine. Although the series didn't score an Emmy nomination for Best Comedy in its final season, it did receive the most nominations of any television comedy (ten), with wins for Leslie Jordan as Outstanding Guest Actor in a Comedy Series, and Megan Mullally, who took home her second Emmy for Best Supporting Actress. For those who may have missed the finale, Lionsgate and NBCUniversal released the finale on DVD a mere twelve days after it aired. At that point, only four seasons had been released on DVD; the final season Region 1 DVDs would not be released until September 2008.

The reviews for the finale were mixed. *Boston Globe* critic Matthew Gilbert felt that the show's "big fat goodbye . . . was sadly bloated and oversized. For every minute of stronger material, there were at least five of flab." For Gilbert, the strongest material was the "touchingly bittersweet" idea that Will and Grace go off to live their own lives only to "develop a healthier intimacy" when their children get married. In her review of the DVD release, *Entertainment Weekly*'s Jennifer Keishin Armstrong wrote: "The series finale gives the feeling of watching all eight years, played at hyperspeed, to fit in an hour, with banter, physical gags, and touching moments, at times mixed to perfection." She also detected Kohan and Mutchnick's "resistance to saying goodbye," which resulted in "a swirl of confusing, unnecessary sequences. . . . By the end, instead of being sad to say adieu, we're just relieved not to have yet another disbelief-suspending flash-forward thrust upon on us."

The finale also gave people an opportunity to reflect on the significant contribution *Will & Grace* made to American culture. In an article reflecting on the upcoming finale, Natalie Finn of *E! Online* included a quote by Neil Giuliano, the current president of the Gay and Lesbian Alliance Against Defamation (GLAAD), who gave the show the recognition it deserved:

> *Will & Grace* has given unprecedented visibility to gay, lesbian, and bisexual people. This is a comedy that created an emotional connection between millions of viewers and its characters. Audiences laugh along with characters like Will and Jack, and a door opened for viewers to have a greater understanding of our lives. For many years to come *Will & Grace* will continue to open hearts and minds as it lives on in syndication.

Putting a Ring on It

Meeting the Mother of *How I Met Your Mother*

How I Met Your Mother (CBS, 2005-2014)
Created by Carter Bays and Craig Thomas
Premiere date: September 19, 2005
9 seasons / 208 episodes
"Last Forever, Parts 1 and 2"
Airdate: March 31, 2014
5.4 rating • 16 percent share • 13.13 million viewers
Directed by Pamela Fryman
Written by Carter Bays and Craig Thomas
Cast: Josh Radnor (Ted Mosby), Jason Segel (Marshall Eriksen), Alyson Hannigan
    (Lily Aldrin), Neil Patrick Harris (Barney Stinson), Cobie Smulders (Robin
    Scherbatsky), Cristin Milioti (The Mother/Tracy McConnell), Lyndsy Fonseca
    (Penny Mosby), David Henrie (Luke Mosby), Bob Saget (Future Ted/voice of
    Ted Mosby)

s series creators Craig Thomas and Carter Bays sat down to record scenes for *How I Met Your Mother*'s series finale in the fall of 2006, they didn't quite know when CBS would need them. Having completed just one season of their much-buzzed about freshman series, Thomas and Bays's decision to jump to the very end was a perfect mirror of their show—a time-hopping labor-intensive endeavor. The series would go on to air nine seasons, find great success in syndication, and catapult its stars to fame. Thus, through the subsequent eight seasons of the show, with finale scenes in the can, Thomas and Bays stretched their love-story-told-in-reverse concept to become more than just a simple gimmick. The series' main character, Ted, would go on to weave the most elaborate tale of how exactly he met his children's mother, filled with endless misdirection, sly hints, constant time-shifting, and the occasional "When is this story going to end?" eye roll from his children. *How I Met Your Mother*, from its very first episode, relied heavily on exactly how it would all resolve, creating a unique television series predicated entirely upon its series finale.

When *How I Met Your Mother* (*HIMYM*) premiered in the fall of 2005 it arrived on the heels of CBS's beloved sitcom *Everybody Loves Raymond*. When *Raymond* left the air, the sitcom left a deep hole in the Monday night comedy block on CBS—the network's closest relative to NBC's once-wildly successful Thursday night "Must See TV" lineup. With *Raymond*'s departure, and a slew of failed prime-time sitcoms spread across all of the major networks, many, including *Variety*, had officially declared the network sitcom "dead and buried." Achieving the level of success that *Raymond* had enjoyed seemed unlikely to critics—especially considering that the previous year's Emmy award winner for Outstanding Comedy Series, *Arrested Development*, was perpetually plagued by being both a critical darling and a ratings bomb. However, the search for a unique twist on the traditional sitcom was a recurring theme across many networks: NBC brought us both *My Name is Earl* and an adaptation of Britain's major hit *The Office*; UPN premiered Chris Rock's *Everybody Hates Chris*; and FX presented *It's Always Sunny in Philadelphia*. While all are categorized within the sitcom realm, each of these shows premiered with the intention of turning traditions on their head—*Earl* with its narrative-framing device of a man in search of karmic redemption, *The Office* with its mockumentary style, *Everybody Hates Chris* with Rock's narration and nostalgic feel, and *Sunny* with its almost-over-the-line situations and language. For *New York Times* television columnist Alessandra Stanley these developments were a necessity as "the Internet and premium cable were making so many innovations—and inroads—that any conventional prime-time sitcom seemed doomed to irrelevance." *HIMYM* found itself firmly in line with its relevance-seeking peers—with the expressed purpose of turning the traditional and tired tropes of the sitcom on its head.

Enter Craig Thomas and Carter Bays. The creators of *HIMYM* had relatively little experience in the creation and development of a television series. Friends from college, and both writers for *The Late Show with David Letterman*, Thomas and Bays based much of the pilot on their own experiences living in New York. Their pilot script was, as *Variety* noted: "One of the most talked-about projects around Hollywood." Given its unusual structure, narrative-framing device, and ambitious number of scenes (whizzing back and forth through time), many feared that the show was doomed to be shredded by network execs—cut down to merely another twenty-somethings *Friends* clone. However, with a combination of Thomas and Bays's determination, and CBS's commitment to finding success after *Raymond*, creative freedom was granted and the show emerged intact. Bays related: "There's been this amazing confidence they've shown in us. They sort of just let us run with it." This creative

"Legen . . . wait for it . . . dary!" The cast of *How I Met Your Mother* hangs out at their favorite spot, MacLaren's: (left to right) Neil Patrick Harris, Cobie Smulders, Josh Radnor, Jason Segel, and Alyson Hannigan.   *Authors' collection*

freedom would prove to be both a blessing and a curse as the series finale approached, but in its initial stages Thomas and Bays's long leash situated the series in a prime position to begin to fill the deep void left by *Raymond*.

The series premiered on September 19, 2005. In its pilot, the voice of Ted Mosby, circa 2030, relays to his two teenage children the story of how he met their mother. Narrated by well-known television dad Bob Saget (*Full House*), the series immediately established itself as a time-hopping love story with lightning-fast scenes, reflective narration in the same vein as *The Wonder Years*, and a crop of familiar and new cast members. Anchored by the pairing of relatively unknown actors Josh Radnor (Ted) and Cobie Smulders (Robin), the show also featured cult-favorite Alyson Hannigan (Lily) of *Buffy the Vampire Slayer* fame, *Freaks and Geeks* alumnus Jason Segel (Marshall), and former child star Neil Patrick Harris (Barney), lovingly remembered as wunderkind doctor Doogie on *Doogie Howser, MD*.

The pilot episode was directed by television veteran Pamela Fryman, known for her work on *Frasier* and *Just Shoot Me!*, and a protégé of legendary sitcom director (and known tastemaker) James Burrows. Fryman, credited with the show's overall style and pacing, would go on to direct all but twelve episodes of the entire series. In the beginning, Fryman was faced with a seemingly impossible task: Thomas and Bays's whopping sixty scene pilot script (fifty more than a traditional sitcom). Fryman had to virtually reinvent how the show would be produced. Recalling to the *Los Angeles Times* in 2008, she said: "We all thought this was a sitcom, but when you pull it apart and see that there are 60 scenes, you realize that the [studio] audience is going to be very bored. And where are we going to put all the sets? We just couldn't do this as a regular multi-camera sitcom." The solution: *HIMYM* merged together multiple styles, taking on traditional multi-camera set design and mixing it with the editing style of a single-camera show, allowing for the full scope of Thomas and Bays's time-hopping concept to be realized. Though a decidedly hybrid show in terms of style, *HIMYM* did stick to one traditional sitcom standard: the laugh track. Finding it impossible to have an audience sustain the grueling sixty-scene, multi-day shooting schedule (Thomas believed they would "blur the line between 'audience' and 'hostage' situation"), the show inserted a pre-taped laugh track, recorded with a live audience who watched an already edited episode. The result: a highly conceptual, innovative show that, to the viewers at home, seemed all the more familiar.

Reception of the premiere was largely positive. *Variety*'s Brian Lowry called it a "bright, cleverly constructed" show, with a "topnotch cast and a sly, too-good-to-give-away twist." Other reviews made the inevitable *Friends* comparison, and some noted that its comic sensibility and sentimentality could potentially wear thin. CBS, however, stood by the show, renewing it for a second season, but hesitant on officially declaring it the successor to *Raymond*—its renewal was not initially announced, landing the show on many critics' "On the Bubble" lists. Coupled with news of its renewal, the network also moved the series from its initial first-season 8:30 p.m. timeslot to the pivotal prime-time kickoff timeslot of 8:00 p.m., thus shifting previous lead-in ratings stronghold *The King of Queens* (then it its final season) to a mid-season premiere date and the 9:30 p.m. timeslot.

As the first season wrapped up and the premiere of the second season loomed, *HIMYM* had established several key storylines that would ultimately drive the eight seasons to follow. No longer was it simply a show about love-lorn Ted in search of his great love, the mother of his children. Marshall and Lily's relationship—most notably their engagement, breakup, re-engagement, marriage, and parenthood—factored largely into the plot of many seasons. Likewise, Robin's ongoing relationship and commitment problems were featured prominently, as was her discovery of her own infertility. Barney also shared the spotlight with his own storylines: the search for his real father and his inability to settle down.

While a gimmick established the main conceit of the show (Ted's framing story told to his grown children), the series emerged strongly as an ensemble effort, leading many of the actors to find success outside of the series—Jason Segel, as a go-to Judd Apatow comedy star (*Knocked Up*, *Forgetting Sarah Marshall*) and Muppets reboot frontman; Cobie Smulders as special agent Maria Hill within the Marvel *Avengers* film franchise; and most notably, Neil Patrick Harris. As the series' lead funnyman, Harris's Barney Stinson was charged with maintaining many of the series' most beloved recurring jokes: his set of unbreakable life rules, the "Bro Code"; ongoing "slap bets" with Marshall; and his own signature catchphrases: "Suit Up!" and "Legendary" (often repeated as "Legen . . . wait for it . . . dary"). Harris emerged as the series' greatest star—and the series' only Emmy-award nominated actor (nominated four times as Barney Stinson, with no wins). Harris utilized his new notoriety to launch himself as the go-to awards show host, subsequently hosting and producing the Tony Awards (2009, 2011, 2012, and 2013), the Emmys (2009, 2013), and the Academy Awards (2015). During the writers' strike of 2008, Harris partnered with Joss Whedon to play the title character in *Dr. Horrible's Sing-Along Blog*, a short live-action comic book series released to wide acclaim exclusively on the Internet. Harris also received a star on the Hollywood Walk of Fame in September 2011.

With Harris as the show's breakout star, the spotlight also turned to the actor's personal life, resulting in Harris coming out of the closet in November 2006, revealing to *People* magazine:

> The public eye has always been kind to me, and until recently I have been able to live a pretty normal life. Now it seems there is speculation and interest in my private life and relationships. So, rather than ignore those who choose to publish their opinions without actually talking to me, I am happy to dispel any rumors or misconceptions and am quite proud to say that I am a very content gay man living my life to the fullest and feel most fortunate to be working with wonderful people in the business I love.

Harris's revelation placed him in the position of being an openly gay actor portraying a womanizing horndog—a role very few had pulled off in the past. In a 2009 profile in *New York Magazine*, Harris noted that he never felt concerned about his romantic storylines on *HIMYM* as coming off as untrue: "No one was ever old-school Hollywood, with a cigar in their mouth, saying 'You can't do this, see! It'll ruin your career, kid'. . . . So long as you're representing yourself well, you're making good choices for good reasons, all of the circumstantial things will vanish." As Harris's star continued to rise with each season of the show, his credibility was never questioned—thus, allowing *HIMYM* to establish itself as a pioneering show not only for its content, but also for its ability to break through stereotypes that had, in the past, proved problematic for other shows.

Riding the breakout success of Harris, and the growing fan base of the show, ratings for *HIMYM* were on the rise. By 2012 (season 7), the show enjoyed its best ratings ever, having, as cited by the Associated Press, the "youngest average audience" on the prime-time network schedule. Likely contributing to this success was the broad-based appeal of the show, evidenced most strongly by the two cable networks that picked up the show for syndication: Lifetime (a network aimed entirely at a female audience), and FX (a network geared toward males, aged eighteen to forty-nine). With syndication broadening the show's audience, by the time it reached its ninth and final season, it became the third-most-watched comedy on network television, trailing just behind ratings juggernaut (and fellow CBS comedy) *The Big Bang Theory*, and ABC's Emmy darling *Modern Family*.

Speculation surrounding the actual timeline for the series' completion ramped up in early 2013, midway through its eighth season. As the cast's contracts were set to expire at the end of the season, lengthy negotiations began—particularly with series star Jason Segel, who was rumored to be the single holdout, reluctant to commit to another season of the show. When Segel reached a deal, the official announcement was made by Nina Tassler, president of CBS entertainment:

> Through eight years, *How I Met Your Mother* has mastered the art of leading-edge comedy, emotional water-cooler moments and pop culture catch-phrases. We are excited for Carter, Craig, Pam Fryman and this amazing cast to tell the final chapter and reveal television's most mysterious mother to some of TV's most passionate fans.

Dana Walden and Gary Newman, chairmen of 20th Century Fox Television (producer of the show), reiterated Tassler's focus on the upcoming "mother" revelation, stating: "Carter Bays and Craig Thomas are masterful and hilarious storytellers, and we have no doubt that they will guide one of the greatest comedies of the last decade to a gratifying conclusion when they finally reveal the identity of the Mother." The stage was set—laser-sharp focus was on the ultimate reveal of "The Mother." With their pre-taped finale moment in the can since season 2, Thomas and Bays, now with even greater pressure to fulfill the series' promise, found themselves in what television critic Alex Sepinwall called a "narrative straightjacket." Knowing that the ninth season would indeed be their last, Thomas and Bays had one more trick up their sleeve, one that they had hinted at in the past. "We've been coy about it; we've gone back and forth about it, but there is no reason why this story ends the moment [Ted] meets her," said Carter Bays in 2008. As the eighth season came to a close, viewers were shocked when, in its final minutes, The Mother, played by breakout Broadway star Cristin Milioti, came onscreen. While lead character Ted technically did not "meet" her, the perpetually misdirected audience was finally in the know. Where the show would go from its eighth season finale was a challenging journey—one that suited the unconventional Thomas and Bays.

The ninth and final season of *HIMYM* would prove to be as ambitious as the show's overall concept. All twenty-four episodes would take place in one single weekend—the weekend of commitment phobic Robin and known bachelor Barney's wedding. Layered into this single weekend would be the flashbacks and flash-forwards the show was known for, establishing a dynamic that Thomas and Bays believed would satisfy the audience. With a nod to the difficulty this involved, Bays noted, "There have been pitfalls in the structure. . . . You give yourself challenges. That's why you get up in the morning." Series lead Josh Radnor had faith in the creators' vision: "They are geniuses at scrambling narratives and playing with time. . . . I knew they were going to find endlessly inventive ways to do that. And not only that, it sounded like a lot of fun." The finale date was set: after 206 episodes, a two-part finale, titled "Last Forever," would air on March 31, 2014.

In part 1, we find the characters at the reception of Barney and Robin's wedding. After a season of "will-they-or-won't-they" speculations surrounding the pair's nuptials, Robin and Barney had tied the knot, leaving Ted's long-held flame for Robin burned out. Ted, ready to move on with his life, decides to leave for a new job in Chicago, exiting the reception after a group hug (reminiscent of *The Mary Tyler Moore Show*'s famous conclusion). The next day, as the gang meets in their favorite bar, MacClaren's, they are surprised to see Ted sitting at their table. After leaving the reception, he spots The Mother, standing beneath her infamous yellow umbrella, at the train station.

What proceeds from this critical moment in the series' timeline is a number of flash-forwards, ultimately covering seventeen years in the lives of the characters. In 2015, we find Ted engaged to The Mother upon the announcement of her pregnancy. In 2016, at a gathering uniting the group, we find that Barney and Robin, whose marriage was the singular focus of the entire ninth season, have secretly divorced. Lily, now expecting her third child with Marshall, worries that this will be the final straw that breaks the group apart—ultimately forcing all to commit to being there for one another for the important moments. Flashing to a few months later, the group celebrates one final Halloween in Marshall and Lily's apartment, where Robin decides that being around her ex-husband Barney, who has returned to his womanizing ways, and her unresolved feelings for Ted, is too much to bear. She decides to leave for good, splintering the series' strongest element: the strength of the group's friendship.

In the series finale, Ted (Josh Radnor) and "The Mother" (Cristin Milioti) finally have their meet-cute under that infamous yellow umbrella.   *Authors' collection*

In part 2, we flash to 2018 and 2019, finding Barney at a crossroads as he discovers he will soon be a father. Ted and The Mother, having been distracted by the birth of both of their children, have not yet married. Robin, unseen by the group since the Halloween party, re-emerges to attend Ted and The Mother's wedding, fulfilling her promise to Lily. It is at this instance that the audience is thrown the ultimate curveball: in a series of images that tells the story of their life together, Ted announces that he will always love The Mother, who, as we learn, becomes terminally ill and passes away in 2024. Immediately, we switch to that fateful night in 2013 at the train station when Ted spots The Mother under her yellow umbrella—the promise of the series becomes fulfilled as the two have their official "meet-cute," finally revealing The Mother as Tracy McConnell. Ted, now seen opposite his children in the setting of his very long story, announces: "And that, kids, is how I met your mother." We then cut back to the kids (in the scenes shot in 2006), who admonish their father, seeing that the point of the story was not to reveal how he met their mother, but instead, a story about his unfulfilled love for their Aunt Robin. Encouraging him to pursue his true love, the kids convince their father to go after Robin, and with their blessing he arrives at her apartment, presenting her with the same blue French horn he had given her in the series' first episode. As the series closes, the viewer is led to believe the love is mutual, and Robin and Ted end on a happy note.

As the credits rolled, audiences were stunned. The very premise of the series, the how and when of the meeting of Ted and The Mother, was seemingly glossed over—favoring instead the reunion of Ted and Robin, their love becoming the central focus of the finale. Reaction was swift, and damning. As the *Washington Post*'s Emily Yahr pointed out in her survey of the finale: "Intense anger is nothing new in terms of highly anticipated series finales of long-running shows with die-hard fan bases." In the case of the finale of *HIMYM*, anger was most certainly the dominant emotion—citing The Mother's death as the most critical component to fuel this anger. As Yahr, along with a host of other television critics, pointed out, after fans had spent the entire season getting to know The Mother—Milioti appeared in fourteen episodes, even taking over the show's narrative in "How Your Mother Met Me"—she is killed off in what seems like mere moments. Adding to this impassioned anger was the swift divorce of Robin and Barney, whose relationship, though long criticized by fans as difficult to believe, was again the focus of the entire ninth season. The Internet lit up with feverish criticism, with the *Daily Beast* calling the finale "bloated . . . with three seasons worth of plot shoved into a single episode." *Vulture*'s Margaret Lyons proclaimed: "*How I Met Your Mother* made a striking, memorable promise in the pilot—that Robin was *not the mother*—and this feels like a promise kept only by a technicality. Congratulations on exploiting that loophole." While *Hitfix*'s Alex Sepinwall agreed with much of the fierce criticism of the finale (calling it "terrible" and "misconceived"), he also conceded that he "very briefly" had sympathy for Thomas and Bays, realizing "they had become victims of their own cleverness." Yet it was that same cleverness that began the entire series, as the hook of Ted referring to Robin as "Aunt Robin" in the pilot was the very element that drew the audience in.

With their audience left feeling overwhelmingly betrayed by the finale (an audience that measured 13.13 million viewers—an all-time high for the series), the stars of the show chimed in with support of the writers' decision. Josh Radnor told *Vulture* that "part of the DNA of the show is they lead you one way and then pull you back." He acknowledged that fans were "grieving for the end of the show. . . . I think when the dust settles people will feel pretty complete." Neil Patrick Harris, in an appearance on *The Late Show with David Letterman*, said: "It wasn't necessarily the happy ending that people were expecting . . . but Carter and Craig knew this ending years ago and had played towards that. And I was a big proponent of it and a big fan of it." Creators Thomas and Bays took to Twitter to thank their fans, despite the negative reaction. In a long series of tweets directed to their fans, Thomas wrote: "Thank you all. I mean it. Every possible reaction to the last 44 minutes. . . . Thank you all. The fact that we have been a TV sitcom that has received this much passion from fans, for 9 years (not just tonight)—thank you. We did a finale about life's twists and turns and that is not always what happens . . . but THANKS. Seriously—no matter what you thought of tonight, THANK YOU . . . you were with us. We love you." Bays put the matter to bed with one short tweet, calling back to one of Barney's signature phrases: "Highest of fives to you all!"

While it took Thomas and Bays nine years to carefully craft their finale, it only took YouTube user Ricardo J. Dylan one day to re-create the ending, posting a three-minute video online that immediately went viral. Called "the perfect fan created ending" by *Entertainment Weekly*, Dylan's "sweet and moving" video featured Ted and The Mother under that same yellow umbrella, as the voiceover relays how happy Ted is to have met their mother, as we fade to black. The next day a petition was filed on Change.org begging the creators to "rewrite and reshoot the *How I Met Your Mother* ending"—it has since been signed by over 22,000 fans. Days after the finale aired, with feelings still raw, Carter Bays took to Twitter again to address the fans. Perhaps inspired by the popularity of Dylan's YouTube clip, Bays announced that an alternate ending would appear on the Complete Series DVD set, calling the new ending "very different." Seen by many as a ploy to sell DVDs, and even worse by many fans as a cop-out that was obviously against the creators' intentions, Bays's announcement was a first for television series finales—a swift and immediate reaction precipitated wholeheartedly by the passion and ire dictated by their fans, truly a watershed moment for the future reception and re-editing of television finales.

Months after the finale aired and CBS's announcement that it would not greenlight a much-hyped series' successor, "How I Met Your Dad" (to star indie darling Greta Gerwig), *Indiewire*'s Liz Shannon Miller posted an article titled, "Time to Forgive the *How I Met Your Mother* finale." In her piece, Miller concedes that "few finales are considered full-on failures, and the general consensus is that *How I Met Your Mother* is one of them." Yet, Miller implores audiences to reconsider their feelings towards the finale, noting that it deserves praise for having "actually surprised us," even if that surprise "was a disappointment." She continues: "But disappointment is expecting that a life has only one love story, that happily ever after only happens once, that surprises, good and bad, happen along the way. *How I Met Your Mother* was never perfect. But then again, whoever said life was?" While the impact of *How I Met Your Mother* on the future of sitcom style and narrative-framing devices cannot yet be known, its complete story, and its creators' freedom and willingness to start from the end of a story and work backwards, will inevitably influence television series to come.

Part 4

All Talked Out

Daytime and Late Night Television

Sunset on Daytime

Closing the Book on Long-Running Soaps

oap opera fans never expect their favorite show to end. Having devoted countless hours, let alone years, watching their favorite daytime drama, their connection to their soap's fictional small-town setting and large ensemble cast of characters is deeply rooted. It's difficult to suddenly have all of that taken away from you, especially if you consider the number of years some of the recently canceled soaps have been on the air: *Guiding Light* (fifty-seven years), *As the World Turns* (fifty-four years), *One Life to Live* (forty-five years), and *All My Children* (forty-three years).

Time is a major factor in determining how a soap opera will end. In some instances, writers and producers are not given sufficient warning their show has been canceled, so they have a limited amount of time to resolve the current storylines and tie up all the loose ends, which does not always happen. Some shows end quietly, while others, ironically, are given a highly publicized send-off by the very same network that pulled the plug on them in the first place. A typical soap opera finale includes a wedding or a celebration of some kind (a homecoming, New Year's Eve, etc.) and some form of a "thank you" and "goodbye" message to their loyal fans.

All My Children (ABC, 1/5/1970–9/23/2011; The OnLine Network, 4/29/2013–9/2/2013) Created by Agnes Nixon; 43 seasons / 10,755 episodes

Agnes Nixon, creator of the ABC soap opera *One Life to Live*, conceived *All My Children* in the 1960s, but didn't get the show on the air until 1970. The soap focused on families living in Pine Valley, a small suburban Pennsylvania town. When the show debuted in 1970, it did not shy away from dealing with topical issues, like the Vietnam War and abortion, and later in its run, drug addiction, gay rights, and AIDS. In a 2011 interview with *Newsweek*'s Maria Elena Fernandez, Agnes Nixon explained, "Current events, for me, all get reduced to people and what makes them do the things they do. What I always wanted was to entertain people, first of all, but I also hope that I taught them a bit and out of that teaching, maybe some people rose out of their prejudices and their fears." The show's legacy is its multi-generational cast of strong female characters: liberal-minded Amy Tyler, affluent and snobbish Phoebe Tyler, matriarchal Ruth Martin, single mother Mona Kane, and her daughter, Erica Kane.

Played by Susan Lucci for the entire run of the show on ABC, Erica Kane is one of daytime television's most iconic characters. Erica started on the show as a manipulative teenage temptress and evolved into a combination of Cleopatra, Scarlett O'Hara, and Bette Davis—a complicated, independent woman who can be a manipulative, self-involved, combative, bitchy seductress, and, at the same time, a caring, loyal friend and mother. Over the course of forty-one years, she was married eleven times to eight different men, though some of her marriages (for whatever reason) were invalid. Erica has a nasty streak, but you can't help but feel sorry for her because she is a survivor who overcame alcohol and pill addiction, survived a plane crash and a car accident, and was raped as a teenager, which resulted in the birth of her daughter Kendall, whom she gave up for adoption. Over the years, Erica still somehow had time to pursue a long list of careers, which included high-fashion model, magazine publisher, cosmetics company mogul, talk show host, and film star. With all of her wealth and fame, it was never clear why she chose to remain in her sleepy hometown of Pine Valley.

Like *As the World Turns*, *All My Children* is a soap opera you thought would run forever. The rumors circulating in early 2011 that *AMC* was headed for cancellation proved to be true when Brian Frons, president of daytime at Disney ABC/Television, made the announcement, on April 14, 2011: the network was axing both *All My Children* and *One Life to Live* and replacing them with two talk shows inspired by *The View* that would be cheaper to produce. *AMC* would air its last episode in September and be replaced by *The Chew*, a show devoted to food and cooking. *One Life to Live* would hand over its time slot the following January to *The Revolution*, a show devoted to "better living" that turned out to be "bad television" and was canceled within six months. According to *Variety* reporter Andrew Wallenstein, ABC's last remaining soap, *General Hospital*, "escaped the chopping block" because it had higher ratings and generated revenue in overseas markets.

The much-anticipated series finale of *All My Children*, watched by 3.475 million viewers, marked the return of many familiar faces: Dr. Joe Martin (Ray MacDonnell) and his wife, Ruth (Lee Meriwether), have moved back home so he can run the hospital now that Pine Valley's resident villain, Dr. David Hayward (Vincent Irizarry), is in trouble with the law; Brooke English (Julia Barr) and Adam Chandler (David Canary) also returned to Pine Valley, where they plan to get married and live in the Chandler mansion, which she purchased with her inheritance from her late aunt Phoebe; Tad (Michael Knight) gets a surprise visit from his son, Jamie (Justin Bruening), and plans to get remarried to his beloved Dixie (Cady McClain). But perhaps the biggest surprise was the return of Adam's beloved twin brother, Stuart (David

All My Children's Erica Kane (Susan Lucci) and husband no. 9 and 10, Dimitri Marick (Michael Nader). *Authors' collection*

Canary), who was shot and presumed dead, only to be brought back to life by Dr. Hayward through his experimental treatment known as the Orpheus Project. Stuart is reunited with his son Scott (Daniel Cosgrove) and his wife, Marian (Jennifer Bassey), who can't believe her husband is back (neither can we).

Meanwhile, Erica's remarriage to Jackson Montgomery (Walt Willey) is off when she admits that she doesn't want to get married, but wants to go to Hollywood to co-write and star in a film about her life. At the Chandler mansion, where everyone has gathered to welcome Stuart back from the dead, she professes publicly that she needs and loves him. Jackson exits like Rhett Butler at the end of *Gone With the Wind* and tells Ms. Kane that, frankly, he doesn't give a damn about what she needs. Erica then does something Scarlett never did—she runs after him.

Tad Martin makes a long, heartfelt toast that sounds as if it should be delivered at a cast and crew farewell party:

> It's because of the love and the help of everybody, everybody in this room, because that's how Pine Valley works. Always has, always will. In tragedy and triumph, we come together. I wish the rest of my kids were here to see this, you know, because this is—this is something to remember, folks. We'll be talking about this for a long time. But then again, I always like to think that no matter what, my family and all my children—they're always with me.

One resident of Pine Valley who is *not* happy is J. R. Chandler (Jacob Young), who has turned into a bitter alcoholic—he lost Babe, the love of his life; he was stripped of his inheritance by his father, Adam; he has experienced uncontrollable rages because of his steroid use; he drove the family company, Chandler Enterprises, into the ground; and he is kept from his son, A J, by his ex-wife, David Hayward's daughter, Marissa, who is now in a lesbian relationship with Erica's daughter, Bianca. During the party, a distraught J. R. hides in a passageway with a gun. At the moment when Erica goes after Jackson, a shot rings out and there is a fade to black.

Whom did J. R. kill?

We eventually find out the answer to this question because, like Stuart Chandler, *All My Children*, along with its sister show, *One Life to Live*, were revived by Prospect Park, which made a licensing deal with ABC to produce new episodes of both soaps that would air on their OnLine Network, beginning in January of 2012. But on November 23, 2011, a few months before the shows were slated to debut, Nellie Andreeva at *Deadline Hollywood* reported Prospect Park announced that they had suspended their plans. According to a company press release, "[T]he contractual demands of the guilds, which regulate our industry, coupled with the program's inherent economic challenges, ultimately led to this final decision." A little over a year later, Andreeva reported that Prospect Park had "inked a deal" with various unions and were putting both shows into production in February of 2013. New thirty-minute episodes of *All My Children* debuted on Hulu, Hulu Plus, and iTunes on April 29, 2013. A total of forty-three episodes were produced for the show's first season, but by November of 2013, the plug was pulled permanently on *All My Children* and *One Life to Live*.

The new episodes picked up five years later with the release of Dr. David Hayward from prison after serving time for shooting J. R., who killed Marissa, his ex-wife (and David's daughter), as David struggled to get the gun away from him. Susan Lucci did not appear on the *AMC* revival; her character was living in Los Angeles while Lucci was busy stirring up trouble on Lifetime's new prime-time soap opera, *Devious Maids*. While new characters were introduced, several *AMC* veterans stayed in or returned to Pine Valley.

During what is likely to be our final visit to Pine Valley, Dimitri Marick (Michael Nader), Brooke's business partner, was pursuing her romantically, but her heart still belonged to Adam; J. R., who was off steroids, was trying to redeem himself, but not everyone is so forgiving; Jesse Hubbard (Darnell Williams) considered opening his own detective agency; and it looks like Tad, who left town, is coming back.

But, alas, without Erica Kane, Pine Valley is just another fictional soap opera town.

Another World (NBC, 5/4/1964–6/25/1999) Created by Irna Phillips and William J. Bell; 35 seasons / 8,891 episodes

Bay City was the setting for this long-running soap opera, originally conceived by its co-creator, Irna Phillips, as a spinoff of her other soap, *As the World Turns*. Unfortunately, CBS had no room on its daytime schedule, so NBC picked up the series, which prevented any characters from crossing over. In her book on the history of *Another World*, Julie Poll includes a quote from Phillips that explains the significance of the show's title: "The events of our lives represent only the surface, and in our minds and feelings we live in many other hidden worlds." In other words, the show's focus was not simply limited to the daily lives of its characters, but their thoughts, feelings, aspirations, fantasies, wishes, dreams, etc., which exist in a whole other sphere. Apparently, there was such a healthy supply of thoughts and feelings in Bay City that *Another World* had to be split into two half-hour soaps. The first of two spinoffs, *Somerset* (1970–1976) (sometimes referred to as *Another World in Somerset*) transported three *AW* characters—Missy Palmer Matthews (Carol Roux), Lahoma Vale Lucas (Ann Wedgeworth), and Sam Lucas (Jordan Charney)—to Somerset, Michigan, a fictional town located in the northern suburbs of Detroit.

James Lipton, best known as the host of *Inside the Actors Studio*, and Agnes Nixon, creator of *All My Children*, contributed to the development of *Another World* in its early years, which lead to the creation of the show's power couple, Mac Cory (Douglass Watson) and the much younger Rachel (Victoria Wyndham), a reformed villainess who was forced to contend with Mac's jealous daughter Iris (Beverlee McKinsey), who was around the same age as his bride. In 1980, Iris moved from Bay City to Houston to star in a second *AW* spinoff, *Texas* (see below). Unfortunately, Watson died of a heart attack in 1989, leaving his on-screen wife, Rachel, a widow with two children, though she would find love a second time with Mac's former rival, Carl Hutchins (Charles Keating).

In the final episode, Cass (Stephen Schnetzer) is visited by the ghost of his late wife, Frankie (Alice Barrett), who gives him her blessing to marry Lila (Lisa Peluso). After the wedding, Rachel and Carl agree, "All's well that ends well." She then walks through the living room looking at the photos she has collected over the years. The final shot is a photograph of Mac Cory (the late Douglass Watson), with a glass of wine in his hand, giving a toast. Ironically, when *Another World* was canceled, several characters from the show—Cass, Lila, Vicky (Jensen Buchanan), Marley (Ellen Wheeler), Donna (Anna Stuart) and Jake (Tom Eplin)—moved over to *As the World Turns*, which was also produced by Procter & Gamble.

As the World Turns (CBS, 4/2/56–9/17/10) Created by Irna Phillips; 54 seasons / 13,858 episodes

After five decades, America said goodbye to the residents of Oakdale, Illinois, when this long-running CBS soap opera stopped spinning. The show's cancellation was not surprising considering CBS had pulled the plug on *Guiding Light* (see below) in 2009. Still, you can't help but feel that the cancellation of *As the World Turns*, even for those who had never seen it, was the death of one of American television's cultural institutions—the title of which was emblematic of the entire genre.

"Good morning, dear. What would you like for breakfast?" asked Nancy Hughes (Helen Wagner) to her husband, Chris (Don MacLaughlin). These were the first lines spoken on *As the World Turns* when television's first half-hour soap opera (as opposed to fifteen minutes) debuted on April 2, 1956. Wagner would play the role of Nancy up until her death on May 1, 2010, seven weeks before the show was scheduled to tape its final episode (the rumor on discussion boards was that the writers were going to end the show by having Nancy repeat the series' first line). Wagner's last appearance aired on June 1, 2010, and the death of her character, the matriarch of the Hughes family, was written into the storyline toward the end of the show's run. Wagner also became part of American television history on November 22, 1963, when CBS news anchor Walter Cronkite interrupted a scene she was performing live with Santos Ortega, who played Grandpa Hughes, to announce that President Kennedy has been shot in Dallas. As the scene was being performed live, the actors were unaware of the interruption and the tragedy that had taken place.

As the World Turns focused on the usual assortment of courtships, marriages, breakups, and tragic accidents, though the show always had a reputation for being somewhat old-fashioned and conservative, especially when more modern soaps, like *All My Children*, *General Hospital*, and *The Young and the Restless*, came along with sexier storylines. But people still watched. For twenty seasons, from 1958–1959 through 1977–1978, *As the World Turns* occupied the no. 1 spot in the daytime drama ratings. The show did eventually catch up to the other soap operas by turning up the volume on the sex and bad behavior, though beginning in the late 1990s, the show's ratings steadily declined. On December 8, 2009, CBS announced that the show was canceled. *New York Times* reporter Bill Carter and Brian Stelter asked CBS president Les Moonves if the cancellation of *ATWT* signaled the end of an era. He could only see it in purely financial terms. "Is it the end of an era?" Moonves asked, "Sort of. Only the special soaps survive. It's certainly the end of the client-owned soap. All good things come to an end, whether it's after 72 years or 54 years or 10 years. It's a different time and a different business."

Now it was time to say goodbye. Dr. Bob Hughes, played by Don Hastings since 1960, served as the voice-over narrator for the final episode, which was heard by 2.8 million viewers. He gives a status report on most of the residents of Oakdale: Barbara (Colleen Zenk) dissolves her relationship with Paul (Roger Howarth); Casey (Billy Magnussen) and Alison (Marnie Schulenburg) leave for Carbondale where he is entering law school; Dusty (Grayson McCouch) and Janet's (Julie Pinson) baby is christened; Carly (Maura West) announces that she and Jack (Michael Park) have a baby on the way; Lucinda (Elizabeth Hubbard) and John (Larry Bryggman) reunite, and Chris (Daniel Cosgrove) proposes to Katie (Terri Conn); Luke (Van Hansis), who lost his lover, Reid, is alone, though he gets to hear Reid's heart beating in Chris's chest, which makes Luke feel better; and, finally, Dr. Bob Hughes, who is retiring, finds it difficult to say goodbye. His wife, Kim (Kathryn Hays), tells him don't say "goodbye, just good night." She tells him to take all the time that he needs. He picks up his nameplate and puts it in his briefcase. He says, "Good night," and walks out. The camera moves to the globe on his desk, which is illuminated and spinning.

ATWT vet Hays told *Entertainment Weekly*'s Lynette Rice that it was very emotional shooting the final scene because literally everyone involved in the show who was there that day was watching. "It was like everyone was holding their breath," she recalled. "In a way, we were all doing it together." Hays was also optimistic about the future of what many people believe is a dying genre: "Maybe soaps will be changed in some way. Or maybe at some point, someone will come along and say that nobody wants to watch reality shows anymore and that maybe we should try telling stories again. Soaps will come back in some way. As far as I'm personally concerned, I feel it was a major privilege to be part of this family."

The Brighter Day (CBS, 1/4/1954–9/28/1962) Created by Irna Phillips; 8 seasons / no. of episodes N/A

"Our years are as the falling leaves. We live, we love, we dream, and then we go. But somehow, we keep hoping that our dreams come true on that brighter day." This message of hope was heard in the opening of this 1950s soap opera, which started as a radio show on October 11, 1948, and continued to run through 1956, two years after the show debuted on CBS. *The Brighter Day* is the story of Reverend Richard Dennis and his sister, Emily Potter, who helps raise her brother's four children: Grayling, his alcoholic son; Althea, an aspiring actress; Patsy, who marries a doctor; and the youngest, Barbara (nicknamed Babby). A fifth child, the eldest daughter, Liz, was married and had moved away when the show was adapted for television. The setting was also changed from Three Rivers to New Hope, Wisconsin, due to a flood. Later in its run, the family moved to Columbus, a college town.

The ratings suffered when the production moved from New York City to CBS's Hollywood studios and the show lost a few key actors/characters during the transition. In September of 1962, *Variety* reported that the show, which also lost viewers when it was moved from an afternoon to a late-morning (11:30 a.m.) time slot, was being axed, along with NBC's *Our Five Daughters*, because the two soap operas "didn't lather up enough sales." The producers did not have sufficient time to wrap up all the storylines, so they employed a device *Soap Opera Digest*'s John Kelly Genovese describes as similar to the Stage Manager's role as the omniscient narrator in Thornton Wilder's play, *Our Town*. Like the Stage Manager, Uncle Walter (Paul Langton), who owned the local hardware store, "stepped before the camera . . . and told viewers who was to leave town, get arrested or shoot themselves."

The Brighter Day was the first soap opera to include an African-American character as a series regular. Rex Ingram was hired to play Victor Graham, an ordained minister, though the show was canceled shortly after he was added to the cast.

Capitol (CBS, 3/29/1982–3/20/1987) Created by Stephen Karpf and Elinor Karpf; 5 seasons / 1,270 episodes

Washington, D.C., was the setting and politics was the backdrop for this CBS soap, which focused on two families living in Jeffersonia, a fictional D.C. suburb, engaged in a long-standing feud: the rich and powerful Cleggs and the middle-class McCandless family. Their respective matriarchs, Myrna Clegg (Carolyn Jones) and Clarissa Tyler McCandless (Constance Towers), are former best friends until they both set their sights on Baxter McCandless (Ron Harper), who ultimately chose sweet Clarissa over the vindictive Myrna. Their lives are further complicated when Baxter, who is presumed dead, resurfaces, and Myrna's daughter, Julie (Catherine Hickland), falls in love and marries Clarissa's son, Tyler (David Mason Daniels).

In terms of viewership, *Capitol* never ranked at the top of the ratings, but lingered in the middle at no. 8 (out of 14 soaps) for most of its run. When the ratings declined, CBS affiliates started to drop the show and so did the network, replacing it with a new soap, *The Bold and the Beautiful.*

In the final episode, Sam Clegg tells his wife, Myrna (then played by Marj Dusay), he wants a divorce, while Clarissa's family say a prayer at the dinner table for the safe return of her former daughter-in-law, Sloane (Debrah Farentino). The show ended with a genuine cliffhanger. Sloane, who married an Arab prince, Ali (Peter Lochran), made the mistake of trying to take her husband's place as ruler of the fictional country of Baraq. Refusing to abdicate the throne when Ali is kidnapped, she is sentenced to death. In the show's last moment, she stands before a firing squad and declares, "Long live, free Baraq! Long live Ali!" The commander tells the squad, "Aim." We cut to a close-up of Sloane's eyes and the screen fades to black. The close-up is then seen over the final credits.

The situation comedy *Soap* (1977–1981) also ended its four-year run with Jessica Tate (Katherine Helmond) being kidnapped by Communist rebels and facing a firing squad. The commander yells, "Ready, aim" and we hear gunshots. (See *Soap* in the appendix to learn how it was later resolved on the spinoff, *Benson*).

Dark Shadows (ABC, 6/27/1966–4/2/1971) Created by Dan Curtis; 6 seasons / 1,225 episodes

Dark Shadows was a Gothic horror soap opera set in Collinsport, a small village in Maine. The town's leading family, albeit one with a curse on them, is the Collinses, who, for generations, have resided in an eighteenth-century estate known as Collinwood. While the soap is set in the present day, the writers also started to explore the history of the Collins family, with stories set in Collinwood in the eighteenth and nineteenth centuries. Joan Bennett, whose movie career had spanned four decades, starred as family matriarch Elizabeth Collins Stoddard. But the most popular character, particularly with teenage viewers, was Barnabas Collins (Jonathan Frid), a 175-year-old vampire who emerges from his unchained coffin in search of the spirit of his beloved wife, Josette du Pres (Mary Cooper), who committed suicide when she discovered she had married a vampire. There is also an evil witch named Angelique (Lara Parker) and a werewolf named Quentin (David Selby).

At the time of its cancellation, the current storyline was set at Collinwood, in the year 1841. Borrowing a plotline from the Shirley Jackson short story "The Lottery," the final storyline revolved around the curse on the Collins family and a lottery that's held every generation that requires the "winner" to spend the night in a locked room where he or she is likely to die or go mad (*Dark Shadows* also "borrowed" from other literary classics, including *The Picture of Dorian Gray*, *The Turn of the Screw*, and *Rebecca*). In the final episode, Catherine (Lara Parker), who was recently married to Morgan Collins (Keith Prentice), spends the night in the room with her lover, Morgan's cousin, Bramwell (Jonathan Frid), when Morgan, enraged that his wife is carrying Bramwell's baby, locks them in. They survive the night and the Collins curse has finally been lifted. Afterwards, Morgan shoots Bramwell, who survives and, with some help, fights Morgan, who falls to his death from the roof of Collinwood.

All is well—until Melanie Collins (Nancy Barrett) is found in the woods with two bite marks on her neck. Is there a vampire on the loose in Collinsport? Apparently not, at least according to the final piece of narration, recited by actor Thayer David. To the haunting melody of Bob Cobert's theme music, the camera turns to a portrait of Barnabas as David's voice reassures us:

> There was no vampire loose on the great estate. For the first time in Collinwood, the marks on the neck were indeed [those] of an animal. Melanie soon recovered and went to live in Boston with her beloved Kendrick. There they prospered and had three children. Bramwell and Catherine were soon married, and at Flora's insistence, stayed on in

Collinwood, where Bramwell assumed control of the Collins business interests. Their love became a living legend. And for as long as they lived, the Dark Shadows at Collinwood were but a memory of the distant past.

The camera turns to a portrait of Barnabas and then moves back into the drawing room toward a window, through which lightning flashes and thunder claps.

Writer Sam Hall, husband of actress Grayson Hall, who played Dr. Julia Hoffman, penned an article for *TV Guide* that answered questions viewers had regarding the fate of the present day characters. Nevertheless, the cult of *Dark Shadows* remained alive by the fans.

Dan Curtis, the creator of *Dark Shadows*, directed and produced two feature-length films while the show was on the air—*House of Dark Shadows* (1970) and *Night of Dark Shadows* (1971). Curtis's later television credits (as director and producer) include the epic mini-series, *The Winds of War* (1983) and *War and Remembrance* (1988–1989), and a short-lived, prime-time revival of *Dark Shadows* (1991), starring Ben Cross as Barnabas Collins and Jean Simmons as Elizabeth Collins Stoddard. A 2012 film directed by Tim Burton, starring Johnny Depp as Barnabas, received mixed reviews and underperformed at the box office in the United States, but did better overseas. The film is part horror film, part comedy, but the film is not scary or funny enough to satisfy die-hard *Dark Shadows* fans, who still remain loyal to the original more than forty years after its demise.

The Doctors (NBC, 4/1/1963–12/31/1982) Created by Orin Tovrov; 19 seasons / 5,280 episodes

The NBC soap opera *The Doctors* started as an anthology series with plotlines that were self-contained within a single episode. After three months, plotlines were expanded over a single week until the show adopted the standard serial format in March of 1964. Each episode started with announcer Mel Brandt's introduction: "And now, *The Doctors*—the program dedicated to the brotherhood of healing." When the show won the Emmy as Best Drama series in 1972 (the first time the award was given) and 1974, "Emmy-winning" preceded "program" in the introduction.

The Doctors revolved around the personal and professional lives of doctors and nurses at Hope Memorial Hospital in the town of Madison, with the usual love affairs, flings, breakups, marriages, divorces, illness, and murder. The show's popularity peaked in the late 1960s and early 1970s, but the ratings started to fall in the late 1970s due, in part, to a change in the show's 2:30 p.m. time slot, which *The Doctors* had occupied for sixteen years. In the early 1980s, *The Doctors* became the lowest rated soap on the air, forcing NBC to cancel the show. Toward the end of its run, the plotlines became more outlandish. The finale wrapped up a major plotline involving the death of bad boy Billy Aldrich (Alec Baldwin), who is murdered by Felicia Hunt (Nancy Stafford) while impersonating her daughter, Adrienne, thanks to a serum created by a French doctor. Dr. Jeff Manning (Michael J. Stark) falls in love with Adrienne, but it's actually Felicia in disguise. When the serum wears off, Felicia ages rapidly. Jeff marries the real Adrienne (also played by Stafford), even though the "Adrienne" with whom he fell in love was actually her mother. Felicia is arrested for murder, though it's later revealed that there was a second shooter—the detective investigating the case, Lt. Paul Reed (Mark Goddard).

The series ended with a combination wedding/New Year's Eve party, where we see, for the last time, the show's major couples. Newlyweds Adrienne and Jeff will live happily ever after. Dr. Matt Powers (James Pritchett, who was with the series from the beginning) and Maggie (Lydia Bruce) announce they are remarrying. Mike (Peter Burnell) and Kit (Hillary Bailey) admit they are in love. Dr. Steve Aldrich (David O'Brien) and Carolee Simpson Aldrich (Jada Rowland) hope 1983 will be a better year (despite the fact that their show has been canceled). In the final moment, Matt makes a toast "to the future" and the clock strikes midnight.

The Edge of Night (CBS, 4/2/1956–11/28/1975; ABC, 12/1/1975–12/28/1984) Created by Irving Vendig; 28 seasons / 7,420 episodes

Irving Vendig, a writer on the *Perry Mason* radio show, was originally hired to adapt Erle Stanley Gardner's *Perry Mason* book series into a daytime drama, but the author refused to give his permission (the prime-time series, starring Raymond Burr, debuted on CBS in 1957). Retaining the original concept of a daytime soap in the tradition of the crime drama/mystery, Vendig created *The Edge of Night*. In their positive review of the soap five years into its run, *Time* magazine described the show's setting, Monticello, as "an average U.S. city" with a "substandard life expectancy" where "crime, litigation, fraud, false arrest, domestic tragedy and incurable disease are commoner than the common cold. In fact, as Keats said of London, Hell is a city much like Monticello." The show's heavy emphasis on crime broadened its appeal. According to Christopher Schemering, author of *The Soap Opera Encyclopedia*, *The Edge of Night* was an immediate hit and 50 percent of its viewership were men.

The show's main protagonist, crime fighter Mike Karr, begins the series as a cop and a recent law school graduate who works his way up to assistant district attorney and, finally, district attorney of Monticello. Played by three actors (John Larkin, Laurence Hugo, and Forrest Compton), Karr is the only character to appear on the series from the beginning to the end. Toward the end of its run, the producers tried to appeal to a younger audience by replacing some of the veteran actors with younger, fresher faces. But *The Edge of Night*'s audience continued to dwindle and on October 29, 1984, *Variety* reported that after twenty-eight years on the air, *The Edge of Night* was canceled due to low ratings. At the time, only 62 percent of ABC's affiliates (106 stations) were even carrying the show.

In the series finale, Miles Cavanaugh (Joel Crothers), ties the knot with thirty-four-year-old virgin Beth Correll (Sandy Faison), who patches things up with her sister, Liz (*Desperate Housewives*' Marcia Cross), who leaves town with Preacher (Charles Flohe), who has broken up with Jody (Karrie Emerson). Geraldine Whitney Saxon (Lois Kibbee) accepts Del Emerson's (Robert Gerringer) marriage proposal, but first he must sign a pre-nuptial agreement

In what seemed like Procter & Gamble's attempt to keep *The Edge of Night* going in case it finds a new home, the series ends with the start of another mystery. Detective Chris Egan (Jennifer Taylor) gets lost in the snowy streets of Monticello and experiences an *Alice in Wonderland*–themed nightmare. She follows Alicia Van Dine (Chris Weatherhead), who disappeared in a snowstorm, into an antique store on Wonderland Lane, where Alicia is knifed in the back by her supposedly imprisoned brother Louis (Jerry Zaks). Donald Hext (Ralph Byers), who died in a fencing duel with Sky Whitney (Larkin Malloy), appears behind Chris. She manages to escape and tries to bring police officers back to the shop, but they can't locate it. Was it real or did she imagine it? Confused and upset, she tells everyone at the post-wedding gathering what happened. We don't hear Mike Karr's reaction to the story because music plays over the dialogue. Sky hears a knock at the door and opens it. He finds a fencing sword—like the one he used in his duel with Donald.

A final message appears on the screen: "Happy Holidays and a fond farewell from the Cast and Crew of *The Edge of Night*."

Guiding Light (CBS, 6/30/1952–9/18/2009) Created by Irna Phillips; 57 seasons / 15,762 episodes

On April 2, 2009, *Variety* ran an article by Michael Schneider with the ominous headline: "Long-running 'Light' Goes Dark at CBS." The "Light" is *Guiding Light* (not *The Guiding Light* as "The" was dropped from the title in 1975), the current record holder for the longest-running drama in American television history. *Light* started on NBC radio on January 25, 1937, and moved over to CBS Radio in 1947, where it ran through June 29, 1956. Meanwhile, the television version debuted on CBS on June 30, 1952. For four years, each episode, which was fifteen minutes in length, could be seen and heard on the same day. The actors first performed live in front of the television camera and then did a live repeat performance for radio later in the day. The location was

Guiding Light's super couple: Reva Shayne (Kim Zimmer) and Joshua Lewis (Robert Newman).   *CBS Photo Archive/Getty Images*

changed to Springfield, a midwestern city, and the focus shifted to the Bauer family.

Guiding Light was the second-highest rated soap throughout the 1960s, right behind *As the World Turns*, though it dropped by a few ratings points in the 1970s with the rising popularity of *General Hospital*. In the early 1980s, the show got a bump in the ratings with a storyline focusing on four high school friends, each a member of one of the show's four core families—Beth Raines (Judi Evans), Phillip Spaulding (Grant Aleksander), Mindy Lewis (Krista Tesreau), and Rick Bauer (Michael O'Leary). Viewers were introduced around the same time to Reva Shayne (Kim Zimmer), who was one-half of the show's super couple with Josh Lewis (Robert Newman). During her years on the show (1983–1990, 1995–2009), Zimmer's character was married nine times to seven different men, presumed dead three times, and diagnosed with manic depression and cancer. While she was being treated with chemo and radiation for leukemia during menopause, she gives birth to her son, Colin. But her most outrageous storyline involved Josh cloning Reva, who is presumed to be dead. Her clone, Dolly, who accelerates in age, captures Reva when she returns to town. Josh rescues Reva and her clone kills herself by taking an overdose of a serum that ages her at an accelerated rate. The clone story, which aired in 1998, actually boosted the ratings, though once the ratings started to steadily decline, budget cuts were made and older characters were written out of the show. Ellen Wheeler (an Emmy winner and former cast member of *All My Children* and *Another World*) also updated the look of *Guiding Light* by redesigning the sets, incorporating more on-location shooting, and shooting the show with a hand-held digital camera. But the ratings kept going down until the show was finally canceled.

Three million viewers tuned in to the series finale, which succeeded in providing some closure to the remaining storylines. There's an impromptu wedding between Remy and Christina, who are having a baby. Rick tells Phillip and Beth that Mindy is moving back to town, which means the Four Musketeers will be reunited. Reva meets Josh at Cross Creek. He's changed his plans and is going to Oklahoma to oversee the new wing of the HB Lewis Hospital. He tells her he loves her, but they both admit they are not yet ready to be together. He promises to come back in a year and meet her at the lighthouse.

One year later, we see most of the characters all together; many of them are now parents. At the lighthouse, Reva and her son, Colin, are reunited with Josh. Reva and Josh profess their love to each other and they drive away in his truck.

Guiding Light fans ultimately got what they want—Reva and Josh (and Colin) driving off together towards the future.

Love Is a Many Splendored Thing (CBS, 9/18/1967–3/23/1973)
Created by Irna Phillips; 6 seasons / 1,430 episodes

This soap opera was based on the glossy 1955 film starring Jennifer Jones as Han Suyin, a doctor of Chinese and European descent who falls in love with an American newspaper correspondent, Mark Elliot (William Holden) in Hong Kong during China's Communist revolution. In adapting the film for television, Irna Phillips, creator of *Guiding Light* and *As the World Turns*, jumps ahead in time with the arrival of Han and Mark's daughter, Mia Elliot (Nancy Hsueh), in San Francisco to study medicine. She meets Mark's family and falls in love with a doctor, though when she finds out he performed an illegal abortion that resulted in her friend's death, she returns to Hong Kong. Another storyline involved a nun, Laura Donnelly (Donna Mills), who has romantic feelings for her sister's boyfriend. In the *Encyclopedia of Daytime Television*, Wesley Hyatt recounts how CBS daytime president Fred Silverman was not pleased with storylines involving an interracial romance, abortion, and a self-doubting nun. In protest, Phillips left the show and the soap continued with less controversial storylines involving a divorce, adoption, custody battles, adultery, nervous breakdowns, etc.

The final episode ends with the outdoor wedding of Joe Taylor (Leon Russom) and Betsy Chernak (Andrea Marcovicci). Spence (Brett Halsey) helps a very nervous Joe out before the wedding. Dr. Peter Chernak (Vincent Baggetta), who is unable to cure his terminally ill wife, Angel (Suzie Kaye Stone), vows to make the most of their remaining time together. Joe and Betsy exchange vows. She reads an excerpt from Elizabeth Barrett Browning and he reads from Walt Whitman. Afterwards, they say goodbye to everyone and go off on their honeymoon. Judson Laire, who plays Dr. Will Donnelly, then steps out of character and addresses the audience directly, thanking them for watching the show:

> There goes Betsy and Joe, off to a new life. I think this is probably the happiest moment for the Donnellys and the Chernaks, the Garrisons, and the Elliots, and the Taylors. But it's a very sad moment for those of us actors who played those characters. I think by now most of you must know that *Love is a Many Splendored Thing* is going off the air with this episode. On behalf of my fellow actors, I would like to tell you how much we enjoyed the privilege of coming into your home for these five and a half years. It's not going to be easy for us. It's hard to say goodbye. But, maybe we'll live on in your memories. It now becomes my sad duty to say goodbye to you on behalf of the entire company—the cast, the crew, the production staff, the writers and the directors . . . all of us. Goodbye, and God bless you.

Love of Life (CBS, 9/24/1951–2/1/1980) Created by Roy Winsor; 29 seasons / 7,316 episodes

Roy Winsor, whose soap-writing career began in radio, created three long-running soaps for CBS in the 1950s: *Love of Life* (1951–1980), *Search for Tomorrow* (1951–1986), and *The Secret Storm* (1954–1974). *Love of Life* was originally set in Barrowsville, New York, though the setting was later changed to another small town, Rosehill, in upstate New York. Barrowsville was home to the Dale sisters—good girl Vanessa, played by Audrey Peters for most of the show's run (1959–1980), and the devious Meg (Tudi Wiggins), whose character was written out in 1958, only to return in 1974 to stir up trouble.

The show was canceled without sufficient time to resolve major storylines, including the trial of Ben Harper (Chandler Hill Harben), who was accused of assaulting his ex-wife, Betsy Crawford (Margo McKenna), who married Ben and became pregnant with his child, unaware that he was a bigamist, married at the time to Arlene Lovett (Birgitta Tolksdorf). Although Arlene divorced him, Betsy refused to marry him and marries Elliott Lang (Ted LePlat), a lawyer, instead. When Ben tries to protect Betsy from a snake with a boat oar, he accidentally hits her, causing her to lose her baby. Betsy leaves the hospital and goes to the courtroom to testify. She tells the truth about the snake, but collapses in the middle of her testimony. Apparently her health had deteriorated to the point that she was on the brink of death. But viewers never learned the fate of Betsy and Ben. The credits roll as the camera moves through an empty studio as we hear Tony Bennett singing "We'll Be Together Again." We then see *Love of Life* director Larry Auerbach, who had been with the show for twenty-eight years, silently walking through the studio. Before exiting, he activates the door to Studio 41, which closes. Fade to black.

Toward the end of its run, there was an attempt to save *Love of Life* by moving the show from the morning to the 4:00 p.m. time slot in most cities. As Auerbach explained in a report that aired on *CBS Evening News with Walter Cronkite*, a 4:00 p.m time slot for a serial is a tough sell to affiliates, who would rather air programs that will appeal to kids watching television after school.

Part of *Love of Life*'s legacy is that it marked the television debut of many future TV stars, including Bonnie Bedelia (Sandy Porter), Bert Convy (Glenn Hamilton), Dana Delany (Amy Russell), Julia Duffy (Gerry Braylee), Paul Michael Glaser (Dr. Joe Corelli), Marsha Mason (Judith Cole), Christopher Reeve (Ben Harper), Roy Scheider (Jonas Falk), and Jessica Walter (Julie Murano).

One Life to Live (ABC, 7/15/1968–1/13/2012; The OnLine Network, 4/29/2013–8/19/2013) Created by Agnes Nixon; 45 seasons / 11,136 episodes

Created by Agnes Nixon, *One Life to Live* broke new ground with its multi-ethnic cast of characters and its treatment of class issues. Like most soap operas, there is a wealthy family at the center of the story, The Lords—Victor, the patriarch, and his daughters Vicki and Meredith—who own the newspaper, *The Banner*, in Llanview, a suburban town outside of Philadelphia. They are surrounded by characters, and, in some instances, entire families from various ethnic and class backgrounds (the Rileys, an Irish-American Catholic family; Jewish lawyer Dave Siegel; the Woleks, a Polish-American Catholic family, etc.). As Christopher Schemering recounts, one early storyline involving Carla Gray, a light-skinned African American woman passing for white who dates a white doctor and a black medical intern, was too controversial for some ABC affiliates, who canceled the soap. But Nixon was adamant about doing socially relevant stories. A storyline about drug addiction even featured scenes that were reportedly taped at a drug rehabilitation center using real recovering addicts. Following the death of her father, Victor (a role originated by Ernest Graves), Victoria (Vicki) Lord (played by Erika Slezak from 1971 to the end of the run of the series), became the show's central character. Her nemesis was her stepmother, the manipulative Dr. Dorian Cramer, played by Emmy winner Robin Strasser. *One Life to Live* became the third highest rated soap on television in the 1980s thanks to a powerful storyline in which Vicki goes on trial for the murder of Marco Dane (Gerald Anthony). Judith Light won two Emmys for her portrayal of Karen Wolek, who took the stand during the Vicki's trial and admitted she was a prostitute. Around the same time, the Buchanan family moved to Llanview and provided the soap with a new patriarch, a Texan named Asa Buchanan (Philip Carey), who bore a close resemblance to J. R. Ewing, the lead character of *Dallas*, which was at the height of its popularity.

Dwindling ratings and rising costs were among the reasons ABC pulled the plug on both *One Life to Live* and *All My Children* (see above). Unlike *AMC*, the series finale of *OLTL*, which was watched by 3.8 million viewers, did not try to resolve some of the outstanding plotlines. Instead, there is a female narrator, though her identity is not revealed until the end.

Meanwhile, Starr Manning (Kristen Alderson) is elated when she is reunited with Cole (Van Hughes), who is alive and has been hired by her father to be her bodyguard. Destiny Evans (Shenell Edmonds) gives birth to Bo (Robert S. Woods) and Nora's (Hillary B. Smith) grandson. Their son, Matthew (Eddie Alderson), tells Destiny he's scared, but he will be there for her and the baby. After Blair (Kassie DePaiva) and Todd (Roger Howarth) make love, Detective John McBain (Michael Easton) barges in with a warrant for his arrest for the murder of Victor Lord Jr. (Trevor St. John). The question involving the paternity of Vicki's twin daughters, Jessica (Bree Williamson) and Natalie (Melissa Archer), is resolved as DNA tests reveal that Clint Buchanan (Jerry Van Dorn) is their biological father. Upon hearing the

Happily Ever After: *One Life to Live*'s Vicki Lord (Erika Slezak) and Clint Buchanan (Clint Ritchie).   *ABC/Photofest*

news, Clint gets down on one knee and proposes to Vicki. In the last scene, the narrator is identified as Allison Perkins (Barbara Garrick), Llanview's resident nutcase. She is holding a manuscript, which she flings at a man tied to a bed—it is none other than Victor Lord Jr.

Unlike *All My Children*, most of the major cast members of *One Life to Live* signed on for the reboot, including the show's star, Erika Slezak. In addition, several actors, including DePaiva, Howarth, Easton, and Kristen Alderson, reprised their characters on *General Hospital*. This sparked a legal battle between ABC and Prospect Park, which accused the network of trying to sabotage their reboot by killing off some of the *OLTL* characters and breaking up a popular couple, John and Natalie, by having John become romantically involved with *GH*'s Sam Morgan (Kelly Monaco, who was Easton's love interest on the *General Hospital* spinoff, *Port Charles*).

Meanwhile, the reboot of *OLTL* ran from April 29, 2013 through August 19, 2013. Prospect Park suspended production indefinitely, so it's unlikely we'll will ever get a chance to revisit Llanview.

Passions (NBC, 7/5/1999–7/7/2007; DirecTV 101, 9/17/2007–8/7/2008) Created by James E. Reilly; 9 seasons / 2,231 episodes

Set in the Eastern seaport town of Harmony, *Passions* was one of television's most original and bizarre soap operas. On one hand, the plotlines involve the same complications one expects to find on a daytime drama (star-crossed lovers, amnesia, adultery, etc.), but with a heavy emphasis on murder and sexual violence (both female and male characters were raped). Characters also died at an alarming rate. At the same time, *Passions* delved deeply into the supernatural with one of its breakout characters being a bona fide witch named Tabitha Lenox, played by British actress Juliet Mills. But *Passions* is best remembered for its camp sensibility, particularly its parodies of popular films and musicals (like *Titanic*, *The Wizard of Oz*, *Wicked*, *The Little Mermaid*, *Brokeback Mountain*) and television series, specifically the 1960s fantasy sitcom *Bewitched*, not only in terms of characters' names (Tabitha, Endora), but an actual character from the show, Dr. Bombay (played by the same actor, Bernard Fox). One of the most unusual pieces of casting was the recurring role of a live-in nurse named Precious, played by an orangutan named BamBam (who was deemed ineligible by the Television Academy for an Emmy nomination).

After eight seasons, NBC canceled *Passions*, which ended its run on the network in 2007, though DirecTV picked up the series and ran original episodes through 2008, when it was finally put to rest. The show's finale was centered around the wedding of Theresa (Lindsay Hartley) and Ethan (Eric Martsolf), but before they say "I do," Father Lonigan (Bruce French) baptizes Tabitha, which rids Harmony of all of its black magic, demons, and evil, transforming Tabitha into a good witch. She then restores Father Lonigan's eyesight and zaps Theresa into a wedding dress so she can walk down the aisle and marry Ethan. After they exchange vows, Theresa turns to the camera and says, "So, after all these years, I have learned one thing for sure. Always follow your passion. Because that, and that alone, will lead you to your happy ending." Ethan winks at the camera. Balloons fall and the actors smile and wave at the camera. Mills is holding a picture of her late co-star, twenty-year-old Josh Ryan Evans, who played Timmy, a doll Tabitha brought to life. Evans, who was only three feet two, due to achondroplasia, a form of dwarfism, died from a congenital heart condition on August 5, 2002 (the same day his character died on the show). A final message appears on a black screen: "From all of us, to all of you . . . Thank you." Cut back to the church where the cast is joined by the entire crew and production staff as a recording of Evans singing "Auld Lang Syne" is played.

Ryan's Hope (ABC, 7/7/1975–1/13/1989) Created by Claire Labine and Paul Avila Mayer; 13 seasons / 3,515 episodes

Ryan's Hope focused on a large Irish-American Catholic family—Johnny (Bernard Barrow) and Maeve (Helen Gallagher) Ryan and their five children—who own a bar and grill in the Riverside area of the Upper West Side of New York City. The Ryans brought a much-needed dose of ethnicity to the predominantly non-ethnic world of daytime drama, though there was a clash of values within the family between Johnny and Maeve and their adult children, who grew up in a very different world than their immigrant parents. Over the course of 13 seasons, most of the Ryan children were recast multiple times (or, in the case of Mary Ryan, murdered), which posed a serious challenge for the writers. In the early 1980s, the show's creators/head writers, Claire Labine and Paul Avila Mayer, were replaced by a new head writer, Mary Ryan Munisteri, who introduced a new family, the wealthy Kirklands, though it didn't help the show's sagging ratings. Labine and Mayer briefly returned to the show, though neither the new writers that followed nor the introduction of teenage characters helped to raise the ratings. *Ryan's Hope* landed at the very bottom of the daytime ratings during its 1987–1988 seasons.

For its final episode, the show returned to its roots with a gathering in the Ryan family pub and Maeve singing a traditional Irish ballad, "Danny Boy."

Ryan's Hope lives on (in a way). Delia Ryan (Ilene Kristen), the show's breakout character, is a master manipulator who gets what she wants and won't let anyone stand in her way. Her many "crimes" include shoving her husband down the stairs and then cheating on him; faking a miscarriage and a mental breakdown; running someone over with a car; and kidnapping a pregnant woman. When she was accidentally shoved down a flight of stairs she lost her vision, but continued to pretend she was blind after regaining her sight. In 2014, Delia was revealed to be the mother of *General Hospital*'s Ava Jerome (Maura West), the daughter of the late mobster Victor Jerome (Jack Axelrod), with whom Delia had an affair. Delia currently resides in New York City, where she runs a pub that looks very, very familiar.

Santa Barbara (NBC, 7/30/1984–1/15/1993) Created by Bridget Dobson and Jerome Dobson; 9 seasons / 2,137 episodes

A soap opera set in Santa Barbara, California, an actual place (a rarity on daytime television), *Santa Barbara* won the Emmy for Best Daytime Drama three years in a row (1988, 1989, and 1990), despite the fact that throughout its nine-year run, the soap ranked no. 10 (or lower) in the Nielsen ratings for daytime soap operas. The show's premise was also unusual because one of the central plots revolved around a character named C. C. Capwell (played by four different actors in flashbacks), who was murdered back in 1979. The show initially focused on the wealthy Lockridge family, whose matriarch, Minx Lockridge was played by Australian actress Dame Judith Anderson, who is best known for playing Mrs. Danvers in Hitchcock's *Rebecca* (1940). But the show's breakout stars were super couple Eden Capwell (Marcy Walker) and Cruz Castillo (A Martinez).

Santa Barbara was never a ratings juggernaut, but it was an international hit, airing in forty-eight countries, including France, where it was shown in prime-time. Still, low ratings led NBC to axe the show in January of 1993. In the final episode, B. J. (Sydney Penny) and Warren (Jack Wagner) are married. Connor McCabe (Charles Grant), who ends up with Kelly Capwell (Eileen Davidson), prevents the mentally unbalanced Andie Klein (Krista Tesreau) (there's one on every soap) from shooting the guests. Wesley Hyatt calls the show's ending "one of the worst close-outs in TV history." The final shot is of producer Paul Rauch walking across an empty soundstage and throwing his cigarette butt on the ground and rubbing it out with his foot. No argument here. But it was the last in a long list of credits, which began, of course, with the main actors appearing onscreen alongside their names. The same is also done for the entire staff and crew—from the producers and writers all the way down to the production assistants. Acknowledging everyone's contribution to the show is a rarity on television—and a classy way to sign-off.

Search for Tomorrow (CBS, 9/3/1951–3/26/1982; NBC, 3/29/1982–12/26/1986) Created by Roy Winsor; 35 seasons / 9,130 episodes

For thirty years, actress Mary Stuart starred as heroine Joanne Gardner Barron Tate Vincente Tourneur (a.k.a. "Jo"), who lived in Henderson, a small midwestern town. Jo was a survivor who endured her share of tragedies—the death of her infant son, the death of several lovers and husbands (including one who went missing, was declared dead, and came back mentally unbalanced), blindness, a gunshot wound, nearly drowning during a flood that devastated the town—and one divorce.

Search for Tomorrow aired in the same time slot (12:30 p.m.) on CBS for thirty years, but the ratings dropped a bit when the network moved it to 2:30 p.m. Procter & Gamble wanted the show's original time slot back, but CBS refused and, despite its respectable ratings, canceled the show. NBC picked up the show and aired it in its original time slot, where it remained for the end of its run.

In the final scene, Jo and Stu Bergman (Larry Haines, who debuted on the show back in 1951) are talking outside on a wintery night. He asks what she's searching for. She replies, "Tomorrow, and I can't wait."

We hear the voice of the show's announcer: "On this, our final telecast, the cast, staff, and crew of *Search for Tomorrow* thank you for your support and your loyalty. We wish you a healthy and happy new year."

Lou Rawls sings, "We'll Be Together Again" as the credits roll with each actor waving or blowing a kiss as his or her name appears on the screen. At the very end, there's Mary Stuart, who says, "Thank you. Thank you all. They were wonderful years."

The Secret Storm (CBS, 2/1/1954–2/8/1974) Created by Roy Winsor; 20 seasons / 5,195 episodes

In the first episode of *The Secret Storm*, Ellen Ames (Ellen Cobb-Hill) dies in a car accident, leaving her husband, Peter (Peter Hobbs), alone to raise their three children. The youngest daughter, seventeen-year-old Amy (Jada Rowland), was the focus of the show's early episodes. Peter eventually marries a woman named Valerie Hill (Lori March).

In the early days of the show, the narrator closed each episode by saying: "You have been watching *The Secret Storm*, the story of the Ames family and deep-rooted emotions, and how these emotions are stirred up to becoming 'the secret storm.'" The Ames family didn't necessarily remain at the foreground of the show's storylines, which broke new ground with a romance between a woman and a Catholic priest. Low ratings prompted CBS to cancel the series after twenty years.

According to John Kelly Genovese, *The Secret Storm* ended with many characters being cured of whatever ailed them: Laurie Reddin (Stephanie Braxton) realizes she isn't crazy and that someone is only making her feel that way; her husband, Mark (David Gale), who is cured of his drinking problem, leaves Laurie and reenters the priesthood; and Mark's brother, Stace (Gary Sandy), is cured of his selfishness. In the final scene, Stace's friend Kevin (David Ackroyd) is cured of his paralysis and is able to walk toward his wife, Amy.

The Secret Storm is perhaps best remembered for a 1968 appearance by Hollywood legend Joan Crawford. When her daughter, Christina, who played twenty-four-year-old housewife Joan Kane, landed in the hospital, her mother briefly stepped into the role. For those who tuned in on those days can attest—Oscar or no Oscar—sixty-four-year-old Joan was not very convincing playing a housewife in her twenties.

Somerset (NBC, 3/30/1970–12/31/1976) Created by Robert Cenedella; 6 seasons / 1,710 episodes

The first official soap opera spinoff, the original title of this 1970s daytime drama was *Another World in Somerset* (the title was shorted to *Somerset* in March 1971). Three characters from *Another World*, Sam Lucas (Jordan Charney), an ex-convict who is now a lawyer, and his wife, Lahoma (Ann Wedgeworth), and Missy Matthews (Carol Roux), traveled an hour outside of Bay City to the mid-sized town of Somerset, located in the suburbs of Detroit, Michigan. Missy only lasted six months; Sam and Lahoma left three years into the run of the show, which focused on crime and mystery stories, including one involving a clown named Jingles who is poisoning innocent young Andrea Moore (Harriet Hall). Underneath the clown mask was the mentally ill Zoe Cannell (Lois Smith), who was convinced that Andrea was trying to steal her husband.

Somerset never matched the success of its sister show, *Another World*. Christopher Schemering attributes the show's demise to an excessive number of writing, producing, and casting changes, the lack of a "core family," and plotlines that were too short and too outlandish.

Texas (NBC, 8/4/1980–12/31/1982) Created by John William Corrington, Joyce Hooper Corrington, and Paul Rauch; 2 seasons / 617 episodes

In an attempt to capitalize on the success of the prime-time soap opera *Dallas*, the co-head writers of *Another World*, John Williams Corrington and Joyce Hooper Corrington, along with the show's executive producer, Paul Rauch, co-created this *AW* spinoff about three Houston families—the Wheelers, the Bellmans, and the Marshalls. In the first episode, the scheming Iris Cory Carrington (Beverlee McKinsey), who spent her time on *Another World* interfering with her father, Mac Cory's (Douglass Watson) relationship with Rachel (Victoria Wyndham), travels to Houston to visit her son, Dennis (Jim Poyner), and is reunited with her former lover, millionaire Alex Wheeler (Bert Kramer), who is really the boy's father. In the end, it didn't matter because Alex was murdered in a mob-related story.

With the departure of McKinsey from the cast, there was an attempt to revamp the show, complete with a new title, *Texas: The Next Generation*, which emphasized younger characters and story arcs classified by Schemering as "love-on-the-run plotlines" straight out of *General Hospital*. On November 24, 1982, *Variety* announced the cancellation of two NBC soaps: *The Doctors* (see above) and *Texas*, which, in the daytime Nielsen ratings, ranked no. 23 and no. 34, respectively. At the end of the show's run, there was a major Christmas miracle when it started snowing in Texas, and Ashley (Pamela Long Hammer), presumed dead, returns home with some help from an angel, in time to deliver her baby.

In the final episode, set on New Year's Eve, Judith Wheeler (Sharon Acker) reveals that she can walk, thus freeing her soon-to-be ex-husband, Grant (Donald May), to marry Reena (Carla Borelli). Victoria Bellman (Elizabeth Allen), who lost her television station (KVIK), gives a farewell speech to her employees, though it doubles as a farewell speech from the producers to the cast. They sing "Auld Lang Syne" and Justin Marshall (Jerry Lanning) raises his glass for a toast: "To Texas!"

One Final Word

Donahue and *Oprah* Sign Off

The Phil Donahue Show/Donahue (1967–1996)

Produced by WLWD-TV (Dayton, Ohio), 1967–1974; WGN-TV (Chicago), 1974–1982; WBBM-TV (Chicago), 1982–1985; WNBC-TV (New York City, 1985–1996)

National Syndication (1970–1996)

Production/Distribution: AVCO Embassy Television (1970–1976), Multimedia Entertainment (1976–1996)

Premiere date: November 6, 1967

29 seasons / 5,515 episodes

Final show aired September 13, 1996

Phil Donahue, host

The Oprah Winfrey Show (1986–2011)

Produced by Harpo Studios

Distributed by King World Productions (1986–2007) and CBS Television Distribution (2007–2011)

Premiere date: September 8, 1986

25 seasons / 4,561 episodes

Final show aired May 25, 2011

Oprah Winfrey, host

In 1992, Phil Donahue celebrated the twenty-fifth anniversary of his talk show with a 90-minute prime-time special. Among the guests were fellow talk show hosts Larry King, Sally Jesse Raphael, Geraldo Rivera, and the "Queen of Daytime" herself, Oprah Winfrey. At the end of the show, he introduced "the heart, the soul, and the brains of *The Donahue Show*"— executive producer Patricia McMillen, who had been working alongside him and warming up his audience before each taping since 1967. Donahue then graciously invited everyone who worked behind the scenes at his show to come up onstage.

Four years later, on September 13, 1996, "The King of Daytime Talk" sat center stage on the *Donahue* set for his final show. He ended his twenty-nine year run as America's preeminent daytime talk show host with a retrospective co-hosted by McMillen. Over the next hour, the pair shared clips of some of their more provocative guests and segments with viewers and the studio audience, which included many of Donahue's personal friends and associates.

Watching Donahue's twenty-fifth anniversary special and his last show is a powerful reminder of the invaluable contribution Donahue—both the show and its host—made to daytime television by providing a forum for an open, frank dialogue about issues and topics that were considered at the time to be too controversial for television, especially during daylight hours. A staunch supporter of the women's rights movement, Donahue shared his microphone with his studio audience, who were mostly women, thereby giving them a chance to voice their opinions. In a 1992 interview with Kathy Haley, Donahue reflected on a question he was frequently asked regarding his studio audience: "Where did you get those bright women in the audience?" According to Donahue, the sexist attitude behind the question was the product of a time when "housewives were condescended to, patronized. Most certainly by the white male figures that were in the power management places of broadcasting. Women cared about soap operas, game shows, covered dishes and fashion."

Donahue's broadcasting career began in Dayton, Ohio, at WHIO-AM-TV, where he read morning news reports on the radio and worked as a reporter for the station's television newscast. In a profile of Donahue, Nimmo and Newsome explain how, as a street reporter, Donahue conducted interviews with two controversial figures: Jimmy Hoffa, a union activist with the International Brotherhood of Teamsters who disappeared in July of 1975, and Billy Sol Estes, a businessman and friend of President Lyndon Johnson who was sent to jail for mortgage fraud. Both interviews were picked up nationally. Donahue hosted his own afternoon call-in radio talk show, *Conversation Piece*, and after a short stint working in sales, he was hired to host his own talk show in Dayton.

The Phil Donahue Show debuted on November 6, 1967, and his early guests included a gynecologist, an undertaker, an anatomically correct "Little Brother" doll, and the controversial founder of American Atheists, Madalyn Murray O'Hair. According to Nimmo and Newsome, while Donahue was interviewing O'Hair, a group of people walked into the studio to watch a variety show that had previously occupied Donahue's time slot. The station management decided to honor their tickets and have them watch Donahue's show instead. During the broadcast, Donahue invited the audience members

Phil Donahue, host of the longest running syndicated daytime talk show in television history (1967–1996).   *NBC/Photofest*

to ask O'Hair questions. He eventually adopted this format in which the audience became active participants in the show. In Kathy Daly's history of the show, aptly titled "From Dayton to the World," Richard Mincer, a producer/director who helped launch the show and later became its executive producer (1968–1985), added that initially the studio audience just sat and watched, but they would feed Donahue questions during the commercial breaks. He eventually had the audience members ask their questions themselves.

After five years in Dayton, *Donahue* moved west and spent the next eleven years in Chicago and then New York City for the remainder of its run, where it originated from Studio 8-G, the future home of *The Rosie O'Donnell Show* and *Late Night with Seth Meyers*. In "From Dayton to the World," McMillen admitted to Kathy Haley that the move to New York City brought "new energy to the show" because "the New York audience was more aggressive and more willing to stand up and say what was on its mind."

For its first three years (1967–1970), Donahue's show aired locally in Ohio until it was nationally syndicated in 1970. A *Variety* ad (January 14,

1970) by the show's syndication company, Avco Embassy, aimed at television stations not currently carrying the show, posed the question, "Have you been programming for the wrong audience?" The ad discourages stations from going after the youth market ("It isn't that American youth will not watch television but rather it doesn't watch very often") and encourages them to pick up *The Phil Donahue Show*, which draws a largely female audience. Women who worked at home raising children and taking care of the house were Donahue's primary target demographic as his show continued to garner high ratings in the country's major television markets, including New York City, where it aired in the mornings on WNBC-TV.

Donahue proved there is an audience on daytime television for intellectual discussion on important social and political issues. His guests include politicians, authors, entertainers, actors, and ordinary people who were making news. A self-proclaimed liberal, Donahue was ahead of his time when tackling topical, controversial, and taboo issues, such as reproductive rights, sex, atheism, abortion, incest, and Holocaust deniers.

One controversial subject Donahue frequently addressed was homosexuality. Historian Charles Kaiser credits Donahue for exploring "every facet of the gay experience" and doing more "than anyone else to turn the exotic into the commonplace." In 1967, he had an "actual homosexual" on his show (Clark Polak, a gay activist and a member of the Mattachine Society), which would be the first of many shows about the topic. This led to Donahue's own realization, despite the teachings of the Catholic Church, that "gayness was not a moral issue." Donahue also addressed the subject of AIDS with activist Larry Kramer in 1982 at a time when the disease received virtually no media attention. His final episode also included footage from another daytime television first—two men exchanging marriage vows and sealing them with a kiss.

Donahue admitted that, at times, he had to feature sensationalistic topics to keep people watching, and on his series finale he shared some of the shows that generated the most viewer mail, including "Transvestite Fashion Show" (1988), "Lesbo-A-GoGo" (1991), and an interview with Joey Buttafuoco (1993), who was all over the news at the time when his sixteen-year-old girlfriend, Amy Fisher, shot his wife, Mary Jo, in the face. Donahue and McMillen admitted there was one show they wish they hadn't done—"Dressing Up Like a Baby for Sexual Pleasure" (1991). Donahue explained that they never actually addressed the issue of sexual pleasure, yet, as McMillen points out, "everyone knew what we were talking about."

In his final episode, Donahue mentioned his first and one of his most famous guests, Madalyn Murray O'Hair, founder of American Atheists, who played an instrumental role in the legal battle banning prayer from public school, Engel v. Vitale, 370 U.S. 421 (1962). McMillen explained that they tried to contact O'Hair but she couldn't be located; they were informed, however, that she was busy traveling, and that she was well. What McMillen and Donahue didn't know was that O'Hair, along with her son and grand-daughter, had been kidnapped and murdered and their bodies mutilated and buried on a Texas ranch.

At a time when the airwaves were saturated with talk shows (the long list of hosts included Oprah Winfrey, Rosie O'Donnell, Ricki Lake, Gordon Elliot, Sally Jesse Raphael, Geraldo Rivera, and Montel Williams), Donahue's rat-ings were sliding, so when the show was not picked up in New York and San Francisco, it was time to pull the plug. Donahue made a highly anticipated return to television with the debut of his new show, *Donahue*, on MSNBC in 2002. The cancellation, after seven months, was supposedly due to low ratings, but as *The Nation*'s John Nichols reported, Donahue's ratings, which were higher than other shows on the network, were not the problem. His firing was due to his opposition to the invasion of Iraq (his show was canceled the night before the invasion) because, according to a memo circulated by NBC, the company feared his show could become a "home for the liberal antiwar agenda at the same time that our competitors are waving the flag at every opportunity." Donahue would go on to co-direct, with Ellen Spiro, *Body of War* (2007), a portrait of an Iraq War veteran, Tomas Young, who answered President George W. Bush's call to duty to fight terrorism after 9/11 and was paralyzed by a bullet during his first week in Iraq.

After twenty-nine years and over 6,000 shows, the end of *The Phil Donahue Show* seemed rather abrupt. As for his final episode, an hour can go by very quickly, and, in the end, it was simply not enough time to pay tribute to the man who had revolutionized the daytime talk show.

In the late 1980s, when *Donahue* was still going strong, the media manu-factured a rivalry between "King of Daytime Talk" Phil Donahue and its new queen, Oprah Winfrey. "Rivalry" is an overstatement because it implies that the two hosts were competing for viewers. In a 1988 article for the *New York Times*, Nan Robertson explained that *Donahue*'s show was currently broadcast in 187 cities across the country, airing in 149 cities in the morning and the remaining 38 in the late afternoon. *The Oprah Winfrey Show* was broadcast at the time in 192 cities, the majority of which (168) aired her show in the late afternoon. When Oprah received her first daytime Emmy the previous year, she acknowledged Phil Donahue in her acceptance speech for smoothing the path for her. She later said that one of the "biggest moments of my life" was when Donahue came up to her table after the ceremony and kissed her and told her she deserved the award. At that moment, she realized that the whole "rivalry" issue had been contrived by the media.

"If there never had been a Phil," Oprah explained, "there never would have been a me. I can talk about things now that I never could have talked about before he came on the air. There's room for both of us."

Oprah Winfrey had enjoyed a quarter-century of creating iconic television moments. From big draw interviews with controversial figures, to buzzworthy celebrity sit downs (or jump up-and-downs, thanks to Tom Cruise's infamous 2005 appearance), to chronicles of her constant struggle with weight (most notably 1988's 67-pound loss), spending an afternoon with Oprah had the promise of the unexpected—a promise only compounded by her unbelievable and elaborate audience giveaways (2004's "You get a car!" rings a bell). Scoring a ticket to *The Oprah Winfrey Show* felt very much like gaining entry to Willy Wonka's chocolate factory—a place where magic certainly did happen. This magic was not only limited to her legions of fans, but also to the books, products, and cultural gurus whom Oprah selected as worthy of her seal of approval. Counted among those catapulted to stardom thanks to her support are financial consultant Suze Orman, interior designer (and make-over king) Nate Berkus, down-to-earth foodie Rachael Ray, television's favorite M.D. Dr. Mehmet Oz, and fellow talk show straight-shooter Dr. Phil McGraw. Oprah's Book Club, launched in September of 1996, recommended seventy books during its fifteen-year run, with each immediately becoming a national bestseller. Choices like Tolstoy's *Anna Karenina*, and John Steinbeck's *East of Eden* revived classics, while Janet Fitch's *White Oleander* went from obscurity to become a Hollywood film starring Michelle Pfeiffer (a fate also dealt to Bernhard Schlink's *The Reader*, with the film version netting Kate Winslet an Oscar). Oprah's ability to anoint a product as a "must-have" item was never more apparent than with her over-the-top "Favorite Things" giveaways. Oprah's annual celebration of her carefully curated list of luxury goods spanned from decadent treats ($40 Williams-Sonoma Croissants, $135 Garrett Popcorn tins), to designer duds (Ralph Lauren cashmere, Tory Burch flats, Burberry jackets), to coveted electronics (Apple's iPad, Sony's 3D television), and all the way to vacations and cars (namely, Volkswagen's new Beetle in 2012). To have Oprah's official stamp of approval meant everything for these brands—bringing them from the luxury sphere to the heartland. Beyond the high-end items, Oprah's generosity also encouraged viewers to donate to her Angel Network (responsible for raising more than $50 million in the show's history), send deserving students to college (through her "world's largest piggy bank" drive), and contribute to the opening of The Oprah Winfrey

Leadership Academy for Girls in South Africa. The cult of Oprah was real and it was powerful—as fellow talk show host Phil Donahue once wrote to Oprah:

> You have carved out a world of huge crowds, where your audience members get cars and the President calls you back! And throughout this fabulous fairyland story, you have held to a noble purpose: you leave a legacy of responsible TV stewardship, a program that brought light to dark places and made us laugh, often at ourselves. There is no match for you in media history. You're not only hot, you're cool, the dream girl for millions of ambitious young women whom you have inspired all over the world.

And as it was time for Oprah to steer the ship to its dock, these same inspired fans, unsure of what was to come of television without its fearless leader, tuned in to see just how it would all end.

The official announcement of the impending end of *The Oprah Winfrey Show* was made on Friday, October 20, 2009. The evening before, Harpo Productions president Tim Bennett spread the word to station owners, hoping to boost ratings for the big announcement. In an e-mail, Bennett said: "The sun will set on the *Oprah* show as its twenty-fifth season draws to a close. . . . As we all know, Oprah's personal comments about this on Friday's live show will mark an historic television moment that we will all be talking about for years to come." Following interviews with both Gabourey Sidibe, star of the recently released film *Precious (based on the novel* Push *by Sapphire)*, and television veteran Ray Romano, Oprah faced her in-studio audience and at-home fans and tearfully announced that the series that launched an empire would come to a close after the completion of its twenty-fifth season. Oprah explained: "So why walk away and make next season the last? Here is the real reason—I love this show. This show has been my life. And I love it enough to know when it's time to say goodbye. Twenty-five years feels right in my bones, and it feels right in my spirit. It's the perfect number, the exact right time." Trusting one's own intuition had been advice Oprah, and her many guests, had dispensed over the course of her long-running show, so it seemed perfectly appropriate for the fearless leader to put her own words into practice. In just eighteen months after this announcement, Oprah Winfrey would stand on that same stage again and speak directly to her adoring fans, but this time, it was a final goodbye.

Before Oprah's parting words were spoken, in the true spirit of the show, an over-the-top decadent celebration was in order. Billed as "Surprise Oprah! A Farewell Spectacular," the two-part episode was shot at Chicago's United Center in front of more than 20,000 adoring fans (the show received nearly 154,000 ticket requests for the episode). In the two penultimate hours of her show, Oprah relinquished the power to her producers, allowing them to create a show filled with surprise guests and performances, all there to bid adieu to their favorite Big O. "I've given up control for the last two days," Oprah said, continuing: "It's a lot to relinquish. I had to pray on that . . . and get a guarantee from [executive producer] Sheri Salata there would be no strippers or dancing people coming out of shells." Oprah's request was honored, and instead, the show's first part was hosted by Tom Hanks, and welcomed guests like Tom Cruise, Madonna, Halle Berry, Queen Latifah, Katie Holmes, and Dakota Fanning, and hosted musical performances by Josh Groban, Rascal Flatts, Patti LaBelle, and pint-sized opera singer Jackie Evancho. Beyonce also appeared, performing her Girl Power anthem "Run the World (Girls)," while Diane Sawyer took to the stage to announce that retail giant Target would rebuild twenty-five school libraries in honor of Oprah's Book Club, as well as plant 25,000 oak trees around the country (to which Oprah joked: "I just gave everybody a tree! You get a tree and you get a tree and you get a tree! Everybody gets a tree!"). In part two, Tom Hanks handed over the hosting duty to Will Smith, who welcomed his wife, Jada Pinkett Smith, to the stage, as well as Oprah's best friend, Gayle King, and Jerry Seinfeld, Rosie O'Donnell, Jamie Foxx, Simon Cowell, Maria Shriver, and Chicago Bulls legend Michael Jordan. Stevie Wonder sang "Isn't She Lovely," Alicia Keys took to the piano to sing "Super Woman," and Oprah protégés Nate Berkus, Dr. Phil, and Dr. Oz paid tribute to their mentor. In the show's final moments, Oprah's own mentor, Maya Angelou, read a poem she had written specifically for the show, and Oprah's longtime partner, Stedman Graham, surprised her onstage (he rarely made such public appearances), introducing the show's most moving performance: a special rendition of "Amazing Grace" by living legend Aretha Franklin. Tears of joy were shed by the media mogul herself, as she proclaimed, "I've never experienced anything like this!" by episode's end. Fans in the arena were elated—the promise that season 25 of *The Oprah Winfrey Show* would "knock your socks off" had definitely come to fruition.

Ads leading up to the finale promised a most memorable hour, with one commercial invoking some of the most memorable television finales (*The Mary Tyler Moore Show*, Johnny Carson's *The Tonight Show*, *Cheers*, *The Cosby Show*, *M*A*S*H*), asking the question: "Where were you?"—seeming to already add Winfrey's exit to television's greatest moments. The final episode of *The Oprah Winfrey Show* aired on Wednesday, May 25, 2011, in a decidedly low-key manner. In a simple pink dress, Oprah stood before a studio audience of just 400 guests and gave it one last go: her last chance to inspire, enlighten, and entertain her dedicated fans. She announced at the top of the show: "Today there will be no guests, no makeovers, no surprises. You will not be getting a car or a tree." She added: "This last hour is really about me saying thank you.

It is my love letter to you. I leave you with all the lessons that have been the anchor for my life, the ones that I hold most precious." What followed were stories about how she ended up on that stage in that very moment, including funny memories of her first gig in Chicago ("a Jheri curl, a bad fur coat . . . and earrings the size of napkins") and moving moments including

Stevie Wonder serenades Oprah during her surprise-filled "Farewell Spectacular."

Barry Brecheisen/Getty Images

a look back on how far she had come from her humble beginnings in rural Mississippi. She recalled her proudest moments on the show (highlighting fellow mogul Tyler Perry's appearance on a show about sexual abuse), and named the secret to the show's success ("my team and Jesus"). She encouraged viewers to follow their own path, begging them: "Don't waste any more time. Start embracing the life that is calling you, and use your life to serve the world." She championed self-reliance ("Nobody but you is responsible for your life") and encouraged her fans to continue to reach out to her—even going as far as to give them her e-mail address (Oprah@Oprah.com, of course). Through tears (or perhaps what Oprah herself would call "the ugly cry"), she concluded her final hour on this most familiar platform by declaring to her audience:

> You and this show have been the great love of my life. I've been asked many times during this farewell season, "Is ending the show bittersweet?" Well, I say, all sweet, no bitter. And here's why. Many of us have been together for twenty-five years. We have hooted and hollered together, had our a-ha! moments, we ugly-cried together and we did our gratitude journals. So I thank you all for your support and your trust in me. I thank you for sharing this yellow brick road of blessings. I thank you for tuning in every day along with your mothers and your sisters and your daughters, your partners, gay and otherwise, your friends and all the husbands who got coaxed into watching *Oprah*. And I thank you for being as much of a sweet inspiration for me as I've tried to be for you. I won't say goodbye. I'll just say, until we meet again. To God be the glory.

As the audience stood and applauded, Oprah exited her main stage. The camera followed her as she walked through the halls of Harpo Studios, greeted her staff, all of whom cheered along as she proclaimed, "We did it!" Then, joined by her loyal cocker spaniel Sadie, Oprah walked off of our television screens, putting her last show into television's great archive.

Reviews of the finale were congratulatory and sincere. *TV Guide* called it "simple, nostalgic, and the perfect way to end a legendary chapter." Myles Tanzer of the *Village Voice* praised the manner in which Oprah delivered her final hour, stating: "Oprah's greatest skill is arguably her ability to have a one-way conversation with millions of people that feels strangely inclusive for the listener. This was a way for Oprah to have one last chance to show off her skills on ABC, and she did it masterfully." Ratings mirrored the words of critics, as the episode raked in more than 16 million viewers, making it the most watched episode of her program in nearly 18 years (the two-part arena extravaganza pulled in 12.3 million and 13 million viewers, respectively). On average, in her farewell month, *The Oprah Winfrey Show* pulled in an audience of at least 8.2 million viewers per episode. The goal of Oprah and her staff, of course, would be that this same near-record breaking audience would tune in to Oprah's newly launched OWN (Oprah Winfrey Network)—a network that just eight months later would launch the prime-time series *Oprah's Next Chapter*, following Miss Winfrey as she navigates through her post-talk show era. OWN has yet to capture the fervent viewership that was so familiar to *The Oprah Winfrey Show*—continuing to experiment with new programming in order to find its voice. The channel can always rely on attracting some viewers as it holds the exclusive rights to the classic *Oprah* episodes—allowing those millions of fans to relive all the sweet, and none of the bitter.

"I Bid You a Heartfelt Goodnight"

Carson and Leno Exit *The Tonight Show*

The Tonight Show Starring Johnny Carson (1962–1992)

Created by Steve Allen, William O. Harbach, Dwight Hemion, Sylvester L. Weaver Jr.

Executive Producer: Fred de Cordova

30 seasons / 2,084 episodes

Final show aired May 22, 1992

50 million viewers

Directors: Bobby Quinn, Steve Purcell

Written by Darrell Vickers and Andrew Nicholls (writing supervisors), Michael Barrie, Jim Mulholland, Bob Keane, Tony DeSena, Bob Dolan Smith, and Tom Finnigan

Ed McMahon, announcer

Doc Severinsen, bandleader

The Tonight Show with Jay Leno (NBC, 1992–2009)

Executive Producer: Debbie Vickers, Joe Medeiros

17 seasons / 3,775 episodes

Final show aired May 29, 2009

11.9 million viewers

Directors: Ellen Brown, Anthony Caleca

Written by Jay Leno, Joe Medeiros, Jack Coen, Beth Armogida, Anthony Caleca, Mike Colasuonno, Larry Jaconson, Michael Jann, John A. Kennedy, Wayne Kline, Jon Macks, Suli McCullough, Andrew McElfresh, Steve Ridgeway, Michael Reidel, John Romeo, Dave Rygalski, Peter Sears, Jim Shaughnessy, Beth Sherman, Jeffrey Spear, Rob Young

John Melendez, announcer

Kevin Eubanks, bandleader

The Tonight Show with Jay Leno (NBC, 2010–2014)

Executive Producer: Debbie Vickers

5 seasons / 835 episodes

Final show aired February 6, 2014

14.6 million viewers

Director: Liz Plonka

Written by Jay Leno, Anthony Caleca, Brian Hartt, Larry Jacobsen, Michael Jann, John A. Kennedy, Mike Loprete, Dave Rygalski, Jon Macks, Andy McElfresh, John Melendez, Steve Ridgeway, John Romeo, Jeffrey Spear, Troy Thomas, Jim Wise, Rob Young

Wally Wingert, announcer

Rickey Minor, bandleader

When Johnny Carson succeeded Jack Paar as the host of NBC's *The Tonight Show*, no one—not even Carson—ever imagined that he would one day become the highest paid entertainer on American television. At the time, he was best known for his short-lived CBS variety show, *The Johnny Carson Show* (1955–1956) and for hosting daytime game shows such as *Earn Your Vacation* (1954) and *Who Do You Trust?* (1957–1963). In his interview with Carson published a day before his debut on *The Tonight Show*, Edgar Penton explained that, according to Carson's press agent, he's received somewhere around seventy requests from newspaper, magazines, and radio shows for interviews with his client. When Penton sits down to talk to Carson, he asks the question repeatedly being asked by interviewers: "What exactly will the show be like?" Carson answers as he has many times already: "It will be an interview show with a little comedy, a little music and a lot of talk. But let's wait until we get on the air and it shapes into its own format before we talk about it. How can we talk about a show which isn't even on the air?"

Carson goes on to say that he will be sticking close to Jack Paar's format, but it will be tailored to his own brand of humor. He mentions how he spends several hours every morning going through the newspaper and magazines looking for "ideas," which, of course, will be source of the topical jokes in his opening monologue. During the interview, Carson, who was often described by his friends as a shy man off-camera, did express his genuine concern about how the show is going to be promoted: "I hope they don't start that barrage of promotion for the show which screams all about how HILARIOUS it's going to be. . . . It's the kiss of death when somebody else tells you about how funny something is going to be." In his unauthorized biography of Carson, author Paul Corkery explained that the host and his team, which included his sidekick from *Who Do You Trust?*, Ed McMahon, and legendary comedy writer Herb Sergeant, adapted the format of the first incarnation of *The Tonight Show* hosted by Steve Allen, simply titled *Tonight*, along with elements from other versions of the show (a discussion with an author, a musical performance, etc.).

Originating from NBC Studios at 30 Rockefeller Plaza in New York City, *The Tonight Show Starring Johnny Carson* debuted on October 1, 1962. Introduced by legendary comedian Groucho Marx, the thirty-three-year-old former gameshow host made his first entrance on *The Tonight Show*'s stage. Johnny's guests that evening were Tony Bennett, Mel Brooks, Joan Crawford, and Rudy Vallee. Initially, the show ran from 11:15 p.m. to 1:00 a.m., although Carson refused to start his monologue until 11:30 p.m. because some local newscasts didn't end until that time; instead, he let Ed McMahon and musical director Skitch Henderson co-host the show's first fifteen minutes. In his review of the first show, *New York Times* television critic Jack Gould observed how Parr's format seemed unchanged, "but Mr. Carson's style is all his own. He has the proverbial engaging smile and the quick mind essential to sustaining and seasoning a marathon of banter." He found Carson's statement that "he was not going to describe every guest as an old and dear friend" to be "a refreshing attitude against prevalent show-business hokum." On the negative side, he felt his questions were "rather orthodox in publicizing their outside interests" and warns the producers against overbooking the show to the extent that some guests have to sit quietly and out of camera range while other guests were being interviewed.

The format remained more or less intact for the next thirty years, although the show did undergo some changes in the 1970s once the show became one of NBC's top moneymakers and its host the network's most valuable asset. In May of 1972, the show moved from New York to NBC's production facility in Burbank, California. When Carson re-negotiated his contract in 1978, his salary was bumped up to $3 million a year and his schedule was cut back to three nights a week (Tuesday through Thursday). A guest host subbed on Monday nights and a rerun aired on Fridays. In 1980, Carson added Friday nights to his hosting duties but the running time of his show was reduced from 90 to 60 minutes.

As a host, Carson was a class act. He was an excellent standup comedian (he didn't write his own monologues, but chose expertly from a list of jokes submitted by his team of writers), a master at ad-libbing, and a terrific interviewer who knew how to put his guests at ease—especially those with little or no talk show experience. Carson was also smart and enjoyed conversing with politicians, authors, and intellectuals such as Robert F. Kennedy, Richard Nixon, Truman Capote, Ayn Rand, Erma Bombeck, Mort Sahl, Margaret Mead, and Gore Vidal. He also liked to showcase new comedic talent and could jump start a comedian's career, especially if, after the comic's performance, he or she was signaled by Johnny to come over to the couch for some impromptu conversation. Among the future stars who received that all-important invitation were Drew Carey, Ellen DeGeneres, Kevin Nealon, Steven Wright, Yakov Smirnoff, and Roseanne Barr.

Carson announced his retirement in May of 1991 and one year later, it was time to say goodbye. The talk show host did it in style with a series of shows in which he invited back some of his favorite people for one last laugh: Roseanne Barr, Mel Brooks, Bob Hope, Bob Newhart, and David Letterman, who was engaged in a high profile battle with Jay Leno to be Johnny's successor. For his penultimate show, Carson invited his two favorite entertainers: Robin Williams, who gave Carson a rocking chair for his retirement, and did his stream-of-conscious comedy about the Los Angeles riots and Vice President Dan Quayle; and the "Divine Miss M," Bette Midler, who first appeared on Carson's show in 1970 (and appeared seventeen more times in the next three years). Midler, who won an Emmy for her appearance on the 1992 pre-finale, sang Cole Porter's "Miss Otis Regrets," a parody of "You Made Me Love You (I Didn't Want to Do It)," and an impromptu duet with Carson, singing one of his favorite songs, "Here's That Rainy Day." She then closed the show with "One for My Baby (and One More for the Road)" to a teary-eyed Mr. Carson. Anyone watching Miss Midler sing might have thought that this was the last show. In fact, in Don Sweeney's backstage history of *The Tonight Show*, Ed McMahon recalled Carson, right before going out on stage for his final show, say, "It just worked last night. We should have just stay home today." He then made a joke about putting on a rerun, but "somehow I don't think that NBC would take too kindly to that." (Carson told the same joke on the air, and perhaps McMahon was confusing Carson's backstage comment with what he said onstage that night.)

Johnny Carson's last show was simple and subdued. It begins with a video montage of Carson entering from behind the curtain. When he finally makes his actual entrance, he receives a minute-long standing ovation. During his monologue, a relaxed Carson sits on a stool (a first for him) and thanks Robin Williams and Bette Midler for their performances on the previous night. We then see a different side of Carson as he mentions that wife, brother, and two of his sons, Chris and Cory, are in the audience and acknowledges how tough it must have been for them to have a father in the spotlight. He also mentions his late son, Rick, a photographer who died tragically in a car accident the previous summer (his photograph of a sunset is the last image at the end of the hour).

During the show, Carson also thanks his loyal announcer, Ed McMahon, and his longtime bandleader, "Doc" Severinsen, for sticking with him all these years; they thank him in return. He also introduces various montages—clips from some memorable moments, and images of favorite guests. There's even an interesting behind-the-scenes piece that reveals to his audience what goes on backstage before a show, from the morning rundown, to the rehearsal, to Johnny's entrance.

Carson ends the show from where he started—center stage, seated on a stool. In his final monologue, Carson reveals that NBC wanted him to do a prime-time special, but he wanted his last show to be in its usual time slot. It's not the star-studded celebration one would expect for Carson's final episode. Yet he managed to have it both ways. He went out with a bang with Williams and Midler on Thursday, and with dignity and class on Friday.

Carson once again thanks his audience and bids them "a very heartfelt goodnight."

While Johnny Carson's 1992 exit personified grace and gratitude, Jay Leno's double exit from his two incarnations of *The Tonight Show* were mired in disgrace and ineptitude. In September of 2004, upon the fiftieth anniversary of the landmark *Tonight Show* franchise, NBC announced that Jay Leno, then the no. 1 host in the late night ratings, would depart in five years, passing the baton to *Late Night*'s Conan O'Brien. The network would have five years to rebrand their show—no small task, but certainly enough time to ease the transition. Leno, having become entangled in a battle for *The Tonight Show* with the previous heir apparent David Letterman, hoped that the five-year lead-in to Conan's takeover would avoid in-fighting and bitterness. Little did Leno know that five years was not nearly enough time to prepare for what was about to transpire.

Jay Leno assumed the post of *Tonight Show* host on May 25, 1992. Leno had regularly substituted for Johnny Carson between 1987 and 1992, even being named a "permanent guest host." The shift to Leno was a contentious one—as many had already accepted David Letterman as the inevitable choice. Letterman had hosted *Late Night* on NBC since 1982, having taken over the 12:30 a.m. timeslot from *Tomorrow Coast to Coast* (better known as *The Tomorrow Show*), hosted by newsman Tom Snyder. Each night as Carson ended, Letterman would begin—making the transition of Letterman into *The Tonight Show* chair a logical next step. When the decision came down to hand the show off to Leno and not Letterman (or Joan Rivers, who had sat in for Johnny nearly a hundred times), Letterman defected to CBS to host *The Late Show with David Letterman*, a direct competitor to Leno's *Tonight* (see appendix). Despite the bitterness that plagued this move (drama enough to sustain both a book and HBO movie—*The Late Shift*, written by *New York Times* reporter Bill Carter), Letterman profited handsomely, having reportedly accepted a $16 million contract from CBS, a far cry from Leno's annual $3

"A very heartfelt goodnight": Johnny Carson ends his thirty-year run as host of *The Tonight Show.*   *NBC/Photofest*

million. Initially, Leno's ratings sagged behind Letterman's—that is until Leno scored the "it" guest of the moment in July 1995. British actor Hugh Grant, who at the time was dating the impossibly gorgeous supermodel Elizabeth Hurley, had been caught with a prostitute named Divine Brown, and thus, was arrested for lewd conduct. On July 10, 1995, Grant appeared on Leno to attempt to repair his image. Leno pulled no punches, starting the interview with: "What the hell were you thinking?" With one line, Leno hooked his audience. From that point on, Leno's *Tonight Show* enjoyed late night's top spot, holding tight to the no. 1 position for nearly twenty years.

When the announcement of the Conan O'Brien changeover came down from network executives in September of 2004, there was a general consensus that this time, as opposed to the perceived Letterman snub, the transition would be seamless. O'Brien had taken over for Letterman when he vacated NBC's *Late Night*, and since had become known for his particular brand of innovative comedy, with adequate ratings that brought a younger audience to the network. O'Brien's humor was razor smart but unquestionably goofy, as the former president of *The Harvard Lampoon* threw his lanky body around the stage, keeping his trademark red coif sky high. Leno, whose training had been in the world of standup, was direct, broad, and punch-line heavy—making him a hit in what *Deadline Hollywood* called "flyover country." The two stood on opposite ends of the comedy spectrum, and NBC execs came to realize that those who tuned in to Jay's *Tonight* might not warm up to O'Brien. Fear that audiences would flee came to a fever pitch in late 2008, as NBC hatched a plan to keep Leno on the network (he was reportedly being "wooed" by both ABC and FOX)—a move that did not sit well with O'Brien. NBC would keep Leno on their payroll—thus preventing him from moving to a competitor's late night timeslot—by giving him a comedy show that would air at 10 p.m. The catch: it would air daily. In Bill Carter's 2010 book on *The Tonight Show* debacle, *The War for Late Night: When Leno Went Early and Television Went Crazy*, he detailed Conan O'Brien's reaction to the new *Jay Leno Show* news:

> He instantly had a bad feeling. After sixteen years of following Jay Leno, after finally being released into the free air of 11:35, Conan had been hit with the news that NBC was reviving the old lineup order. This was more like a time shift than a programming change; certainly it wasn't a commitment to a new star over the old. It amounted to going from daylight savings time back to eastern standard time—move the clocks back an hour.

But O'Brien, assured that he was still being bestowed the honor of hosting the one and only *Tonight Show*, moved forward with hope. He concluded his run on *Late Night* on February 20, 2009, literally taking an axe to his set—and then handing out pieces to members of his loyal audience.

Leno's supposed last stint as *The Tonight Show* host aired on May 29, 2009. He welcomed Conan O'Brien as his final guest, telling the audience "I couldn't be prouder of him." Leno graciously passed the torch on to O'Brien, as highlights from his seventeen years as host played. Leno confirmed for his audience that he would indeed be returning to the network for his 10:00 p.m. gig, joking (at ratings-plagued NBC's expense): "I'm going to a secluded location where no one can find me: NBC's prime-time." James Taylor was the final musical guest, serenading the audience with "Sweet Baby James," as per Leno's request. In the final moment of the show, he brought 68 children to the stage, introducing them as "the greatest thing we've ever done." He revealed that each of those children had come from a set of parents who met because they worked on Leno's *Tonight Show*. An estimated 11.9 million viewers tuned in for this touching moment, not nearly as many as watched Carson's final bow, but the *New York Times* pointed out in their recap of the episode that "unlike Mr. Carson, Mr. Leno is not retiring."

Conan O'Brien debuted his version of *The Tonight Show* on June 1, 2009, to a solid audience of 9.2 million. Plans to debut Leno's new series moved forward, and on September 14, 2009, *The Jay Leno Show* premiered. Cosmetically, as Bill Carter details in his account of the premiere, things were different. There would be no desk, a move that Carter called "entirely out of respect for Conan." Instead, Jay would sit across from his guest in comfortable chairs. Jerry Seinfeld was Jay's first guest, ribbing him with the line: "You know, in the nineties, when we quit a show, we actually left." Leno's debut brought in 18.4 million viewers, doubling the numbers O'Brien brought in. But numbers did not stay steady, eventually falling to an average of 5 million just a month later. Local NBC affiliates were not pleased—weaker numbers for Leno meant weaker numbers for their nightly 11:00 p.m. broadcasts, which the *Los Angeles Times* deemed "crucial for local stations [drawing] upon them for a third of their revenue." Affiliates threatened to run their own news broadcast at 10:00 p.m. in place of Leno, a move that worried NBC execs. Talk of cancellation ran rampant, but, according to Bill Carter, Conan O'Brien was cautious. His fears were realized in January 2010, when it was announced that NBC intended to move Leno back to the 11:35 p.m. time slot he had held for nearly twenty years, planning a half-hour version of the revamped *Jay Leno Show*, thus bumping the official *Tonight Show* (still hosted by O'Brien) to a 12:05 a.m. start time. O'Brien was incensed, penning a widely circulated letter criticizing this decision. His letter, addressed simply to "People of Earth," stated:

> After only seven months, with my *Tonight Show* in its infancy, NBC has decided to react to their terrible difficulties in prime-time by making a change in their long-established late night schedule. Last Thursday, NBC executives told me they intended to move *The Tonight Show* to 12:05

Jay Leno passes *The Tonight Show* baton to fellow NBC late night host Conan O'Brien (but not for long) on May 29, 2009.   *NBC/Getty Images*

> to accommodate *The Jay Leno Show* at 11:35. For 60 years *The Tonight Show* has aired immediately following the late local news. I sincerely believe that delaying *The Tonight Show* into the next day to accommodate another comedy program will seriously damage what I consider to be the greatest franchise in the history of broadcasting. *The Tonight Show* at 12:05 simply isn't *The Tonight Show*. . . . My staff and I have worked unbelievably hard and we are very proud of our contribution to the legacy of *The Tonight Show*. But I cannot participate in what I honestly believe is its destruction.

He closed with a joke ("Have a great day, and for the record, I am truly sorry about my hair"), but there was nothing funny about how serious the NBC late night programming problems had become.

Forced to choose between Leno and O'Brien, NBC ultimately went with Leno. Conan O'Brien's final *Tonight Show* aired on January 22, 2010—just seven months after its debut. Leno would take over the reins again in March, following NBC's coverage of the Winter Olympics. Despite being on the receiving end of a raw deal (and being prohibited from appearing on television until September 2010), O'Brien landed on his feet, securing the new late night spot at cable's TBS, a deal that allowed him to finally control his own destiny. *Conan* debuted in November 2010. Leno, in the meantime, fell back into his old routine, with *Saturday Night Live* alumnus Jimmy Fallon continuing his gig as *Late Night*'s host, a post he inherited from O'Brien in March of 2009.

As Leno retread familiar ground, ratings numbers did not bounce back. By October 2010, Leno resigned the no.1 spot in late night to a familiar foe: David Letterman. As the ratings battle continued, a new contender entered the ring, as ABC's Jimmy Kimmel (host of *Jimmy Kimmel Live!*) was moved from 12:05 a.m. to 11:35 a.m., making him a direct competitor to both Leno and Letterman. In addition, as the *Los Angeles Times* reported in August 2012, Comedy Central's *The Daily Show with Jon Stewart* and *The Colbert Report* were surging in popularity—particularly in the all too coveted 18–49 demographic. Leno's contract kept him in the host's seat only through September 2013. As Letterman, Leno, and Kimmel jockeyed for the no.1 spot, NBC considered its options, knowing that this time any move with Leno would have to be final.

The decision came in April of 2013, just as Leno had firmly recaptured the top spot. Jimmy Fallon would replace Jay Leno as host of *The Tonight Show* as of spring 2014. NBC's chief executive Steve Burke remarked: "We are purposefully making this change when Jay is No. 1, just as Jay replaced Johnny Carson when he was No. 1." But this time, *The Tonight Show* would face a complete transformation, moving the show from Burbank to its original home at New York's Rockefeller Plaza. This transition would make a Leno re-return nearly impossible, as moving his entire crew cross-country was unlikely, and Leno, having made it clear in the past, was fiercely loyal to his own. Leno's second "last" *Tonight Show* was planned for February 6, 2014, nearly four years since his return.

Leno's final hour was jam-packed with celebrity guests: Oprah Winfrey, Garth Brooks, Carol Burnett, Kevin Bacon, and even President Barack Obama, who jokingly appointing Leno as his "new Ambassador to Antarctica." Billy Crystal was also a guest, just as he had been when Leno made his permanent host debut in 1992 (Crystal poked fun at his friend, saying: "Let me get this straight—you're moving to 9 o'clock?"). Crystal then led a star-studded rendition of *The Sound of Music*'s "So Long, Farewell," with many celebrities adding their own lyrics (Kim Kardashian mustered: "So long, farewell, last night I told my folks, 'Now I won't be the butt of Leno's jokes'"). In the end, Leno became overcome with emotion as he thanked his fans (14.6 million of whom tuned in, Leno's best numbers since 1998) and his crew. He wished his successor well ("I'm really excited for Jimmy Fallon"), as he let Johnny Carson's words end the night: "I bid you all a heartfelt good night."

And, this time, he meant it.

Part 5
Saying Goodbye

"Good Night, Seattle"

Frasier Crane Signs Off

Frasier (NBC, 1993–2004)

Created by David Angell, Peter Casey, and David Lee
Premiere date: September 16, 1993
11 seasons / 264 episodes
"Goodnight, Seattle, Parts 1 and 2"
Airdate: May 13, 2004
16.3 rating • 25 percent share • 33.7 million viewers
Directed by David Lee
Written by Christopher Lloyd and Joe Keenan
Cast: Kelsey Grammer (Frasier Crane), David Hyde Pierce (Niles Crane), John Mahoney (Martin Crane), Jane Leeves (Daphne Moon), Peri Gilpin (Roz Doyle), Enzo (Eddie)
Guest Stars: Laura Linney (Charlotte), Wendie Malick (Ronee Lawrence), Harriet Sansom Harris (Bebe Glazer), Anthony LaPaglia (Simon Moon), Tom McGowan (Kenny Daly), Edward Hibbert (Gil Chesterton), Patrick Kerr (Noel Shempsky), Robbie Coltrane (Michael Moon), Richard E. Grant (Stephen Moon), Jennifer Beals (Dr. Anne Ranberg), Jason Biggs (Dr. Hauck)

elevision spinoffs are very hit-and-miss. There's no guarantee anyone will be tuning in when a character from a popular television series is given a show of his or her own. A handsome, dim-witted womanizer with his own catchphrase ("How *you* doin'?"), Joey Tribbiani (Matt LeBlanc) was funny as a member of a six-character ensemble on *Friends*. But on his spinoff, *Joey* (2004–2006), the character proved to be too one-note to watch on a weekly basis as his personality, a mixture of cluelessness and male bravado, lost its charm. If it's any consolation to the producers of *Joey*, their show was not the exception, but one in a long list of failed sitcoms spun-off from long-running, hit comedies: *Joanie Loves Chachi* (1982–1983) from *Happy Days* (1974–1984), *The Golden Palace* (1992–1993) from *The Golden Girls* (1985–1992), *AfterMASH* (1983–1984) from *M*A*S*H* (1972–1983) and

The Ropers (1979–1980) and *Three's a Crowd* (1984–1985) from *Three's Company* (1977–1984), just to name a few.

The news of a *Cheers* spinoff for the sitcom's resident psychiatrist, Dr. Frasier Crane, came as a bit of a surprise when J. Max Robins and Jim Benson reported in *Variety* that NBC Entertainment president Warren Littlefield announced in a closed session with the NBC affiliates that Kelsey Grammer would be starring in his own series beginning in the fall. Since season 3, the over-educated, pompous, and insecure Dr. Crane was a fish-out-of-water among the beer-and-pretzel crowd that frequented the Boston watering hole (why the psychiatrist chose to hang out there was never made clear). Like the gang at *Cheers*, many viewers found Frasier irritating. But it's a testament to the talents of Kelsey Grammer and the *Cheers* writers that they were able to create a character who, despite his highfalutin, condescending demeanor was also humane and, at times, even likable.

Dr. Frasier Crane was introduced in season 3 as a "friend" of Diane Chambers (Shelley Long) when she returned to Boston after her recent stay in a sanitarium, recovering from her tumultuous breakup with Sam Malone (Ted Danson). Diane hoped Frasier could help Sam, a recovering alcoholic who had fallen off the wagon after their breakup, but Sam soon finds out that Frasier is actually Diane's lover, which is complicated by the fact that Sam and Diane are still hot for each other. In the season 3 finale, Frasier proposes to Diane and the couple leave for Italy, though a phone call from Diane prompts Sam to get on a plane to stop the wedding. At the start of season 4, Diane, who left Frasier at the altar, is in a convent while her jilted lover is back in Boston, drowning his sorrows. Sam retrieves Diane from the convent and she goes back to work at Cheers, while a depressed Frasier loses his job and develops his own drinking problem. Over time he turns his life around and then meets, falls in love, and marries a psychiatrist, the steely, equally neurotic Dr. Lilith Sternin (Bebe Neuwirth). Together they have a son, Frederick, though their marriage eventually falls apart. In the pilot for *Frasier*, we learn that Frasier and Lilith are now divorced and their son is living with his mother in Boston. In turn, Frasier has moved to Seattle, where he is now hosting his own call-in radio show.

Frasier is the second spinoff of the long-running, highly rated sitcom *Cheers* (the first spinoff, *The Tortellis* [1987], which focused on Carla Tortelli's [Rhea Perlman] obnoxious ex-husband, Nick [Dan Hedaya] and his family, only lasted half a season). The creators of *Frasier*, former *Cheers* writers David Angell, Peter Casey, and David Lee, co-created the NBC comedy *Wings* (1990–1997), which was in its fourth season when *Frasier* debuted. Following a similar formula as *Cheers*, *Wings* was a workplace comedy set in a two-airline airport on the island of Nantucket, Massachusetts. One airline is owned and operated by two brothers (Steven Weber and Timothy Daly), who are surrounded by oddball characters. Nantucket is forty-five minutes by plane from Boston, which made it easy for *Cheers* cast members to make crossover appearances on *Wings*: Norm (George Wendt) and Cliff (John Ratzenberger) took a fishing trip on the island ("The Story of Joe"); Frasier and Lilith visited Nantucket ("Planes, Trains, and Visiting Cranes") to conduct their seminar on how to ride the "Crane Train to Emotional Well-being"; and Rebecca

Frasier's ensemble cast: (left to right) David Hyde Pierce, Peri Gilpin, Kelsey Grammer, Jane Leeves, John Mahoney, and Moose. *Authors' collection*

(Kirstie Alley) appeared in an episode when *Wings* characters visited Boston ("I Love Brian").

Before Ted Danson made his final decision not to return to *Cheers* for a twelfth season, Grammer decided he wanted to star in his own series. While Paramount liked the idea of a *Frasier* spinoff, Angell, Casey, and Lee preferred to create a whole new character for Grammer to play. In his interview with the Archive of American Television (AAT), David Lee recalls their initial idea was to have Grammer play a wealthy, eccentric man (a Malcolm Forbes type) who is paralyzed after a motorcycle accident and now running his empire from his bedroom. Paramount didn't think a sitcom in which the main character is bedridden for life would work and once again suggested a *Frasier* spinoff. Borrowing an unproduced story idea from *Cheers* in which Frasier subs for a radio psychiatrist, the trio relocated Frasier to Seattle, where he hosts *The Dr. Frasier Crane Show*, which airs weekdays from 2:00 p.m.–5:00 p.m. on a fictional radio station, KACL 780 AM (the call letters "ACL" stand for Angell, Casey, and Lee). The radio station was originally going to be the focus of the series, but they were concerned the show would be too much like *WKRP in Cincinnati* (1978–1982). Drawing on their own personal experiences caring for their elderly parents, they decided to give Frasier a home life that would be disrupted when his father, Martin (John Mahoney), a retired police officer shot in the line of duty, must move into his son's bachelor penthouse, along with his Jack Russell terrier, Eddie (Moose), and a full-time, live-in caregiver, British-born Daphne Moon (Jane Leeves).

The inclusion of Frasier's father must have surprised die-hard *Cheers* fans because as Sam Malone reminds him when he visits Frasier in Boston ("The Show Where Sam Shows Up") and meets Martin for the first time, he once revealed that his deceased dad was a research scientist ("Two Girls for Every Boyd"). Frasier explains that he and his father were arguing over the phone when Martin called him a "stuffed shirt" and hung up on him. He was mad at Martin, so he told people his father was deceased (and figuring he's dead by this time, he told people he was a research scientist).

There are shades of Neil Simon's *The Odd Couple* in Frasier and Martin's relationship, with Frasier playing the obsessive, finicky Felix Unger to Martin's casual, carefree Oscar Madison—the kind of guy you can imagine having a few beers with the gang down at Cheers. British-born Mahoney did do a guest spot on *Cheers* as jingle writer Sy Flembeck ("Do Not Forsake Me, O' My Postman") and Peri Gilpin, who plays Frasier's loyal radio producer, Roz, appeared as a reporter at the end of the show's final season ("Woody Gets an Election"). The show's creators knew Frasier's pretentious demeanor might be too hard to take on a weekly basis and, as David Angell explained to Jefferson Graham, author of the official companion to *Frasier*, "That cartoony, pompous Frasier Crane would not carry a series. We needed to find ways to pop that pomposity and deal with some real emotion." Consequently, Martin was given zero tolerance for his sons' snobbery and the ability to know exactly how to get under their skin.

Another surprise for *Cheers* fans (and Sam Malone) was learning that Frasier also has a brother, Dr. Niles Crane (David Hyde Pierce), who is the mirror image of Frasier. According to N. F. Mendoza's *Los Angeles Times* profile of Pierce, the actor's photo was spotted by casting director Sheila Guthrie, who, amazed by his resemblance to Grammer, showed the photo to the show's producers. Although there had been no discussion of Frasier having a younger brother, they decided to cast Pierce, who appeared as a senator's suicidal son-in-law on the short-lived NBC sitcom *The Powers That Be* (1992–1993), in the role (no audition required). Pierce was aware of his resemblance to his future sitcom sibling. He told Graham he recalled first seeing Grammer when they were appearing in separate plays at the Long Wharf Theatre in New Haven. "We had our meals at the same place and I went in to have dinner," Pierce recalled, "and he (Grammer) was sitting at the table and I looked at him and thought I was already eating."

But the similarity between Frasier and Niles is not limited to their physical appearance. Both of the Crane brothers are psychiatrists, though Niles, who is even stuffier and more uptight than Frasier, does not hide his disapproval of his brother's job as a radio shrink. They are both self-proclaimed connoisseurs of French cuisine, fine wine, classical music, theatre, and the opera and, when the opportunity arises, they can be fiercely competitive. The brothers compete to be the next "Corkmaster" of their local wine club ("Whine Club"), a member of an exclusive men's club ("The Club"), and even to buy the best present for their father's birthday ("The Gift Horse"). Niles also has his own troubles in the form of his wife, Maris, who, like Vera, Norm Peterson's wife on *Cheers*, doesn't appear on camera (the closest we get is a glimpse through a shower curtain ["Voyage of the Damned"] and in a flashback ["Rooms with a View"] in which she is covered with bandages after surgery). Still, we feel like we know Maris because her neurotic, codependent behavior and her long list of medical problems are the butt of many jokes. After a two-year separation, Maris and Niles divorce so he can at last marry the woman he's been pining for since he first laid eyes on her—Daphne ("The Ring Cycle").

The addition of Niles made the inclusion of their father all the more necessary. Frasier and Niles's mother, Dr. Hester Crane, a research psychiatrist who inspired her sons to enter the profession, is deceased, though she did appear on an episode of *Cheers*. Played by four-time Emmy winner Nancy Marchand, who is best remembered as Tony Soprano's manipulative mother,

Livia, on *The Sopranos* (1999–2007), Hester threatens to kill Diane Chambers if she marries her son. Over time, we do learn more about Hester Crane, whose ghost makes an appearance in a memorable episode ("Don Juan in Hell, Parts 1 and 2"), in which Frasier comes to terms with his track record of failed relationships. Hester, along with Frasier's first wife, Nanette Guzman (Dina Spybey), a future guitar-strumming child entertainer known as "Nanny G"; his second wife, Dr. Lilith Sternin; and his runaway bride Diane Chambers all appear in Frasier's hallucination, in which he comes to the realization that he must put his failed relationships behind him before he can move forward in his life. In particular, Neuwirth is a welcome familiar face when she reprises her *Cheers* role as Frasier's ex-wife in a dozen episodes during the series run, sometimes accompanied by their son, Frederick (Trevor Einhorn), who doesn't spend as much time as one would expect with his father.

The show's pilot ("The Good Son") establishes the long history of tension between Frasier and his father when his old man has to move into Frasier's meticulously, tastefully decorated penthouse apartment (Frasier explains that nothing matches because the style is "eclectic") along with his shabby, worn-out recliner, and Eddie, the dog whose habit of staring at Frasier is a running joke. Frasier has trouble dealing with his father's intrusion and finally loses his temper. The episode poignantly concludes with Martin calling into Frasier's radio show. Admitting that he has trouble expressing his feelings to his son, he eventually tells Dr. Crane he appreciates what he's doing for him.

Critics who were skeptical that *Frasier* couldn't live up to the legacy of *Cheers* were pleasantly surprised. *Variety* critic Tony Scott praised the show's premise, witty script, and performances. He was certain the show would be "one of the season's winners" and credited Grammer for making the "pompous Frasier Crane . . . sympathetic, funny, and, with the writers' sharp help, quotable." *Los Angeles Times* critic Howard Rosenberg agreed, calling it "cleverly written with a quality cast that bodes well for the future." *USA Today* critic Matt Roush credited the show for keeping "a bit of *Cheers* alive . . . with an arch and often funny new setup." *New York Times*' critic John J. O'Connor points out that even through the pairing of odd couple Frasier and Martin is "not the season's most original concept," *Frasier* is "one of the few new series likely to survive. And deservedly, not just because it follows *Seinfeld*."

Frasier landed the coveted 9:30 p.m. time slot after *Seinfeld* on NBC's "Must See TV" Thursday night schedule, though the show moved to NBC's Tuesday night comedy block at the start of season 2, and then, throughout its run, back and forth between Thursday and Tuesday. The show managed not only to survive the scheduling changes, but for nine of its eleven seasons, *Frasier* was a Top 10 comedy among adults 18–49, which is the reason NBC used it when it needed an anchor show on Tuesday and Thursday nights. *Frasier* also stayed in the Top 20 for seasons 1–9 (its personal best was no. 3 in season 6), and then dropped down to no. 26 in season 10 and no. 35 in season 11.

In terms of its comedic style, the main source of the show's humor is the irony surrounding Frasier's character. He is a psychiatrist who, by profession, uses his knowledge and insight into human behavior to analyze his patients and help them solve their problems. At the same time, Frasier's neurosis and superior attitude makes it difficult for him to resolve conflicts within his own family, come to terms with his own feelings, and deal with awkward social situations.

The complications that arise for the characters are created through the use of stock comic devices, such as cases of mistaken identity (Frasier, Niles, and Roz's boyfriend are all thought to be gay on more than one occasion), situations spiraling out of control, or misinterpretion of an event.

The *Frasier* finale opens on a plane, where Frasier strikes up a conversation with a fellow nervous flyer (and psychiatrist) Dr. Anne Ranberg (Jennifer Beals). Frasier admits it's been an eventful three weeks. To keep their minds off the bumpy flight, he accepts her generous offer to listen to his story (the fact that he is telling it to a psychiatrist is a nice touch). The flashback begins with his goodbye to Charlotte (Laura Linney), the matchmaker he hired and with whom he fell in love. But Charlotte had already bought back her old business from her ex-husband and is moving back to Chicago. They find saying goodbye difficult and, surprisingly, the woman who seems to be the soul mate Frasier has been looking for is gone within the episode's first twelve minutes.

The attention then shifts to family matters. Niles and a very pregnant Daphne receive a surprise visit from three of her eight brothers—Simon (played by Australian-born Anthony LaPaglia, reprising the role that won him an Emmy), Michael (Robbie Coltrane), and Stephen (British actor Richard E. Grant)—who love to booze it up and make themselves comfortable wherever they land. Niles is worried his son will grow up to be like one of the Moon brothers, while Daphne fears he might be a little Niles or Frasier. They are all looking forward to the upcoming wedding of Martin and Ronee (Wendie Malick), though apparently Martin screwed up the dates and booked the room for May (on Eddie's birthday) rather than July. As a result, Frasier and Niles agree to take over and throw them an impromptu wedding.

The wedding sequence is classic *Frasier*. The brothers Crane have planned the event in what can only be described as way, *way* over the top, complete with Chinese acrobats, a gospel choir, and a cannon. Everything begins to fall apart when the air-conditioning unit breaks down during a heat wave and a series of other catastrophes, including the Moon brothers getting the flower girl drunk, and a crash involving a truck transporting "large, un-diapered

"Hello, Seattle": Frasier Crane (Kelsey Grammer) is on the air.   *Authors' collection*

cattle." To top it all off, Eddie accidentally swallows the ring, forcing Niles and Daphne to take the pooch to the local vet. The hijinks continue in the vet's office, where it's Dr. Hauck's (Jason Biggs) first day on the job. The ring is retrieved, but Daphne's water breaks and she is forced to give birth in the vet's office with the help of a registered nurse who happened to be in the waiting room. Finally, Ronee and Martin arrive and decide to get married in the vet's office, with Frasier officiating. Roz gets some good news the following day when she is made the new station manager of KACL.

And so, Frasier finally gets what he's wanted since the pilot—to have his apartment all to himself—yet he realizes that everyone's else's life is moving forward. So he calls his agent, Bebe (Harriet Sansom Harris), and tells her that he is going to accept the new gig he's been offered in San Francisco, which will also include appearances on television. Frasier then reluctantly agrees to go see Bebe's "face man," though he is unhappy with the results. Still, that evening, he assembles his family and friends to break the news that he is moving to San Francisco. But before he tells them, he starts giving away his prized possessions. This sudden display of generosity and their misinterpretation of a phone message from Bebe's doctor left on Frasier's answering machine, lead them to believe that Frasier is dying.

Frasier finally shares the good news of his imminent move, much to his family's relief. He then offers an emotional goodbye to the people who mean the most to him by reciting a few lines from Alfred, Lord Tennyson's poem, *Ulysses*, in which the titular hero, having returned home, expresses his desire to once again go and explore the world ("To strive, to seek, to find, and not to yield"). The poem serves as a sound bridge to the scene in which Frasier says goodbye to his Seattle listeners (and the viewers at home) as all of the characters watch through the glass partition: "I have loved every minute with my KACL family and all of you. For eleven years you have heard me say, "I'm listening." Well, *you* were listening too. And for that I am eternally grateful. Good night, Seattle."

It's a series finale, so there has to be a twist. Frasier has finished recounting his past few weeks to Dr. Ranberg as their plane lands, but—and here's the twist—Frasier is not in San Francisco, but in Chicago, where it is implied that he is planning to surprise Charlotte (Laura Linney). He asks Dr. Ranberg to "wish him luck."

So did Frasier decide not to take the job in San Francisco, or is he just going to surprise Charlotte with a visit? His final request to "wish him luck" implies that this trip is more than a visit.

As to be expected, the ending generated plenty of chatter on message boards as viewers expressed how much they loved or hated it, or were just simply confused. Whatever the reaction, it seemed a fitting finale to a sitcom that always managed to maintain an air of dignity even when relying heavily on farcical situations. Its characters grew over the course of eleven seasons and this was not only conveyed by the life-changing decisions they made, but in subtler ways. In the show's pilot, a moving man (Cleto Augusto), much to Frasier's horror, arrives with Martin's weathered old recliner, which is then parked in the center of Frasier's living room. In the final episode, the same moving man (played by the same actor) arrives to pick up Martin's chair and take it to Martin and Ronee's new home. This time, Frasier tells the moving man "to be careful with it."

The *Frasier* finale was the no. 1 show of the week with 33.7 million viewers tuning in. Although it didn't come close to the 52.46 million who tuned in to watch the *Friends* finale the week before (see chapter 5), the *Frasier* series finale was a classy ending to a classy show—even Niles and Frasier would have approved.

20

Canceled!

Liz Lemon Exits *30 Rock*

30 Rock (NBC, 2006–2013)
Created by Tina Fey
Premiere date: October 11, 2006
7 seasons / 138 episodes
"Hogcock!" / "Last Lunch"
Airdate: January 31, 2013
3.0 rating • 5 percent share • 4.8 million viewers
Directed by Beth McCarthy-Miller
"Hogcock!" written by Jack Burditt and Robert Carlock
"Last Lunch" written by Tina Fey and Tracey Wigfield
Cast: Tina Fey (Liz Lemon), Tracy Morgan (Tracy Jordan), Jane Krakowski (Jenna
     Maroney), Alec Baldwin (Jack Donaghy), Jack McBrayer (Kenneth Parcell),
     Scott Adsit (Pete Hornberger), Judah Friedlander (Frank Rossitano), Katrina
     Bowden (Cerie), Keith Powell (Toofer), Kevin Brown (Dot Com), Grizz
     Chapman (Grizz), John Lutz (J. D. Lutz), Maulik Pancholy (Jonathan)
Guest Stars: James Marsden (Criss), Salma Hayek (Elisa Padriera), Julianne Moore
     (Nancy Donovan), Nancy Pelosi (herself), Alice Ripley (herself), Richard
     Belzer (himself), Ice-T (himself), Savannah Guthrie (herself), Al Roker (him-
     self), Conan O'Brien (himself), David Garrison (Dr. Carlock), Marceline Hugot
     (Kathy Geiss), Seth Kirschner (Shawn), Sue Galloway (Sue), Paula Pell (Paula
     Hornberger), Jack Burditt (The Colonel), Bethany Hall (Bethany), Jim Downey
     (Downey), Remy Bond (Janet), Dante Hoagland (Terry), Barrett Doss (Eliza
     Lemon), Maggie Geha (Inga), Bonnie Swencionis (Sam)

In the fall of 2006, NBC added two new series to their prime-time lineup that were set backstage at a live sketch comedy series à la *Saturday Night Live*. The first, *Studio 60 on the Sunset Strip* (2006–2007) was an hour-long comedy-drama created by Aaron Sorkin. The series' title doubled as the title of the live comedy show-within-the-show, broadcast from the Sunset Strip on the fictional National Broadcast System (NBS) network. Back in October

2005, Josef Adalian reported in *Variety* that Sorkin's pilot sparked a bidding war between NBC and CBS, with the "Peacock network" the victor after agreeing to pay $2 million per episode. This made *Studio 60* the most expensive first-year drama in NBC history.

The second series, *30 Rock*, was the brainchild of *Saturday Night Live* head writer Tina Fey, who had a four-year deal to develop new television series for NBC. According to *Time* magazine television critic James Poniewozik, the first show Fey pitched was set behind-the-scenes at a cable news network. Kevin Reilly, president of NBC Entertainment, encouraged Fey to write about what she knew, so she returned with a pilot for a single-camera comedy in which she plays Elizabeth Miervaldis "Liz" Lemon, producer of *The Girlie Show*, a live sketch comedy show on NBC. The series' title and setting, 30 Rock, is short for 30 Rockefeller Center, the Art Deco skyscraper that houses the National Broadcast Company's corporate headquarters and the studios for *The Today Show*, MSNBC, and NBC's late night talk shows. *30 Rock* was filmed at Silvercup Studios in Long Island City in Queens, New York, though the episodes in season 5 ("Live Show") and season 6 ("Live from Studio 6H") were broadcast live with a studio audience from 30 Rock's Studio 8H, the long-time home of *Saturday Night Live.*

In the pilot episode, Liz Lemon's world is turned upside down when her new boss, Jack Donaghy (Alec Baldwin), the network's new vice president of East Coast Television and Microwave Oven Programming, orders her to add Tracy Jordan (Tracy Morgan) to the cast of *The Girlie Show*. A comedian with a reputation for exhibiting bizarre, erratic, and inappropriate behavior, especially in public (i.e., walking naked through LaGuardia Airport, biting Dakota Fanning's face, etc.), Tracy is certifiable. For Liz, who, as the show's executive producer has enough on her plate, he is a handful. For Jenna Maroney (Jane Krakowski), *The Girlie Show*'s narcissistic star (and Liz's best friend), he's a major threat, especially when Jack insists the show's title be changed to *TGS with Tracy Jordan.*

A real casting change occurred off-camera before *30 Rock*'s debut when Krakowski was hired to replace former *Saturday Night Live* cast member Rachel Dratch. Two months before *30 Rock* debuted, *Variety*'s Michael Schneider reported that Dratch, who has known Fey since they were Second City cast members back in Chicago, would no longer be playing Jenna DeCarlo. Instead, Dratch would be featured in an assortment of roles, such as no-nonsense cat wrangler Greta Johanssen, who appears in the pilot and several other episodes. As a result, the pilot was re-shot with Krakowski taking over the role of Jenna DeCarlo, who was renamed Jenna Maroney. Dratch eventually left the show after season 1, but made guest appearances in season 5 on the "Live Show" episode and in an hour-long episode celebrating *30 Rock*'s 100th episode ("100").

In her autobiography, *Girl Walks Into a Bar: Comedy Calamities, Dating Disasters, and a Midlife Miracle*, Dratch sets the record straight by answering the question that everyone kept asking her: "SO WHAT HAPPENED WITH *30 ROCK?*!" According to Dratch, the original pilot of the series included real comedy sketches, but when they were all cut when the pilot was rewritten,

The talented Tina Fey—creator, star, and executive producer of *30 Rock*. *Authors' collection*

they no longer need an actual sketch performer (like Dratch) in the role, but a "sitcom ingénue type," like Krakowski, who had played office assistant Elaine Vassal on *Ally McBeal* (1997–2002). Dratch admitted that the idea of playing different characters was "unique" and it felt more comfortable for her than solely playing a "diva type."

But the Internet told a completely different story. "The general opinion seemed to be that it wasn't about 'sitcom' or 'sketch,'" Dratch writes. "It was about attractiveness. It was about Pretty. The Internet, magazines, and news stories all gingerly speculated that I had been replaced by a more attractive actor and that this was the *only* reason I had been replaced." Although Dratch believed this was not the case, she reminded herself when she did have moments of self-doubt that her comedy idols—Gilda Radner, Lily Tomlin, Jean Stapleton, and Carol Burnett—would hardly be classified as "hotties." She also commented on the matter in this way: "I had always been pretty sure that comedy was about producing a laugh and not a boner. Now I had to produce laughs *and* boners? When did the rules change?"

The cast of *30 Rock* also featured actor/comedian Judah Friedlander as slovenly staff writer Frank Rossitano and two more of Fey's Second City cast mates from the 1990s: Jack McBrayer as Kenneth Parcell, the overly zealous NBC page who loves television, and Scott Adsit as Pete Hornberger, *TGS*'s low-key executive producer. Also in the cast were Katrina Bowden as Cerie, Liz's beautiful, but not terribly competent, assistant; Keith Powell as Toofer Spurlock, a Harvard graduate and the lone African American writer on the *TGS* staff; and Maulik Pancholy as Jonathan, Jack's doting assistant who hates Liz and was only hired when a sedated Jack mistook the Indian American for *The Sixth Sense* director M. Night Shyamalan.

A television series set in the wacky world of broadcasting is not entirely a new concept. Over the years, there have been "behind-the-scenes" sitcoms of a comedy-variety show (*The Dick Van Dyke Show* [1961–1966]), talk shows (*The New Dick Van Dyke Show* [1971–1974], *The Larry Sanders Show* [1992–1998], *Life with Bonnie* [2002–2004]), morning shows (*Good Morning, Miami* [2002–2004]), how-to shows (*Home Improvement* [1991–1999]), television news programs (*The Mary Tyler Moore Show* [1970–1977], *Murphy Brown* [1988–1998], *Less Than Perfect* [2002–2006]), as well as a radio news show (*NewsRadio* [1995–1999]), Top 40 AM stations (*WKRP in Cincinnati* [1978–1982]/*The New WKRP in Cincinnati* [1991–1993]), and a sports network (*Sports Night* [1998–2000]). *Studio 60* creator Sorkin has had great success with shows set behind-the-scenes of such places as the White House (*The West Wing* [1999–2006]), an ESPN-type sports show (*Sports Night*), and a cable news network (*The Newsroom* [2012–2014]). But two behind-the-scenes shows with similar settings on the same network was a tough sell for NBC, which hoped

West Wing fans would watch *Studio 60*, and *Saturday Night Live* fans would tune in to see Fey, Morgan, and, popular and frequent *SNL* host Baldwin. Unfortunately, it didn't happen for either show.

The *30 Rock* pilot received mixed reviews by the television critics, with the highest marks going to Baldwin and Morgan. The first line of *New York Times* critic Alessandra Stanley's review reads: "Nothing very funny happens on '30 Rock' until Alec Baldwin enters the room, and suddenly this new NBC sitcom comes alive." For *Pittsburgh Post-Gazette* TV critic Rob Owen, "'30 Rock' is amusing enough before Morgan makes his entrance," but "it's much funnier after his arrival." As for Tina Fey—the sitcom star—some critics were not so keen on her performance. *Washington Post* critic Tom Shales, a longtime champion of *SNL* who co-authored (with James Andrew Miller) a history of the show, believed the "one gaping and highly visible flaw" in Tina Fey's "show about herself starring herself as herself" was Tina Fey: "Called upon to act, she unfortunately tends to fade into the wallpaper. It's not good when the star of the show appears to be just hanging around." Shales liked the rest of the cast, but he was not impressed by the overall show: "For all the rewriting and reworking, the show needs a better premise and funnier dialogue, and, most of all, a more commanding performer in the starring role." Ironically, for her portrayal of Liz Lemon, Fey would go on to win an Emmy, two Golden Globes, and four Screen Actors Guild Awards. As Liz might say, "Suck it, Shales."

By comparison, *Studio 60* received high praise from many critics, several of whom—Tim Goodman (*San Francisco Gate*), Melanie McFarland (*Seattle Post-Intelligencer*), Matthew Gilbert (*Boston Globe*), to name a few—called it one of, if not the best, new show of the season. But by the time *30 Rock* premiered, four episodes of *Studio 60* had aired (on Monday at 10:00 p.m., opposite *C.S.I. Miami* [2002–2012]) and each week its viewership declined. *Chicago Tribune* media columnist Phil Rosenthal reported that the "most-hyped show of the new TV season . . . has become the 'biggest disappointment.'" An estimated 7.74 million viewers, 60 percent fewer viewers than the 13.4 million who tuned in to the pilot, saw the fourth episode.

30 Rock found itself in a somewhat similar situation. *Variety*'s Rick Kissell reported the ratings for the premiere were decent (8.13 million viewers), but viewership dropped by 20 percent, making *30 Rock* and the sitcom it preceded, *Twenty Good Years* (2006), which disappeared from the schedule after four episodes, the two lowest rated comedies on the major networks. But as he told *Variety* reporter Josef Adalian, NBC president Kevin Reilly still believed in *30 Rock* and decided it needed a better time slot, so he added the show, along with *Scrubs* (2001–2010), to NBC's "Must See TV" Thursday night schedule. Reilly told *Variety*'s Josef Adalian that after watching several completed episodes, he was confident that *30 Rock* would find an audience on

The cast of *30 Rock* toasts their seventh and final season: Seated (left to right): Jack McBrayer, Alec Baldwin, Tracy Morgan. Back Row (left to right): Tina Fey and Jane Krakowski.   *Authors' collection*

a new night. In December, Adalian reported that *30 Rock*, the network's last remaining "bubble show" (meaning it could either be canceled or picked up for more episodes), which had recently scored its second-best rating among adults 18–49, was picked up for a full season. Later that month, *Variety*'s Michael Learmonth also reported that in an effort to recruit new viewers, particularly college students home from the holidays, NBC was planning to stream the first seven episodes of *30 Rock*, along with the critically acclaimed yet low-rated *Friday Night Lights* (2006–2011), on nbc.com until first-run episodes resumed in January.

In addition to Reilly's support for the series, there are several other reasons *30 Rock* continued for seven seasons and a total of 138 episodes: many major television critics included *30 Rock* on their 2006 "Best of Television" list; Lorne Michaels, whose association with NBC dates back to the mid-1970s, was the show's executive producer; and Tina Fey was (and is) a major talent whose impersonation of vice presidential candidate Sarah Palin on *SNL* gave the sitcom a much needed ratings boost in season 3. *30 Rock* was also an Emmy magnet, winning Best Comedy Series three years in a row for seasons 1, 2, and 3. Over seven seasons, the show picked up sixteen Emmys and a stagger-ing 103 nominations. More importantly, the show's low ratings did not tell the whole story. In late December of 2006, Nielsen Media Research started publishing the results of monitored viewers who were recording programs on their Digital Video Recorder (DVR) and watching it at another time (known as "time-shifting"). According to the television ratings website Zap2it, *30 Rock* was the fourth-most time-shifted new series on television (*Studio 60* was no. 1) with 7.5 percent additional viewers added to its total audience.

The term "postmodern" may be overused and misused by academics and pop culturists, but it is certainly applicable to *30 Rock* due to the distinct manner in which Fey experimented with the sitcom form. Over the course of a twenty-two minute episode, a new conflict is introduced, followed by a series of complications, which leads to a final resolution. Order is once again restored—at least until next week's episode. But *30 Rock* never followed this formula. There's conflict, but minimal plot (and it's not necessarily linear or logical), which leaves plenty of time for jokes—and there are lots of them. The result is a highly fragmented half hour that caters to viewers with short attention spans. In his aptly titled essay, "The Sitcom Digresses," Ross Simonini examines how sitcoms like *30 Rock*, *Arrested Development*, *Scrubs*, and the animated comedy *Family Guy* "explore their situations through collage and a restless stream of consciousness" by using verbal digressions (like, "Remember the time . . ." or, "What would it be like if . . ."), which lead to one or more cutaways to events in Liz's childhood and high school years, usually contradicting how she remembers the past.

30 Rock also qualifies as postmodern because it is a hyperconscious (acutely aware of itself) situation comedy set behind-the-scenes of a fictitious television comedy, both of which air on an actual network. At the same time, we can only assume that the network that pays Fey and Baldwin for their services bears no resemblance to the loony bin where Liz works. (Or does it?) The line separating the real NBC and *30 Rock*'s NBC is often blurred, particularly with the numerous guest appearances by NBC personalities, such as NBC news anchor Brian Williams; NBC comedy veterans Jerry Seinfeld, Kelsey Grammer, and cast members from the 1980s sitcom *Night Court* (1984–1992) (Harry Anderson, Markie Post, and Charles Robinson); and hosts of *Today* (Savannah Guthrie, Matt Lauer, Al Roker, Meredith Vieira) and the network's late night talk shows (Conan O'Brien, Jimmy Fallon).

We are also reminded in every episode when Liz Lemon takes her obliga-tory elevator ride up to the top of 30 Rock to engage in another absurd exchange with Jack Donaghy that American television is, first and foremost, a business. For instance, *30 Rock* poked fun at the placement of products in television series by calling viewers' attention to it. When Jack remarks to Liz about his new Verizon phone ("Somebody to Love"), she remarks, "Well, sure, that Verizon Wireless service is just unbeatable. If I saw a phone like that on TV, I would be like, 'Where is my nearest retailer so I can get one?'" Then, without missing a beat, she talks directly into the camera and asks, "Can we have our money now?" In another meeting, Jack informs Liz and her staff they will need to integrate General Electric products into their show ("Jack-Tor"). Liz and Pete interrupt the conversation, remarking how great the Diet Snapple they are drinking tastes.

In an age when the media is controlled by brand-conscious conglomerates, it is surprising (and refreshing) that NBC and General Electric allowed *30 Rock* to bite the corporate hand that fed them. *30 Rock* even went so far as to parody the 2009–2010 media-fueled feud between Conan O'Brien and Jay Leno over hosting *The Tonight Show*, which resulted in O'Brien leaving the network (rather than moving his show to midnight to accommodate Leno's new show) and Leno getting his old job back. In *30 Rock*'s version ("Khonani") Jack must mediate a feud between two NBC janitors over their late night work schedules.

Another major change that occurred at NBC while *30 Rock* was on the air was the purchase of General Electric's remaining 49 percent of NBC Universal by Comcast, thereby making the largest cable television provider in the United States the sole owner of NBC. On *30 Rock*, G. E. sells NBC to the fictional cable company Kabletown, which becomes Jack's new employer. As Josh Wolk at *Vulture* notes, the episode in which Liz and Jack watch the General Electric sign being replaced at the top of 30 Rock with Kabletown's logo ("Operation Righteous Cowboy") aired the same day that NBC employees had a town meeting with their new boss, Comcast Cable president Steve Burke, who is now the chief executive officer of NBC Universal.

The two-part finale of *30 Rock* ("Hogcock!" and "Final Lunch") is really a *three*-part finale that begins the previous week in an episode ("A Goon's Deed in a Weary World") in which Jack and Liz are finally given the opportunity to move on with their lives—away from *TGS with Tracy Morgan*, NBC, and 30 Rock.

Jack manages to secure his position as the new CEO of Kabletown ("Game Over") by outsmarting his former archenemy Devon Banks (Will Arnett) and teenager Kaylie Hooper (Chloë Grace Moretz). The current CEO, Hank Hooper (Ken Howard), names his granddaughter Kaylie as his successor, but Jack gets the job because he remembers to send Hank a Happy 70th Birthday card while little Kaylie forgot because she was too busy scheming with Devon behind Jack's back.

Jack's next job ("A Goon's Deed in a Weary World") is to hire someone to take over as the new president of NBC. With some help from Kenneth, who is back in his page uniform, he tries to figure out which of the five finalists is right for the job. In true postmodern fashion, *30 Rock* "borrows" from the plot of the 1971 film musical *Willy Wonka & the Chocolate Factory* (based on Roald Dahl's children's book, *Charlie and the Chocolate Factory*). The five candidates resemble the five children from the story, yet none of them really, really, *really* loves television as much as simple-minded Kenneth, whom Jack appoints as the new head of the network. Meanwhile, Liz learns *TGS* has been canceled due to bad press over a recent lawsuit by Hazel (Kristen Schaal), the nutjob intern. Jack says he will stick with *TGS* if it can turn a profit, so Liz plans to save the show by convincing the Kabletown board to keep them on the air. While all of this is going on, her husband, Criss (James Marsden), tells her that their adopted twins are set to arrive by plane that day. When the cast and crew of *TGS* find out that Liz was planning to sacrifice being there when her kids arrive in order to save the show, they decide to return the favor and, as a way of thanking Liz for all that she's done, quit the show, so Liz can rush to the airport to join Criss to meet their adopted twins, Janet and Terry.

"A Goon's Deed" would have been a satisfying series finale. In true *30 Rock* fashion, there is no shortage of silly moments: the *Willy Wonka* plotline; Tracy and Jenna's idea for a feature film entitled *Heads of State*, in which they play conjoined twins elected co-president of the United States; and Liz's attempt to save the show by securing a reprehensible new sponsor, Bro Body Douche, whose owner insists on changing the show's title to *Man Cave*. But there are also a few emotional moments one expects to find in a series finale, like Jack's speech to Kenneth when he is appointed the new president of NBC; and the cast and crew's thank you to Liz, who we see hugging her adopted children for the first time.

While *30 Rock*'s frenetic pacing resumes in the two-part finale, there are, once again, a few moments in which the characters wear their hearts on their sleeves, particularly Liz and Jack, both of whom find themselves at a crossroads in their lives. Liz is miserable being a stay-at-home mom, while her husband, Criss, would rather be a stay-at-home dad than work as a receptionist in a dentist's office. Back at 30 Rock, Jack questions whether he is truly happy and with some help from his "Wheel of Happiness Domination," he manages to fill, in a minute-long montage, some of the voids in certain aspects of his life, like "Family," "Faith," "Philanthropy," and "Sex & Relationships." Still, despite the pleasure diehard Republican Jack gets ticking off Occupy Wall Street protestors and Congresswoman Nancy Pelosi (who makes a cameo) when his zillion-dollar salary as the head of Kabletown is made public, he's still not happy with the one thing that has always meant the most to him— work. He decides to resign as CEO of Kabletown, which confuses and upsets Liz, who has been listening to Jack for seven years about how work is the

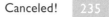

only thing that really matters. He blames Liz for "worming her way" into his brain with "her endless handwringing and feelings." Jack later tries to make amends, but Liz can hold a grudge, which turns Jack into an emotional mess.

Meanwhile, Tracy and Jenna are having problems adjusting to post-*TGS* life: he is lost without Kenneth, who is now busy running the network, and Jenna is discovering she is not as young or as big of a star as she believes. But they both get to return to *TGS* one last time when Kenneth informs Liz that there's a clause in Tracy's contract that if he is in fewer than 150 episodes of *TGS*, NBC has to pay him a penalty of $30 million. He's been in 149, so Liz is contractually obligated to produce one more episode of the show. Consequently, the gang gets back together for a last goodbye. Only Tracy is M. I. A., forcing Liz to hunt him down at the same strip club where they had their first meeting. They have a poignant exchange in which Tracy admits that he ran out because he didn't want to have to say goodbye (like his father did when he went out for cigarettes and never came back). The conversation

Shades of *St. Elsewhere*: NBC's new network president Kenneth Parcell (Jack McBrayer) and his snow globe. *NBC/Photofest*

between Liz and Tracy seems like one Fey and Morgan would have had now that *30 Rock* is over, particularly when Liz admits they probably won't be hanging out together in the future. "Tracy, you frustrated me, and you wore me out," she admits. "But because the human heart is not properly connected to the human brain, I love you, and I'm gonna miss you. But tonight might be it."

Liz and Jack also have a final moment. After watching a video message that sounds like a suicide note, Liz races to a pier where she sees Jack jumping into the water. Actually, he is jumping on to his yacht, ready to sail away. Liz tells him she loves him. He says the same (in a less direct manner) and admits that for the past seven years she was the one thing that made him consistently happy. Jack leaves, yet suddenly turns his boat around because he has had a brainstorm—see-through dishwashers!

You sense this is all being done more for the cast and crew of *30 Rock*, but that's okay. *TGS* ends with the entire cast and crew of *30 Rock* (minus Fey) in front of the camera. Tracy Jordan (or is it Morgan) looks into the camera and says, "Thank you, America. That's our show. Not a lot of people watched it, but the joke's on you—'cause we got paid anyway."

Fey and co-writer Tracey Wigfield, who won an Emmy for "Last Lunch," treat us to an epilogue. Pete, who had faked his own death, is found by his wife, Paula. Liz is back at work producing a new sitcom for Tracy's wingman, Grizz, called *Grizz & Herz*. Jenna tries to steal Broadway star Alice Ripley's Tony Award. Liz has remained friends with Jack, who gets his dream job—CEO of General Electric—and Tracy, whose father has finally come home from getting cigarettes. Finally, in a wink to the finale of another NBC show, *St. Elsewhere* (see chapter 8), there's another twist: we see an image of 30 Rockefeller Center inside of a snow globe Kenneth is holding in his hand while listening to a young woman pitch her idea for a show based on her great, great grandmother, Liz Lemon. Fortunately, Kenneth likes the idea!

"High-five a million angels!" exclaims *TV Guide* reporter Joyce Eng, who is happy to report that *30 Rock*'s finale received its best rating in almost a year. People tuned in to the finale—4.8 million to be exact—which is not bad considering *30 Rock* faced off against two high-rated shows: *The Big Bang Theory* (17.5 million) and *American Idol* (13.7 million). The critics who often doubled as fans of the show were also over the moon about the finale. *People* magazine television critic Tom Gliatto praised the hour as "one of the most delightful series wrap-ups I can remember." James Poniewozik of *Time* magazine called the finale, which made him cry, "sharp, nostalgic, funny and heartfelt" and cited Liz and Jack's goodbye "as fine a declaration of platonic love as a sitcom has ever done." Poniewozik also makes an important observation regarding Liz and Jack's "work-love," which "has always been one of the most important points of the show: a love that's about respect, mutual concern, and high regard." He also retracts his earlier criticism regarding Fey's acting, crediting the "onetime writer" for mastering "the physical and verbal jump rope required by the very demanding show she created" (to set the record straight, Fey did begin her comedy career performing in Chicago as a member of Second City). The *New York Times*' Alessandra Stanley called Fey "a pioneer who resists being taking too seriously" and implies that as a female writer starring in her own network series, she paved the way for Mindy Kaling (*The Mindy Project*), Lena Dunham (*Girls*), Whitney Cummings (*Whitney*), and Amy Poehler (*Parks and Recreation*). Stanley also notes that Fey is better at writing and impersonating Sarah Palin than acting, mostly because she was "never convincing as a loser." *A loser?* That's a bit of a simplification. Jack Donaghy's description of Liz was far more accurate: "I got you: New York third-wave feminist, college educated, single, and pretending to be happy about it, over scheduled, undersexed, you buy any magazine that says 'healthy body image' on the cover, and every two years you take up knitting . . . for a week."

In the past, networks have thrown in the towel on low-rated series halfway through the first season. But in this case, perhaps NBC just couldn't bring itself to shut down a show named after its own headquarters. Fey's decision to title the show *30 Rock* does sound like something cooked up by Jack and Liz.

21

Clocking Out

Closing *The Office*

The Office (NBC, 2005–2013)
Created by Ricky Gervais and Stephen Merchant
Adapted for U.S. television by Greg Daniels
Premiere date: March 24, 2005
9 seasons / 187 episodes
"Finale"
Airdate: May 16, 2013
3.2 rating • 5 percent share • 5.7 million viewers
Directed by Ken Kwapis
Written by Greg Daniels
Cast: Rainn Wilson (Dwight Schrute), John Krasinski (Jim Halpert), Jenna Fischer
     (Pam Beesly-Halpert), Ed Helms (Andy Bernard), Angela Kinsey (Angela
     Martin), Oscar Nuñez (Oscar Martinez), Craig Robinson (Darryl Philbin),
     Phyllis Smith (Phyllis Lapin-Vance), Brian Baumgartner (Kevin Malone), Ellie
     Kemper (Erin Hannon), Creed Bratton (Creed Bratton), Leslie David Baker
     (Stanley Hudson), Paul Lieberstein (Toby Flenderson), Catherine Tate (Nellie
     Bertram), Kate Flannery (Meredith Palmer)
Guest Stars: Steve Carell (Michael Scott), Mindy Kaling (Kelly Kapoor), B. J. Novak
     (Ryan Howard), Andy Buckley (David Wallace), Michael Schur (Mose Schrute),
     Nancy Walls Carell (Carol Stills), Rachael Harris (Rachael)

When it comes to American pop culture embracing British imports, four young mop-topped lads from Liverpool immediately come to mind. Creating a sensation in the States that began in 1964, John, Paul, George, and Ringo ushered in a time in American history when a "British Invasion" was considered a good thing. Along with the Beatles came the Rolling Stones, beloved superspy James Bond, and mod fashion icon Twiggy—American audiences were ready and willing to embrace all things England. Even television joined in the act, as Norman Lear's cultural sensation *All in the Family* was inspired by a British sitcom called *Till*

Death Us Do Part (BBC1, 1965–1975), and Charles Prince of Wales and Lady Diana Spencer's 1981 nuptials shattered ratings records. However, the road for British imports didn't always go the way of successes like the Spice Girls or Simon Fuller's *Pop Idol*, and with every profitable story there are an equal number of failed projects. Hoping to tap into the success (and fan base) of its megahit *Friends*, NBC adapted famed British sitcom *Coupling* in 2003, only to find it flop after just four episodes. Expectations were not high when NBC dipped its foot back across the pond in 2005 with an adaptation of the quirky British hit *The Office*. But NBC, wasting away in fourth place among its prime-time network counterparts, was willing to take the risk. Eight years later, throngs of fans lined the streets of Scranton, Pennsylvania—and this time, it wasn't to welcome the Fab Four, but instead, the fictional characters of their favorite television show, the employees of paper company Dunder Mifflin.

Before television audiences came to know the staff at Dunder Mifflin, Ricky Gervais and Stephen Merchant brought British audiences the employees of Wernham Hogg Paper Company—a two-season, twelve episode series (plus a two-part Christmas special and *The Office Revisited* [2013]) that premiered in the United Kingdom in July 2001. With a style similar to Christopher Guest's iconic mock rock 'n' roll documentary *This Is Spinal Tap* (1984), Gervais and Merchant (both writing and directing the series, with Gervais as its star) welcomed cameras into the halls of Wernham Hogg and, with that, a new genre of television: the mockumentary. While following the mundane day-to-day exploits of bored office workers does not immediately bring to mind riveting television, Gervais and Merchant's style used the device of the breaking-the-fourth-wall, and direct-to-camera character asides, allowing the audience to have a look inside the minds of their favorite characters. Breaking through that wall led to a breakthrough in television comedy. Gervais and Merchant's show was a hit, winning critical acclaim both in the UK and abroad, including a win for both the show and Gervais (as Best Actor) at the 2004 Golden Globes.

Months before the Globes, the show was officially sold to NBC for a pilot commitment, a decision that the *New York Times* called "a desperation move by [a network] which finds itself in fourth place after years at the top with hits like *Friends* and *Frasier*." Desperate or not, it was a gamble for NBC, who had only just struck out with their attempt to import *Coupling*. But NBC execs remained cautiously optimistic. Kevin Reilly, then president of prime-time development at the network, told *The Hollywood Reporter*: "Workplace comedies are a staple of TV. Unfortunately, most office comedies have all the reality leeched out of them. In *The Office*, Ricky Gervais and Stephen Merchant have created a show that perfectly captures the universal experience of the daily grind." With Gervais and Merchant committed to staying on as executive producers and show consultants, Greg Daniels, co-creator of FOX's animated comedy *King of the Hill*, was tapped to write the pilot—a script that was largely based on the pilot of the British series, even to the point of lifting exact lines. Fears that the show's humor would not translate in America were soon quashed when the UK *Office* premiered to raves on BBC America—but a new fear, the fear that audiences would never welcome anyone other than Ricky Gervais in the lead role, became very real. It was clear that NBC would need to land a major comedy player to fill Gervais's deep shoes.

Enter Steve Carell. Trained with the successful Chicago Second City comedy troupe, Carell appeared as a correspondent on *The Daily Show with Jon Stewart* from 1999 to 2005 and voiced half of Robert Smigel's animated "Ambiguously Gay Duo" on *Saturday Night Live* (the other half voiced by *Daily Show* and Second City colleague Stephen Colbert). At the time of casting for Daniels's *The Office*, Carell was unavailable—he was already cast as a supporting player on NBC's midseason comedy *Come to Papa*, based on the work of standup comic Tom Papa. This problem quickly resolved itself as *Come to Papa* was canceled after airing only four episodes. With Carell officially cast as the lead in the American adaptation of *The Office*, NBC charged forward with casting the rest of the ensemble, a process future cast member Angela Kinsey called "not conventional," in part due to its focus on finding relative unknowns (Kinsey: "For once, not being a prominent face on TV was a help."). With realism as its main concern, it was imperative that the actors be believable as employees at a mid-sized paper company based in its new home of working-class Scranton, Pennsylvania—or in the words of Leslie David Baker, who went on to play *The Office*'s beloved curmudgeon Stanley Hudson: "You don't want an office where everybody is 20 years old. It's unrealistic. *The Office* looks like real offices. Everybody is not looking like they just stepped off the cover of *Vogue*." With its rookie cast and newly hired director Ken Kwapis, a television veteran with credits including many offbeat sitcoms (*The Larry Sanders Show, Malcolm in the Middle*, and *The Bernie Mac Show*), *The Office* was ready for its midseason premiere on March 24, 2005.

Ricky Gervais's cringe-worthy branch manager David Brent was now Carell's Michael Scott; Rainn Wilson's Dwight Schrute filled in for Mackenzie Crook's strange, power-hungry Gareth Keenan; Jenna Fischer's Pam Beesly sat in for Lucy Davis's receptionist Dawn Tinsley; and shaggy-haired prankster Tim Canterbury (previously played by Martin Freeman, of future *Sherlock* and *The Hobbit* fame) became John Krasinski's shaggy-haired Jim Halpert. The show did not open with blockbuster ratings, or wild critical acclaim. Initial reviews were cautious, suggesting that the overly faithful version of the BBC series may seem unappealing to diehard fans. The *New York Times* called it "very funny for viewers who never saw the original." *Entertainment Weekly*'s

Gillian Flynn added: "For aficionados, it won't work: You can't help but see Gervais' roly-poly ghost in every scene." Flynn continued: "*The Office* lacks the aching subtlety of the BBC version. . . . As every office drone knows, a copy is never quite as perfect as the original." The *Washington Post*'s Tom Shales bluntly stated: "Steve Carell as boss Michael Scott is simply not as good as Ricky Gervais as the boss in the British prototype." As these early reviews make clear, overcoming the hurdle of endless comparisons to the original BBC version would prove most challenging for the show, especially considering the success of the previous incarnation on both BBC America and rising DVD sales. Series creator Greg Daniels, however, was hopeful, noting: "It's going to be a process, a long road. There are two constituencies—those who love the English show and who should like this show because it has a lot of the same qualities, and the general audience. I think that they will learn to like the show. I don't expect them to love it right off the bat." Luckily for Daniels, NBC agreed, and renewed the show for a second season, counting on the upcoming summer release of Carell's feature film *The 40 Year Old Virgin* to catapult its lead to super-stardom—and their gamble paid off. *Virgin* was the breakout hit of the summer of 2005 (grossing $21.4 million on its opening weekend, $109 million total), and Carell became a household name—just in time for the second season of the show to premiere on September 20, 2005. Ratings soared—Dunder Mifflin was on its way.

The Office went on to win the Emmy for Best Comedy Series in August 2006, and became the flagship show of NBC's Thursday night lineup. Carell's ultimately loveable Michael Scott began to break free of the lingering shadow of Gervais's David Brent; John Krasinski and Jenna Fischer's Jim and Pam wooed audiences with their will-they-won't-they mating; and Rainn Wilson's sci-fi nerd, beet-enthusiast Dwight was truly an American original. Much of the credit was rightly given to Greg Daniels and his writing staff for differentiating the show from its predecessor. Upon the show's celebration of its 100th episode in 2009, UK co-creator Stephen Merchant agreed:

> Ricky and I did everything ourselves . . . so there's no way we could have sustained that momentum. And syndication is not an option [in the UK], so you can't invest in a show in the hopes of paying everyone later. We're these little old ladies running a tea shop in Devon, while the American show has a momentum and ambition and energy. It's the Henry Ford model, but something special is coming out the other end.

The success of the show continued to buoy Carell's growing film career (*Evan Almighty* [2007], *Get Smart* [2008], *Despicable Me* [2010]) while the series regulars all became stars in their own right—with Krasinski, Fischer, Wilson, and season 3 additions Ed Helms (Andy Bernard) and Rashida Jones (Karen

Filippelli) all finding roles in feature films. But it was this same catapult to stardom that resulted in the announcement fans dreaded: Steve Carell would exit the series at the end of his existing contract, making the show's seventh season (2010–2011) Michael Scott's last.

Saying goodbye to Michael Scott would take a complete restructuring of the series, a fact that led many to suggest ending the show with Carell's exit. But executive producer Paul Lieberstein (pulling double duty as Dunder Mifflin's head of HR Toby Flenderson) saw things differently: "I hear from both, from people who don't want to watch without Steve and from people who say, 'Great ensemble. Keep going' . . . it's not obvious to me we should stop. When Michael Jordan left the Bulls, nobody said the Bulls should stop. They didn't say, 'Shut down the franchise.'" NBC's president of Prime-time Entertainment, Angela Bromstad, echoed Lieberstein: "Not to diminish the departure of Steve, because that will impact the show, but we have tremendous faith in the writers and actors to keep it alive." Opting not to say goodbye to Carell in the season finale (which was scheduled to air on May 19, 2011), America said goodbye to their beloved Michael Scott on Thursday, April 28, in an extended 50-minute episode titled "Goodbye, Michael." In one of the episode's final moments, Michael, ready to board a plane to join his fiancée, Holly Flax (Amy Ryan), in Colorado, unplugs his microphone pack and hands it over to the unseen documentary crew, but not before saying, "Hey, will you guys let me know if this ever airs." *Entertainment Weekly* called it "nothing short of perfect." *Rolling Stone*'s television critic Rob Sheffield supported Michael Scott's curtain call, particularly how unique his exit was: "In the old days, when a star left a still-thriving hit show, they'd celebrate by killing him or her off," instead *The Office*'s Michael "took a brave step into maturing." Sheffield then named Michael Scott "the most influential sitcom character of the past decade."

After Carell's departure, the show struggled to find its footing, instead opting to entertain a revolving door of celebrity special guests (one of which included a brief appearance by Ricky Gervais as David Brent). Comedy megastar Will Ferrell initially took over for Carell, appearing as DeAngelo Vickers, substitute regional manager of the Scranton branch. But after only four episodes, Ferrell exited the series, replaced by James Spader's Robert California. Dunder Mifflin, mirroring the show itself, went through its own transition—merging with printer company Sabre and assisting in the opening of a Florida retail store. While ratings remained relatively on target (the show remained NBC's highest rated scripted series), the transitional season could not recapture Carell's magic. As the season came to a close, NBC officially announced that the next season, the show's ninth, would indeed be its last. Immediately, speculation of Carell's return began.

Carell's will-he-won't-he dance around the question of whether Michael Scott would appear in the series finale became regular news. In multiple interviews, Carell denied any desire to head back to Scranton to reprise his role as the now former branch manager: "I figured the character would go back and visit everybody, but he wouldn't do it on camera at this point. . . . I think he had grown past the idea of being in the documentary, that was my take on it. That he had said goodbye to that aspect of his life, and that's not what was important to him. I just thought, yeah he'd go back and visit, but he wouldn't want the camera crew to be documenting it."

Executive producer Greg Daniels added fuel to the fire claiming, "Steve is very much of the opinion that the 'Goodbye, Michael' episode *was* his goodbye . . . and that [this season] is the goodbye the rest of the show gets to have." Carell's generosity toward his former colleagues remained headline entertainment news, leading outlets to report mere weeks before the finale that any appearance by Carell would be highly unlikely. But the rumor mill continued to churn when Steve Carell made a surprise appearance at the official *Office* wrap party, held in Scranton on Saturday, May 4, 2013, less than two weeks before the finale was set to air. The send-off, held all across the city, brought nearly all of the series' stars to town, complete with a downtown parade, and capped off with a massive celebration in the city's PNC Field baseball stadium. It was at the stadium, in front of a sold-out audience, that Steve Carell appeared alongside his former cast mates, telling the crowd, simply, "Thank you, Scranton. This is all because of you." Carell's appearance ignited fans—and on the evening of May 16, they would finally get their answer.

The final scenes of the penultimate episode of *The Office* ("A.A.R.M.") find the gang from Dunder Mifflin meeting up after work to watch the first episode of *The Office: An American Workplace*, the documentary series they have all starred in for the past nine years. As we enter the finale (prosaically titled, "Finale"), a year has passed, and the documentary crew has returned to film DVD extras. The characters reunite in Scranton for Dwight and Angela's wedding as well as a panel discussion on their now fully aired documentary. Andy, who was fired in the previous episode, has since become both a viral sensation (for all the wrong reasons) and an admissions officer at his beloved Cornell University. Darryl Philbin (Craig Robinson) has become successful within the Austin-based sports marketing agency Athlead that Jim founded (but subsequently left). Stanley is enjoying retirement in Florida, while Nellie Bertram (Catherine Tate) returns stateside after moving to Poland, and Toby is a struggling author in New York. Kevin Malone (Brian Baumgartner) has been fired from Dunder Mifflin and now runs a local Scranton bar, while office oddball Creed Bratton (convincingly portrayed by real-life oddball

Creed Bratton) remains MIA, though he has reportedly faked his own death. Back at the office, Dwight now runs the show as regional manager, while Oscar Martinez (Oscar Nuñez) plans his own state senate campaign from his desk. Jim and Pam remain in their previous jobs, as do Angela, Phyllis Lapin-Vance (Phyllis Smith), Meredith Palmer (Kate Flannery), and Erin Hannon (Ellie Kemper).

On the eve of Dwight's wedding, Jim is revealed to be "bestest mensch" (best man), and is charged with the task of organizing the bachelor party. Performing the required "gutten pranks" ("good deeds"), Jim treats the gang to Dwight's favorite activities (shooting bazookas in an empty field and smoking cigars) as well as a terribly orchestrated lap dance from a stripper Dwight mistakes for his waitress (why won't she just read him the specials?). Across town, the women, joined by Angela's sister Rachael (Rachael Harris), gather at the Schrute farmhouse for their own bachelorette party, only to discover that the male stripper they hired is actually Meredith's teenage son, Jake. Distracted by the aftermath of Jake's performance, Phyllis leaves the door open and Dwight's cousin Mose (played by former co-executive producer Michael Schur) kidnaps Angela, a family tradition previously unknown to Angela. Dwight, realizing that Mose has followed strict Schrute-family protocol, goes in search of Angela with his bachelor party in tow, discovering that Mose has selected Kevin's bar as the place to settle the score before releasing Angela. Jim, knowing that Dwight would avoid Kevin at all costs, encourages Dwight to finally bury the hatchet with his previous co-worker (his final "gutten prank"), and the two reconcile. After Dwight buys a round for the bar, he goes to the parking lot to liberate Angela, who has been trapped in Mose's trunk during her abduction (and she's not happy about it).

The following morning, the current and former employees of Dunder Mifflin (including CEO David Wallace, played by Andy Buckley) reconvene at the Scranton Cultural Center for a panel discussion on their documentary. As they all reunite on the stage, looking out into an empty auditorium, they wonder if anyone saw the series at all—when, suddenly, they discover a tremendously long line of excited and adoring fans. The Q&A begins shortly thereafter, with highlights that include David Wallace's hatred of the documentary, Erin reuniting with her birth-parents (expertly played by special guests Joan Cusack and Ed Begley Jr.), and Pam fielding many questions about Jim—namely, the marital troubles they encountered in the final year, as Jim's involvement with his business expanded. Pam, fighting off a crowd of Jim admirers, admits that while her relationship had its ups and downs, "it got deeper and it got stronger." The panel discussion concludes, and the audience gives their beloved Dunder Mifflin employees a round of applause.

Angela (Angela Kinsey) and Dwight (Rainn Wilson) marry per the Schrute family tradition: while standing in their own graves.   *NBC/Photofest*

The gang, now joined by old flames Kelly Kapoor (Mindy Kaling), accompanied by her doctor-husband, and Ryan Howard (B. J. Novak), now a father to baby Drake, attend Dwight and Angela's wedding. As the guests filter in to Schrute Farms, Jim confesses to Dwight that he can no longer be the "bestest mensch" as strict Schrute law dictates that the position must be held by someone older than the groom. Just as Dwight argues with Jim, he turns to see

Michael Scott, now aged with salt and pepper hair, standing in the doorway. Through tears Dwight says, "I can't believe you came," to which Michael, as only he could, replies: "That's what *she* said." Despite Carell's many interviews to the contrary, Michael Scott had returned to Scranton to stand alongside his beloved "Assistant to the Regional Manager." Post-ceremony, Michael, looking on at the smiling faces of Jim and Pam, Dwight and Angela, relates to the camera crew: "I feel like all my kids grew up and they married each other. It's every parent's dream." The wedding continues, as co-workers dance and reconnect—none more so than Kelly and Ryan, who run off together, abandoning their husband and son, respectively.

Jim and Pam return home following the wedding, only to find realtor Carol Stills (Michael's former girlfriend, played by Carell's real-life wife, Nancy Walls) showing their home to prospective buyers. Jim is caught completely off guard, as Pam explains that she has had the house on the market for some time. The couple admiring their house agrees to buy it, and Pam's romantic gesture pays off—the Halperts can now leave Scranton for Austin so that Jim can go back to his dream job at the company he started. The Halperts rejoin the wedding revelers at the after party held in the Dunder Mifflin warehouse. There, Pam reveals her final mural—a painted history of the branch, complete with each character beautifully represented. After an official photo is taken (cleverly including both the cast and the crew of *The Office*—even Greg Daniels has a cameo), the staff sneaks up to the offices, where Jim and Pam break the news of their departure to Dwight. Dwight refuses to accept their resignation, opting to fire both Halperts instead, offering a very generous severance package. The employees gather together for one last hurrah, as a bearded Creed leads the group in a sweet song. Each character bids farewell to the camera crew, and it is Pam who has the last word: "I thought it was weird when you picked us to make a documentary, but all in all, I think an ordinary paper company like Dunder Mifflin was a great subject for a documentary. There's a lot of beauty in ordinary things. Isn't that kind of the point?" As Pam's words hang in the air, she removes the watercolor she painted of Dunder Mifflin's office building—the very one that Michael had purchased at her art show many years earlier ("The Business School"). And with that, the lights go out on Dunder Mifflin.

Reception of the finale initially focused on Carell's surprise appearance. After months of denials, Carell stepped back into his role as Michael Scott to bid adieu to the series that helped make him a star. His appearance, coupled with Jim and Pam's bittersweet farewell to the office that set the scene for their great love story, packed the emotional punch fans were hoping for. James Poniewozik of *Time* admitted that the finale "used every device in the emotional-comedy playbook: a wedding, reunions, flashback footage, a romantic gesture, a goodbye song," but that ultimately the series close was "touching, sweet, funny, messy, a little manipulative . . . and in the end, it worked." *Variety*'s Brian Lowry called it "a nostalgic, bittersweet experience for anyone who admired the show along the way." For *New York Times*' Mike Hale, the series capper was "festive and sentimental," while "[working] hard to provide resolutions or at least comic grace notes for many in the cast." Hale also noted that *The Office* refrained from closing out on a "high-concept twist" à la the *Seinfeld* trial, the *Frasier* plane ride, or the *Newhart* bad dream (for more on those see chapters 4, 19, and 24), opting instead for "an episode that was in keeping with the show's modest, utilitarian style." The finale saw a ratings bump for the series, averaging just about 5.7 million viewers (the show's biggest audience since January 2012).

The lingering effects of *The Office* on the television landscape are numerous. Originally intended to be a spinoff, *Parks and Recreation*, co-created by *The Office*'s Greg Daniels and Michael Schur, became a star-making vehicle for *Saturday Night Live*'s Amy Poehler, borrowing all of its mockumentary style from its predecessor. ABC's five-time Emmy Award-winning comedy megahit *Modern Family* uses a direct-to-camera interview style that owes a great debt to *The Office*. Yet, beyond simply the technical influences, *The Office* also ushered in a type of sitcom that did not rely solely on the punch line, the laugh track, or the volleying setup of a traditional joke. *The Office*, though a contemporary of more traditional sitcoms like *Everybody Loves Raymond*, *How I Met Your Mother*, and *Two and a Half Men*, ushered in a new era of television comedy. It embraced the subtle moments, the awkward glances, and a style of cringe-inducing comedy that, with the help of Gervais's strong foundation, paved the way for highly praised (but frequently ratings-challenged) shows like *30 Rock*, *Community*, *New Girl*, *Brooklyn Nine-Nine*, and *The Mindy Project* (created by *The Office*'s own Mindy Kaling).

While the workplace sitcom had been perfected and overworked by countless predecessors (*The Mary Tyler Moore Show*, *Murphy Brown*, *NewsRadio*, *The Drew Carey Show*, *Spin City*, *Just Shoot Me!*, just to name a few), *The Office*, with its unique style, subtle charm, and graceful storytelling, emerged as a ground-breaking addition to the genre. In the series finale, Pam, reflecting on her time at Dunder Mifflin as it comes to an close, admits: "It's like a long book that you never want to end, and you're fine with that, because you just never, ever want to leave it." Luckily for fans, long after the fluorescent lights of *The Office* have been shut off, and the staff has clocked out, syndication and countless streaming sources allow fans to continue peering into the cubicles at Dunder Mifflin.

"I Couldn't Help but Wonder"

Carrie-ing on Without *Sex and the City*

Sex and the City (HBO, 1998–2004)
Created by Darren Star
Based on the book by Candace Bushnell
Premiere date: June 6, 1998
6 seasons / 94 episodes
"An American Girl in Paris (Part Deux)"
Airdate: February 22, 2004
10.6 million viewers
Directed by Tim Van Patten
Written by Michael Patrick King
Cast: Sarah Jessica Parker (Carrie Bradshaw), Kim Cattrall (Samantha Jones),
    Kristin Davis (Charlotte York Goldenblatt), Cynthia Nixon (Miranda Hobbes),
    Chris Noth (Mr. Big), David Eigenberg (Steve Brady), Evan Handler (Harry
    Goldenblatt), Jason Lewis (Jerry "Smith" Jerrod), Mikhail Baryshnikov
    (Aleksandr Petrovsky), Mario Cantone (Anthony Marantino), Lynn Cohen
    (Magda), Anne Meara (Mary Brady), Carole Bouquet (Juliet)

Before it was commonplace for HBO to dominate the Emmy Award nominations, the pay-cable network was best known for hosting professional boxing matches and comedy specials. Early original programming for the network, namely comedies *Dream On* (1990–1996) and *The Larry Sanders Show* (1992–1998), were cult hits at best, failing to grab a wider, national audience. Capitalizing on the lack of censor oversight on its network (and the creative freedoms that allowed), HBO pushed the envelope with fast-talking, no-holds-barred sports agent Arliss Michaels (Robert Wuhl) in *Arliss*, as well as taking audiences to *Oz*, a prison that makes *Orange Is the New Black* look like a country club. Just as the channel became synonymous with water-cooler programming, cable television had hit its peak—finally eclipsing traditional networks in viewership by the summer of 1998 (with 40 million viewers versus a continuously slipping 37 million for the networks). The time was right for HBO to separate itself from the cable television pack—and Darren Star's adaptation of Candace Bushnell's racy sex column was just the ticket.

Candace Bushnell, best known for her weekly column for the *New York Observer*, had adapted her work to novel form with her 1997 best-seller *Sex and the City* (published by Warner Books). Following the exploits of Bushnell's alter-ego Carrie Bradshaw (also a sex columnist with the initials C.B.), *Sex and the City* chronicled just that—sex in Manhattan—taking readers into parties, bars, and clubs in the bustling metropolis, all in search of love and lust. Bushnell's urban sex diaries hit a nerve with Darren Star, a television executive producer best known for bringing audiences the racy soaps *Beverly Hills, 90210*, and *Melrose Place*. Bushnell's characters were a perfect fit in Star's world—glamorous socialites navigating an even more glamorous zip code. Star initially pitched the idea to ABC in hopes that the major network would seize the opportunity to host a boundary-pushing female-centered show—an arena the network was familiar with, having broadcast Marlo Thomas's *That Girl* (1966–1971). But *Sex and the City* was too racy for network television and ABC passed, leading Star to head to perhaps the only network able to aptly portray Bushnell's tales: HBO. At the time of Star's pitch, HBO's original programming was brimming with testosterone—capitalizing on the same boxing and comedy-special audience it had long worked to build. Shows like *Dream On*, *The Larry Sanders Show*, and *Arliss* all focused on what Gary R. Edgerton and Jeffrey P. Jones's *Essential HBO Reader* called "psychiatric journeys into the tortured male ego." The time was right for a female-centered, genre-pushing show and Bushnell and Star's creation was the perfect remedy. Looking back on the process of finding the right home for his show, Star said: "*Sex and the City* belongs on HBO. . . . I can't think of another place that would give us the freedom to produce this candid and comical take on contemporary sex and relationships." In the summer of 1998, HBO was ready to launch Star's comedy, reaching out to an entirely new (and powerful) audience: women.

As the show approached its premiere date, series star Sarah Jessica Parker, whose most notable credits to that date were the movies *Honeymoon in Vegas* (1992), *The First Wives Club* (1996), and the painfully '80s sitcom *Square Pegs* (1982–1983), worried that the edgy, sexy style of the book would be too much for television viewers. Parker told *Entertainment Weekly*: "I'm slightly nervous. . . . I don't know if people will find it saucy and smart or if they're going to say, 'Well, this is just completely inappropriate. Who are these dirty awful people who would pollute our airwaves?'" Luckily for Parker (along with Star and Bushnell), 2.75 million viewers tuned in to see just how offended they would be. While raking in HBO's highest ratings to date for an original program, *Sex and the City* was not a right-out-of-the-gate critical hit. The *Washington Post*'s Tom Shales called it a "hopeless bummer," adding that "these are supposedly hip, chic, fashionable New Yorkers, but for the most part they are freakish shrieking bores." The *New York Times'* Caryn James was a bit more kind, calling it "fresh and funny," but also adding "irritating" and "self-important" to the mix. But blockbuster ratings proved to be enough for HBO, who threw its support behind Star's creation, allowing its viewers to continue to be ushered in to the "Age of un-innocence" by their surrogate gal-pal, Parker's Carrie Bradshaw.

Along with Carrie came the sexual escapades of prim and proper Charlotte York (played by *Melrose Place* veteran Kristin Davis), unapologetic feminist lawyer Miranda Hobbes (Cynthia Nixon), raunchy man-eater Samantha Jones (Kim Cattrall), and Carrie's main love interest Mr. Big (*Law and Order*'s Chris Noth). Just as the ensemble became household names, with gaggles of fans declaring "I'm a Carrie" or "I'm a Charlotte," HBO rolled out another show about living in the shadow of New York—David Chase's *The Sopranos*. Premiering in January of 1999, just six months after *Sex and the City*'s debut, Chase's mob drama would overtake *Sex and the City*'s water-cooler freshness, becoming the most talked about, transformative television show for HBO—often cited as the beginning of a new golden age of television (with triple the ratings of *Sex and the City*, with 7.5 million tuning in). *The Sopranos* dominated the conversation, and catapulted HBO to new realms, making the cable network an official tastemaker. *Sex and the City*, briefly thought to be HBO's hallmark series, was now, as the *New Yorker*'s Emily Nussbaum noted, downgraded to merely a "guilty pleasure . . . pigeonholed as a sitcom." But Star, along with executive producer and writer Michael Patrick King, were determined to differentiate their series from any run of the mill rom-com— and with costume designer Patricia Field on their side, the series found its footing.

Fashion figured prominently into every aspect of the series. Carrie's world was a virtual runway, whether her catwalk was the hottest NYC club, or merely a side street in Greenwich Village. Field gave each character her own voice through her clothes and accessories—none more iconic than Carrie's pink tank-top-tutu combination from the show's opening credits. Carrie's love of shoes made designers Manolo Blahnik, Jimmy Choo, and Christian Louboutin household names, with Carrie's Manolos appearing as a major plot point in episodes like season 6's "A Woman's Right to Shoes." While footwear may have been Carrie's main obsession, the girls also appeared frequently with cocktails in hand, ushering in the popularity of the pink, flirty Cosmopolitan. Viewers lived vicariously through the fashion-loving,

The ladies of *Sex and the City*: (left to right) Miranda Hobbes (Cynthia Nixon); Charlotte York (Kristin Davis); Carrie Bradshaw (Sarah Jessica Parker); and Samantha Jones (Kim Cattrall).   *Authors' collection*

cocktail-swilling New York fantasy that was the life of Carrie Bradshaw and her equally chic friends. Yet, while the fashion and lifestyle was enviable, writers also struck a chord with fans by presenting love as messy and complicated. Charlotte's almost too perfect marriage finds itself on the rocks as she has trouble conceiving. Career-obsessed Miranda unexpectedly finds herself pregnant by her underachieving bartender boyfriend. Samantha struggles with breast cancer and the realities of aging. Carrie's will-they-won't-they relationship with Big sabotages all of her other promising relationships, and constantly stands in the way of her happiness. This mix of style and substance led the show to win a major Emmy (2001's Outstanding Comedy Series)—the first for *any* cable series, even its peer *The Sopranos*, which didn't bring home the Drama gold until 2004. *Sex and the City* remained the only cable series to win the Emmy for Best Comedy for nearly fifteen years (HBO recaptured the top prize for *Veep* in 2015).

As *Sex and the City* entered its sixth season in June of 2003, fans knew the end was near. HBO had announced that the sixth season would indeed be its last, but in one final treat for fans, the network split the season into two parts. The first part would air twelve consecutive episodes through September, and the second would air eight additional episodes premiering in January 2004, thus bringing the final season up to twenty episodes—the most ever for any season of the series. Season 6 brought many new changes for the four notoriously single women living in Manhattan—most notably, they all found themselves in relationships. Charlotte, newly converted to Judaism, finds herself ready to tie the knot with her divorce lawyer, Harry Goldenblatt (Evan Handler). Miranda reveals her true feelings for Steve (David Eigenberg) at their son's first birthday party, and like Charlotte, makes it legal (but then has to, gasp, move to Brooklyn!). Samantha, ever the monogamy phobe, meets sexy young waiter-turned-actor Jerry Jerrod (Jason Lewis), whom she rebrands as "Smith Jerrod" and unexpectedly meets her perfect match. Carrie, who strikes out yet again with fellow writer Berger (Ron Livingston), meets famous (and mysterious) Russian artist Aleksandr Petrovsky (played by dance legend Mikhail Baryshnikov). Carrie and The Russian's romance is passionate and fast, with Carrie ready to commit despite his questionable womanizing past. As the final episode approached, each of the four women were in committed relationships—a fact that caused fans to wonder if the pioneering love and lust fantasy had gone soft. The show's touchstone had always been surviving the single life in the big city—following the third season the foursome even appeared on the cover of *Time* with the giant headline: "Who Needs a Husband?" On the eve of the finale, fans wondered if eternal single girl Carrie Bradshaw would join her friends in marital bliss.

The final episode, titled "An American Girl in Paris (Part Deux)" aired on February 22, 2004. The audience joins Carrie who, in the previous week's episode, had decided to leave Manhattan to move to Paris to live with The Russian. Carrie struggles to find herself within Aleksandr's world, even lunching (unexpectedly) with his ex-wife—the impossibly beautiful Juliet (played by model and former Bond girl Carole Bouquet). Back in New York, Charlotte shops with best friend (and former wedding planner) Anthony (Mario Cantone) and considers how much her world will change, as she and Harry prepare to meet the North Carolina couple who have agreed to give up their unborn child. The Goldenblatts are crushed when they learn that the couple has changed their mind, but are put back together again when they learn they are still eligible for an adoption from China. Samantha struggles with the side effects of chemotherapy, namely her diminished sex drive. As Smith heads off to shoot a movie in Canada, Samantha tries to push him away, only to find that he cannot be deterred. Smith returns early from filming to profess his love for Samantha, and the two make passionate love. Steve and Miranda, adjusting to married life and their new residence in Brooklyn, face the failing health of Steve's mother, Mary (played by comedy legend Ann Meara). Discovering that Mary has indeed had a stroke, Miranda agrees to allow her mother-in-law to move in to their new home—a big step for the uncompromising (and unsentimental) lawyer.

Back in Paris, Carrie's adjustment to her new life continues to be difficult, even though it is briefly brightened when she encounters fans of her work at a Parisian bookstore. Invited to a party in her honor, Carrie excitedly asks Aleksandr to escort her, but again, his art (and anxiety) takes precedence over their relationship. Agreeing instead to join him at an early presentation of his art show, Carrie is disappointed (though not surprised) when he ignores her. Rifling through her vintage handbag, Carrie discovers her iconic "Carrie" necklace, the very one she previously believed to be lost. Ever the romantic, she takes it as a sign that she's found herself—and Paris is not where she belongs. She quickly leaves Aleksandr's gallery in hopes of rejoining the bookstore party, but she's too late. Back with Aleksandr, she vents her frustrations. She has left New York, her career, her friends—and now, with Aleksandr busier than ever, she "walks the streets of Paris alone." He tries to avoid their inevitable confrontation and, as she stands in his way, he accidentally hits her. As Carrie stands shocked and embarrassed, he apologizes. It's then that Carrie takes a stand. She lays it all out: "Maybe it's time to be clear about who I am. I am someone who is looking for love. Real love. Ridiculous, inconvenient, consuming, can't-live-without-each-other love . . . and I don't think that love is here." Carrie admits that moving to Paris was a mistake, and leaves their hotel suite. She struggles in the hotel lobby to book another room, only to run into Mr. Big, who, in the previous episode, had made his intentions known to Miranda, Charlotte, and Samantha, all of whom encouraged him to head to Paris to "go get our girl." Carrie breaks down, and when Big hears about the slap, he angrily storms upstairs to confront The Russian, with Carrie chasing close behind. Unable to convince him to back down, Carrie uses the only weapon in her arsenal—her impossibly high-heeled shoes. She trips Big and as they both tumble onto the ground, they laugh hysterically. In the next scene, we see them walking through the streets of Paris. Carrie, still stunned by Big's presence in France, asks: "How did you even get here?"

to which he responds: "It took me a really long time to get here . . . but I'm here. Carrie, you're the one." They kiss as Carrie pleads: "I miss New York. Take me home." Soon after, Carrie is reunited with the girls, giving us one final monologue:

> Later that day I got to thinking about relationships. There are those that open you up to something new and exotic, those that are old and familiar, those that bring up lots of questions, those that bring you somewhere unexpected, those that bring you far from where you started, and those that bring you back. But the most exciting, challenging and significant relationship of all is the one you have with yourself. And if you can find someone to love the you
> *you* love, well, that's just fabulous.

And with that, Carrie's bedazzled cell phone rings, with the caller ID reading "John," and we hear Big's voice, who tells Carrie his house in Napa is on the market: "Look out New York, I'm a' comin'."

As the credits roll on the series finale, all four women had found their happily-ever-after. Fans who longed for Carrie to end up with Big rejoiced. Critics, on the other hand, struggled to make sense of the all-too-tidy ending of a series that celebrated the messy, uncertain lives of four perpetually single women. David Kronke of the *Los Angeles Daily News* called it "awfully moony for such a generally cynical series." The *Washington Post*'s Jennifer Frey found herself "swooning and groaning simultaneously." *The New Yorker*'s Emily Nussbaum accused the show of "[pulling] its punches" by letting "Big rescue Carrie." She continued: "It honored the wishes of its heroine, and at least half of the audience . . . but it also showed a failure of nerve, an inability of the writers to imagine, or to trust themselves to portray any other kind of ending—happy or not." But, luckily for critics and fans alike, Carrie's final moments, neatly tied up in a perfect bow, would not be the last we'd hear from Miss Bradshaw.

As the finale pulled in a series record 10.6 million viewers, *Sex and the City* solidified itself as the cultural phenomenon it always proclaimed to be. No sooner had the show ended when the tease of a movie version lingered in the air, with series star Parker fanning the flames. "It's very important to me that we are dignified and graceful in our exit from the series," she told reporters two weeks before the finale. She continued: "After that, if we hear a cry from the public, I think we have to respond to that, if we can do right by them." As Parker's promise still hung in the air for diehard fans, new fans discovered the show through its migration into syndication—a first for a pay-cable series, especially one as boundary pushing (and sexy). But HBO was well prepared for this transition. Producers of the series had already filmed scenes that would pass muster with basic cable standards—a necessity

"Carrie, you're the one." Big (Chris Noth) puts his heart on the line after ambushing Carrie (Sarah Jessica Parker) in Paris. *Authors' collection*

for the show's marketability to foreign markets. With even more edits made by U.S. basic-cable markets for language and content, what emerged was a watered-down, sanitized version of HBO's cutting-edge show. David Bianculli of the *New York Daily News* described it best when he wrote: "The gist of each story line is there, but some of the edgiest observations and funniest jokes are gone, and Kim Cattrall's catty character, Samantha, has had her claws trimmed way back, if not removed entirely." The appeal, of course, was roping in an even larger audience through syndication—an audience who did not subscribe to HBO or had not purchased the series' DVDs, a market perhaps as great as 60 million viewers. This audience, as Bianculli deduced, wouldn't "know any better when they see the diluted versions." Initially syndicated on TBS (who promoted the run as "five nights of great sex"), the show also found a home on E!, WGN, the CW, and Oxygen. By June of 2004, *Sex and the City* was a hit on basic cable—only four months after fans thought their favorite girls were gone forever.

As fans never really disconnected with the show's characters, it came as no surprise that three years after it had come to a close, there was still buzz surrounding a possible movie. New Line Cinema confirmed, in the summer of 2007, that they were indeed close to sealing the deal (with tabloids naming Cattrall's salary negotiations as the lone holdup), and by the fall of 2007, the ladies had returned to the streets of Manhattan to begin filming the official *Sex and the City* movie. Michael Patrick King, writer and director of the new film version, credited the love of fans as the leading factor in the creation of the film: "The fact that I knew I had an enormous amount of love in the world for these characters was sort of the thing that overpowered the fear of, 'You're going to fail.' The fact that the fans wanted to see the girls more than I was afraid to write them was a big deal." While King's tribute to fans was touching, the financial boon to be had from the movie also motivated producers. Fashion houses jockeyed for costume designer Patricia Field's attention. They knew that whatever Carrie and the girls wore in the film would become instant trends. The show never shied away from label dropping, and on the big screen every fashion detail would instantly come alive.

The film opened on May 30, 2008, and grossed a whopping $57 million dollars in its opening weekend, stealing the top spot from Harrison Ford's fourth foray as action star Indy in *Indiana Jones and the Kingdom of the Crystal Skull*. *Sex and the City* (the movie) clocked in at 145 minutes—what would ultimately make up five episodes of the television version. It opens with Big and Carrie, blissfully happy in New York. They have the perfect Fifth Avenue apartment, the perfect relationship, and now, the perfect fairy-tale ending: a wedding in the storied halls of New York's gorgeous Public Library. As Carrie enters, wearing an impossibly fashionable Vivienne Westwood wedding gown, with a jaunty blue bird festooned to her head (just one of her eighty-one outfits featured in the film), she waits for her prince to come, only to find that in the last moments, Big has chickened out. Carrie is devastated, and retreats to Mexico, accompanied by her concerned best friends Miranda, Charlotte, and Samantha. As Carrie tries to put herself back together, Miranda discovers Steve has cheated and must make the ultimate decision on the fate of her marriage. Samantha, having moved to Los Angeles with star-on-the-rise Smith, finds herself painfully bored and unhappy. While Charlotte, whose fertility struggles dominated her storylines in the television series, has unexpectedly found herself expecting. Each vignette expands and builds upon the television series, delving even more deeply into the messy nature of relationships. Favoring the imperfect over the neat, wrapped-in-a-bow television ending, the movie, for *New Yorker* critic David Edelstein, was "what the series finale should have been." While in the end Carrie did get the happy ending she desired (a quiet, private wedding ceremony reuniting her with her soul mate, Big), the struggle along the way better captured the spirit of the series than the 2004 television swan song. Fans agreed, and the film ultimately grossed $152 million in the U.S. and another $260 million internationally. By February of 2009, the stars, along with writer-director-producer King, had signed on for the sequel, to be released in May 2010.

Ultimately, the sequel did not fare as well as its predecessor, failing to grab the top spot from *Shrek Forever After* (that series' fourth installment), grossing only $31 million in its opening weekend. Yet, the franchise continued to grow. In January 2013, the CW premiered *The Carrie Diaries*, a *Sex and the City* 1980s prequel penned by Bushnell. Despite critical praise, the show was canceled after two seasons, having aired only twenty-six episodes. Although these extensions of the franchise failed to reach the same blockbuster status as the original series and its first big-screen adventure, their existence speaks to the power of the series' initial concept: a show about women for women, with a blunt, in-your-face style that was at times effortlessly charming, seductive, sly, moving, and, ultimately, very funny. One single 45-minute series finale was hardly enough to close the book on Carrie Bradshaw, and there's still no telling if every chapter has been written.

Part 6
The Best TV Series Finales

"It's a Long Way to Tipperary"

Mary Tyler Moore and Friends Share a Group Hug

Mary Tyler Moore a.k.a. *The Mary Tyler Moore Show* (CBS, 1970–1977)

Created by James L. Brooks and Allan Burns
Premiere date: September 19, 1970
7 seasons / 168 Episodes
"The Last Show"
Airdate: March 19, 1977
25.5 rating • 45 percent share • 30 million viewers
Directed by Jay Sandrich
Written by James L. Brooks, Allan Burns, Ed. Weinberg, Stan Daniels, David Lloyd
and Bob Ellison
Cast: Mary Tyler Moore (Mary Richards), Ed Asner (Lou Grant), Gavin MacLeod
(Murray Slaughter), Ted Knight (Ted Baxter), Georgia Engel (Georgette
Baxter), Betty White (Sue Ann Nivens)
Guest Stars: Valerie Harper (Rhoda Morgenstern), Cloris Leachman (Phyllis
Lindstrom), Vincent Gardenia (Mr. Coleman), Robbie Rist (David Baxter)

Mary Tyler Moore, or as it is more commonly known, *The Mary Tyler Moore Show*, was the first situation comedy to have an official series finale. Up to that point, most sitcoms typically ended with an episode that could have aired at any point during the show's final season. In the process, the creative team behind an aptly titled "The Last Show" set the comedic bar high for all the sitcom finales that would follow. The same can be said for the series itself. *Mary Tyler Moore*, along with two other CBS comedies that debuted within the next two years, *All in the Family* (1971–1979) and *M*A*S*H* (1972–1983), revolutionized a genre overrun in the 1960s by fantasy-based comedies (featuring such oddities as a talking horse, a flying nun, a domesticated witch, and a genie in a bottle) and sitcoms set in small, sleepy towns like Mayberry and Hooterville. The creative minds behind *Mary Tyler Moore*, *All in the Family*, and *M*A*S*H* proved that a situation comedy could be intelligent, topical—and funny.

Mary Tyler Moore (henceforth referred to as *MTM*) debuted in the middle of CBS's "Rural Purge," a four-year period (1969–1972) when the network cleared their prime-time schedule of rural-themed shows ("everything with a tree," quipped *Green Acres*' Pat Buttram), along with series watched by viewers who were older and/or resided in rural parts of the country. *The Beverly Hillbillies* (1962–1971), *Petticoat Junction* (1963–1970), and its sister show, *Green Acres* (1965–1971), along with variety shows like *Hee Haw* (1969–1971) and *The Glen Campbell Goodtime Hour* (1969–1972), were replaced by shows that appealed to the most desirable demographic group to advertisers, namely young, educated urban dwellers with disposable incomes.

A few months before the start of the 1970–1971 television season, *New York Times*' Fred Ferretti reported that CBS president Robert D. Woods, in an "unprecedented" move, made some last-minute changes to the network's fall schedule that included moving *MTM* from Tuesday to the more desirable Saturday night comedy block, which would be the show's permanent home for the next seven years. Woods and new vice president for programming Fred Silverman reportedly made the change based on their positive reaction to the pilot. The strategy worked. In its freshman year, *MTM* ranked no. 22 in the overall ratings. For the next four seasons, it ranked among the Top 11 shows.

MTM also marked a more significant turning point in the portrayal of women on television, which had not yet reflected the social impact of feminism on the lives of American women. The women of *MTM* were far from the typical stay-at-home wives and mothers who populated American television since the 1950s, nor were they career women who were just biding their time until they found the man of their dreams. Rhoda (Mary Richards's neighbor and friend, played by Valerie Harper) did eventually get married (and her own series), but she and her husband, Joe (David Groh), eventually separated and divorced. As Harper admitted in her autobiography, *I, Rhoda*, her TV alter-ego "was funnier divorced than she had been married, that was undeniable."

The feminist ideals embodied by Mary Richards were hardly radical, but characteristic of a brand of feminism dubbed by critic Bonnie Dow as "lifestyle feminism." Mary Richards would be the first in a series of young, attractive, single, working women with no steady romantic partner in their lives. As Jennifer Keishin Armstrong, Robert S. Alley and Irby B. Brown explain in their respective, detailed backstage histories of the series, Mary Richards was originally a divorcée, but the CBS brass were concerned that

America would think that "Laura Petrie" (Moore's character on *The Dick Van Dyke Show* [1961–66]) had divorced her television husband, Rob, and moved to Minneapolis. So Mary Richards is a single woman who, in the pilot, officially ends her two-year relationship with her marriage-phobic boyfriend. Now she is nervous, yet ready, to start a life for herself in Minneapolis with a new apartment, a new job, and new friends. Most important of all, her entire existence did not revolve around finding Mr. Right, as *New York Times* columnist Joyce Purnick explained in a 1991 editorial:

> Mary Richards made it all O.K.—O.K. to be single, O.K. to be over 30, O.K. to be independent. She even made it acceptable to stay home and watch her if you had a mind to, rather than go out on a date, the once-obligatory date that women used to say that they had even when they didn't.

Mary Richards didn't spend much time alone. She was constantly surrounded by her neighbors Phyllis Lindstrom (Cloris Leachman) (seasons 1–5) and the aforementioned Rhoda Morgenstern (seasons 1–4); and her co-workers at WJM-TV Channel 12's *6 O'Clock News*: her cantankerous boss, Mr. (Lou) Grant (Ed Asner); caustic news writer and confidante, Murray Slaughter (Gavin MacLeod); and buffoonish anchorman Ted Baxter (Ted Knight), who were later joined in season 4 by the man-hungry hostess of *The Happy Homemaker*, Sue Ann Nivens (Betty White). Moore's supporting cast was comprised of seasoned actors with resumes that included stage, film, and television credits, though Asner, Knight, and Leachman were considered interesting cast choices because they were best known for dramatic, rather than comedic, roles (during season 2, Leachman won an Academy Award for Best Supporting Actress for her work in Peter Bogdanovich's *The Last Picture Show* [1971]). The cast also included Georgia Engel as Ted's sweet, ditzy girlfriend (and later, his wife), Georgette Franklin (seasons 3–7). Engel was only twenty-four when she was cast on the show, though she had appeared on Broadway and was nominated for a BAFTA (British Academy Award) for a supporting role in Milos Forman's *Taking Off* (1971).

As on most workplace sitcoms, Mary's co-workers became her substitute family. The main plotline (known in the industry as the "A" story) typically revolved around either Mary's personal or professional life, but with an emphasis on her personal relationships with her co-workers rather than work-related stories. The writers also managed to intersect the two in creative, unexpected ways, with Mary usually caught in the middle. For instances, she encourages Mr. Grant to hire Rhoda to decorate his apartment ("The Square Shaped Room")—and it's a disaster. Two seasons later, Rhoda fills in for an ailing Mary as Mr. Grant's date—and they hit it off. In a classic episode ("The

Lars Affair") Phyllis enlists support from Mary when she confronts Sue Ann, who is having an affair with her (never-seen) husband, Lars.

During its seven seasons, *MTM* picked up twenty-nine Emmys, including four for Moore (three for Best Actress in a Comedy, and one for Actress of the Year in a series) and multiple statues for supporting actors Asner (3), Harper (3), Knight (2), Leachman (2), and White (2). The Television Academy also bestowed writing Emmys for what are now considered some of the show's classic episodes: "Support Your Local Mother," written by series creators Allan Burns and James L. Brooks, which introduced the character of Rhoda's mother, Ida (Nancy Walker); "The Lou and Edie Story," written by Treva Silverman (the first solo female writer to win an Emmy for comedy), a bittersweet episode that focused on Lou Grant's crumbling marriage; and "Will Mary Richards Go to Jail?" by Ed. Weinberger and Stan Daniels, in which America's sweetheart spends a night in the hoosegow with a pair of hookers when she won't reveal a news source. But the show's most memorable (and funniest) half-hour is "Chuckles Bites the Dust," which offers a comical reflection on the subject of death when WJM-TV's resident clown, Chuckles, who, while dressed as Peter Peanut, is shelled to death by a rogue elephant named Jocko during a parade. Murray, Mr. Grant, and Sue Ann can't stop cracking peanut jokes at Chuckle's expense, which angers Mary who chastises her colleagues for being so insensitive. At the funeral, it's Mary, in one of Moore's best moments, who gets a case of the giggles during the preacher's eulogy when he starts naming Chuckles's characters (Mr. Fee-Fi-Fo, Billy Banana, Aunt Yoo-Hoo) and recites the late clown's catch phrase: "A little song, a little dance, a little seltzer down your pants." When the preacher asks Mary to stand up and encourages her to laugh, she bursts into tears. The episode ranked no. 1 in *TV Guide*'s 1997 list of the "100 Greatest Episodes of All Time."

Burns, Brooks, Weinberger, Daniels, Lloyd, and Bob Ellison received another writing Emmy for episode no. 168—the best series finale in sitcom history. It opens with Mr. Grant on the phone with the new owner of WJM-TV, who asks him to evaluate Ted as an anchorman. Mr. Grant tells him to watch the show and decide for himself. When Mr. Grant, Ted, Murray, and Mary are called up to the office of the new owner, Frank Coleman (Vincent Gardenia), everyone is shocked when he decides to keep Ted and fire the "rest of you guys" (plus Sue Ann). Mary is especially devastated (she even calls Mr. Coleman to make sure he was including her as one of the "guys" and if he meant to fire her—"*especially* you," he tells her over the phone). To cheer Mary up, Mr. Grant empties the $800 from the petty cash box to fly in Rhoda and Phyllis.

In his interview for the Archive of American Television, James L. Brooks described how everyone was pleased with the ending and everything was

The cast of the *Mary Tyler Moore Show* shoots the series finale: (left to right) Gavin McLeod, Ed Asner, Mary Tyler Moore, Ted Knight, Betty White, Georgia Engel, Valerie Harper, and Cloris Leachman.   *CBS Photo Archive/Getty Images*

going well during the emotional last week. Each character was given a moment to express his or her feelings. Lou Grant, who was not known for wearing his heart on his rolled-up sleeves, tears up and tells everyone, "I treasure you people." In his official on-air goodbye, Ted unknowingly gives his colleagues a less than cheery send-off by reciting the lyrics to an old World War I British marching song, "It's a Long Way to Tipperary." Brooks recalled that there was one thing they initially overlooked, prompting Moore to do something she had only done one other time in seven seasons—she asked to speak with him about the script. Moore pointed out that the writers had given all of the characters a farewell speech, but didn't write anything for her. They quickly remedied the situation by writing what would be the emotional high note of the episode. She keeps telling Mr. Grant that she has something to say, but he keeps putting her off until the final scene. Richards finally get her moment, though her heartfelt speech sounds like it's coming as much from Moore as her television alter ego:

I just wanted you to know that sometimes I get concerned about being a career woman. I get to thinking that my job is too important to me. And I tell myself, "The people I work with are just the people I work with and not my family." Last night I thought, what is a family anyway? They're just people who make you feel less alone and really loved. And that's what you've done for me. Thank you for being my family.

The show's final scene is also remembered for the moments that followed. Mary and her family join in a group hug and because no one wants to let go, the group shuffles over to Mary's desk to get some Kleenex. When they exit out the door, they sing, "It's a Long Way to Tipperary." Mary sadly pokes her head back in and takes one last look. She smiles and then turns out the light. In the original broadcast, she returned during the final credits with roses in one hand and a microphone in another to introduce "the best cast ever." One by one, they come out and take a final bow. Since then, other situation comedies, including *Newhart*, *Full House*, *Family Ties*, all ended with a final bow.

Like the WJM-TV's *6 O'Clock News* team, the show's fans were having a hard time saying goodbye. In his tribute, *New York Times* critic John J. O'Connor compared the series to a "dazzling collection of what are really one-act plays," with casting, writing, and direction that "have been outstanding—far beyond the point [of] reasonable expectation." O'Connor also credits Mary Richards for "almost singlehandedly" transforming "the TV image of the 'unmarried working woman,' the once 'unnatural' spinster, into an attractive character of intelligence, verve and independence."

Steve Berg reported in the *Los Angeles Times* that the people who reside in Mary's adopted city of Minneapolis, Minnesota, were especially sad to say goodbye to the woman who put their city on the map. According to co-creator Allan Burns, Minneapolis was chosen because Moore, who was born in Brooklyn and raised in Los Angeles, seems like she is from the Midwest. As for the city, Burns said it was scenic, politically progressive, and a cultural center. There was also the weather, which, according to Burns, "makes a writer salivate. You have all those weather jokes." According to author Jennifer Keishin Armstrong, fans of the show can visit Mary Richards's old stomping grounds (as seen in the opening title sequence). Her list of "Mary Richards' Best of Minneapolis" include the IDS Crystal Court, where Mary is seen riding the escalator and having lunch; McGladrey Plaza, the skyscraper used as the exterior of WJM-TV; the Nicollet pedestrian mall, specifically at 7th Street, where she tossed her hat in the air (a statue, compliments of TVLand, marks the spot); and the Victorian house at 2104 Kenwood Parkway, where she first lived (along with Rhoda and Phyllis), which has been restored and is now almost unrecognizable.

After *MTM* signed off, *Rhoda* continued for its fourth and final season. Moore's supporting cast members moved on to their own series with mixed results. On *The Betty White Show* (1977–1978), White played television actress Joyce Whitman, who resurrects her career as the star of a weekly cop series, *Undercover Woman*, which is directed by her ex-husband (John Hillerman). Georgia Engel co-starred as Whitman's ditzy best friend and roommate. The show was produced by MTM Enterprises, as was Ted Knight's first sitcom, *The Ted Knight Show* (1978), in which the former anchorman starred as the head of a high-class (and legitimate) escort service. The show lasted only six episodes. In Knight's second series, *Too Close for Comfort* (1980–1987), he played a cartoonist and overprotective father who shares a two-family house with his attractive adult daughters. The show ran for three seasons on ABC and then new episodes aired in syndication, though the show was revamped and its title changed to *The Ted Knight Show*. Gavin MacLeod moved from one hit to another when he was cast as Merrill Stubing, captain of *The Love Boat* (1977–1987).

Mary Tyler Moore did eventually return to CBS's prime-time lineup, first as the star of *Mary* (1978), a Sunday night variety show along the same lines as *The Carol Burnett Show* (1967–1978), which had ended its eleven-season run earlier in the year. Moore even had her own group of repertory players that included Swoosie Kurtz, David Letterman, and Michael Keaton. The show was yanked from the schedule after three outings, but returned with a new format and title, *The Mary Tyler Moore Hour* (1979). In this variety show/sitcom hybrid, she plays Mary McKinnon, the popular star of a fictional variety series, *The Mary McKinnon Show*. The supporting cast of the backstage comedy consisted of Mary's personal secretary, the show's producer, etc., plus guest stars like Lucille Ball, Bea Arthur, and Dick Van Dyke playing themselves as guests on McKinnon's show. The show was canceled at the end of the 1978–1979 season.

Moore did return in the 1980s with two sitcoms, the first of which, *Mary* (1985–1986), featured her as a divorced consumer advocate who worked for a tabloid newspaper; and in the second, *Annie McGuire* (1988), she played a divorced Deputy Coordinator of Human Relations for a Manhattan borough president who falls in love with a widower. In between her four post-*MTM* series, Moore received four Emmy nominations for her work in mini-series and made-for-TV movies, winning her seventh playing against type as the head of a black market baby ring in *Stolen Babies* (1993). She was also cast against type again as the icy mother in Robert Redford's acclaimed motion picture *Ordinary People* (1980), for which she received an Oscar nomination. In 1980, she won a special Tony Award for her onstage portrayal of quadriplegic artist who sues for her right to die in *Whose Life Is It Anyway?*

But Mary Tyler Moore will forever be Mary Richards, and when we think of her, we can't help but flash back to that final scene in the newsroom when Moore and the finest cast in the history of television comedy said goodbye.

Critic Tom Shales summed it all up beautifully: "The last episode of *The Mary Tyler Moore Show* was probably the funniest sad good-by that 30 million people ever said to friends good and true and vicarious."

It Was Only a Nightmare

Newhart Wakes Up

Newhart (CBS, 1982–1990)
Created by Barry Kemp
Developed by Sheldon Bull
Premiere date: October 25, 1982
8 seasons / 184 episodes
"The Last Newhart"
Airdate: May 21, 1990
18.7 rating • 29 percent share • 29.5 million viewers
Directed by Dick Martin
Written by Mark Egan, Mark Solomon, and Bob Bendetson
Cast: Bob Newhart (Dick Loudon/Bob Hartley), Mary Frann (Joanna Loudon),
    Peter Scolari (Michael Harris), Julia Duffy (Stephanie Vanderkellen), Tom
    Poston (George Utley), William Sanderson (Larry), Tony Papenfuss (Darryl
    no. 1), John Voldstad (Darryl no. 2), Thomas Hill (Jim), William Lanteau
    (Chester), Kathy Kinney (Miss Goddard), David Pressman (Mr. Rusnak)
Guest Stars: Gedde Watanabe (Mr. Tagadachi), Sab Shimono (Sunatra),
    Shuko Akune (Sedaka), Frank Kopyc (Ed), Christie Mellor (Rhonda), Nada
    Despotovich (Zora), Lisa Kudrow (Sada), Candy Hutson (Baby Stephanie),
    Suzanne Pleshette (Emily Hartley)

O n *The Bob Newhart Show* (1972–1978), comedian Bob Newhart plays Dr. Bob Hartley, a psychologist with a thriving practice in Chicago, where he lives with his schoolteacher wife, Emily (Suzanne Pleshette), in a high-rise apartment. The sitcom, produced by Mary Tyler Moore's production company, MTM, and created by *The Mary Tyler Moore Show* writer/producers David Davis and Lorenzo Music, was tailor-made for Newhart's comedic talent. Capitalizing on Newhart's dry wit, deadpan delivery, and slight stammer, Dr. Hartley was the comedic straight man to his wife, friends, and dysfunctional patients. The show ran for six seasons and made Newhart, best known for his comedy albums and appearances on talk shows and comedy-variety shows (including his own in 1961), into a major sitcom star.

Newhart returned to television four years later in another sitcom produced by MTM, this one bearing his last name only. In an interview for the Archive of American Television (AAT), he recalled how around the time he was considering returning to television, he got the initial idea for the series during a hotel stay in Seattle, where he was performing his standup comedy act. While sitting in the hotel cafeteria with his wife Ginny, he wondered what *The Bob Newhart Show* would have been like if it was set in a hotel, where his character would interact with the employees and the guests, to whom he would always have to be nice. Newhart shared the idea with his agent, Artie Price, who put his client together with comedy writer (*Taxi*) Barry Kemp. Kemp asked Newhart how he would feel if, instead of a hotel in Seattle, his character would be running an inn in Vermont. Afraid the idea might not measure up to his first sitcom, Newhart procrastinated an entire weekend before reading the script, which he thought was "a great piece of writing and a great idea." In his AAT interview, Newhart revealed that he considered having his new show be a continuation of *The Bob Newhart Show*, but realized it would be creatively advantageous to start with a new premise and an entirely new cast of characters.

Newhart's new show did have something in common with his first sitcom—the absence of children as he had no interest in heading a family sitcom. He recounted that he was given a script for *The Bob Newhart Show* in which Emily is pregnant. He told the producer he liked the script, and then asked, "So, who are you going to get to play Bob?" They did, however, do an episode of *The Bob Newhart Show* in which Emily (Suzanne Pleshette) and his secretary, Carol (Marcia Wallace), both announce that they are pregnant ("You're Having My Hartley"), only to reveal that it was all Bob's nightmare.

In the new series, Dick Loudon (Newhart) is a former advertising executive turned successful how-to author (his books include *Building Your Own Patio Cover* and *Know Your Harley*), who moves from New York City to Vermont with his wife, Joanna (Mary Frann), to be the new proprietors of The Stratford, a colonial inn. As Dick explains in his talk on the history of the Stratford to the ladies of the Daughters of the War for Independence (DWI), many of their ancestors stayed at the inn during the winter of 1775. He also reveals, somewhat reluctantly, that at the time the Stratford was a brothel. Dick and Joanna learn another interesting fact about the Stratford: the corpse of Sarah Newton, a young woman accused of being a witch and hanged in 1692, is buried in their basement because she was refused a church-sanctioned

"Welcome to the Stratford Inn"—the cast of *Newhart*: (top left, clockwise) Peter Scolari,
Tom Poston, Mary Frann, Bob Newhart, and Julia Duffy.   *CBS/Photofest*

cemetery burial. The episode ("Mrs. Newton's Body Lies A-Mould'ring in
the Grave") marked the introduction of three backwoods brothers—Larry
(William Sanderson), his brother Darryl (Tony Papenfuss), and his other
brother Darryl (John Voldstad)—who are hired to dispose of the body, though
in the end Dick decides it's best to let Mrs. Newton's corpse stay put.

In addition to Larry and his brothers, the supporting characters include
George Utley (Tom Poston), the Stratford's befuddled handyman, whom
Poston describes in an interview for the AAT, as a "guy whose book of instructions started to fade"; Leslie Vanderkellen (Jennifer Holmes), a wealthy
Dartmouth graduate who works as the Stratford's maid because she wants
to see what it's like to be "average"; and Kirk Devane (Steven Kampmann), a
compulsive liar who owns the Minuteman Café and Souvenir Shop next door
to the inn, which is later sold to Larry, Darryl, and Darryl. Leslie departs after

season 1 and is replaced by her cousin Stephanie Vanderkellen (Julia Duffy), a shallow, spoiled, materialistic heiress who left her husband after two days of marriage and is cut off financially from her parents. Kirk is written out of the show after season 2 when he marries a professional clown, Cindy Parker (Rebecca York), and leaves town. In season 3, Dick is hired to host *Vermont Today*, a talk show on the local television station, WPIV-TV. His producer, the fast-talking, disingenuous Michael Harris (Peter Scolari), falls in love with and eventually marries Stephanie (his pet names for her are "Cupcake" and "Muffin"). Together, Stephanie and Michael are the quintessential 1980s yuppie couple. In season 8, Stephanie's rich parents buy WPIV-TV for their infant granddaughter, also named Stephanie ("Child in Charge"). Michael gets a promotion, but it's the owner, baby Stephanie, who calls all the shots—including cancelling Dick's show in the middle of an interview with Senator George McGovern—with an assist from her parents, who interpret their infant daughter's wordless sounds. In a classic *Newhart* moment, Dick, in an effort to get his show back, must carry on a conversation with the unintelligible infant.

Much of the show's humor stems from Dick's reactions to the eccentric townspeople and their odd customs. Although Dick makes an effort, he continues to make the occasional *faux pas*, such as the time he voices skepticism regarding the local legend of the Great White Buck ("The Buck Stops Here"), which, if spotted, brings good luck to the town. Unfortunately, when Dick spots the town's good luck charm, he accidentally kills it with his car, bringing bad luck to the town.

To alleviate their fears, Dick agrees to publicly humiliate himself by wearing antlers on his head and performing the dance known as "The Rite of the Dancing Wood Nymph." While Dick is exasperated with the townspeople, Joanna is amused by their eccentricities and finds them endearing.

One of the show's running gags is the weekly appearance of Larry and his two silent brothers. Their entrance begins with Larry introducing himself: "Hi, I'm Larry. This is my brother Darryl, and this is my other brother Darryl." Creator Barry Kemp, in his interview for the AAT, said the brothers are "sharing one brain and Larry has most of it." Originally, they were slated to appear in only one episode, but after several appearances they were officially bumped up to recurring characters.

We also never really know the name of the rural Vermont town the Loudons call home, but it is assumed to be Norwich, which is located on the Connecticut River, opposite Hanover, New Hampshire, home to Dartmouth College. In the opening sequence, we follow what we assume to be Dick and Joanna's car as it makes its way to the Stratford Inn, which is seen in the final shot. In his AAT interview, Barry Kemp revealed that the footage, which they purchased for $800 is actually made up of outtakes from the 1981 film, *On Golden Pond*, directed by Mark Rydell. The passengers riding in the car are not Dick and Joanna, but the film's stars, Henry Fonda and Katharine Hepburn. The inn seen in the opening title sequence and the exterior shots at the start of each episode is the Waybury Inn in East Middlebury, Vermont. Built in 1810, the Waybury sits at the base of the Green Mountain National Forest.

Newhart performed well in its first season (1982–1983), ranking no. 12 in the ratings. The show would remain in the Top 25 for the next five seasons, despite the fact that, over the course of eight seasons, CBS changed its time slot fourteen times. In his autobiography, *I Shouldn't Even Be Doing This: And Other Things That Strike Me as Funny*, Newhart complained about the network's handing off his time slot to other sitcoms; he even considered ending the show after season 6, which, according to his contract, he had the option of doing. "I thought it was unfair to the show," Newhart writes. "We had established 9:00 p.m. as a hit time slot, and they were acting cavalierly toward a successful show. Nobody seemed to know when we were on—not even us." Newhart adds that in the middle of the show's eighth season, he decided it was time to end the series once and for all. *Variety* ran a story on March 5, 1990, stating that CBS wanted the show to continue, but, according to Mel Blumenthal, senior executive vice-president at MTM, it is "just not economically feasible to continue"; an additional season wasn't needed for the syndication package, which already contained 184 episodes. One point missing from the story, but included in a shorter version that appeared in *Weekly Variety* on March 7, 1990, was that Bob Newhart was willing to do a ninth season, but could not reach an agreement with MTM, suggesting that the reason it wasn't "economically feasible" was due to Newhart's renewal demands. In an interview with Robert Blanco, of Scripps Howard News Service, Newhart made it clear that he would most likely return to do another series for CBS, but he would not be working with MTM in the future. Without going into details, he said that his "renewal demands" were not "outrageous" as MTM was claiming. "But it has to end sometime and it seems appropriate," he said. "I just wish it hadn't ended with such acrimony."

The finale episode of *Newhart* opens with a town meeting on the morning of the town's 216th birthday celebration, which includes a production of the musical *Fiddler on the Roof*. At the end of the meeting, Mr. Tagadachi (Gedde Watanabe), a Japanese businessman, offers to buy the entire town so he can build a 5,000-room resort and golf course. They turn down his offer, but when he offers each resident a million dollars for their house, everyone does a complete 180—except for Dick, who refuses to sell the Stratford Inn. In the next scene, Stephanie, Michael, George, Larry, Darryl, and Darryl say goodbye to the Loudons. They are soon joined by the townspeople, who file in one by one with their suitcases, singing "Anatevka," the song sung at the end of *Fiddler* by the poor Jews who are ordered by the Czar to leave their village. Of course the Jewish villagers in *Fiddler* aren't leaving with a million dollars in their pocket.

Five years later, the Stratford Inn is still standing, but it's been transformed into a Japanese inn complete with a Japanese maid and handyman, who are less than enthusiastic about working there. Dick is miserable and admits he made a mistake by refusing to sell the Stratford. Meanwhile, Joanna, dressed in a kimono and a black wig, has assimilated and started playing golf (a running joke, because the Stratford now sits in the middle of a golf course; each time a golfer yells, "Four!," everyone in the inn ducks). The Loudons get a surprise visit from their friends, who, as Stephanie explains, agreed to meet there on this day five years earlier to see if Dick and Joanna "are still alive." Larry and the two Darryls introduce their wives—three Long Island princesses named Rhonda, Zora, and Sada (the latter played by an almost unrecognizable Lisa Kudrow). All three women begin to tell Dick and Joanna how they met their husbands when, for the very first time, the Darryls break their silence, yelling, "Quiet!" The group admit that they all miss their town and have decided to move into the Stratford, despite Bob's objections. But no one is listening to poor Bob, and he storms out of the inn, only to get hit on the head with a golf ball. The scene fades to black.

What follows put *Newhart*'s ending on many "Top Ten" lists of the best series finales. We then hear Newhart waking up from a dream and turning on the lamp next to his bed. He wakes up the person next to him, who turns on her light, and we see that it is Newhart's first television wife, Emily Hartley (Suzanne Pleshette). Bob begins to tell Emily about the dream he had in which he was an innkeeper in this little town in Vermont where nothing made sense ("the maid was an heiress, her husband talked in alliteration, the handyman kept missing the point of things, and then there were these three woodsmen, only one of them talked."). She tells him no more Japanese food before bedtime. He then mentions the beautiful blonde he was married to—and tells Emily she should wear more sweaters (like Joanna Loudon).

The episode concludes with the cast taking their final bows and singing, "For he's a jolly good fellow" to Newhart, followed by the cutting of a large farewell cake. Then, instead of ending with the usual company logo (of Mimsey, the cat, meowing), when Mimsey meows we hear the voice of the two Darryls yelling, "Quiet!"

Newhart's inventive, hilarious ending was completely unexpected, mostly because they were able to keep Pleshette's cameo a closely guarded secret. In fact, the original script contained a scene that was never shot, in which Bob goes to heaven and meets God, played by George Burns (the veteran comedian had played the Deity in three films in the late 1970s). The information was leaked to the tabloids and, sure enough, stories did appear in the paper about Bob dying and meeting God in the show's final episode. In his interview with AAT, Newhart explained that Pleshette, the writers, the producers, and the production designer were the only ones who knew about the twist ending. The cast was not told until the day of shooting. To keep the moment a surprise for the in-studio audience, Pleshette remained hidden in her trailer all day, and a screen (called a floater) was placed over the *The Bob Newhart Show* bedroom set. The moment the scene was revealed, the audience members, who immediately recognized the familiar setting, gasped and started applauding.

Newhart also admitted that they knew the ending was risky: "We were apprehensive . . . because *St. Elsewhere* was received negatively because people were saying we devoted all of our time to this show and cared about these people and now you're telling us it's a dream." It's understandable why Newhart thought the ending was risky. The ending of *St. Elsewhere* (see chapter 8), in which it's revealed the entire series was in the imagination of an autistic child, angered some of the show's fan base who didn't appreciate the implication that the series they had been watching for the past six seasons was essentially a fake. But the situation with *Newhart* was entirely different: a situation comedy has more leeway than a medical drama to have some fun with the audience, even a drama laced with humor like *St. Elsewhere*. Also, there is a thematic connection between the ending of *Newhart* and the past seven seasons because throughout the show, the oddball neighbors and their local customs have been the constant source of frustration for poor Dick, who reaches a breaking point when everyone decides they are going to stay at his inn, which is in the middle of a golf course. Most important of all, the ending of *Newhart* relies on the viewer's knowledge of the comedian's first television series, so the audience is essentially "in on the joke." This is not the case with *St. Elsewhere*, which, ironically, was known to include many references to other television series and to popular culture in general. The twist at the end of *St. Elsewhere* may have had a thematic connection to the rest of the series in the minds of the writers, but not in the minds of the audience, who were left scratching their heads and wondering what the hell just happened.

Newhart credits the idea for the ending to his wife, Ginny, as did Suzanne Pleshette and the episode's director, Dick Martin. But the three writer/executive producers who penned the finale—Mark Egan, Mark Solomon, and Bob Bendetson—remember it differently. In a May 1995 *Entertainment Weekly* cover story about the "Best Closers and Cliff-Hangers of All Time," Erika K. Cardozo and Bruce Fretts report that it was Ginny Newhart who "dreamed up" that "brilliant gag—a goof on *Dallas*' Bobby's-death-was-all-a-dream ploy." A few weeks later, *EW* published a response from Egan, Solomon, and Bendetson, claiming this was not the case: "To set the record straight, the final episode of *Newhart* was not 'dreamed up' by Bob's wife, Ginny. She had absolutely no connection with the show. We should know. We wrote and produced the Emmy-nominated script (with special thanks to Dan O'Shannon)."

Authorship aside, the series finale of *Newhart* has deservingly earned a special place in American popular culture. Since then, the scene has been parodied several times, even by Bob Newhart himself. After the final credits at the end of his second hosting stint on *Saturday Night Live* (on February 11, 1995), Newhart wakes up in bed as Bob Hartley, who then wakes up Emily (Pleshette, in a surprise cameo) and tells her he had a horrible dream in which he hosted *Saturday Night Live*. "*Saturday Night Live?*" Emily asks. "Is that show *still* on?"

More recently, an "alternate ending" of *Breaking Bad* was posted on YouTube in which actor Bryan Cranston wakes up in bed in a panic as Hal, his character on *Malcolm in the Middle* (2000–2006), next to his TV wife, Lois (Jane Kaczmarek), and proceeds to describe his bad dream, which is essentially the plot of *Breaking Bad* ("I was this meth dealer . . .").

Two years later, Newhart did return to CBS in another sitcom, *Bob* (1992–1993), in which he plays Bob McKay, creator of a 1950s comic book superhero, "Mad Dog." The character is revived when a company buys the rights, only they want Mad Dog to be a vigilante rather than a superhero. In the second (and final) season, the comic book premise was scrapped and Bob is hired to run a greeting card company, where he works for the former owner's wife, Sylvia Schmitt (Betty White). Four years later, Newhart co-starred with Judd Hirsch in a short-lived sitcom, *George & Leo* (1997–1998), about two men, George Stoody (Newhart) and Leo Wagonman (Hirsch), who become in-laws when George's son, Ted (Jason Bateman), marries Leo's daughter, Casey (Bess Meyer in the series' first three episodes; Robyn Lively for the rest). The show was canceled due to low ratings.

During his long career, Newhart has been the recipient of many awards, including the Peabody, three Grammys (for his comedy albums), and the Mark Twain Prize for Humor. He was also inducted into the Academy of Television Arts & Sciences Hall of Fame. The one award that seemed to elude him, despite his eponymous roles in two highly successful series, was the Emmy. But that all changed when he guest-starred on the hit situation comedy *The Big Bang Theory* (2007–present), playing Arthur Jeffries, a former kids' show television host who went by the nickname Professor Proton. In 2013, he received the Emmy for Outstanding Guest Actor in a Comedy Series. The understated comedian was humbled by the attention. But for his generations of fans, the honor was long overdue.

The Apocalypse Has Been Postponed

Buffy the Vampire Slayer and Angel Save the World

Buffy the Vampire Slayer (The WB, 1997–2001; UPN, 2001–2003)
Created by Joss Whedon
Premiere date: March 10, 1997
7 seasons / 144 episodes
"Chosen"
Airdate: May 20, 2003
2.9 rating • 5 percent share • 4.9 million viewers
Written and Directed by Joss Whedon
Cast: Sarah Michelle Gellar (Buffy Summers), Nicholas Brendon (Xander Harris),
    Emma Caulfield (Anya Jenkins), Michelle Trachtenberg (Dawn Summers),
    James Marsters (Spike), Alyson Hannigan (Willow Rosenberg)
Special Guest Stars: Anthony Stewart Head (Giles), Eliza Dushku (Faith Lehane),
    Nathan Fillion (Caleb), David Boreanaz (Angel)
Guest Stars: Tom Lenk (Andrew Wells), Iyari Limon (Kennedy), Sarah Hagan
    (Amanda), Indigo (Rona), D. B. Woodside (Principal Robin Wood), Felicia Day
    (Vi)

Angel (The WB, 1999–2004)
Created by Joss Whedon and David Greenwalt
Premiere date: October 5, 1999
5 seasons / 110 episodes
"Not Fade Away"
Airdate: May 19, 2004
3.3 rating • 5 percent share • 5.3 million viewers
Directed by Jeffrey Bell
Written by Joss Whedon and Jeffrey Bell

Cast: David Boreanaz (Angel), James Marsters (Spike), J. August Richards (Charles Gunn), Amy Acker (Winifred "Fred" Burkle/Illyria), Andy Hallett (Lorne), Mercedes McNab (Harmony Kendall), Alexis Denisof (Wesley Wyndam-Pryce)

Guest stars: Vincent Kartheiser (Connor), Christian Kane (Lindsay McDonald), Dennis Christopher (Cyvus Vail), Sarah Thompson (Eve), Julia Lee (Anne Steele), Leland Crooke (Archduke Sebassis), Stacey Travis (Senator Helen Brucker), Adam Baldwin (Marcus Hamilton), Pee Pee Demon (Ryan Alvarez), David Figlioli (Bartender), Mark Colson (Izzy)

 television series achieves cult status when its dedicated fan base remains loyal to "their show" long after the series finale airs. Die-hard *Star Trek* fans, better known as Trekkies, turned a science-fiction series that ran for three seasons on NBC (1966–1969) into one of Hollywood's most successful entertainment franchises spanning nearly five decades. Fans of *Arrested Development* (2003–2006) played an instrumental role in resurrecting the defunct FOX comedy that was canceled after three seasons due to low ratings, only to return seven years later with new episodes available for streaming on Netflix. *Veronica Mars* (2004–2007) fans (a.k.a. "Marshmallows") partially financed a 2014 theatrical film based on the teen detective series by contributing to a Kickstarter campaign that raised $5.7 million. In addition to *Star Trek* and *Veronica Mars*, other fan-based cult series that made the leap from the small screen to a theatre near you include *The Twilight Zone* (1959–1964)/*Twilight Zone: The Movie* (1983), *Twin Peaks* (1990–1991)/*Twin Peaks: Fire Walk with Me* (1992), *The X-Files* (1993–2002)/*The X-Files* (1998) and *The X-Files: I Want to Believe* (2008), and *Firefly* (2002)/*Serenity* (2005).

Many of the shows listed above, and most cult television shows in general, are science fiction, fantasy, and horror series (or a combination of any two, or all three) because these genres have the most dedicated, active fan bases. At the same time, a television series about space travel, paranormal activity, or vampires is not necessarily guaranteed a cult following. Most cult shows are created by writers and producers who put an original spin on a traditional genre—visionaries like Rod Serling (*The Twilight Zone*, *Night Gallery* [1969–1973]), Gene Roddenberry (*Star Trek*), David Lynch (*Twin Peaks*), Chris Carter (*X-Files*, *Millennium* [1996–1999]), and Joss Whedon (*Buffy the Vampire Slayer* [1997–2003], *Angel* [1999–2004] [co-creator], *Firefly* [2002–2003]), *Dollhouse* [2009–2010], *Marvel's Agents of S.H.I.E.L.D.* [2013–present]).

With *Buffy the Vampire Slayer* and its spinoff, *Angel*, Whedon took a popular, classic horror subgenre, the vampire film, and modernized its mythology with a gender reversal. Female characters in traditional horror films are limited mostly to the role of victim—the girl who is watched, stalked and terrorized by "the monster" and, if she is lucky, saved by the male hero. But the character of Buffy Summers directly challenges this sexist, patriarchal representation of women. Buffy is the slayer, who, as the opening narration of seasons 1 and 2 explain, was destined since birth to protect the world from evil: "Into every generation a slayer is born; one girl in all of the world, a chosen one. She alone will wield the strength and skill to fight the vampires, demons, and the forces of darkness; to stop the spread of their evil and the swell of the number. She is the Slayer." Buffy is a modern-day action hero who possesses recuperative powers and superhuman strength, agility, and reflexes. Consequently, when an equally powerful vampire hurls Buffy across the room, The Slayer can immediately stand up without a scratch on her and continue fighting. Buffy spends her evenings in the graveyard patrolling for vampires, who are reduced to dust by staking them in the heart, but in the daylight she faces a different form of horror, better known as high school.

Buffy entered the annals of popular culture with the 1992 feature film *Buffy the Vampire Slayer*, written by Whedon and directed by Fran Rubel Kuzui; however, there are some differences between the title character in the film and her television counterpart. The film version of *Buffy* stars Kristy Swanson as a high school cheerleader at a San Fernando Valley high school who is told by a mysterious stranger named Merrick (Donald Sutherland) that she is The Slayer—the Chosen One—who has certain physical and sensory abilities to combat vampires. As her "Watcher," Merrick trains and guides Buffy as she assumes her official duties. Over the course of the film, she transforms from a shallow, superficial, self-involved high school cheerleader with no value system into a bona fide hero, even if it means losing her boyfriend and jeopardizing her social standing at school. In the film's climax, Buffy defeats the local Vampire King (Rutger Hauer) and his loyal minion (played by Paul Reubens, in a hilarious supporting role) with some help from her new beau, Pike (Luke Perry, in his first major film role).

The horror-comedy was a modest hit, yet it didn't leave much of an impression on the critics. Calling the film's style "rudimentary" and its tone "flat," *Variety* critic Todd McCarthy called *Buffy* "a bloodless comic resurrection of the undead that goes serious just when it should get wild and woolly." *New York Times* critic Janet Maslin described *Buffy* as "a slight, good-humored film that's a lot more painless than might have been expected" and Whedon's script, "uneven, but bright." *Rolling Stone* critic Peter Travers wrote: "*Buffy* is amusing for a time but its destiny is to die in a disappointing, long-winded conclusion. The second half feels stretched out and muddled, as if screenwriter Joss Whedon drove a stake through his script."

Apparently, Whedon's experience working on his film felt like someone drove a stake through his heart. In a 2001 interview with Tasha Robinson

The cast of *Buffy the Vampire Slayer* pose for a final photo: (left to right) Michelle Trachtenberg, Sarah Michelle Gellar, Anthony Head, Eliza Dushku, Nicholas Brendon, and Alyson Hannigan.
Authors' collection

for The A.V. Club, he candidly revealed his frustration working with actor Donald Sutherland, who, according to Whedon, was allowed by the director to rewrite his dialogue to the point that it didn't make sense. "It didn't turn out to be the movie that I had written," Whedon explained. "They never do, but that was my first lesson in that. Not that the movie is without merit, but I just watched a lot of stupid wannabe-star behavior and a director with a different vision than mine—which was her right, it was her movie—but it was still frustrating." Whedon also shared something his wife told him after the premiere that he dismissed at the time as naïve: "You know honey, maybe a few years from now, you'll get to make it again, the way you want to make it!" What Whedon was so sure could never happen did when Gail Berman, an executive at Sandollar, the company that co-produced the film and owned the rights, phoned Whedon three years later to tell him they were planning to turn *Buffy* into a television series. Sandollar was contractually obligated to contact Whedon, never expecting him to sign on for the series.

In movies, the director has creative control, but in television it's the writer/producer. Consequently, the television version of *Buffy the Vampire Slayer* reflected Whedon's original vision, which he describes in the DVD commentary of the show's pilot episode, "Welcome to Hellmouth":

> The first thing I thought of when I thought of Buffy—the movie—was the little blonde girl who goes into a dark alley and gets killed in every horror movie. The idea of Buffy was to subvert that idea, and create someone who was a hero where she had always been a victim. That element of surprise, that element of genre-busting is very much at the heart of both the movie and the series.

Whedon also made some smart changes when adapting the film for television, most notably in regards to the character of Buffy. As played by Sarah Michelle Gellar, Buffy is not a vapid, shallow, popular cheerleader, but a modest, somewhat self-conscious, emotionally vulnerable teenager, who is also a strong, fearless, sassy, kick-ass vampire slayer. She arrives in Sunnydale, California, to make a fresh start and some new friends (the rumor around the halls of Sunnydale High School is that she was responsible for a gymnasium fire at her last school). What Buffy doesn't find out until she meets her Watcher (and school librarian), a British gentleman named Rupert Giles (Anthony Stewart Head), is that Sunnydale is an epicenter of demonic and supernatural activity and Sunnydale High School is built on the "Hellmouth," a portal between earth and hell. Buffy befriends two of her classmates, nerdy Xander Harris (Nicholas Brendon) and brainy Willow Rosenberg (Alyson Hannigan), who, along with the school's queen bee, Cordelia Chase (Charisma Carpenter), provide her with the assistance and support she needs to carry out her duties as The Slayer. Their nickname is the "Scooby Gang" or "Scoobies," an homage to the teenagers who solve mysteries in the Hanna-Barbera cartoon *Scooby-Doo*. Using Giles's extensive collection of ancient reference books, they conduct research to help Buffy combat whatever vampire, demon, or creature she's battling that week.

Buffy is a champion when it comes to slaying, but it interferes with her social life and any chance she has for a healthy, normal relationship. This explains why she found herself in the middle of a three-way love triangle with two vampires: Angel (David Boreanaz), the vampire with a soul, whom Buffy describes to Giles after their first meeting as "dark, gorgeous, in an annoying sort of way," and badass Englishman Spike (James Marsters), who has a love/hate relationship with Buffy. After season 3, Angel departs for Los Angeles (to star in the *Buffy* spinoff, *Angel*), while Spike eventually becomes a loyal ally to Buffy and, as a member of the Scoobies, plays a key role in *Buffy's* near-apocalyptic series finale.

In addition to the series regulars, the fictional universe of *Buffy*, dubbed Buffyverse by the show's fans (a term also adopted by Whedon), is inhabited by a long list of characters, a combination of humans and the walking dead, each with their own complex and detailed backstories: Daniel "Oz" Osbourne (Seth Green), Willow's first boyfriend, a guitarist who is very chill, except when the moon is full and he turns into a werewolf; Anya (Emma Caulfield), a former vengeance demon, whose oddness, due mostly to her lack of social skills, serves as the show's comic relief; Drusilla (Juliet Landau), a vampire sired by Angel and Spike's lover, who kills Kendra (Bianca Lawson), the slayer who takes Buffy's place when she is temporarily deceased; Faith (Eliza Dushku), Kendra's slayer replacement, who begins as Buffy's nemesis but later emerges as a valuable ally; and Andrew Wells (Tom Lenk), an annoying former classmate who joins the Scoobies in the final season.

Buffy the Vampire Slayer became one of the "anchor shows" (the top rated show in a lineup) of The WB, a new network co-owned by Time Warner and Tribune Broadcasting that debuted on January 11, 1995 with the premiere of *The Wayans Brothers* (1995–1999), a situation comedy starring Shawn and Marlon Wayans. Although The WB would be home to several long-running sitcoms starring African-American comedians (*The Steve Harvey Show* [1996–2002], *The Parent 'Hood* [1995–1999] [starring Robert Townsend], and *The Jamie Foxx Show* [1996–2001]), after two years on the air, The WB also started to cater more to the teen market. Their schedule included family-oriented dramas (*7th Heaven* [1996–2007], *Everwood* [2002–2006], *Gilmore Girls* [2000–2007]), and shows about high school (*Dawson's Creek* [1998–2003], *One Tree Hill* [2003–2012]) and college students (*Felicity* [1998–2002]) starring young, attractive, and mostly unknown actors. In addition to *Buffy*, there were also science fiction, fantasy, and horror shows featuring young characters: *Charmed* (1998–2006), a fantasy about three sisters who also happen to be witches (but the good kind); *Roswell* (1999–2002), a modern-day sci-fi show about three teenage aliens living on earth; *Smallville* (2001–2011), which recounts the early years of Clark Kent leading up to his transformation into Superman; and the long-running *Supernatural* (2005–present, now on The CW), which focuses on two brothers who fight supernatural beings.

After three seasons, Buffy, the Scoobies, and the rest of the class of '99 graduate from Sunnydale High School, though the commencement exercises culminate with Buffy leading her fellow graduates against an army of vampires and an Olvikan, a giant demonic snake, which Buffy and Xander blow up, destroying their school in the process. The first of the two-part season 3 finale ("Graduation Day") aired four weeks after the Columbine High

School massacre (on April 20, 1999). At the last minute, The WB chose to replace the second part with a repeat. WB president Jamie Kellner explained the rationale for the network's decision to the Associated Press: "Given the current climate, depicting acts of violence at a high-school graduation ceremony, even fantasy acts against a 60-foot serpent and vampires, we believe, is inappropriate to broadcast around the actual dates of these time-honored ceremonies." *Salon* critic Charles Taylor criticized The WB for pulling what he called a "PR stunt" that had an "inescapable air of Big Daddy condescension." *Buffy* fans, who wrote protest letters and took out ads in trade magazines, did eventually get to see "The Graduation, Part 2" three months later (on July 13, 1999), though the episode did air as scheduled in Canada, which resulted in bootleg copies circulating around the Internet. In response, Whedon told Kevin V. Johnson at *USA Today*, "OK, I'm having a Grateful Dead moment here, but I'm saying 'Bootleg the Puppy.'"

After high school, Buffy and Willow enroll at University of California at Sunnydale while Xander retreats to his parents' basement. Willow falls in love with a fellow Wiccan named Tara (Amber Benson), Xander has his first real adult relationship with vengeance demon Anya, and Buffy dates Riley Finn (Marc Blucas), who is the teaching assistant for her psychology class. Riley is also a key player in the season 4 plotline, which focuses on a highly classified, experimental government program (known as "The Initiative") that involves planting microchips in vampires to make them harmless. But chaos ensues when The Initiative is taken over by a bio-mechanical demonoid named Adam (George Hertzberg) whose plans to take over the world are thwarted by Buffy.

In season 5, Buffy battles Glorificus (or Glory) (Clare Kramer), a god who was banished from the hell dimension and needs "The Key" to open the portal so she can return. The Key turns out to be Buffy's mystical little sister, Dawn (Michelle Trachtenberg), whom The Slayer saves by sacrificing her own life. Buffy dies, but is resurrected in season 6 by Willow, who develops a serious addiction to magic. When Willow's girlfriend, Tara, is killed by a bullet meant for Buffy, Willow uses black magic in the process to seek revenge, but is stopped by Xander from destroying the world.

One major change that occurred at the start of season 5 was *Buffy*'s move from The WB to UPN (United Paramount Network). At the time, *Buffy* was the third highest rated series on The WB (behind *7th Heaven* and *Dawson's Creek*) and it was the network's "anchor show" on Tuesday nights, with about 4.5 million viewers tuning in each week. Like the teenage stars on *Dawson's Creek*, the actors on *Buffy* were also important to The WB brand. In a *Variety* story dated April 23, 2001 (with the comical headlines "UPN Sinks Teeth into WB's 'Buffy'" and "UPN Becomes the 'Buffy' Payer"), Josef Adalian explains it was purely a matter of economics. UPN agreed to pay an average of $2.33 million per episode as part of a two-year/forty-four episode deal, which is $500,000 more per episode than The WB offered. Whedon was also displeased by the remarks WB President Jamie Kellner made about *Buffy* in an *Entertainment Weekly* article by Lynette Rice in which he downplayed the show's importance to the network: "Nobody wanted the show; it didn't perform [at first] but we stuck with it. . . . It's not our No. 1 show. It's not a show like 'ER' that stands above the pack." Whedon was quick to point out that while *Buffy* may not be their no.1 one show, it "put the WB on the map critically. . . . For [the WB] to be scrambling to explain why it's not cost efficient—it's their second highest rated show. They need to step up and acknowledge that financially."

Variety's Rick Kissell reported that *Buffy*'s debut on UPN, on October 2, 2001, attracted its second largest audience (7.65 million). The two-hour season 6 opener also achieved its best ratings ever among ages 18–49 and 18–34 year olds, which indicates the show's audience was not limited to teenagers. In his assessment of the move to UPN at the end of the 2001–2002 season, *Variety* reporter Josef Adalian concluded that both networks actually benefited in the end. *Buffy*'s strong performance at UPN during season 6, along with the *Star Trek* prequel *Enterprise* (2001–2005), definitely increased UPN's overall viewership and added some much-needed cache to their programming lineup. Adalian contends that the show's departure did not put a major dent in The WB's overall ratings and definitely saved the network the millions of dollars it would have shelled out to pay for the series. During its second season at UPN, Adalian reported that the show's current season—its seventh—would be Gellar's last, though there was some speculation that there could be a second *Buffy* spinoff, but it never materialized.

Written and directed by Whedon, the series' finale ("Chosen") had a lot of ground to cover (Buffy and company had approximately forty-three minutes of screen time to save the world), beginning with what would be Buffy and Angel's last big scene together on the show. They are interrupted by Caleb (Nathan Fillion), a deranged defrocked priest and part-time serial killer, whom Buffy kills by splitting him in two with a scythe. But Caleb's death takes a back seat to the exchange between Buffy and Angel. Buffy realizes that she has feelings for Spike. More importantly, she shares a revelation about what she sarcastically calls "her stellar history with guys": "I always feared there was something wrong with me, you know, because I couldn't make it work. But maybe I'm not supposed to." She then launches into a metaphor, comparing herself to cookie dough that has not yet done baking: "I'm not finished becoming whoever the hell it is I'm gonna turn out to be. I make it through this, and the next thing, and the next thing, and maybe one day I turn around and realize I'm ready. I'm cookies. And then, you know, if I want someone to eat—or enjoy warm, delicious cookie me, then, that's fine. That'll be then. When I'm done."

In the audio DVD commentary, Joss Whedon credits writer Marti Noxon for coming up with the cookie analogy and admits that this scene was shot quickly because he only had David Boreanaz for seven hours. As a demonstration of how well-versed *Angel* writers were in Buffyverse, the character makes reference to the cookie analogy in a season 5 episode ("The Girl in Question") when he and Spike are led to believe that Buffy is going out with their mutual enemy, The Immortal. "But she's not finished baking yet," he tells Spike. "I gotta wait till she's done baking, you know, till she finds herself, 'cause that's her drill. I'm waitin' patiently, and meanwhile, The Immortal is eatin' cookie dough." Of course, Spike (and certainly some audience members) has no idea what he's talking about.

The Buffy-Angel scene does serve another purpose. He gives her an amulet, which will be important to the climactic ending to the series.

After slaying what seemed like hundreds of vampires, demons, and bizarre creatures (*Buffy* fans estimate the final death count to be around 200), Buffy and the Scoobies must face off with the ultimate villain, The First Evil (also known as "The Infinite Evil" or "The Evil" for short), which made its first "appearance" back in season 3 ("Amends"). The First Evil is a tall order because it is an omnipresent entity that is the embodiment of all the evil that exists in the world. It does not have a body of its own (in its true form, it appears like a large demon-like creature wearing a white robe), but it

Spike (James Marsters) and Buffy (Sarah Michelle Gellar) save the world in the series finale of *Buffy the Vampire Slayer*.   *Authors' collection*

is all-powerful, with the ability to take the form of any person, living or dead, along with his or her memories, and be selectively seen or heard by humans. In an attempt to undermine the Scoobies' loyalty to Buffy and lower their morale before the impending battle, The First Evil plays mind games with the people closest to her by impersonating Buffy and people from their past: Drusilla appears to Spike; the late Mrs. Summers (Kristine Sutherland) to her daughter, Dawn; and Willow is visited by a dead Sunnydale student, Cassie Newton, who pretends to be delivering a message from Tara, who says she wants Willow to attempt suicide so they can be together (fortunately, Willow is too smart for that). The Scoobies have some backup: a small army of young women who are future slayers (nicknamed "The Potentials") because their coordination, agility, and speed far exceeds the average teenage girl and, like Buffy and the other slayers, they have dreams about past slayers and supernatural premonitions.

Aware of its impending destruction, the citizens of Sunnydale abandon their town. At first, Buffy appears uncertain about what to do, but then takes control of the situation and devises a plan in which she divides everyone into groups and arms herself with the Scythe, a weapon that was devised by a group of women for The Slayer to kill the last demons to walk the earth. The Slayers and the Potentials use drops of their blood to enter the Hellmouth underneath Sunnydale High School and Willow uses white magic on the Scythe to release its power and transform the Potentials into Slayers. Buffy and Spike enter the Hellmouth. She is armed with the Scythe and he is wearing the crystal amulet on a silver chain that Angel gave to Buffy at the start of the episode with very little information about it (no instructions are included) except to say, "It's very powerful and probably very dangerous . . . it bestows strength to the right person who wears it." Buffy and Spike battle the First Evil and save the world when he uses the amulet to open a hole at the top of Sunnydale High, which destroys the Hellmouth and its residents (including poor Spike). Buffy and everyone else (except Anya, who is killed in the battle) escape by bus as the Hellmouth and all of Sunnydale implodes, leaving a giant crater. The episode ends with Buffy and the Scoobies standing on the road, looking at the crater. Dawn asks Buffy, "What are we gonna do now?" Close-up on Buffy, who has no answer. She smiles slightly. In his director's DVD commentary, Whedon explains the significance of the final shot: "Because what this shot is ultimately about, is what a lot of the show is about, which is, that the story goes on. That there is closure, but not a closing. That's what we've seen is a life being formed, like the cookie dough speech explains. This is a life in progress, a life that in some way is just beginning. Like that smile."

"Chosen" was seen by 4.9 million viewers and received an Emmy nomination for Outstanding Special Visual Effects for a Series, bringing the series'

Buffy (Sarah Michelle Gellar) looks toward the future in the final scene of *Buffy the Vampire Slayer*.   *Authors' collection*

total to fourteen nominations and two wins in 1998 for Outstanding Makeup for a Series (for "Surprise/ Innocence") and Christophe Beck for Outstanding Music Composition for a Series (Dramatic) for "Becoming, Part I."

Fans were generally pleased with the finale. On a website devoted to Buffy entitled the Phi-Phenomenon.org/buffy, an anonymous fan ranks all 144 episodes based on information obtained from postings around the web of *Buffy* fans' best, worst, favorite, etc. (to qualify, sources had to rank a minimum of ten episodes). "Chosen" is ranked as the no. 6. The no. 1 episode—and certainly the most original—was "Once More, With Feeling," a musical episode written and directed by Whedon, in which Sweet, a tap-dancing demon in a Zoot suit (played by three-time Tony winner Hinton Battle) puts a spell on all of Sunnydale which makes its residents express their innermost feelings and reveal their secrets in song.

The superfan at Phi-Phenomenon.org also offers a detailed critique of every episode, including "Chosen," which he "does not see as a great episode or even a near-great episode by *Buffy* standards." One major complaint pertains to how the episode included three *deus ex machina*: the amulet supplied by Angel; Buffy's Scythe, which was introduced in the previous episode ("Touched"), but also appears in *Fray*, Joss Whedon's 2003 comic book about a Slayer hundreds of years in the future; and Willow's ability to use the Scythe to magically transform The Potentials into Slayers. The author also observes how the series finale lacks the suspense, which, in the finales of season 1–6, came from not knowing how the heroes will defeat the villain at the last minute. In "Chosen" the First Evil never comes close to succeeding.

Buffy's fandom remains active and the series continues to receive critical attention from academics, particularly by Third-Wave feminists. Buffyverse has been the subject of college courses and numerous critical books and essays in the fields of gender studies, media studies, family studies, genre studies, theology, psychology, and philosophy. In 2001, David Lavery and Rhonda V. Wilcox founded *Slayage: The Online Journal of Buffy Studies*, a quarterly academic online journal. *Slayage*, which continues to publish two issues a year, later changed its name to *Slayage: The Journal of Whedon Studies*

Association and includes essays on television series and films written, directed, and/or produced by Joss Whedon. As expected, the show's creator appreciates the attention *Buffy* has received. In a 2003 *New York Times* interview, Whedon expressed his gratitude to academics who are *Buffy* fans: "I think it's great that the academic community has taken an interest in the show. I think it's important for academics to study popular culture."

Buffy's spinoff, *Angel*, follows the vampire to Los Angeles, where he sets up Angel Investigations (also known as Team Angel), a detective agency specializing in cases involving the supernatural. The show is darker than *Buffy* in part because it's in the neo-noir tradition: it deals with

Angel (David Boreanaz), a vampire with a soul, moves to Los Angeles (and gets his own series).   *Authors' collection* the underside of urban life in present-day Los Angeles where evil lurks in the form of both mortals and demonic visitors from another dimension. There is also the fact that, unlike *Buffy*, the show's title character can't go out into the daylight.

Angel's motivation for establishing his agency stems from his troubled past. Born in 1727 and sired in 1753, Angel's reputation as a sadistic killer earned him the nickname "The Scourge of Europe." When Angel feeds on the daughter of a clan of Romanian gypsies, he is cursed by having his soul restored to him. Guilt-ridden for his crimes against humanity, Angel lives a desolate and lonely life, yet he is committed to protecting the innocent from vampires and demonic forces. After living in Sunnydale (for three seasons of *Buffy*), Angel relocated to Los Angeles, where, by chance, he meets up with Cordelia Chase, who helps him establish Angel Investigations. Over the course of five seasons, Angel's crew consists of an odd mix of mortals and demons.

As Angel and his co-workers fight evil for a living, the show delves more deeply into the mythology of demonic force, oftentimes building on what had previously been established in Buffyverse. In addition to Cordelia, several characters introduced on *Buffy* appeared as regular or recurring characters on *Angel*: Spike, who died in the *Buffy* series finale, is resurrected by the amulet; Darla, Angel's sire and former lover; Drusilla, who sired Spike; Harmony Kendall (Mercedes McNab), a shallow, self-involved former classmate of Buffy's whose personality hasn't changed since being bitten by a vampire during the attack at graduation ("Graduation Day 2"); and Wesley Wyndam-Pryce (Alexis Denisof), a demon hunter who briefly replaced Giles as Buffy's Watcher despite his incompetence. In addition, several *Buffy* characters—Buffy, Willow, Oz, Faith, and Andrew—appeared in one or more episodes.

Although it's more open ended than *Buffy*'s series finale, the ending of *Angel* ("Not Fade Away") is more satisfying because instead of fighting a non-corporeal entity like The First Evil, Angel's target is a group known as the Circle of the Black Thorn, a secret society whose evil and powerful members are entrusted to bringing on the apocalypse. The Circle answers to three unseen Senior Partners—known as the Wolf, the Ram, and the Hart—who have been banished from this dimension. The Circle is served by Wolfram & Hart (so-named after the Senior Partners), an international law firm that defends mobsters, murderers, etc.—the lowest of the low, both human and demonic. At the start of season 5, the Circle, thinking that Angel and his team have come over to the dark side, gives Angel Investigations control of Wolfram & Hart. Angel is then able to join the Circle, who want him on their side because, according to the Shanshu Prophecy, a vampire with a soul will play a pivotal role in the apocalypse and be rewarded by being turned back into a mortal. But the Prophecy doesn't specify which side the vampire will be on. Consequently, in the ultimate display of loyalty, Angel signs a parchment renouncing his claim to the reward.

In the finale, Angel and his crew—Spike, Wesley, Gunn (J. August Richards), and Illyria (Amy Acker)—eliminate the members of the Circle and their minions. Angel, with some help from his son, Conner (Vincent Kartheiser), defeats Marcus (Adam Baldwin), a child of the Senior Partners and their liaison to Wolfram & Hart, by biting him, thereby ingesting his blood which gives him his superhuman strength. We see the members of the Circle of the Black Thorn go down one by one (with one casualty, Wesley, who dies in Illyria's arms). Lorne (Andy Hallett), the singing demon who, along with Spike, served as the show's comic relief, and Lindsey (Christian Kane), a sleazy lawyer (and sorcerer) who worked for Wolfram & Hart's Special Projects Division, manage to eliminate the Sahrvin demon clan. Afterwards, Lorne follows Angel's instructions and shoots a surprised Lindsay, whom Angel felt he could never trust.

After the assassination scenes, and the lengthy showdown between Angel and Marcus, Angel and his crew congregate in an alley, ready to face off with an army of demons (including a dragon, on which Angel calls dibs).

Angel's final word to his team: "Let's go to work." Fade to black.

As we see what they are up against, the lack of closure was certainly a brazen choice. Considering how much they are outnumbered, it's unlikely any of them had a chance of surviving. The ending seems like the kind of cliffhanger that would continue in the next season opener. "The word 'cliffhanger' is really a misnomer here," Whedon told Ethan Alter in an article for *TV Guide Online*. "This was not the finale grace note after a symphony the way the *Buffy* finale was. We are definitely still in the thick of it [at the end]. But the point of the show is that you're never done; no matter what goes down, the fight goes on."

Whedon, the creative team at *Angel*, and the show's fans were surprised when The WB canceled the show. *Variety's* Josef Adalian described the network's decision not to renew the show for season 6 "a head-scratcher" considering it is the network's second highest rated hour among viewers ages 18–34 (behind *Smallville*) and fourth among ages 12–34. The show's ratings had also been solid this year, despite competition on Wednesday nights. According to WB president Jordan Levin, the network needed to make room for new shows and free up time slots so that shows can be repeated on other nights. A heartbroken Whedon said that while he understood why the decision was made from a business standpoint, it still doesn't make sense: "I thought that if a show was really good and doing really well [in the ratings], it was renewed. I was apparently misinformed." Whedon described the show's cancellation to

TV Guide's Ethan Alter as a "horrible blow. . . . Basically, we were told that we were old and in the way, [even though] ratings were higher than what they'd been." But he was touched by the outpouring of support he received from *Buffy* fans: "For them to react that strongly to what had always been perceived as the bastard child of the *Buffy* franchise was really important to me."

The fans were not so quick to give up. An ad in *Variety* on March 15, 2004, paid for by "the international community of ANGEL fans," made an emotional plea to The WB:

> ANGEL has been saving the world for years. Now he needs your help.
>
> Smart, funny, dark, and yet eternally hopeful, ANGEL has gained a devoted following and impressed critics. As good as things have been in the past, the fans feel the best is yet to come.
>
> We've banded together from all over the fan base and the world to ask the WB to reconsider its decision to cancel ANGEL. We'll follow ANGEL to wherever on your schedule you can find a home for it.
>
> Don't drive a stake through our hearts. Renew ANGEL, and keep one of the best hours of television on the air. If you can't see your way clear to do that . . .
>
> Looking for a few (million) good viewers? We'll follow ANGEL to hell . . . or ANOTHER NETWORK

Both *Buffy* and *Angel*'s narratives continued—in comic book form—in a series published by Dark Horse Comics, which also included offshoots for various characters, including Willow and Spike. *Buffy the Vampire Slayer Season Eight* is set a year after the series ended, in which Buffy and Xander are at the helm of a command station that oversees 500 slayers who are stationed throughout the world. In *Angel: After the Fall*, the main characters are still alive (even Wesley returns, though he is forced to work for Wolfram & Hart and the Partners), but the city of Los Angeles has been sent to hell—literally.

26

Dearly Departed

RIP *Six Feet Under*

Six Feet Under (HBO, 2001–2005)
Created by Alan Ball
Premiere date: June 3, 2001
5 seasons / 63 episodes
"Everyone's Waiting"
Airdate: August 21, 2005
3.89 million viewers
Directed by Alan Ball
Written by Alan Ball
Cast: Peter Krause (Nate Fisher), Michael C. Hall (David Fisher), Frances Conroy
(Ruth Fisher), Lauren Ambrose (Claire Fisher), Freddy Rodriguez (Federico
"Rico" Diaz), Matthew St. Patrick (Keith Charles), Justina Machado (Vanessa
Diaz), James Cromwell (George Sibley), Rachel Griffiths (Brenda Chenowith)
Guest Stars: Kathy Bates (Bettina), Jeremy Sisto (Billy Chenowith), Joanna Cassidy
(Margaret Chenowith), Richard Jenkins (Nathaniel Fisher), Tina Holmes
(Maggie Sibley), Peter Macdissi (Olivier Castro-Staal), Chris Messina (Ted
Fairwell), Kendré Berry (Durrell Charles-Fisher), C. J. Sanders (Anthony
Charles-Fisher), Tim Maculan (Father Jack), Becky Thyre (Marcie), James
McDonnell (Dr. Frank)

Alan Ball was no stranger to death. At just thirteen, the future Oscar winner—Best Screenplay for the Best Picture winner *American Beauty* (1999)—had witnessed his own sister's death, sitting alongside her in the car she crashed. Ball told the *Baltimore Sun*: "When my sister died, death stuck its face in mine and said, 'Uh, hello.' And I've been living with that ever since." Choosing to stick to the industry adage of "write what you know," Ball tackled his lingering feelings of loss by channeling them into the HBO show *Six Feet Under*—a series he created, wrote, and directed. The series followed the Fisher family on the heels of the death of their patriarch, Nathaniel Fisher (Richard Jenkins), who, like Ball's sister, dies in a car accident in the pilot episode. But in the world of Alan Ball, whose *American*

Beauty screenplay had stunned audiences with its bitter dark humor, there must be an added twist. For the Fisher family, death was not a foreign concept. Nathaniel Fisher, ironically, is driving a hearse at the time of his death—having spent his life as a funeral director. Ball's bitter irony of Nathaniel's untimely death sets the stage for a series that continued to haunt its fans for five seasons, bringing the reality of death to audiences weekly.

Each episode of Ball's series opened with a death—setting the tone of the rest of the episode, and at times, shocking audiences with its wicked twists. Death by elevator, lightning, overdose, gang shooting, and yes, even a shockingly gruesome encounter with a dough mixer, were not uncommon within the *Six Feet Under* universe. Ball would pick up each episode following this death, bringing the family and relatives of the deceased to the receiving room of Fisher and Sons funeral home. Deeply closeted David Fisher (Michael C. Hall) has the run of the place, while reluctant prodigal son Nate (Peter Krause)—returning to Los Angeles for good following his father's death—is unsure if undertaking is indeed his calling. Though he toys with the idea of heading back to his organic farming life in Seattle, a chance encounter with attractive stranger Brenda (Rachel Griffiths) keeps him intrigued enough to stick around. Younger sister Claire (Lauren Ambrose), still in high school at the series start, languishes in her own teenage funk, moodily making her way to school via a lime-green vintage hearse. Ruth (Frances Conroy), the family matriarch, struggles to come to grips with the loss of her husband, overcome with the guilt she feels for being unfaithful. Upon the series premiere, critics wondered if *Six Feet Under*'s view on the living would be too dark for audiences, though most assured viewers that they were not in for an hour-long sob fest, wracked with morbid curiosity. "Whatever you might expect from a series about morticians," the *New York Times* Caryn James wrote in her review, "Forget it." She continued: "Mr. Ball has created an amazing dark comedy, full of dry humor and deflected emotions." Ken Tucker of *Entertainment Weekly* couldn't resist making the deeply ironic connection featured in the series, stating: "Ball draws parallels between the embalming profession and the formaldehyde effect of repressed emotions." Ball's parents, like the Fishers, suffered immensely following his sister's death—his mother's mental state requiring hospitalization and his father seeking comfort in alcohol. The real and raw emotion imparted on screen was felt by critics and viewers alike, as the *Washington Post*'s Tom Shales noted: "It's great, and it's merrily macabre, and it's eerily teleportational, and at times, as it should under the circumstances, it hurts like hell." These conflicting (and intriguing) responses to the show's premiere paid off in its numbers, bringing in about 5 million viewers. HBO knew they had a strong show to complement its megahit *The Sopranos*—or as the *Chicago Tribune*'s Steve Johnson put it: "[*Six Feet Under*] is proof that

The Fisher family in "happier" times. Seated (left to right): Ruth Fisher (Frances Conroy), and David Fisher (Michael C. Hall). Standing (left to right): Nathaniel Fisher (Richard Jenkins), Claire Fisher (Lauren Ambrose), and Nate Fisher (Peter Krause).   *Authors' collection*

HBO can find poetry not just in the pluggin 'em but in the planting 'em too." Perhaps *The Sopranos* would rack up a high death count in their upcoming season, but as long as *Six Feet Under* was around the Fishers would be there to handle the arrangements.

Subsequent seasons of the series delved more deeply into David's suppressed sexuality (particularly in dealing with LAPD boyfriend Keith, played by Michael St. Patrick), as well as thoroughly dissecting Nate and Brenda's on-again-off-again relationship. Claire moved from high school to art school, piling up a multitude of dysfunction along the way. Ruth, meanwhile, searches for higher purpose, famously seeking out a self-help seminar in season 2 that specialized in self-actualization by imagining yourself as "the architect of your life." The characters grew amidst their own grief following their father's death, achieving a new normal at the Fisher & Sons funeral home—especially when assistant mortician Rico (Freddy Rodriguez) emerges as a power player in the rescuing of the business from corporate takeover, earning him a controlling interest ("Welcome to Fisher and Diaz").

By November of 2004, the series was poised to begin shooting its fifth season when HBO announced that the current set of episodes would indeed be the show's last (*Variety*, never resisting a good pun ran with the headline: "Ball to Put "Six Feet" Under"). Executive producer Alan Poul was at peace with the decision, stating: "All of us feel very good about it. Our biggest concern has always been to get out while we're still fresh, and at our peaks as storytellers." And at this peak of storytelling, Poul, Ball, and their writing staff set in motion events that would forever alter the imprint of the series. David, finally out, adopts two children with boyfriend Keith, while Claire finds happiness in new love Ted (Chris Messina). Ruth busies herself in light of the discovery that her new husband, George (James Cromwell), is obsessed with the possibility of a nuclear holocaust. Despite these developments, no storyline trumped that of Nate and Brenda, who, after four seasons of psychologically torturing each other, marry, suffer a miscarriage and then find themselves with child again. Nate, conflicted with the prospect of another child (his first child, daughter Maya, was with now deceased wife Lisa), begins to spend time with George's daughter Maggie (Tina Holmes), intrigued by her quiet, Quaker beliefs. After he and Maggie begin their affair, Nate collapses, suffering a massive stroke, believed to be connected to the arteriovenous malformation (AVM) in his brain that he had removed at the end of season two. Appearing to recover, thus giving the Fishers hope, Nate passes unexpectedly. His death rocks the family, turning their lives upside down in the final two episodes leading up to the finale. As each is haunted by the spirit of Nate (not unlike Nate's constant visions of his own father throughout the series), closure seems beyond their reach.

The series finale aired on August 21, 2005. As per usual, the episode would begin with a death, signifying the jumping off point for the episode (and at times, the overall theme). In the opening scenes of the series finale, however, the audience bears witness to a birth, as Brenda prematurely gives birth to a daughter. As Brenda struggles, Ruth, seated alongside her in the delivery room, promises that the baby will be fine. Moments later the baby girl is born unresponsive. She is rushed out of the room, as Brenda calls out: "Where are they taking her?" And then, the white screen appears: Willa Fisher Chenowith (2005–). The lack of an "end" date left fans cautiously optimistic. Ruth, at the hospital, calls home in hopes of reaching Claire. On the answering machine, Ruth breaks down—following Nate's untimely death she simply cannot bear "to lose another child." Ultimately, Willa survives, though is not quite out of the woods. Throughout the finale episode Brenda is haunted by Nate, who fills her head with the idea that Willa will not make it—there is something wrong that Brenda just cannot see ("She's damaged," Nate growls). Brenda brings Willa home but continues to be plagued with a crushing sense of fear and doubt. It is only after Brenda buries the hatchet with Ruth—agreeing to mutually help each other through Nate's absence and forgo the custody battle over Maya—that she sees a vision of Nate (with his father, who introduces himself to Brenda) holding baby Willa, promising Brenda that they all will make it. Ruth, likewise, is pulled from the brink of a deep depression thanks to a phone call with George's daughter Maggie, who was with Nate when he suffered his stroke. "Was he happy?" Ruth asks, to which Maggie tearfully responds, "He was." Ruth breathes a life-saving sigh of relief.

Meanwhile, David's emotions following his brother's death get the best of him and Keith suggests that David move out of their home. Their adopted sons listen in, concerned, as the family they always dreamed of seems to be decaying before their very eyes. David returns to live with Ruth at the funeral home, an especially tense place given Rico's renewed interest in selling the entire business. Rico talks David and Brenda (now representing Nate's interest in the company) into finally putting the business on the market, celebrating the financial boon this will bring him (he owns 25 percent of the business, which is valued at minimally $3 million). David, meanwhile, struggles with the idea of what he will do with his life, finally realizing that it

Brenda (Rachel Griffiths) and Ruth (Frances Conroy) make amends in the series finale of *Six Feet Under*.

Everett Collection

is only at the funeral parlor that he belongs. He drops the bomb on Rico, who insists that if David won't sell he must buy him out—an option David decides to go with after he and Keith reconcile and decide to pour their life savings into the business (and a much-needed upgrade to Ruth's time-warped home).

Claire continues seeing Ted (Chris Messina), who has supported her photography from the very beginning. She receives a promising job offer in New York, discovering that it was Olivier (Peter Macdissi)—her painfully narcissistic mentor—who recommended her. After deciding to take the leap and head east, Claire is moved by her mother's fragile state and offers to stay in Los Angeles, but Ruth insists (even making it easier thanks to some unfrozen trust money). When Claire finds out that the job is no longer available due to a business consolidation, she intends to stay put, only to be visited by Nate who encourages her to go ("Ah, who cares," he tells her. "Go anyway"). She heeds his advice and packs up to go to New York. The family gathers for a final dinner at the funeral home—as the camera whips through the gorgeously remodeled house—reminiscing about their favorite "Nate moments," ending with a tribute toast. The next morning Claire awakes to Nate in her room. He implores her to "get up . . . c'mon everybody's waiting" (a nod to the episode's title). Outside the funeral home, she tearfully says goodbye to Ruth, David, Keith, and their sons Durrell and Anthony. As she pulls out of the driveway and onto the freeway, Sia's "Breathe Me" plays, as the series breaks into its final montage.

The finale montage, cited by *Vulture* as "the most satisfying TV ending ever," visits with each character one last time, fulfilling the show's final season promise that "Everything. Everyone. Everywhere. Ends." The audience catches glimpses of lives well lived. Ruth spends time with Bettina (Kathy Bates) at her sister's home in cozy Topanga Canyon. David teaches his son the funeral business. The family gathers to celebrate Willa's first birthday (a welcome sight, given the opening scene of the episode). Keith and David are married, as their grown sons look on. And then, as Claire's car goes into hyper drive the years begin to speed up, bringing the audience to each character's true end—a fitting resolution for a show that opened every episode with a death. Ruth is first, glimpsed lying weak in a hospital bed. She rolls over to see a vision of her husband Nathaniel, and then her son Nate, who smiles at her. She closes her eyes, as Claire, David, and George reel over her passing. The screen reads: Ruth O'Connor Fisher (1946–2025). At the cemetery, Claire is reunited with lost love Ted, as David's aged son leads the burial service. Keith is up next, devastatingly shot by an array of bullets as he exits a "Charles Security" armored truck—Keith Dwayne Charles (1968–2029). Intermixed into the death sequence, Claire marries Ted, after both are beyond middle aged. David, attending a picnic in the park, watches on

Claire (Lauren Ambrose), David (Michael C. Hall), and George (James Cromwell) sit at Ruth's (Frances Conroy) bedside as she takes her final breath.   *Authors' collection*

as young men play football, catching a glimpse of lost love Keith amid the huddle. He falls backwards as the screen reads: David James Fisher (1969–2044). Rico, spotted on a cruise ship with wife, Vanessa, grabs his arm and collapses, befallen by a sudden heart attack—Hector Federico Diaz (1974–2049). Brenda, seated opposite her droning brother Billy (Jeremy Sisto), appears to die of boredom, a death that fully embraces the show's ability to inject dark humor amidst so much tragedy—Brenda Chenowith (1969–2051). And in the final death, the camera pans through an apartment adorned with photos of the past in neat square frames, finally settling on a very old woman lying in bed with a shock of white hair and a haunting pair of blue eyes— Claire Simone Fisher (1983–2085). The audience rejoins Claire in her car, and a close-up of those same blue eyes—still young and filled with promise— as the car speeds by, driving into the endless horizon.

For Alan Ball, the finale sequence was "the perfect way to end the show," admitting that after hearing Sia's "Breathe Me," he created the scene around the song. Ball chose to end the series on Claire, letting her character live past the century mark, because she was "the artist." He continued: "Claire is the one who sees the story. She sees the bigger picture. And because the series started with somebody in a car ending their life, I wanted to do somebody in a car driving off into their new life." Nearly 4 million fans tuned in to see Ball's bookended series finale, a season best in terms of ratings. Following the episode's broadcast, HBO posted obituaries for each of the characters, elaborating on the circumstances of their death, as well as the lives they lived (David's entry was of particular interest, as he enjoyed performing in local theater productions following his retirement). Unsurprisingly, most of the characters were given a proper memorial service at Fisher & Sons Funeral Home. The episode has since appeared on countless lists of "the best series finales," with many citing the death montage as the crowning achievement in series finale history. In no other show was it so poetically fitting to employ the use of "everybody dies" as a means to say goodbye—and it's likely, there never will be another quite like it again.

27

Bye-Bye Baltimore

Cutting *The Wire*

The Wire (HBO, 2002–2008)
Created by David Simon
Premiere date: June 2, 2002
5 seasons /60 episodes
"-30-"
Airdate: March 9, 2008
Directed by Clark Johnson
Story by David Simon and Ed Burns
Written by David Simon
Cast: Dominic West (Detective James "Jimmy" McNulty), John Doman (William A. Rawls), Aidan Gillen (Thomas "Tommy" Carcetti), Clark Johnson (Augustus "Gus" Haynes), Deirdre Lovejoy (Rhonda Pearlman), Tom McCarthy (Scott Templeton), Clarke Peters (Lester Freamon), Wendell Pierce (Detective William "Bunk" Moreland), Lance Reddick (Cedric Daniels), Andre Royo (Reginald "Bubbles" Cousins), Sonja Sohn (Shakima "Kima" Greggs), Seth Gilliam (Ellis Carver) Domenick Lombardozzi (Thomas "Herc" Hauk), Gbenga Akinnagbe (Chris Partlow), Jamie Hector (Marlo Stanfield), Neal Huff (Michael Steintorf), Jermaine Crawford (Duquan "Dukie" Weems), Corey Parker Robinson (Leander Sydnor), Tristan Wilds (Michael Lee), Michael Kostroff (Maurice "Maury" Levy), Michelle Paress (Alma Gutierrez), Reg E. Cathey (Norman Wilson), Michael Kenneth Williams (Omar Little, credit only), Isiah Whitlock Jr. (Clayton "Clay" Davis, credit only)
Guest Stars: Jim True-Frost (Roland "Prez" Pryzbylewski), Peter Gerety (Judge Daniel Phelan), Amy Ryan (Beatrice "Beadie" Russell), Paul Ben-Victor (Spiros "Vondas" Vondopoulous), Bill Raymond (The Greek), Delaney Williams (Jay Landsman), Marlyne Afflack (Nerese Campbell), Steve Earle (Walon), Maria Broom (Marla Daniels), Hassan Johnson (Roland "Wee-Bey" Brice), Method Man (Melvin "Cheese" Wagstaff), Kwame Patterson (Monk Metcalf), Anwan Glover (Slim Charles), Al Brown (Stan Valchek)

Before David Simon reinvented the genre, the basic premise of a cop show was simple: a crime is committed, a cop hunts the bad guy, same cop catches bad guy, and justice is served—all in the span of a tidy televised hour. *Neat* and *efficient*, however, were not words in Simon's vocabulary. Having shadowed the Baltimore Police Department's Homicide Unit during his stint as a journalist for the *Baltimore Sun*, Simon knew a thing or two about real crime—crime that was anything but the glamorous, polished version to which television audiences had grown accustomed. Simon's book detailing his experience on the gritty inner-city streets of Baltimore, *Homicide: A Year on the Killing Streets* (1991), provided the basis for two television shows: NBC's *Homicide: Life on the Street* (1993–1999), and HBO's *The Wire* (2002–2008). NBC's *Homicide* won three Peabody awards, four Emmys, and launched the careers of Andre Braugher (now back in his role as a cop in Fox's comedy *Brooklyn Nine-Nine*), Richard Belzer (whose character, Munch, made the crossover to NBC's *Law and Order: Special Victims Unit*), and Melissa Leo, who would go on to win an Academy Award for her role in David O. Russell's *The Fighter*. Simon's *The Wire* won one Peabody, took home no Emmy statuettes, and its cast, while lauded for their realistic portrayal of cops, criminals, and politicians alike, count the show, for the most part, as their most notable role (with the exception of Idris Elba, whose lead role on the BBC's *Luther* has garnered praise). However, when placed side by side in the halls of television's past, *The Wire* emerges as Simon's crown jewel—a series that completely reinvented the cop show and was often called the best show on television during its run, and perhaps, of all time. *The Wire* did not attract awards or high ratings, instead it carried with it a passionate circle of critics and a rabid fan base. The series, cited for its hyper-realistic portrayal of what Simon called "life on the streets," carried the torch of its predecessor *Homicide*, and then ran circles around it. Stylistically—in its cinematography, writing, and sound—it portrayed police work and the inner workings of urban drug organizations (both from supply and distribution channels) as they actually existed, forgoing the high-production value flash, swelling musical scores (or any score), and dramatic monologues often featured in crime shows. Instead, Simon's *The Wire* quietly revolutionized television—hiding from the glaring spotlight of ratings juggernauts, all the while reinventing the genre and winning over all who sought it out.

The Wire premiered on HBO on June 2, 2002, two years after David Simon brought the pay-cable network an adaptation of his own book *The Corner*, which won the Emmy for Outstanding Miniseries in 2000. Like *The Corner*, *The Wire* took its viewers into the lives of the residents of West Baltimore—a part of town known for its drug-slinging and poverty—as well as into the world of the cops

Detectives Bunk Moreland (Wendell Pierce) and Jimmy McNulty (Dominic West) of HBO's
The Wire.   *Authors' collection*

that guard their streets. The key to Simon's series was acknowledging the similarities between these two different worlds, or as the *New Yorker* noted: "The drug trade emerged as its own intricate bureaucracy, a hierarchy that subtly mirrored that of the police department." Simon protested that *The Wire* not be referred to as a "cop show," continuing: "The whole cop-show logic is to see a bad guy arrested before the last commercial break . . . you wonder who is a bad guy and what's the point?" Figuring out the bad from the good was made that much more difficult by Simon's choice to litter the screen with as many characters as he could fit—dissecting each one as the season went along. For Neil Genzlinger of the *New York Times*, this could give the series a sense of being "choppy and confusing," but, he continued, "[by] not giving viewers the traditional 'This is who's who and what's what' opening, *The Wire* is determined to be as different as possible from *Law and Order*, *CSI*, and all the other network police dramas." For the *Chicago Tribune*'s Steve Johnson, Simon's choice to differentiate his show from the existing cop lineup was the perfect fit: "*The Wire* is compelling in its complexity, heart-rending in its humanity, and surprising in the ways it finds to spin the conventions of cop drama. Following *The Sopranos* and *Six Feet Under*, it's worthy of the title of

HBO's next dramatic series." Within the confines of HBO, Simon's work was safe—he could portray the streets of Baltimore as he knew them, without the expectation of any embellishments to be added. *Variety* called the audience for *The Wire*'s June premiere "solid, but not spectacular," adding that the resulting viewership was "more-than-satisfactory." The network paired the premiere with the season 2 finale of *Six Feet Under*, hoping to win over a built-in audience. Numbers were strong enough to satisfy HBO execs, and by January 2003, *The Wire* was safely headed towards its second season.

When season 2 premiered, it took fans by surprise—the focus had now shifted away from the first season's main characters. Season 1 had told the story of Detective Jimmy McNulty (Dominic West) and his determination to take down the Barksdale gang, known drug kingpins of West Baltimore. The season was split between following the inner workings of the Baltimore Police Department and the dealings within the Barksdale organization, led by Avon Barksdale (Wood Harris) and up-and-comer Stringer Bell (Idris Elba). Yet, these storylines took a backseat in season 2 in favor of detailing the decaying status of Baltimore's working middle class—particularly those who worked at the waterfront. Union dock workers turned to drug smuggling in order to get by, supplying the dealers that viewers had come to know in the previous season. This switch to a new perspective for *The Wire* furthered the cause of many critics who championed the series as being "novelistic," approaching television in a new way. Each season would feel like a new chapter in David Simon's latest book on inner-city Baltimore. All angles would be covered within Simon's universe, contributing to his vision of the series representing "the decline of the American empire." To cover the entire swath of that empire meant focusing each season on a different layer: season 1 covering the cops and dealers; season 2 focusing on the dockworkers; season 3 delving more deeply into the drug trade, combined with the backdoor politics of the upcoming mayoral race; season 4 shifting to the public education system, sending former cop **Roland "Prez" Pryzbylewski (Jim True-Frost)** from the beat into the classroom; and, finally, season 5 going straight to the source—the media, that is—chronicling the stories that make it and don't make it past the desks of the dwindling array of journalists that work at the *Baltimore Sun* (Simon's former haunt). To cover that much ground within the confines of television's small screen was no small task for Simon, and thus, he brought on board an elite group of writers, including novelist Dennis Lehane (known best for *Mystic River* and *Gone Baby Gone*—both adapted for the screen with A-list actors), D.C. detective fiction writer George Pelecanos, author turned screenwriter Richard Price (*Clockers, The Color of Money*), and series co-producer and Simon's main collaborator Ed Burns, a retired Baltimore homicide detective turned school teacher. Critics likened storylines to Dickens, Tolstoy, and even Shakespeare, with Simon citing Greek mythology as a main influence ("We've basically taken the idea of Greek tragedy and applied it to the modern city-state," he told the *New Yorker*). As the fifth and final season approached, fans and critics elevated the series to monumental levels, or as *Variety*'s Brian Lowry put it: "When television history is written, little else will rival *The Wire*." Lofty expectations hit new heights, as the series finale was set to premiere in March 2008.

The final episode opens as Baltimore mayor (and gubernatorial hopeful) Tommy Carcetti (Aidan Gillen) discovers that the "Red Ribbon Killer"—the serial murderer he promised to bring to justice—was an invention of Baltimore detectives Jimmy McNulty and Lester Freamon (Clarke Peters) as a means to bring more funding (and illegal wiretapping) to their continued pursuit of drug kingpin Marlo Stanfield (Jamie Hector). Freamon, believing his and McNulty's secret is safe, goes on with his other case (tracking down a courthouse mole), presenting his evidence to Chief Drug Prosecutor Rhonda Pearlman (Deirdre Lovejoy), who subsequently reveals to Freamon that the jig is up. When he brings this news to McNulty, his partner wonders why this is the first they are hearing of this, suggesting that the bigwigs' reluctance to bring this to light (for fear of jeopardizing the election) will work to their

Much of *The Wire*'s fifth season took place in the newsroom of the *Baltimore Sun*: (left to right) Gus Haynes (Clark Johnson); Mike Fletcher (Brandon Young); Alma Gutierrez (Michelle Paress); and Scott Templeton (Tom McCarthy).   *Authors' collection*

advantage. Meanwhile, *Sun* journalist Scott Templeton (Tom McCarthy) falsi-fies a story about witnessing a homeless man about to be kidnapped (possibly by the fictitious Red Ribbon Killer, known for preying on the homeless), and his editor Gus Haynes (played by *Homicide: Life on the Street* vet and director of the finale, Clark Johnson) sees right through it. The story grows more troublesome when a homeless man does end up murdered, complete with a white ribbon tied around his wrists, suggesting that McNulty and Freamon's fictional killer has inspired a copycat. Detectives Bunk (Wendell Pierce) and Kima (Sonja Sohn) join McNulty at the scene of the crime, where McNulty finds himself racked with guilt. His superiors Cedric Daniels (Lance Reddick) and William Rawls (John Doman), already in the know on McNulty's crime, press him to settle this case once and for all, as it will, in fact, be his last one on the force. McNulty does ultimately find the copycat killer—thanks to somewhat un-*Wire*-like convenient evidence—and Rawls begs him to get a signed confession from his perp for all of the Red Ribbon killings. McNulty only files charges on the two murders the copycat did commit, and the killer is sent to a psychiatric hospital as he is unfit to stand trial. The mayor stages a splashy press conference celebrating the victory of ridding the streets of the Red Ribbon Killer, hoping this will seal his fate as the next governor of Maryland. McNulty is asked to surrender his badge, while Freamon sets off into retired life. Daniels, now commissioner of Baltimore PD, is asked to cook the books by Mayor Carcetti's chief of staff Michael Steintorf (Neal Huff) to make it seem that crime has gone down under Carcetti's leadership. Daniels refuses, and then retires from the department, opting instead to go back to practicing law.

For the characters that litter the streets of West Baltimore, the conclusion of the series finds them in equally compromising positions. Marlo walks away from the charges that resulted from the illegal cop wiretap, all thanks to a mutually agreed upon deal by Pearlman and his defense lawyer Maury Levy (Michael Kostroff), whose hands are just as dirty as his clients (as are Levy's private investigator cohort Herc [Domenick Lombardozzi]). Marlo's men, however, are not dealt a similar fate, as Chris (Gbegnga Akinnagbe) and Monk (Kwame Patterson) take the fall, while Cheese (Method Man) is murdered by Slim Charles (Anwan Glover) while out on bail. For Marlo, being free is just a different type of life sentence, as he is shut out of the business he loves (not unlike the fate of Detective McNulty). The Greek (Bill Raymond) and Vondas (Paul Ben-Victor) remain in the distribution game (or as TV critic Alan Sepinwall put it: "Same as it ever was—'always business'"). Former junkie Bubbles (Andre Royo) finally emerges from his sister's base-ment—ready to rejoin society, clean, no longer confined to his literal pit of despair. On the street, another junkie is born, as Dukie (Jermaine Crawford) shoots up, despite having promised his former teacher Prez that he would go to college (and borrowing money from him to do so). After the death of Omar Little (Michael Kenneth Williams)—undoubtedly the fan favorite and perhaps the most memorable character of the series—Michael (Tristan Wilds) takes a page from Omar's playbook and begins ripping drug dealers off left and right (Sepinwall calls him the new "Robin Hood of West Baltimore").

At the newspaper—the primary focus of season 5—Gus is sent back to the copy desk, as punishment for his supposed vendetta against Templeton (and his fictitious homeless abduction story), while editor James Whiting (Sam Freed) and managing editor Thomas Klebanow (David Costabile) move forward with Templeton's story. Mike Fletcher (Brandon Young), who just ran his profile on recovering addict Bubbles, takes over for Gus as city editor, and Alma Gutierrez (Michelle Paress), having also accused Templeton of fabricating his story, is relinquished to the lesser county bureau.

The series closes with one final montage, as series theme song "Way Down in the Hole," performed by the Blind Boys of Alabama, plays in the background (the same song used for season 1's credits). McNulty, having found peace with girlfriend Beadie (Amy Ryan), does his penance as he picks up the homeless man he stowed away during the Red Ribbon Killer case. Driving back into Baltimore with his new passenger, McNulty gets out of his car to gaze at the city skyline. In the next series of shots, we see the new state of affairs on the streets and in the suites of Baltimore. New crews fill the corner, as Freamon enjoys retirement with stripper-turned-good girl Shardene (Wendy Grantham). Herc buys a round at the bar, and Templeton officially wins the Pulitzer for his news story. Vondas renegotiates terms with newly in charge Slim Charles, as The Greek inconspicuously listens in. Carcetti becomes governor of Maryland, as Gus looks on in the newsroom, watching Mike handily take over the city desk beat. Stan Valchek (Al Brown) is officially announced as the new commissioner of the Baltimore PD, as former prosecutor Rhonda Pearlman takes her seat on the bench. Wee-Bey Brice (Hassan Johnson)—who was imprisoned in season 2—joins Chris as they hold their own court in the prison yard, as Rawls is officially announced as head of the Maryland State Police (thanks to Carcetti). Bubbles joins his sister at the dinner table, as young Kenard (Thuliso Dingwall) is led into a squad car (perhaps for Omar's death). Various shots of the streets of Baltimore, much the same as it always was, fly by as we revisit each season's most memorable haunts. Finally, we land back on McNulty, who re-enters his car, telling Larry: "Let's go home." As he drives away, the final shot lingers on the Baltimore skyline at sunset.

The episode barely brought in a million viewers—which at the time accounted for just 5 percent of HBO's subscribers. Critics, however, tuned in by the droves; they found it fitting that in a series so chock-full with memorable characters, Simon chose the city of Baltimore to fill the screen in the final shot. After all, Simon had said: "We knew that the ultimate star of the narrative was Baltimore, and by extension the American city, and by extension America." A number of critics immediately compared *The Wire*'s final episode to another HBO series finale—*The Sopranos*. For Adam Sternbergh of Vulture.com (*New York Magazine*) *The Wire* finale "was the anti-*Sopranos*: an almost absurdly exhaustive festival of closure." (For more on *The Sopranos* black-out ending, see chapter 11). The true finality of the series was fitting given the propensity of critics (and viewers alike) to compare the series to a novel. No stone was left unturned, which seemed all the more appropriate as the show's creative force, David Simon, was first and foremost a journalist. "Simon, the newspaperman, likes stories, told right to the end," wrote *Vulture*'s Sternbergh. The same dense storytelling filled with countless characters that scared off Emmy voters (or any casual viewer, really) allowed for a supremely satisfying swan song for *The Wire*. As images of Baltimore passed by, there was a sense that life goes on the streets, no matter whether we are watching, or if we cease to check in. Alessandra Stanley of the *New York Times* touched on this aspect of the finale, stating: "A few deserving people came out ahead, or at least even, but nothing really changed: the drug trade thrives and the system in Baltimore drifts on, corrupt and self-sustaining, held together by convenience and a lie too big to bring down." Stanley concluded, "*The Wire* ended at just the right time: too soon."

The episode was appropriately titled "-30-," shorthand used by journalists to indicate where their story ends—and this was indeed where the ink would dry on David Simon's *The Wire*.

One Last Knock

Walter White's Final Days on *Breaking Bad*

Breaking Bad (AMC, 2008–2013)
Created by Vince Gilligan
Premiere date: January 20, 2008
5 seasons / 62 episodes
"Felina"
Airdate: September 29, 2013
10.3 million viewers
Directed and written by Vince Gilligan
Cast: Bryan Cranston (Walter White), Aaron Paul (Jesse Pinkman), Anna Gunn
    (Skyler White), Betsy Brandt (Marie Schrader), RJ Mitte (Walter White Jr.),
    Jesse Plemons (Todd), Laura Fraser (Lydia Rodarte-Quayle), Dean Norris
    (Hank Schrader, credit only), Bob Odenkirk (Saul Goodman, credit only)
Guest Stars: Matt L. Jones (Badger Mayhew), Charles Baker (Skinny Pete), Adam
    Godley (Elliott Schwartz), Jessica Hecht (Gretchen Schwartz), Michael Bowen
    (Uncle Jack Welker), Kevin Rankin (Kenny)

W hen AMC wanted to make their first move into original programming, Matthew Weiner's *Mad Men*, a virtual time-machine back
to 1960s New York, was the perfect fit. The network was already
known for its classic Hollywood fare—be it a Marx Brothers marathon, or a
Katharine Hepburn showcase—and Jon Hamm's dashing Don Draper was
a familiar leading man. Known for its first twenty years as American Movie
Classics, AMC (part of Rainbow Entertainment Services) rebranded itself to
accommodate *Mad Men*–like programming beginning in 2007. This move,
designed to differentiate the channel from peers like Turner Classic Movies,
aimed to marry original programming like *Mad Men* with their existing library
of classics films. Films like Hitchcock's stylish *North By Northwest*, starring
Cary Grant as a New York ad man on the run, would transition seamlessly to
the prime-time dealings at *Mad Men*'s smoke-filled Sterling Cooper agency.

Mad Men premiered in July of 2007 to rave reviews, garnering a Golden Globe for Best Drama and Best Actor just six months after its first episode, followed by its first of four consecutive Emmys for Best Drama. But *Mad Men* (see appendix), while ground-breaking and stylish in its own contemporary way, felt nostalgic—at first a perfect fit for the network, but not enough for a complete rebrand. AMC needed a show set in modern times that would also parlay off of their existing treasure trove of Hollywood classics. Enter Vince Gilligan and *Breaking Bad*.

The premise for *Breaking Bad* was easily explained: a high school chemistry teacher named Walter White learns he has terminal cancer and decides to start cooking meth as a side job to supplement his lost income. Creator Vince Gilligan, whose previous credits included eight seasons writing for *The X Files* (1993–2002), originally pitched the show to FX, then the recent home to edgy dramas like *The Shield, Nip/Tuck*, and *Rescue Me*, but (in his words) it was "dead in the water." When he brought the series to AMC, they jumped at the chance to add it to their emerging original lineup. Production and tax incentives brought the series to New Mexico, and suddenly, the story of Walter White's journey from bland chemistry teacher to meth-cooking kingpin, combined with the deserted, dusty landscape of Albuquerque, transformed the series into the story of an unapologetic, ruthless cowboy. The show fit easily into the category of "spaghetti western"—a film genre born in Italy (thanks to director Sergio Leone) and known best for its morally questionable heroes, over the top violence, and stop-at-nothing villains. For AMC, a show that recalled the flavor and substance of Leone's masterpieces (*A Fistful of Dollars* [1964], *A Few Dollars More* [1965], *The Good, The Bad and the Ugly* [1966]—all starring Clint Eastwood) tapped right into their base audience. This sentiment was echoed by Ed Carroll, president of Rainbow Entertainment Services (AMC's parent company), who said: "You're always looking to drive home the message that this show is uniquely suited to this network, and at AMC we're developing quality original series that have high production values and work with our movie library." But AMC knew that in order to sell the series to their audience they would need a leading man as compelling as Eastwood. Luckily for the network, Gilligan already had a cowboy in mind—funny man and sitcom veteran Bryan Cranston.

Based on Cranston's résumé, he was a very unlikely choice for Walter White. Known for his Emmy-nominated work as the patriarch of a dysfunctional brood on FOX's comedy *Malcolm in the Middle* (2000–2006), Cranston also famously appeared on *Seinfeld* (1989–1998) as the re-gifting dentist Tim Whatley. His credits, while long and storied, did not immediately read Walter White. White was meant to be a villain the audience roots for—a no-good bad guy à la Eastwood, or, more apt, Dexter Morgan of Showtime's *Dexter*

The dynamic duo of AMC's *Breaking Bad*: Walter White (Bryan Cranston, right) and Jesse Pinkman (Aaron Paul).   *Authors' collection*

(2006–2013). But Gilligan insisted. He had previously worked with Cranston on one episode of *The X-Files* in its sixth season, titled "Drive." Cranston played an anti-Semitic criminal on the run who kidnaps David Duchovny's Mulder and forces him to drive west, away from the harmful radiation that is slowly killing him. Cranston's ability to bring humanity and sympathy to an otherwise loathsome role left a lasting impression on Gilligan. This sense of sympathy was crucial to maintaining an audience—after all, who would root for a man who commits truly heinous acts if there was no way to latch on to the lighter side of his darkness? For Gilligan it was simple: "[On *The X-Files*], we had this villain, and we needed the audience to feel bad for him when he died. . . . Bryan alone was the only actor who could do that, who could pull off that trick. And it is a trick. I have no idea how he does it." But Cranston, though fully on board with the series, knew it would be a tough sell, telling the *Los Angeles Daily News*: "They were thinking, and rightfully so, 'Wait a minute. The goofy dad? He's not right for this guy. This guy is a weighty, deep kind of character.'" Luckily for millions of fans to come, AMC took Gilligan's word and signed on to casting Cranston.

Breaking Bad premiered on Sunday, January 20, 2008—having the misfortune of being broadcast opposite a nail-biting overtime showdown between two Super Bowl hopefuls: the New York Giants and Green Bay Packers (New York won). Despite being up against the pig-skinned ratings juggernaut, the show had a respectable audience of just about a million viewers. The success of *Mad Men* had led viewers to AMC, and thus *Breaking Bad* arrived with the cache of what AMC had banked on: high quality production value married with high caliber, complicated storytelling. The pilot followed Walter White as his metamorphosis from chemistry teacher to meth producer begins—or as Gilligan put it: from "Mr. Chips to Scarface." Cranston's Walt learns that he is suffering from inoperable lung cancer on the heels of his recently celebrated fiftieth birthday. Meanwhile, Walt has also been invited to ride along with his DEA agent brother-in-law Hank (Dean Norris) on his next big bust. Realizing how much money is typically confiscated from these crime scenes, it dawns on Walt that this could be a lucrative enterprise. Walt knows that his treatment will be expensive, and that his breadwinning status in his home is in jeopardy, especially considering that his wife, Skyler (Anna Gunn), is pregnant. During the ride along, Walt recognizes one of the criminals who manages to elude the cops—a former student turned burnout Jesse Pinkman (Aaron Paul). Tracking Jesse down, Walt attempts to convince him to get into the game, or face the wrath of his DEA agent brother-in-law. Pinkman reluctantly agrees, and the two scheme to buy an RV to use as a mobile meth lab. Gathering (read: stealing) lab equipment from his high school, Walt, with Jesse's help, successfully cooks meth, which turns out to be the purest form Jesse has ever seen. With this promising development, Walt and Jesse move forward with their money-making plan. The rest of the episode follows along as Walt and Jesse's plan becomes increasingly complicated. Walt's last scene, coming home to his wife a newly bold and confident man, leads viewers to believe that Walt does not need the meth to get a high—just the mere making of it, and the profits to be gained, are plenty.

Early reviews were overwhelmingly positive. *Washington Post* critic Tom Shales dubbed the show an instant "cult hit," calling it "a mondo-bizarro, dark-as-midnight, bitterly bleak tragicomedy." Shales continued: "Viewers who like to tiptoe over to the dark side now and then—at least once a week—are bound to find Walter White's wonderland of woes worth a visit or two, or many more." *LA Weekly* critic Robert Abele called the show "sharp if unsettling" and likened it to a "low-key indie you'd discover at Sundance." Robert Lloyd of the *Los Angeles Times* put it simply: "completely gripping." Praise for Cranston's portrayal of Walter White dominated the reviews, as did Aaron Paul's performance as Walt's sidekick, the "lost doggish" Jesse Pinkman. AMC knew that while the show was not going to break ratings records—a fact that would become a short-lived problem—it was worth the investment. By May of 2008, just two months after the first season's seven episodes wrapped (truncated by one episode due to the 2008 Writers Guild Strike), AMC renewed the series for a full thirteen-episode order. For Charlie Collier, executive vice president and general manager of AMC, it was a no brainer: "*Breaking Bad* is a powerful, intelligent and thought-provoking series that clearly resonated with viewers and critics alike." AMC launched the second season of *Breaking Bad* on March 8, 2009, premiering alongside a month-long "March Badness" film festival—a series that celebrated bad guys viewers loved, including such films as Eastwood's *Dirty Harry* (1971) and Charles Bronson's vigilante hit *Death Wish* (1974).

Ratings soared in the second season, with nearly 40 percent more viewers tuning in. Viewers clamoring to keep current with what was considered "must see TV" sought out the first seven episodes of the series—a trend that would continue to multiply the audience of *Breaking Bad* with every season. *Breaking Bad*'s streaming presence was the biggest game changer, as fans flocked to Netflix to catch up on what critics deemed the not-to-be-missed cult gem. While Netflix viewership is not measured in the same manner as traditional broadcast television, the numbers that did exist painted a fascinating picture. According to the streaming service, fans became as easily addicted to the series as Walt's "blue sky" meth customers, with 73 percent of subscribers who watched the first episode eventually finishing the entire first season. Subsequent season numbers only grew greater, climbing into the range of an 85 percent chance of completion. This surge in Netflix viewership inevitably led to bigger and bigger audiences tuning in to the show's original broadcasts on AMC. Once viewers were "caught up" on Netflix, it was time to turn to prime-time weekly broadcasts—and *Breaking Bad*'s ratings soared. *Time* magazine's TV critic James Poniewozik explained this phenomenon, citing "the ease of access, the narcotic pleasure vortex of bingeing, the potential for hooking new viewers—is, in chemistry terms, an accelerant"—and Walter White knew a thing or two about chemistry.

Binge watching *Breaking Bad* in preparation for upcoming seasons (particularly the final season) became en vogue. *New York Magazine*'s television critic Emily Nussbaum wrote an article titled "My *Breaking Bad* Bender" chronicling her experience binge-watching the first three seasons in preparation for the fourth season premiere in July 2011. Her conclusion: "Binge watching a show like *Breaking Bad* is probably the purest way to watch a great series." The overarching narrative—Walt's slow transition from Walter White, the reluctant criminal to the murderous (and loving it) drug kingpin known only as "Heisenberg"—lent itself to consecutive episodes being gobbled up in one sitting. Seen on Netflix, plowing through episode after episode, Walter White turned into Michael Corleone of *The Godfather* (1972)—and fans couldn't resist clicking *play* when each following season felt like *The Godfather: Part II* (1974), a sequel that nearly eclipses its original. Even celebrities admitted to being among the dedicated Netflix bingers, as a leaked e-mail from acting royalty Sir Anthony Hopkins to series star Bryan Cranston attested. Hopkins wrote: "I just finished marathon watching *Breaking Bad* . . . [and] your performance as Walter White was the best acting I have seen—ever." Hopkins continued: "From what started as a black comedy, descended into a labyrinth of blood, destruction and hell. It was like a great Jacobean, Shakespearian (*sic*) or Greek Tragedy." With fans like Hopkins counted among its flock, *Breaking Bad*'s plethora of Emmy awards (two for the series, two for Anna Gunn's Skyler White, three for Paul's Pinkman, and a whopping four for Cranston) catapulted the show to legendary, history-making status. For creator Vince Gilligan, Netflix fans were what ultimately kept the show afloat. After picking up the Emmy for Best Drama in 2013, Gilligan told the press: "I feel like Netflix kept us on the air. It's a bold new era in television, and we've been fortunate to reap the benefits of the technological developments." He added, "I don't even think our show would have lasted beyond season 2 without video streaming on demand, social media and the Internet component." When AMC announced that the series would conclude after the end of its fifth season, slow-to-adapt television fans rushed to get in one last binge. Luckily for those pressed for time, the fifth and final season would be split into two parts: the first airing from July to September 2012 and the last a year later, from August to September 2013.

In the pilot episode Walter White, then standing in front of a classroom filled with his students, explained the fundamentals of his subject matter: "Chemistry is . . . well, technically it's the study of matter, but I prefer to see it as the study of change." By the beginning of the series' fifth and final season, Walter White had undergone unbelievable change. Once fearful of those who may track him down, knocking down his door, he had become (as he told his shocked wife in season 4's "Cornered"), "the one who knocks." Walt's ruthlessness grew with each season, reaching new heights with his insistence that Jesse take out innocent lab assistant Gale Boetticher (David Costabile), and, in perhaps the most famous sequence in the show's history, assisting in the death of Los Pollos Hermanos meth emperor Gustavo "Gus" Fring (Giancarlo Esposito)—a gruesome death-by-explosion that leaves the ever-polished, but two-faced, Gus with literally half a face. No longer working in Gus's shadow, Walt must strike out on his own if he wishes to continue in the business—an inevitable fate given Walt's insatiable thirst for power.

Throughout the series, Walt manages to outsmart his DEA agent brother-in-law Hank, as well as most of his family and friends, including his sticky-fingered, but suspicious, sister-in-law Marie (Betsy Brandt), and his naïve and trusting teenaged son Walt Jr. (RJ Mitte). Walt's wife, Skyler, having discovered his secret in early season 3, covered for Walt's frequent disappearing act (and sudden financial windfall) by painting him as a gambling addict. By season 4, Skyler becomes a willing participant, laundering his money through their recently acquired car wash. But as the audience settles in to the beginning of the final season, Skyler cannot cope with her involvement, acting out and attempting suicide (her desperate effort to protect her children). Meanwhile, Walt charges forward with his new meth-dealing enterprise, with Jesse in tow, and Gus's former chief enforcer, Mike Ehrmantraut (Jonathan Banks), handling the distribution. Assuming the identity of exterminators, Walt, Jesse, and new assistant Todd (Jesse Plemons), use a tented home, prepared for fumigation, as their new mobile meth lab. Business booms—but after a death-defying train robbery (one that is crucial to maintaining their chemical supply), Todd kills an innocent young bystander, leading Jesse and Mike to want out. When Jesse and Mike sell their shares to a Phoenix-based meth dealer, Walt also cuts himself into the deal, refusing to get out of the game. Meanwhile, the DEA, having uncovered Gus Fring's true identity following his death, closes in on Fring's associates in search of the infamous "Heisenberg"—associates that are protected by Mike's hush money. Walt demands that Mike disclose the names of those associates, and Mike refuses, leading Walt to shoot him in retaliation. Walt's killing of Mike signals that there is no turning back now—Walt has completely transformed into the (no-longer) fictional Heisenberg. Walt eventually gets the names from Gus's other associate Lydia Rodarte-Quayle (Laura Fraser), an easily rattled businesswoman with international connections. In "Gliding Over All," the final episode of the first half of season 5 (episode 8), Walt gives the names to Todd's uncle Jack (Michael Bowen), a known criminal in a biker gang with connections inside multiple prisons. In a scene eerily similar to Francis Ford Coppola's staging of the iconic baptism murder sequence in *The Godfather*, the audience watches as one-by-one each of Fring's imprisoned associates is taken out—each death more gruesome than the last. All the while, Walt, alone, looks out the window of his home, knowing he is now safe, as Nat King Cole's "Pick Yourself Up" plays in the background. Just as the audience settles in to the notion that Walt has freed himself from being caught, by episode's end, Hank, now without any leads in the hunt of Heisenberg, discovers Walt's secret in the most unlikely of places—while reading a book, sitting on the toilet. The book (Walt Whitman's collection of poetry, *Leaves of Grass*) includes an inscription all too familiar to Hank—one written by long-dead Fring cook Gale Boetticher.

Fans reeled over the shock of Hank's discovery amid Walt's foolproof protection measures. The series had a mere eight episodes left—just enough to witness the fallout, and the imminent destruction of Walter White. Expectations for the final eight episodes were soaring as it premiered in August of 2013. The show had just been nominated for thirteen Emmy awards and Walter White's final chapter had only just begun. Gilligan and his writers cut right to the chase when it came to the previous season's revelation, wasting no time in setting up Hank and Walt's first showdown. In the final moments of the episode "Blood Money" (season 5, episode 9), Walt warns Hank to "tread lightly." Tim Goodman of *The Hollywood Reporter* called it "the kind of cinematic television moment that pays off enormously . . . [a] goose-bump inducing, let's-do-this!, pumped-up-kicks kind of hysteria that was like a shot of adrenaline directly into the heart." The final showdown between Hank and Walt would have to wait until the fourteenth episode, "Ozymandias"—eventual winner of the 2014 Emmy for Best Writing for a Drama Series. The episode finds Hank wounded from a shootout with Walt's associates, led by Todd's uncle Jack. Hank, with the help of Jesse, had lured Walt to a deserted location with the threat of digging up Walt's buried fortune—a threat which forces Walt to call in backup. As Hank lay wounded, Walt begs Jack to spare him, promising him the buried money, but Hank, keenly aware of how a criminal like Jack operates, knows he's a goner. Before Walt can stop him, Jack puts the final bullet in Hank. Five and a half seasons had led up to this point, and while fans and critics speculated that body bags would be filled in the final season, Hank's untimely death—not at the hands of Walt—was truly shocking. Walt's responsibility for Hank's death resonated with fans—even *Game of Thrones* creator George R. R. Martin took to his blog, "Not a Blog," to add his voice to the chorus of stunned fans. He wrote: "Talk about a gut punch. Walter White is a bigger monster than anyone in Westeros." By the episode's end Skyler figures out Walt's involvement in Hank's death and attacks him with a knife, only to be subdued by their son. Walt escapes and skips town, shepherded away with a new identity, care of his trusty lawyer Saul Goodman (Bob Odenkirk). With just two episodes left, the series' final showdown was an uncertain one. With Hank out of the picture, who would be Walt's final adversary?

The finale episode aired on Sunday, September 29, 2013. Titled "Felina" (a character in the episode-featured song "El Paso," but also, cleverly, an anagram for the word "finale"), the episode finds Walt back in Albuquerque, after having spent a significant amount of time hiding in a cottage in rural New Hampshire. As teased through flash forwards throughout both parts of the fifth season, viewers are led to believe that Walt has returned to exact revenge on his enemies, and set the record straight with his family. Walt's revenge storyline takes him to the lavish home of his former colleagues and friends Gretchen and Elliott Schwartz. There, he threatens the couple, with the help of former street-level dealers Badger (Matt L. Jones) and Skinny Pete (Charles Baker), promising death if they didn't agree to see that his family gets every penny they deserve. Walt's revenge also extends to former business partner and distributor, Lydia Rodarte-Quayle. She has proven to be untrustworthy and disloyal, so Walt must eliminate the threat Lydia poses to his family, particularly in the implication of Skyler's association with Walt's dealings. Lydia's fate is death by poisoning—a death aided by Walt's hidden vile of ricin (hidden since season 4), a final loose end tied up neatly by Gilligan. In the meantime, Walt evades the cops and visits Skyler, finally confessing that, despite his constant insistence, his drug-dealings were purely a selfish enterprise. He admits to her: "I did it for me. I liked it. I was good at it. And I was really . . . I was alive." With that, Walt is ready for his final showdown: taking out Jack and his gang (Jesse included).

Walt arrives at the biker gang compound under the guise of getting back in the game. Todd, now a major player in the organization, warns Walt: "You really shouldn't have come back, Mr. White." When a gun is pulled on him, Walt demands the return of Jesse—only to find that the gang has not partnered with Jesse as he believed, but instead has imprisoned him, literally keeping him on a leash. Upon seeing Jesse's fate, Walt tackles him to the ground, protecting him from the gunfire showering the gang members, thanks to Walt's pre-rigged machine gun mounted on his car. The bullets kill most of the gang, sparing Todd and Jack who eventually die at the hands of Jesse and Walt, respectively. Walt, having been injured in the spray of bullets, gives Jesse a gun, tempting him to take him out. "Do it," Walt begs, continuing: "You want this." But just as Gilligan and his staff had surprised fans and critics throughout the entire run of the series, Jesse, though entirely justified in his desire to take out Walt, spares his former partner, opting instead to escape, triumphantly, in a blaze of glory. Walt, however, is not as fortunate. The police begin to descend on the complex, as Walt strides through the meth lab— a trail of his own blood following behind him. He pauses, stopping to admire the equipment, holding the lab gas mask like a trophy. Badfinger's 1972 hit "Baby Blue" plays in the background echoing the words "Guess I got what I deserved." The camera then reveals Walt splayed out on the floor, as the police enter and stand over his dead body.

As the credits hit the screen, fans flocked to the Internet to dissect every moment. Twitter spiked with *Breaking Bad*–related tweets, with AMC measuring approximately 1.24 million tweets from more than 600,000 individual users. Bryan Cranston's tweet thanking the fans for their loyalty was retweeted nearly 53,000 times. The show dominated Twitter's worldwide and U.S.

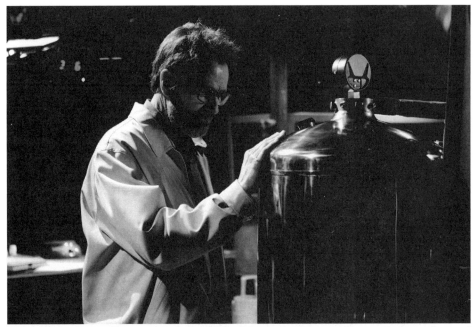

Walter White (Bryan Cranston) feels the thrill of the cook one more time on the series finale of *Breaking Bad*.   *Authors' collection*

trending topics list with hashtags including: #GoodbyeBreakingBad, #AMC, #BreakingBad, #BreakingBadFinale, #Heisenberg, #HelloGretchen, and #GoodbyeLydia. Beyond social media, in terms of actual broadcast numbers, the ratings exploded. The series finale was viewed by a record 10.3 million viewers, breaking every ratings record in *Breaking Bad*'s history, and increasing more than 300 percent from the season 4 finale (thanks largely to those last-minute bingers). AMC's president Charlie Collier was thrilled:

> *Breaking Bad* is simply unique. It all starts with Vince Gilligan who really only ever asked for one thing—the opportunity to end the show on his own terms. That is exactly what Vince did last night and, as always, brilliantly so. Congratulations to Vince and to every single person involved in this remarkable journey. We're proud that AMC will forever be known as the birthplace and home of this iconic show and, at the same time, we tip our Heisenberg hat to the fans who made this a truly shared experience.

Likewise, Gilligan felt the show went out soaring, carried along by diehard fans, telling *Entertainment Weekly*: "People have asked me, 'Does it make you want to go on and do a bunch more episodes now?' Just the opposite. It makes me think, through quite a bit of good luck being involved, we really did pick the right moment to exit the stage." In 2010, *Time* magazine's James

Poniewozik called the show "a drama that has chosen the slow burn over the flashy explosion"—and the finale proved just that. As each season, and each Netflix binge, slowly led fans to the dark underworld of Walter White, just as it came to an end all that time had paid off—the finale's record-breaking ratings firmly cemented the episode as an instant classic.

Critics overwhelmingly agreed. *Vulture*'s/*New York Magazine*'s Matt Zoller Seitz praised the episode itself, stating: "It's amazing that any episode of TV could feel so rock-solid yet be so fluid in its possible meanings. It's happy. It's sad. It's neat. It's messy. Walt won. Walt lost. Walt won and yet he lost." Damon Lindelof, creator of *Lost* and self-confessed "huge fan and zealot of *Breaking Bad*'s Church of Awesomeness," reviewed the finale for *The Hollywood Reporter*, calling it "fantastic . . . not a false beat." Lori Rackl of the *Chicago Sun Times* called it "equal parts suspenseful and satisfying [delivering] heart-breaking flashbacks and closure. . . . More about resolution than redemption." Andrew Romano of *The Daily Beast*, who had previously not listed the series on his list of the "finest television shows of all time," walked back on his words: "Sunday's series finale was such a perfect, A-1 piece of televisual filmmaking—and such an unparalleled valedictory achievement, especially when you compare it to the endings of other Great Cable Dramas—that I think I'm ready to reconsider my earlier assessment."

Beyond the critics, and the flurry of tweets, the series stars were enormously pleased with the finale. Aaron Paul organized a screening of the finale episode in the famous Hollywood Forever Cemetery, raising $1.8 million for charity from the event's ticket sales (the event sold out online in about one minute). Bryan Cranston joined Paul at the event, as did Vince Gilligan and most of the cast, as they assembled for a panel following the screening, moderated by late night host Jimmy Kimmel. The cast unanimously agreed that Walt's final moments fit the show perfectly, with Jonathan Banks, famous as the show's now-dead enforcer Mike Ehrmantraut, threatening the crowd: "If anyone bitches and moans about how the show ended, tell them to come see me." Later in an interview with *Entertainment Weekly*, Paul called the finale "100 percent satisfying," with Cranston adding "unapologetic" to his critique. Cranston continued: "I think this is the best ending. A real satisfying ending. And I'm so grateful for that." Weeks after the finale aired, a video of Cranston and Paul reading the finale script together went viral (now available on the complete series DVD set). Paul is triumphant when his Jesse Pinkman escapes from danger, and Cranston, upon reading Walt's final moments, reminded fans that comedy is inherently in his DNA, deadpanning: "So I guess there won't be a sequel." Cranston was partially right, as the *Breaking Bad* universe inhabited by his beloved Walter White would continue on—but this time as the prequel *Better Call Saul*, starring Bob Odenkirk's Saul, long before he became Walter White's trusty lawyer. Speculation of Cranston and Paul reprising their roles by guest-starring on the series, which launched in February 2015, still runs rampant.

The finale episode of *Breaking Bad* ensured the legacy of the show. On air for a mere five seasons, airing just 62 episodes, the series' entry into television history's unquestionable classics enriches what it means to be considered among the greats. No longer did it mean airing for a decade, amassing more than a hundred episodes—storytelling and high caliber acting reigned triumphant. Vince Gilligan named the series *Breaking Bad* after a phrase with Southern origin meaning "to raise hell"—but for fans, and television historians alike, the phrase could also be turned to mean "defy authority," or "completely dominate." *Breaking Bad* certainly lived up to the promise of its title, scoring a well-deserved space as a ground-breaking show for both its content and its binge-worthy status, all the while doing it in its own way—just as Walter White would have wanted it.

Appendix

Below are additional series finales worth mentioning (many of which rank within the top-twenty-most-watched finales of all time). While the finales of many of these series tied up all the loose ends, some shows left their loyal viewers dissatisfied, particularly when they were left hanging with major questions left unanswered. Also included are some of television's most unusual and unexpected series finales.

ALF, "Consider Me Gone" (NBC, 3/24/1990, 21.7 million viewers) Directed by Nick Havinga. Story by Ian Praiser. Teleplay by Steve Pepoon, David Silverman, Stephen Sustarsic, and Victor Fresco

ALF (Alien Life Form) intercepts a radio broadcast in Melmacian (his native language) and connects with Skip and Rhonda, two of his former friends. They tell ALF that they bought a new planet, where they plan to resurrect Melmac. ALF decides to join them, breaking the news to his human family, the Tanners—Willie and Kate (Max White and Anne Schedeen) and their kids, Lynn and Brian (Andrea Elson and Benji Gregory). The Tanners throw ALF a grand going away party to mark the occasion, complete with emotional goodbyes. When ALF goes to meet Skip and Rhonda's ship, he is captured by the Alien Task Force, who have been after ALF since he first crash landed on Earth. The finale ends as the words "To Be Continued . . ." come on screen—but there was to be no continuation, as NBC pulled the plug on the series. Fans were assured that ALF survived the Alien Task Force's probes and experiments when NBC aired *Project: ALF* six years later in 1996, a television-movie that settled the storyline once and for all (ALF was imprisoned but not mutilated by scientists, and finally saved by two officers who liberate him).

Alias, "All the Time in the World" (ABC, 5/22/2006, 6.7 million viewers) Directed by Tucker Gates. Written by Drew Goddard and Jeff Pinkner.

The spy/action-adventure series concludes with Agent Sydney Bristow (Jennifer Garner) wrestling with her mother, Irina Derevko (Lena Olin), on a skylight. As Irina tries to grab the Horizon (an artifact that grants its beholder immortality), she falls to her death. Thanks to the power of the Horizon, Sloane (Ron Rifkin) is now immortal, but he is trapped in an underground cavern for eternity thanks to Jack Bristow (Victor Garber), who seals it off with explosives. In the end, Sydney and Vaughn (Michael Vartan) are living happily on the beach with their two kids.

All in the Family, "Too Good Edith" (CBS, 4/8/1979, 40.2 million viewers) Directed by Paul Bogart. Written by Harriett Weiss and Patt Shea.

At the end of end of season 8, Mike and Gloria Stivic (Rob Reiner and Sally Struthers) moved to California, where he got a teaching job. In the final season, Archie and Edith Bunker (Carroll O'Connor and Jean Stapleton) suddenly find themselves parents again when Edith's cousin Floyd (Marty Brill) leaves his daughter, Stephanie (Danielle Brisebois), indefinitely with the Bunkers.

Meanwhile, Archie is now co-owner of a tavern. In the series finale, Edith, who is diagnosed with phlebitis and told by her doctor to stay off of her feet, risks her health to prepare the food for the St. Patrick's Day celebration at Archie's tavern. Archie insists that she come down to the bar and serve the food, but she collapses on the stairs because she can't walk. What follows is a beautifully written and acted scene in which Archie tells Edith he's upset that she didn't tell him she was sick.

"I've been blowing my own horn for a lot of years, and I'm gonna tell you something" Archie says, "I ain't nothing without you."

For once, Edith has the last word: "You know something, Archie, you're a pip. A real pip."

The Bunkers lived on in the show's spinoff, *Archie Bunker's Place*, though Stapleton only appeared in five episodes in season 1. In the season 2 opener, we learn that Edith died of a stroke and Archie must adjust to life without her.

Ally McBeal, "Bygones" (FOX, 5/20/2002, 11.5 million viewers) Directed by Bill D'Elia. Written by David E. Kelley.

Ally (Calista Flockhart) has grown closer to her long-lost, biological ten-year-old daughter, Madison (Hayden Panettiere), who suffers from major stress, so Ally decides to move back to New York with her. Meanwhile, Richard Fish (Greg Germann) marries actress Liza Bump (Christina Ricci). Some familiar faces—Georgia Thomas (Courtney Thorne-Smith) and Renee Raddick (Lisa

Nicole Carson)—return for the wedding and there's plenty of tears when Ally says, "Goodbye."

American Horror Story: Murder House, "Afterbirth" (FX, 12/21/2011, 2.8 million viewers) Directed by Bradley Buecker. Written by Jessica Sharzer.

In the previous episode ("Birth"), Vivien Harmon (Connie Britton) gave birth in the house to twins, one of whom lives and the other is stillborn. Vivien suffers from severe hemorrhaging from the delivery and dies, leaving her husband, Dr. Ben Harmon (Dylan McDermott), a psychiatrist, distraught over the loss of his wife and daughter Violet (Taissa Farmiga), who committed suicide in the house. The ghosts of Vivien and Violet encourage Ben to take the surviving newborn and leave the house. But before Ben can leave, Hayden (Kate Mara), with help from the other vengeful ghosts in the house, hang him from a chandelier and make it look like suicide.

When a new family moves in, Ben and Vivien, who don't want anyone else to suffer in the house, scare then away. Tate (Evan Peters), the psychotic teenage ghost who raped and impregnated Vivien and failed to save Violet, wants to be forgiven for his sins (like gunning down innocent kids at his school). But when he tries to impress Violet by trying to kill a teenage boy who moves in with his family, she wants nothing more to do with him. When Ben, Vivien, Violet, and their stillborn baby celebrate Christmas, Tate waits outside watching, determined to win back Violet's love.

Four years later, their neighbor, Tate's mother, Constance (Jessica Lange), who is raising Vivien's surviving baby (and her grandson), Michael, comes home to find that the toddler has killed his nanny. "Now what am I going to do with you?" she asks Michael, who, despite his innocent demeanor, is likely to grow up to be like his father, Tate.

American Horror Story: Asylum, "Madness Ends" (FX, 1/23/2013, 2.5 million viewers) Directed by Alfonso Gomez-Rejon. Written by Tim Minear.

In 1971, Lana Winters (Sarah Paulson), who is now an investigative reporter on television, sneaks into Briarcliff Asylum with her camera crew in an attempt to rescue Sister Jude (Jessica Lange), who is being held captive there. But Kit (Evan Peters) has already rescued her and she is living with him and his family.

Lana gave the son she bore after being raped by serial killer Dr. Oliver Thredson (Zachary Quinto) up for adoption. She later killed Thredson, who murdered her lover, Wendy (Clea Duvall). In the present day, Lana's son, Johnny (Dylan McDermott), has become a serial killer himself. When she is interviewed about her career at her home in New York City, Johnny sneaks into her house by posing as a member of the television crew. When the camera crew leaves, he stays behind. She recognizes him from a police photograph. When he puts a gun to her head and threatens to kill her, Lana says he's not a killer like his father. He lowers the gun and starts crying. She takes it and shoots him in the head.

American Horror Story: Coven, "The Seven Wonders" (FX, 1/29/2014, 4 million viewers) Directed by Alfonso Gomez-Rejon. Written by Douglas Petrie.

Five witches—Zoe (Taissa Farmiga), Madison (Emma Roberts), Misty (Lily Rabe), Cordelia (Sarah Paulson), and Queenie (Gabourey Sidibe)—compete to be the new head witch (known as the "Supreme"), who must perform seven acts of magic. Zoe and Misty both die while performing one test. Queenie tries to revive Zoe, but can't. Madison refuses to even try and decides to leave, but Kyle (Evan Peters), who was in love with Zoe, strangles Madison and kills her. Cordelia performs the seven acts of magic (including reviving Zoe) and becomes the new Supreme. Zoe and Queenie are the new Council of Witchcraft and Kyle is the new butler. Cordelia also regains her sight and later appears on television and reveals the coven to the world. A tearful Cordelia agrees to allow Myrtle (Frances Conroy) to be burned at the stake as punishment for murdering the two other members of the Witches Council.

Cordelia reconciles with her mother, Fiona (Jessica Lange), who dies of cancer. Papa Legba (Lance Reddick), an ancient voodoo spirit, banishes Fiona to hell, where she is living in a country cabin with her former lover, The Axman (Danny Huston). Legba also sentences Madame Delphine LaLaurie (Kathy Bates) and Marie Laveau (Angela Bassett) to the same hell. The hateful, racist Delphine is locked in a cage in her own torture attic where she must watch Marie Laveau torture her innocent daughters in front of her.

In the final scene, Cordelia, Zoe, and Queenie reopen the school and welcome a new group of young witches.

American Horror Story: Freak Show, "Curtain Call" (F/X, 1/21/2015, 3.27 million viewers) Directed by Bradley Buecker. Written by John J. Gray.

When no one shows up to see the talentless rich kid/psychopath Dandy Mott (Finn Wittrock) perform, the freaks tell him he's boring and quit the show. Dandy gets his revenge by walking through the freak show grounds and gunning down everyone he sees, including Paul (Mat Fraser), Toulouse (Drew Rin Varick), Legless Suzi (Rose Siggins), and Amazon Eve (Erika Ervin). Jimmy Darling (Evan Peters) returns to the freak show, where Desiree (Angela Bassett) is the only survivor. Afterwards, afraid for their lives, Siamese twins Bette and Dot Tattler (Sarah Paulson) have no choice but to marry Dandy. But the twins, along with Desiree, Jimmy, and Penny (Grace Gummer) get their revenge on Dandy by drugging him, stripping him down to his BVDs, putting him in a glass tank, and filling it with water. As they watch him drown, Desiree observes, "You may look like a motion picture dreamboat, but you're the biggest freak of them all."

Meanwhile, Elsa Mars (Jessica Lange) has become a major television star with her own show. Her old boyfriend and the doctor who saved her life, Massimo Dolcefino (Danny Huston), visits her and reveals that he is dying. She is unhappy with her life. The snuff film she was in has surfaced and it will

Presenting Miss Elsa Mars: Jessica Lange in *American Horror Story: Freak Show.*   *Authors' collection*

surely end her career. Having heard that all the freaks have died, she agrees to perform on Halloween. During her performance, she summons Edward Mordrake (Wes Bentley), who, earlier in the season, killed Twisty the Clown and transported him to hell after hearing about all the terrible things he did. He kills Elsa during a live telecast (but nobody else can see him), but instead of taking her to hell, he transports her to a freak show where she is reunited with her dead freak friends and performs.

As for the surviving freaks, they live happily ever after. Desiree is married and the mother of two children. Bette and Dot are pregnant and enjoying married life with their husband, Jimmy.

Barney Miller, "Landmark, Part 3" (ABC, 5/20/1982) Directed by Danny Arnold. Written by Jeff Stein, Frank Dungan, and Tony Sheehan.

When the building housing the 12th precinct is declared a national landmark, a developer buys it to take advantage of the tax credit. Captain Barney Miller (Hal Linden) has been promoted to deputy inspector, and the other men are reassigned to precincts around the city. After Barney turns off the lights one final time, a message appears on the screen for the show's loyal viewers: "Goodbye and Thank You from All of Us at the Ol' One Two."

Battlestar Galactica, "Daybreak" (SyFy, Part 1, 3/13/2009; Parts 2 and 3, 3/20/2009, 2.4 million viewers) Directed by Michael Rymer. Written by Ronald D. Moore.

The smart and imaginative reboot of the 1978 science fiction series concludes with a three-part episode that brings some closure to the battle between the Cylons, artificially intelligent beings created by and indistinguishable from humans, and the 30,000 or so humans that survived after the Cylons exterminated most of the human race. The remaining humans are aboard the Battlestar Galactica, which is under the command of Admiral William "Bill" Adama (Edward James Olmos). After defeating the Cylons, the human race lands on a planet Adama calls Earth. Instead of colonizing, they decide to spread out and integrate themselves with the humans living there, essentially choosing civilization, but without the existing technology.

Admiral Adama takes President Roslin (Mary McDonnell), who is dying, on a ride across the continent of Africa in a Raptor, during which she dies (her last words are "So much life"). He buries her on a hilltop where he plans to build a cabin so he can visit her grave.

There is still a mystery surrounding who or what exactly was the show's heroine, Kara "Starbuck" Thrace (Katee Sackhoff). She seems to have a psychic connection to Earth, but once they arrive she says goodbye to Admiral Adama and tells his son Lee (Jamie Bamber) that she's leaving because her job (leading the humans to earth) is done. She then disappears without leaving a forwarding address.

Beverly Hills, 90210, "The Penultimate"/"Ode to Joy" (FOX, 5/17/2000, 16.8 million viewers) "The Penultimate" directed by Michael Lange. "Ode to Joy" directed by Kevin Inch. Written by John Eisendrath.

David (Brian Austin Green) and Donna (Tori Spelling) get married. Donna's maid of honor, Kelly (Jennie Garth), breaks off her engagement with Matt (Daniel Cosgrove) and reconciles with Dylan McKay (Luke Perry), who serves as David's best man. In the final scene, Steve Sanders (Ian Ziering), Valerie Malone (Tiffani-Amber Thiessen), and Andrea Zuckerman (Gabrielle Carteris) join them on the wedding dance floor. Jason Priestley appears in a cameo as Brandon Walsh via a video message.

The Big C, "The Finale" (Showtime, 5/20/2013, 390,000 viewers) Directed by Michael Engler. Written by Jenny Bicks and Darlene Hunt.

When Cathy Jamison's (Laura Linney) insurance will no longer pay for her stay at a hospice, she goes home to die. Her estranged father, Bud (Brian Dennehy), and friend Andrea (Gabourey Sidibe), who has accepted an internship with designer Isaac Mizrahi, pay her a visit. Her non-conformist brother, Sean (John Benjamin Hickey), donates his kidney to a wealthy man, but he is sickened when the man thanks him by giving him a Rolex watch.

Cathy's dream comes true when her son Adam (Gabriel Basso) surprises her by earning his diploma. When her husband, Paul (Oliver Platt), goes out and returns with flowers, he is told by her hospice worker that she passed away. In the end it's revealed that Cathy's therapist is a "higher being." When we last see Cathy, she is floating in a swimming pool with her neighbor, Marlene (Phyllis Somerville), who died of Alzheimer's.

Big Love, "Where Men and Mountains Meet" (HBO, 3/20/2011, 1.565 million viewers) Directed by Dan Attias. Written by Mark V. Olsen and Will Scheffer.

Bill's mother, Lois (Grace Zabriskie), developed dementia due to a sexually transmitted disease she contracted from her husband, Frank (Bruce Dern). Frank grants Lois her final wish to have a merciful death by injecting her with a lethal drug. Bill (Bill Paxton) is released from jail on bail and goes back to the Utah State Senate to advocate for a bill to legalize polygamy. Bill is murdered by his neighbor Carl Martin (Carlos Jacott), who guns him down at close range because Bill re-sodded Carl's lawn, which he misinterprets as Bill implying that he can't take care of his family. Bill's wives, Barb (Jeanne Tripplehorn), Nicki (Chloë Sevigny), and Margie (Ginnifer Goodwin), rush out of the house. Barb, who became a priest, gives him a final blessing before he dies in their arms. Eleven months later, Bill's son is married and his daughter has named her child after him. Margie departs on a mission to Central America to help the poor. She says goodbye to Barb and Nicki. They embrace in the dining room and the ghost of Bill can be seen in the background, seated in his spot at the head of the table.

The Bob Newhart Show, "Happy Trails to You" (CBS, 4/1/1978) Directed by Michael Zinberg and Peter Bonerz. Written by Glen Charles, Les Charles, and Lloyd Garver.

Dr. Bob Hartley (Bob Newhart) decides to close his practice in Chicago and move to Oregon with his wife, Emily (Suzanne Pleshette), where he has accepted a teaching job at a small college.

Boston Legal, "Last Call" (ABC, 12/8/2008, 9.9 million viewers) Directed by Bill D'Elia. Teleplay by David E. Kelley. Story by David E. Kelley and Susan Dickes.

After cigar-chomping, womanizing Denny Crane (William Shatner) discovers that his Alzheimer's disease is progressing rapidly, he proposes marriage to his best friend (and law firm partner) Alan Shore (James Spader) in order to ensure that Alan retains power over Denny's estate and medical decisions. Alan accepts, and Denny responds: "It'll be great . . . like jumping the shark," with a wink to the audience. When they apply for a marriage license they are immediately sued by a local chapter of the Gay and Lesbian League who see the marriage as the sham it is—but Alan and Denny beat the injunction and move forward with their plans. Meanwhile, Shirley (Candice Bergen) and Carl (John Larroquette) plan their own nuptials, as the firm (Crane, Poole & Schmidt) is sold to Chinese buyers and will become Chang, Poole & Schmidt. In addition to fighting for their right to marry, Alan also gives his final argument in the case regarding Denny's access to experimental treatment not yet approved by the FDA, which moves the judge to rule in his favor. In the last scene, Shirley and Carl along with Alan and Denny have a double wedding.

The Closer, "The Last Word" (TNT, 8/13/2012, 9.8 million viewers) Directed by Michael M. Robin. Written by James Duff and Mike Berchem.

Deputy Police Chief Johnson's (Kyra Sedgwick) pursuit of her nemesis, lawyer/serial rapist Philip Stroh (Billy Burke), ends when she guns him down in her kitchen. She resigns from the Los Angeles police force, making way for her successor, Captain Sharon Raydor (Mary McDonnell) and the show's spinoff, *Major Crimes* (2012–present).

Dallas, "Conundrum, Parts 1 and 2" (CBS, 5/3/1991, 33.3 million viewers) Written and Directed by Leonard Katzman.

In the early to mid-1980s, *Dallas* ruled prime-time as the highest rated show on television for three seasons (1980–1981, 1981–1982, 1983–1984) and the second highest rated for two seasons behind *60 Minutes* (1982–1983) and *Dynasty* (1984–1985). The nighttime soap also achieved the highest rating on record at the start of season 4 when an estimated 83 million viewers, representing 53 percent of U.S. households and 76 percent of the U.S. television audience, tuned in to the "Who Done It" episode to find out the identity of "Who shot J. R.?" in the season 3 cliffhanger.

By the early 1990s, *Dallas* sunk to no. 61 in the ratings. Still, loyal viewers remained curious about the fate of J. R. Ewing, the man America loved to hate, when *Dallas* ended its fourteen-season run with a two-part episode that was watched by 33 million viewers. It was the show's highest rated episode since 1987.

It's not such a wonderful life for J. R. Ewing (Larry Hagman) in the series finale of the long-running soap. After selling his shares of Ewing Oil to his nemesis, Cliff Barnes (Ken Kercheval), in order to acquire Weststar Oil, his plot fails and he ends up losing control of both companies on the same day. His son, John Ross, has moved to London to be near his mother, J. R.'s ex-wife, Sue Ellen (Linda Gray) and his new stepfather.

1980s TV villains we love to hate: *Dallas*'s J. R. Ewing (Larry Hagman) and *Dynasty*'s Alexis Morell Carrington Colby Dexter Rowan (Joan Collins). *Authors' collection*

All alone at Southfork, J. R. goes on a drinking binge. Borrowing the plot from Frank Capra's 1946 film, *It's a Wonderful Life*, a man named Adam (Joel Grey), who J. R. assumes is an angel, visits him and shows him what everyone's life would have been like if he was never born. His brother Gary (Ted Shackelford) became a successful lawyer and met his wife, Valene Clemens (Joan Van Ark). His brother Bobby (Patrick Duffy) has a gambling problem that led to his divorce from his wife and children. The Ewing born in J. R.'s place, Jason (Patrick Parkhurst), is a sleazy real estate developer who tricked Bobby and Gary out of selling their stakes of Ewing Oil and Southfork Ranch, which he turned into "Southfork Estates," a development of tract houses. J. R. feels sorry for Ray Krebbs (Steve Kanaly), who has to work as a ranch hand and in a bar to make ends meet, yet still is a happy man with a wife and two kids. Ex-wife Sue Ellen is a famous actress and ex-wife #2 Cally (Cathy Podewell) is in an abusive relationship. As for his nemesis, Cliff Barnes, he becomes vice president of the United States, then president when the current P.O.T.U.S. has a stroke.

At the end of the episode, Adam encourages J. R. to kill himself. With the gun in his hand, he looks in the mirror and sees that Adam is not an angel, but the devil. As Bobby returns to the ranch to check on his brother, a shot rings out and Bobby runs into the room and is shocked by what he sees. Did J. R. really do himself in?

Five years later the question is answered with a two-hour made-for-TV movie entitled *Dallas: J. R. Returns* (1996), which is set several years after "Conundrum," at the end of which J. R. fired at the mirror and not himself. J. R. is up to his old tricks in his attempt to seize control of Ewing Oil. He fakes his own death, but Bobby and Sue Ellen are on to his scheme. They now control Ewing Oil, but J. R. is currently chairman of the board of Weststar Oil, and Sue Ellen and John Ross return to Southfork. In the end, J. R. reveals to John Ross that this was exactly what he was going for all along. The story continues in a second television movie, *Dallas: War of the Ewings* (1998), in which J. R. schemes to gain control of Ewing Oil, which is complicated by the discovery of oil on Ray Krebbs's ranch. In 2004, the cast reunited for a series retrospective, *Dallas Reunion: The Return to Southfork.*

Dallas was revived on TNT for three seasons (2012–2014), though the focus was on the next generation of Ewings, J. R.'s son, John Ross Ewing III (Josh Henderson); Bobby and Pam's adopted son, Christopher Ewing (Jesse Metcalfe) (his mother is Pam's sister, Kristin Shepard—the answer to "Who shot J. R.?"); and Cliff Barnes and Afton Cooper's daughter, Pamela Rebecca Barnes (Julie Gonzalo). Hagman, Duffy, and Gray reprised their respective roles and there were appearances by other former cast members as well. The series essentially ignored the events in the two made-for-TV movies. After the death of Larry Hagman on November 23, 2012, J. R. was shot to death off-camera in season 2 ("The Furious and the Fast") and he was buried in the following episode ("J. R.'s Masterpiece"). In the final episode of the season, it's revealed that Steve "Bum" Jones (Kevin Page) was hired by J. R., who was dying of cancer, to kill him so it could be pinned on Cliff Barnes. Although his daughter Pam knows he's innocent, she lets him stay in jail because he was behind an explosion at an oilrig, which caused her to lose her baby.

Dynasty, "Cache 22" (ABC, 5/11/1989, 14.7 million viewers) Directed by David Paulsen. Written by David Paulsen (as Samuel J. Pelovitz)

By its ninth and final season (1988–1989), *Dynasty* ranked no. 57. But at the peak of its popularity (season 5, 1984–1985), this prime-time sudser was the highest rated show of the season, with an estimated 21.2 million households tuning in to watch rich bitch Alexis Colby (Joan Collins) make life miserable for her ex-husband, oil tycoon Blake Carrington (John Forsythe), and his lovely wife, Krystle (Linda Evans).

Krystle spends much of season 9 in the hospital after having a brain tumor removed. The surgery leaves her in a coma. Meanwhile, back at the Carrington mansion, a body found at the bottom of the lake on their property is identified as Roger Grimes, a man Alexis was having an affair with when she and Blake divorced. Their daughter, Fallon (Emma Samms), who is haunted by memories of Grimes, becomes romantically involved with the detective investigating the case, Sergeant John Zorelli (Ray Abruzzo). Fallon remembers that she shot Grimes when she saw him beating his mother and her late grandfather, Tom Carrington, hid Grimes's body in a mine under the lake to protect his granddaughter. The twist to the story is that the mine also contains stolen Nazi treasure hidden there by her grandfather. The person who discovered the body was a diver hired by Alexis's cousin, Sable Colby (Stephanie Beacham).

In the finale episode, an argument between Alexis and Sable gets nasty when Alexis's son Adam (Gordon Thomson) reveals that Sable is pregnant by Alexis's lover, Dex (Michael Nader). When a fight erupts, Adam pushes Dex into Alexis, breaking a railing, and the two fall over a second-floor balcony. Fallon and her half-sister, Krystina (Jessica Player), venture into the tunnel and are followed by Roger Grimes's son, Dennis (Jeff Kaake), who takes them hostage. When she steals his gun and fires it, the tunnel caves in. Blake finds out that Captain Handler (John Brandon), who is investigating the murder of Roger Grimes, is behind the search for the treasure. They both pull guns on each other; both Handler and Blake are shot.

Dynasty ended with all the lives of all the major characters hanging in the balance. Their fate is revealed in *Dynasty: The Reunion*, a four-hour miniseries, which aired on ABC on October 20 and 21, 1991. Some characters are completely off the canvas (Dex Dexter, Sable Colby), while others return: Blake and Alexis's gay son, Steven (played the actor who originated the role, Al Corley), and Kirby Anders (Kathleen Beller), the daughter of the Carringtons' majordomo, who is now working in Paris as a translator for the Consortium, who managed to steal Blake's company while he was serving time for killing Captain Handler. The plot revolves around the Consortium, an organization headed by the ruthless Jeremy Van Dorn (Jeroen Krabbé), who has a doctor hypnotize Krystle so she will assassinate Blake (she doesn't), kidnap Jeff (John James), and use Alexis to get inside the Carrington mansion to kill Blake. But he's no match for The Carringtons, who celebrate their victory over Van Dorn and the Consortium with a family dinner with everyone present—even Alexis.

ER, "And in the End . . ." (NBC, 4/2/2009, 16.4 million viewers) Directed by Rod Holcomb. Written by John Wells.

The medical series concludes just as it began, literally, with scenes from the pilot episode recreated by the current team of doctors. The episode focuses on the opening of Dr. John Carter's (Noah Wyle) medical clinic for underprivileged families, a celebration that reunites many of County General's most beloved past residents, including Peter Benton (Eriq La Salle), Elizabeth Corday (Alex Kingston), Kerry Weaver (Laura Innes), and Susan Lewis (Sherry Stringfield). Rachel Greene (Hallee Hirsh), daughter of the deceased Dr. Mark Greene (Anthony Edwards), visits County General as a candidate for the hospital's medical teaching program. As the ER fields multiple cases, Dr. Carter takes Rachel under his wing, just as her father did for him. In the final moments, as victims of an explosion are wheeled in, Carter calls Rachel along to assist, asking, "Dr. Greene, you coming?"—a statement that, like the pilot episode, reminds fans that life will go on at County General.

Everybody Loves Raymond, "The Finale" (CBS, 5/16/2005, 32.9 million viewers) Directed by Gary Halvorson. Written by Philip Rosenthal, Ray Romano, Tucker Cawley, Lew Schneider, Steve Skrovan, Jeremy Stevens, Mike Royce, Aaron Shure, Tom Caltabiano, and Leslie Caveny.

Raymond Barone (Ray Romano) has a routine procedure (his adenoids are removed), but when he doesn't readily wake up from the anesthesia, everyone begins to panic. Raymond eventually wakes up and the doctor explains to the family that the complication may have been due to hypertension. Meanwhile, the idea that they almost lost Raymond takes its toll on his wife, Debra (Patricia Heaton); his parents, Marie (Doris Roberts) and Frank (Peter Boyle); and his brother, Robert (Brad Garrett).

Family Ties, "Alex Doesn't Live Here Anymore" (NBC, 5/14/1989, 36.3 million viewers) Directed by Sam Weisman. Written by Susan Borowitz, Katie Ford, Marc Lawrence, and Alan Uger.

Everyone's favorite young Republican Alex P. Keaton (Michael J. Fox) says goodbye to his family and heads to New York to fulfill his lifelong dream of working on Wall Street.

Felicity, "Back to the Future" (The WB, 5/22/2002, 3.7 million viewers) Directed by Lawrence Trilling. Written by Jennifer Levin and Josh Reims.

After creator J. J. Abrams already tied up the series' loose ends in the fourth season's college graduation episode, "The Graduate," the WB ordered an additional five episodes. What resulted was a story arc following Felicity (Keri Russell) as she travels back in time to settle the series' ultimate question: Should she choose Noel (Scott Foley) or Ben (Scott Speedman)? Having initially selected Ben, only to end up heartbroken, she then chooses Noel, setting off a chain of events that eventually leads to his untimely death. In the finale episode, Felicity tracks down the original writer of the spell that sent her back in time in hopes that he can reverse it, which he does successfully. Felicity reunites with her true love, Ben, and the couple, along with the rest of the college gang, attend Noel's wedding.

Friday Night Lights, "Always" (DirecTV 101 Network, 2/9/2011 and NBC, 7/15/11, 3.5 million viewers) Directed by Michael Waxman. Written by Jason Katims.

Christmastime in Texas. As the East Dillon Lions head to the state championship, Coach Eric Taylor (Kyle Chandler) and his wife, Tami (Connie Britton), weigh an important decision: Should they move to Philly, where Tami has a promising job offer, or stay in Dillon, so Coach can take over the reins of a "super" team combining the best of his East Dillon Lions and the Dillon Panthers (his former team)? Their daughter Julie (Aimee Teegarden) is also facing an important decision when her boyfriend, Matt Saracen (Zach Gilford), arrives in town and proposes marriage (thanks to a pep talk from his trusty friend Landry [Jesse Plemons]). Julie accepts, but the couple soon finds that not getting Coach's blessing first was a fatal error ("The answer to your question is 'no.' The answer to your question is going to be 'no' today. It's going to be 'no' tomorrow. And it'll probably be 'no' until the sun burns out"). When Julie protests and begs her parents to reconsider, she tells them they are her role models because they can always make their relationship work—this sinks in for Coach, who, until then, was completely against moving to Philly. Tim Riggins (Taylor Kitsch) makes up with his brother Billy (Derek Phillips) and decides to stay in Texas—which works out nicely when his ex-girlfriend Tyra (Adrianne Palicki) returns from college for one last fling. The championship game is finally underway—and with just three seconds left on

Friday Night Light's Coach Taylor (Kyle Chandler) and Tami Taylor (Connie Britton).
Authors' collection

the clock and trailing by five, the Lions put the ball in the air. As the ball hangs there (courtesy of a freeze-frame), the next shot is of a Philadelphia Pioneer football player catching the ball—Coach and Tami have moved for Tami's job. In a set of closing scenes, Tim and Billy continue to bond, as Julie and Matt are seen together in Chicago. Buddy Garrity (Brad Leland) has taken over the "super team" operations, while Becky (Madison Burge) kisses Luke (Matt Lauria) as he heads off for the army. Luke gives Becky his championship ring (the Lions caught the pass and won!). Coach and Tami walk off the field together in the closing shot.

Repeatedly snubbed by the Television Academy, both Kyle Chandler and Connie Britton were finally nominated for their leading roles on *Friday Night Lights* at the 2011 Emmy Awards. Britton was bested by *The Good Wife*'s Julianna Margulies, but Chandler was triumphant. In his speech, he thanked the people of Austin, Texas, for helping to "bring the show to life," but forgot to thank his onscreen wife, Connie Britton, and, for that matter, his offscreen wife. Backstage, he finally remembered to thank these two important women in his life and career.

Full House, "Michelle Rides Again, Parts I and 2" (ABC, 5/23/1995, 24.3 million viewers) Directed by Joel Zwick. Story by Marc Warren and Dennis Rinsler. Part I written by Adam I. Lapidus. Part 2 written by Carolyn Omine.

Michelle (Mary-Kate and Ashley Olsen) learns to ride a horse, only to be thrown off and left unconscious. In the two-part hour-long episode, Michelle is rushed to the hospital, with Danny (Bob Saget), Joey (Dave Coulier), and Jesse (John Stamos) in tow. They discover that the fall has left Michelle with amnesia, though the doctor suspects it's temporary. The family tries to pick up the pieces (and put them back together for Michelle), as Stephanie (Jodie Sweetin) struggles with kissing her "Romeo" in her school production of *Romeo and Juliet,* and D. J. (Candace Cameron) prepares for her senior prom. Joey and Jesse consider the possibility of their own late night television show, but in light of Michelle's accident they decide family is more important than career. On the night of D. J's prom, Michelle gets her memory back, as D. J. is whisked away to her big dance by a surprise date—her goofy (but loveable) ex-boyfriend Steve (Scott Weinger).

The Golden Girls, "One Flew Out of the Cuckoo's Nest" (NBC, 5/9/1992, 27.2 million viewers) Directed by Lex Passaris. Written by Mitchell Hurwitz, Don Seigel, and Jerry Perzigian.

Dorothy (Bea Arthur) and Lucas Hollingsworth (Leslie Nielsen) pretend they are in love to get back at Lucas's niece Blanche (Rue McClanahan); in the midst of this hoax, Dorothy and Lucas realize they have feelings for each other, get married, and move to Atlanta. In the spinoff, *The Golden Palace* (1992–1993), Sophia (Estelle Getty), Rose (Betty White), and Blanche invest in a Miami hotel and end up running the place—but only for twenty-four episodes.

Gunsmoke, "The Sharecroppers" (CBS, 3/31/1975, 30.9 million viewers) Directed by Leonard Katzman. Written by Earl W. Wallace.

Gunsmoke ended its run in 1975 after twenty years on air and over 600 episodes. Its final hour followed Deputy Festus Haggen (Ken Curtis), who accidentally shoots a man, and then has to help out the man's wacky family on their farm. The hour did not serve as a traditional series finale in the sense of providing closure to a storyline or characters. Instead, the episode ran as a regular, run-of-the-mill installment to preserve the possibility of extended syndication. At the time of its final broadcast, *Gunsmoke* was the longest running prime-time show in television history (eventually bested by *The Simpsons*).

Home Improvement, "The Long and Winding Road, Part 3" (ABC, 5/25/1999, 35.5 million viewers) Directed by John Pasquin. Written by Bruce Ferber, Lloyd Garver, and Marley Sims.

Al (Richard Karn) and Trudy (Megan Cavanagh) get married in Tim (Tim Allen) and Wilson's (Earl Hindman) backyard (the fence comes down for the occasion). *Tool Time*'s new producer, Morgan (Danny Zorn), offers Tim a raise and the title of executive producer, but Tim doesn't like what Morgan has done with the show and quits. Jill (Patricia Richardson) accepts a new job in another city, but she is hesitant to go because she will miss their house, so Tim takes the house apart and takes it with them. And most important of all, viewers finally gets to see Wilson's face.

I Married Dora, "The Millionaire's Club" (ABC, 1/8/1988) Directed by Peter H. Hunt. Written by Linda Morris and Vic Rauseo.

This short-lived sitcom is best remembered for the last moment in the show's finale in which the characters break the fourth wall. The show's premise revolves around Peter Farrell (David Hugh Kelly), a single dad, who marries his housekeeper, Dora Calderon (Elizabeth Peña), an illegal alien, to prevent her from being deported. In the final scene of the last episode, Peter accepts a job overseas, leaving his two children in Dora's care. He boards the plane, but suddenly reappears in the airport and tells Dora and his family, "It's been canceled."

"The flight?" Dora asks.

"No, our series," he replies. And the entire cast waves at the camera, which pulls back to reveal, in case you didn't know it, that you've been watching a sitcom.

¡Adios, Dora!

Knot's Landing, "Just Like Old Times, Parts 1 and 2" (CBS, 5/13/1993, 19.6 million viewers) Directed by Jerome Courtland. Part 1 written by Lisa Seidman. Part 2 written by Ann Marcus.

Valene Ewing (Joan Van Ark), presumed to have died in a car accident, escapes her kidnappers and returns to Seaview Circle, where she is reunited with her husband, Gary (Ted Shackelford). Abby's (Donna Mills) attempt to take over the Sumner Group fails. She shocks everyone when she drives into the cul-de-sac while the Mackenzies and the Ewings are having a barbecue to celebrate Valene's return and announces that she's buying her old house and moving back home. Abby, standing face-to-face with her longtime nemesis Karen (Michele Lee), casually asks, "Just like old times, isn't it?" The saga continued in the mini-series, *Knots Landing: Back to the Cul-de-Sac* (1997).

The Larry Sanders Show, "Flip" (HBO, 5/31/1998) Directed by Todd Holland. Written by Peter Tolan and Garry Shandling.

Garry Shandling played fictional late night talk show host Larry Sanders in this HBO comedy that featured real celebrities who appeared as guests on the talk show. In the one-hour series finale, which received Emmys for writing and directing, it's Larry's last show (Jon Stewart is taking over), but Larry can't seem to get anyone to appear on it (and the ones who are booked—Tom Petty, Greg Kinnear, and Clint Black—are fighting in the green room). For his last show, his guests include Carol Burnett and Ellen DeGeneres, who expose Larry for lying to both of them about who he asked first, and Sean Penn and Tim Allen, who leave during the commercial break. Hank (Jeffrey Tambor) embarrasses himself as he tries to give a heartfelt goodbye. Clint Black sings a farewell song, and after the show, Hank is upset that his time was cut short. He argues with Larry and Arthur (Rip Torn), but they make up at the end as they sit on the *Larry Sanders* set for one last time.

The Late Show with David Letterman (CBS, 5/20/2015, 13.76 million viewers) Created by David Letterman.

After twenty-two seasons and 4,263 episodes, the lights went out at the Ed Sullivan Theatre in New York City, as audiences said goodbye to beloved late-night talk show host David Letterman. The host, who once seemed to be *The Tonight Show* heir apparent (see chapter 18), had found a home on CBS as their top late night go-to guy, garnering a loyal fan base and six Emmys for Outstanding Variety, Music or Comedy Series (1994, 1998–2002). After Letterman's 2014 announcement of his impending retirement, the search for a replacement sparked many rumors of potential hosts (including Jerry Seinfeld, Neil Patrick Harris, Chelsea Handler, and *The Daily Show*'s Jon Stewart) but the gig eventually went to Comedy Central's *Colbert Report* host, Stephen Colbert.

On the last broadcast of Letterman's *Late Show*, fans were treated to a star-studded celebration which began as only Letterman could imagine it, with Gerald Ford's famous quip: "Our long national nightmare is over," then repeated by former presidents George W. Bush and Bill Clinton, and current president Barack Obama. Letterman even made a callback to his famous *Tonight Show* snub, opening his monologue with: "It's beginning to look like I'm not gonna get *The Tonight Show*." The show also featured a behind-the-scenes look at the creation of the daily show, and a special thank you to his wife and son (perhaps a nod to Johnny Carson, as he featured similar segments on his final bow on late-night). Also featured was one last, and memorable, Top 10 list, complete with ten celebrity guests reading each entry. Guests included Alec Baldwin, Barbara Walters, Steve Martin, Jerry Seinfeld, Jim Carrey, Chris Rock, NFL superstar Peyton Manning, Tina Fey, Bill Murray, and Julia Louis-Dreyfus, who garnered the biggest laugh from the audience when she quipped: "Thanks for letting me take part in another hugely disappointing series finale," receiving a disappointed glare from *Seinfeld* co-star Jerry Seinfeld. As Dave's favorite band The Foo Fighters played him off, the television legend said his final goodbye: "For the last time on a television program, thank you and good night."

Little House: The Last Farewell (NBC, 2/6/1984) Written and directed by Michael Landon.

Little House on the Prairie was canceled at the end of season 9 (it was retitled, *Little House: A New Beginning* and focused more on Laura [Melissa Gilbert] and Almanzo [Dean Butler] than the Ingalls family). The residents of Walnut Grove are forced out of town by a railroad tycoon, Nathan Lassiter (James Karen), who owns the land. Union soldiers are called in to force them to evacuate. But the good people of Walnut Grove don't go quietly. Lassiter may own the land, but he can't take their town, which they blow up with explosives.

Mad Men, "Person to Person" (AMC, 5/17/2015, 3.3 million viewers) Written and Directed by Matthew Weiner.

Taking a page from its AMC colleague *Breaking Bad*, *Mad Men* split its seventh and final season into two installments (with a year hiatus between the two parts). Matthew Weiner's 1960s advertising drama, winner of four consecutive Emmys for Outstanding Drama Series (2008–2011), finally closed the book on Madison Avenue's mystery man Don Draper (Jon Hamm) on May 17, 2015.

The final season finds boutique agency Sterling Cooper Draper Pryce absorbed into corporate bigwig firm McCann Erickson. Don, finally about to get a crack at monster accounts like the coveted Coca-Cola, disappears from his desk, retreading old ground as he runs away from any new sense of authority. As Don heads west to find himself (under the initial guise of tracking down hopeless waitress-turned-damsel-in-distress Diana, played by Elizabeth Reaser), he leaves behind his former co-workers, who also struggle to cope with their changing business landscape as they enter the new promising decade of the 1970s.

Peggy Olsen (Elizabeth Moss) worries how she will be perceived in the new office, but after a pep talk from an unlikely source, Roger Sterling (John Slattery), she arrives at McCann Erickson confident and ready to take charge (toting along Bert Cooper's erotic nineteenth century Japanese painting "The Dream of the Fisherman's Wife" for added effect). Pete Campbell (Vincent Kartheiser) finds himself fitting in nicely with the corporate mucky-mucks, only to be propositioned by former colleague Duck Phillips (Mark Moses) to jump the McCann ship for a promising opportunity at Leer Jet (the only catch—it's in Wichita). Roger, feeling responsible for the McCann takeover, retreats into semi-retirement, prepping his will (which will now include Joan's son Kevin, proving once and for all that he is the father) and settling down with Marie Calvet (Julia Ormond), mother of Don's newly minted ex-wife Megan (Jessica Paré). Joan Harris (Christina Hendricks) struggles to be taken seriously at McCann, regularly being propositioned and insulted by her sexist co-workers. When she takes her sexual harassment complaints all the way up to the boss, Jim Hobart (H. Richard Greene), Hobart is less than sympathetic and ultimately demands Joan's resignation, opting to buy out her controlling interest in the company rather than deal with her problems.

On the home front, Don's ex-wife Betty Francis (January Jones) copes with her terminal lung cancer diagnosis, as daughter Sally (Kiernan Shipka) returns home from boarding school to deal with the family crisis (both of her own will, and due to the insistence of her long-suffering stepfather, Henry, played by Christopher Stanley). Betty sees that her condition has caused her little girl to accelerate toward adulthood, and thus entrusts Sally with the arrangements for her own funeral—going as far as to put in writing her specific dress requests, ending the letter on a heartbreaking note: "Sally, I always worried about you, because you marched to the beat of your own drum. But now I know that's good. I know your life will be an adventure. I love you, Mom." Don, still away as part of his most recent disappearing act, is completely unaware of Betty's condition.

The series finale is titled "Person to Person"—a retro phrase used to describe a phone call that is connected directly by an operator. The theme of phone calls factors prominently in the episode, as Don places three important calls. The first is to his daughter Sally. Hoping to update her on his current whereabouts and the plans for his continued (seemingly aimless) adventure, Don is shaken to the core when Sally betrays her mother's trust and tells him that Betty is dying. Soon after, Don places his second call to ex-wife Betty, insisting that he come home, but she refuses. In a heart-wrenching conversation, the pair, once passionately in love, says goodbye. Don, unable to accept this, escapes yet again, arriving at the California doorstep of Stephanie (Caity Lotz), the niece of his deceased friend Anna Draper (the woman who allowed him to take her husband's name). Stephanie then convinces Don that he seems lost and should accompany her to a New-Age retreat (reportedly based on the Esalen facility located on California's Big Sur coastline).

With Don now participating in classes like "Psychotechnics" and "Divorce: A Creative Experience," the rest of the Sterling Cooper Draper Pryce gang copes with their new realities. Newly unemployed Joan, inspired by a free-lance gig with former co-worker Ken Cosgrove (Aaron Staton), decides to strike out on her own, forming a production company. She attempts to lure Peggy to join her, but instead opts to run the business herself—even if that means losing her new beau Richard (Bruce Greenwood). Pete, having reconciled with ex-wife Trudy (Alison Brie), heads off to Wichita to begin his promising new career with Leer Jet, while Roger runs off to Quebec with his new wife, Marie. Meanwhile, Peggy digs deep into her new position at McCann, only to find the love of her life has been right under her nose all along—artist, and longtime co-worker, Stan Rizzo (Jay R. Ferguson). The two share the episode's most romantic moment, as he runs from one end of the office floor to her door to plant a long, lustful kiss on her lips.

Before Peggy and Stan share their big moment, she is the recipient of Don's last "Person to Person" phone call. On the other line a broken, tormented Don bids farewell to Peggy, whom he long doted on as his protégée (whether he admitted it or not). Peggy pleads with Don to come home, but Don is destroyed, and instead simply says goodbye. In the "all is lost" moment of the final episode, Don sits in on one final seminar, listening to the sad story

Mad Men's Don Draper (Jon Hamm) has a final moment of inner peace (and inspiration).

AMC/Photofest

of Leonard (Evan Arnold), a man who feels invisible. Leonard's story reso-
nates with Don, who has long struggled with his own identity, having been
born the poor, orphaned Dick Whitman, and transformed himself into the
suave, adman Don. He embraces Leonard, and in this moment, Don is freed.
The final moment of the episode finds Don, clean-shaven and calm, meditat-
ing on a grassy mountaintop. As his meditation circle hums their
"Ohmmmms" a bell rings, and the next shot is the first frame of the iconic
1971 Coca-Cola "Hilltop" commercial featuring the memorable jingle "I'd
Like to Buy the World a Coke." As images of the characters in the mega-
famous ad pass by, we recognize them as being inspired by Don's fellow
retreat members, and the grassy hilltop that serves as the setting for the song
is a virtual copy of Don's retreat. Ending the episode on this note implies that
in Don's moment of clarity—at the very moment he felt free to be himself—
he dreamt up the most famous advertisement of all time.

A near-record audience of 3.3 million viewers tuned in to see the finale
of *Mad Men* (the third most-watched episode of its seven-season run). In a
move similar to TVLand's choice to suspend programming during *Seinfeld*'s
series finale, AMC sister stations IFC, WE tv, Sundance, and BBC America
followed suit, running a slideshow of images from the series, with the note:

"It's the end of an era. Everyone at [IFC/WE tv/Sundance/BBC America] is watching the *Mad Men* series finale on AMC. Come join us!" Many critics highlighted the general "happy ending" motif of the episode (with the exception of Betty's sad demise), while fans debated as to whether or not Don's moment of clarity was a stroke of genius or a cynical commentary on the ability of advertising to profit from any (and every) human emotion. In an interview with the *Hollywood Reporter*, series creator Matthew Weiner, who had long remained tight-lipped about the ending of his series, called the accusation of cynicism "disturbing," opting instead to see Don's moment of clarity as "something that's very pure . . . coming from a good place." Series star Jon Hamm told the *New York Times* that he was "struck by the poetry" of the final scene, interpreting Weiner's ending as a "serene moment of understanding. . . . [Don] realizes who he is. And who he is, is an advertising man." Meanwhile, as *Mad Men* rarely presented real ads on the show, reporters quickly seized upon the opportunity to track down the original creator of the "Hilltop" ad—actual former McCann Erickson employee Bill Backer. When asked what Backer thought about the series using his iconic ad for its last moments, he told CNN, "I don't care. . . . I didn't see it."

MacGyver, "The Mountain of Youth" (ABC, 5/21/1992, 22.3 million viewers) Directed by William Gereghty. Written by Brad Radnitz.

In the fictional country of Kabustan, MacGyver (Richard Dean Anderson) meets with businessman Jack Dalton (Bruce McGill) and joins him on his quest to find the Fountain of Youth. Upon finding the Fountain, it suddenly stops running, and MacGyver suspects foul play. As they follow the water upstream, they come upon Kabustani soldiers, and have to retreat. Soon, MacGyver uncovers the Kabustanis' plan to turn the Fountain's water into resources to make H-bombs. MacGyver finds security footage proving this and steals the videotape, stashing it away for safe-keeping. When he and Jack are captured for attempting to foil the Kabustani plan, he uses a piece of a test tube (previously filled with magic Fountain water) to cut them to freedom (as only MacGyver could). On the run, MacGyver and Jack snatch up the hidden videotape and flee in hopes of outrunning their captors. But before he can go, MacGyver must stop the water from making it to the Kabustanis, and, upon this attempt, causes the entire pump house to explode. Amidst the explosion, MacGyver escapes with Jack, as Jack decides to keep the Fountain a secret (but not before taking one vial for himself).

Monk, "Mr. Monk and the End, Parts I and 2" Part I (USA, 11/27/2009, 5.8 million) and Part 2 (12/4/2009, 9.4 million) Directed by Randy Zisk. Written by Andy Breckman.

After a series-long search, Detective Adrian Monk (Tony Shalhoub) reveals the killer of his wife, Trudy (Melora Hardin), to be her law professor, Ethan Rickover (Craig T. Nelson), who is now a judge and a nominee for the State Supreme Court. Trudy, who didn't know Rickover was married, got pregnant, but the baby, who was delivered by a mid-wife, Wendy Stroud, died shortly after the birth. Fearing she will jeopardize his future career, Rickover kills Trudy with a car bomb, and Wendy, who is buried in his yard. All the while, Monk is dying from exposure to a poisonous toxin planted by someone working for Rickover. Once Rickover's crime is exposed, the judge kills himself and Monk is cured with the antidote. The twist is that Trudy's baby did live and was put up for adoption by Wendy. Monk meets his wife's daughter, Molly Evans (Alona Tal), who is a film critic for a Monterey County newspaper.

Michelle Kung reported in the *Wall Street Journal* that the final episode was the most watched episode of an hour-long drama series in basic cable history, breaking the record of the series finale of *The Closer*, which was watched by 9.2 million viewers.

Mr. Belvedere, "Mr. Belvedere's Wedding, Parts I and 2" Part I (ABC, 7/1/1990) Part 2 (7/8/90, 13.8 million viewers) Part I directed by Don Corvan. Part 2 directed by Don Corvan and Rob Stone. Part I written by Dennis Snee. Part 2 written by Beth Roberts.

British butler Mr. Belvedere (Christopher Hewett) marries Louise (Rosemary Forsyth), who must return to her work in Africa, so he must say goodbye to his employers, the Owens family. In the final scene, which mirrors the end of each episode in which Belvedere writes in his journal, Mr. Belvedere, living in Africa, writes a postcard to the Owens family.

Murphy Brown, "Never Can Say Goodbye, Parts I and 2" (CBS, 5/18/1998, 17.5 million viewers) Part I directed by Steve Zuckerman. Part 2 directed by Barnet Kellman. Written by Diane English.

Murphy (Candice Bergen) decides to leave *FYI*, but not before firing her last secretary (a guest appearance by Bette Midler). Having completed her chemotherapy for breast cancer six months earlier, Murphy must undergo one last scan to be proven cancer free. When the scan finds something worth exploring, she goes under the knife again. In an out-of-body experience, Murphy goes to heaven and lands a major interview: God (played by comedian Alan King). God tells her to make the best with what she has, and as she comes out of the surgery she discovers it was just a cyst and thus, decides to return to *FYI*. Upon her return, she finds that life has moved on without her. Returning to her townhouse, she discovers that her son has called her former handyman Eldin (Robert Pastorelli), who returns to propose marriage to Murphy (she ignores the proposal, but will accept a few touchups on his paintjob).

One Day at a Time "Off We Go" (CBS, 5/21/1984) and "Another Man's Shoes" (5/28/1984) Directed by Noam Pitlik. "Off We Go" written by Perry Grant, Dick Bensfield, and George Tibbles. "Another Man's Shoes" written by Perry Grant and Dick Bensfield.

Ms. Ann Romano (Bonnie Franklin) takes a job in London and bids adieu to her family, friends, and Indianapolis. The final episode ("Another Man's Shoes") was intended as a pilot for a spinoff for the Romano's super, Dwayne Schneider (Pat Harrington Jr.), who decides to move away to raise his niece and nephew following the death of his brother.

One Tree Hill, "One Tree Hill" (The CW, 4/4/2012, 2 million viewers) Written and Directed by Mark Schwahn.

The Tree Hill gang gathers to celebrate the tenth anniversary of nightclub Tric, an event that includes performances by series stars Haley James Scott (Bethany Joy Lenz), Chris Keller (Tyler Hilton), and real-life musician Gavin DeGraw. Nathan (James Lafferty) has returned home after his European kidnapping to reconnect with his wife, Haley, and their young son, Jamie (Jackson Brundage). Julian (Austin Nichols) buys Brooke (Sophia Bush) her childhood home and promises her a new shot at the perfect life. Clay (Robert Buckley) and Quinn (Shantel VanSanten) get full custody of Clay's son Logan (Pierce Gagnon) and decide to marry. Marvin "Mouth" McFadden (Lee Norris), having been left $500,000 by Dan Scott's estate, sets up a sports scholarship in memory of Jimmy Edwards and Keith Scott, both victims of season 3's school shooting. In the final moments, the series flashes to the future, as the gang enters the Tree Hill gym to cheer on a now high-school-aged Jamie Scott as he continues in the family basketball star tradition.

Oz, "Exeunt Omnes" (HBO, 2/23/2003) Directed by Alex Zakrzewski. Written by Tom Fontana.

Chris Keller (Christopher Meloni) tells Beecher (Lee Tergesen) he loves him, but when he rejects his advances, Keller yells, "Beecher, don't!" and commits suicide by throwing himself over a railing, thereby implicating Beecher in his "murder." Meanwhile, a package sent by Keller, containing anthrax, kills six members of the Aryan Brotherhood working in the mailroom.

Parks and Recreation, "One Last Ride" (NBC, 2/24/2015, 4.15 million viewers) Directed by Michael Schur. Written by Michael Schur and Amy Poehler.

After a final season jump three years into the future, former Pawnee Parks Department workaholic Leslie Knope (Amy Poehler) has climbed her way

Leslie Knope (Amy Poehler) and Ben Wyatt (Adam Scott) walk the halls of Pawnee's City Hall in the *Parks and Recreation* series finale.   *Authors' collection*

from small-time local government to become the head of the Midwest branch of the National Parks Services. In the series finale, Leslie makes the move to the big time: accepting a job with the Department of the Interior. This, coupled with Andy (Chris Pratt) and April's (Aubrey Plaza) upcoming move to D.C., forces the Pawnee gang to get together for their final goodbyes—only to be interrupted by a concerned citizen who begs them to fix one last broken swing. They all agree, and as Leslie works with each of her cherished employees, the episode flashes to the future. No-nonsense office assistant Donna (Retta) has moved to Seattle, becoming a successful real estate agent, while, mogul-in-training Tom Haverford (Aziz Ansari) writes a best seller (*Failure: An American Success Story*) and becomes a motivational speaker. April and Andy have a baby, and Garry Gergich (Jim O'Heir) serves ten terms as mayor of Pawnee, dying at the advanced age of 100 (his funeral, yet another flash forward, features Leslie flanked by Secret Service . . . Madam President?). Ron Swanson (Nick Offerman) gives up his construction business and invests in a whiskey company, only to be lured back to government work by Leslie, who puts him in charge of Pawnee's newest national park. Ben Wyatt (Adam Scott) becomes an Indiana congressman, and he and Leslie become D.C. bigwigs, until they are lured back to Indiana with the promise of running for governor—but which one will run? Heading back to Pawnee to reunite with the old gang (including former cast members Rashida Jones and Rob Lowe), Ben convinces Leslie that *she* should be the candidate. In the final flash forward, Leslie accepts an honorary doctorate from Indiana University, promising more for her future. The final shot brings the audience back to the Pawnee park, now with a shiny new swing, as Leslie stands proudly looking forward.

Party of Five, "All's Well . . . That Ends Well" (Fox, 5/3/2000, 6.5 million) "All's Well . . ." directed by Steven Robman. ". . . That Ends Well" directed by Ken Topolsky. Written by Christopher Keyser and Amy Lippman.

At the weekly family dinner at Salingers' Restaurant, Bailey (Scott Wolf), Julia (Neve Campbell), and Claudia (Lacey Chabert) all announce their plans to leave town. Charlie (Matthew Fox) decides to sell the Salinger family home and divide the money among his siblings. He, his wife Kirsten (Paula Devicq), and his little brother Owen (Jacob Smith) move into a new house. To help Daphne (Jennifer Aspen), who is the mother of his child, Charlie makes her boyfriend, Luke (Charles Esten), a partner in his furniture business.

Peyton Place, Season 5, Episode 54 (6/2/1969) Written by Del Reisman. Directed by Everett Chambers.

Dr. Mike Rossi (Ed Nelson) is arraigned for the murder of Carolyn's (Tippy Walker) ex-husband Fred (Joe Maross) and the case will go to trial despite the efforts of his lawyer, Steven Cord (James Douglas), to create reasonable doubt. Meanwhile, Lew (Glynn Turman) considers giving himself up for his involvement in a hit-and-run in New York City, yet he wonders if they think a respectable, white doctor like Mike Rossi killed a man, does a black man have any chance at justice? In the end, he agrees to turn himself in and Mike Rossi sits alone in a jail cell, wondering what is going to happen to him. Unfortunately, the show was canceled and the question was not immediately answered.

Picket Fences, "Three Weddings and a Meltdown" (CBS, 4/24/1996, 11.1 million viewers) Directed by Mel Damski. Written by Nick Harding, Nicole Yorkin, and Dawn Prestwich.

Three couples tie the knot in a triple wedding: Police officers Kenny (Costas Mandylor) and Maxine "Max" Stewart (Lauren Holly), Carter Pike (Kelly Connell) and Sue (Sheila McCarthy), and Doug and Selma Wambaugh (Fyvush Finkel and Edith Fields), who get remarried after Doug gets her off for murder. Sheriff Jimmy Brock (Tom Skerritt) and his wife, Dr. Jill Brock (Kathy Baker), who were having marital problems, reconcile at the wedding.

The Practice, "Adjourned" (a.k.a. "Cheers") (ABC, 5/16/2004, 10.9 million viewers) Directed by Jeannot Szwarc. Written by David E. Kelley.

The law firm closes and everyone moves on: Eugene (Steve Harris) is a judge; Jimmy (Michael Badalucco) and Jaime (Jessica Capshaw) start their own firm; Ellenor (Camryn Manheim) takes a break to raise her daughter; Alan Shore (James Spader) continues to work for Denny Crane (in the spinoff, *Boston Legal*); and Bobby Donnell (Dylan McDermott) is left all alone, crying in his office.

Quantum Leap, "Mirror Image – August 8, 1953" (NBC, 5/5/1993, 20.6 million viewers) Directed by James Whitmore Jr. Written by Donald Bellisario.

A mysterious bartender (Bruce McGill, who had played a different role in the first episode) reveals to Dr. Sam Beckett (Scott Bakula), a quantum scientist, that he can actually control the leaps he has been taking through time to make the world a better place. He then tells Sam that he can go home anytime he wants. The last leap we see him take is back in time to visit Al's wife, Beth (Susan Diol), to assure her that Al (Dean Stockwell), who was a prisoner of war at the time, is alive. As a result of his visit to Beth, she doesn't remarry and she and Al have a happy life together with their four children. The image cuts to black and a message appears on the screen: "Beth never remarried. She and Al have four daughters and will celebrate their 39th wedding anniversary in June. Dr. Sam Becket never returned home." (Note: "Becket" should be spelled "Beckett"). Why doesn't he make it home? We never find out. Apparently the show's creator, Donald Bellisario, was hopeful that the show would be renewed.

The Shield, "Family Meeting" (FX, 11/25/2008, 1.8 million viewers) Directed by Clark Johnson. Written by Shawn Ryan.

Regarded by critics as one of the best crime dramas in recent years, the series finale did not disappoint. For six seasons we have been following the Strike Team, an anti-crime unit in the Farmington district of Los Angeles that resorts to illegal tactics to control the gang problem. Their team leader, Vic Mackey (Michael Chiklis), is a ruthless, corrupt officer of the law who justifies breaking it in order to put away hardened criminals. In the series finale, it looks like he and the members of the disbanded Strike Team are all going down, but Vic cuts a deal and admits to all of the crimes they've committed, including the murder of a member of his team, Detective Terry Crowley (Reed Diamond), who was sent by his commander to build a federal case against the Strike Team for colluding with a drug lord. In exchange for the information, Vic is granted immunity, but his two former teammates, Shane Vendrell (Walton Goggins), whom Vic tried to have killed, and Ronnie Gardocki (David Rees Snell), are certain to be put away for life.

A desperate Shane calls his pregnant wife, Mara (Michele Hicks), and son, Jackson (Miles Greenberg), into the room for a "family meeting." We later see that Shane not only committed suicide, but poisoned Mara and his son as well. After Vic lies to Ronnie and tells them they were both granted immunity, the police come and take Ronnie away.

When Vic's ex-wife, Corrine (Cathy Cahlin Ryan), first heard about the horrible crimes Vic committed, she agrees to help him. But when Corrine learns that Vic tried to kill Shane and Mara, she agrees to help the police build a case against her ex-husband. When Vic gets immunity, she and her children are put into the witness protection program.

All alone with his gun: *The Shield*'s Vic Mackey (Michael Chiklis).

Authors' collection

As for Vic, it's his worst nightmare come true when he is assigned a desk job, shuffling paper at the ICE (Immigration and Customs Enforcement). In the final scene, in which there is no dialogue, Vic, after hours at his desk, hears police sirens and goes to the window to see police cars speeding by. Back at his desk, he looks at photos of his wife and kids. He is teary-eyed, though a defiant look comes over his face. He uses a key to open the bottom of his desk, takes out a gun, slides it in the back of his pants, and walks off. When *Entertainment Weekly*'s Michael Ausiello asked the show's creator, Shawn Ryan, where Vic was going, Ryan said he "viewed Vic as a shark. He's someone, who, in order to survive, has to move forward. Is he going to pursue his own sort of police work on his own time? Is he going to do something postal? I don't know. But I do think the shark swims forward."

Soap, Season 4, Episode 22 (ABC, 4/20/1981) Directed by J. D. Lobue. Written by Susan Harris and Stu Silver.

Susan Harris's controversial sitcom was suddenly canceled by ABC after season 4, so the one-hour finale consisted of a series of cliffhangers that were never resolved. In the final moment, Jessica Tate (Katherine Helmond) is facing a firing squad in South America—but we never know what happened. Two years later, on an episode of the *Soap* spinoff *Benson* ("God, I Need This Job," 9/30/1983), an overworked Benson (Robert Guillaume), sees Jessica's apparition, who reveals she is lying in a coma somewhere in South America.

That '70s Show, "That '70s Finale" (Fox, 5/18/2006, 10 million viewers) Directed by David Trainer. Written by Gregg Mettler.

New Year's Eve, 1979—literally the last day of the '70s. The gang gathers to celebrate, reminiscing about their best times together, as Kitty (Debra Jo Rupp) debates the idea of making a move with her husband, Red (Kurtwood Smith), to Florida. Eric (Topher Grace) is en route back home to Wisconsin from Africa, but is late because he missed his flight. Meanwhile, Michael Kelso (Ashton Kutcher) returns from Chicago unexpectedly. In a sweet gesture, Red returns all of the money Hyde (Danny Masterson) had paid the Formans over the years for rent, which Hyde then uses to buy Red season tickets to the Green Bay Packers. Having those coveted tickets makes Red reconsider the move to Florida, and Kitty happily agrees to remain in Wisconsin. Donna (Laura Prepon), missing Eric, waits outside in hopes he will return, and when he does the two reconcile with a passionate kiss. In one final joint-passing circle, the gang makes their final revelations of the '70s: Fez (Wilmer Valderrama) admits he's dating Jackie (Mila Kunis), Eric gives Kelso a present for his daughter, and Hyde realizes how many brain cells they've lost over the years. The final shot shows the Forman basement empty, as the gang counts down the New Year upstairs. When they reach *one*, a license plate appears on screen with "That 70s Show" written on it, with a tag labeled "1980." The opening credits then run again, as the gang all sing along as they had done for eight seasons.

3rd Rock from the Sun, "The Thing That Wouldn't Die, Parts 1 and 2" (NBC, 5/22/2001, 11.9 million viewers) Directed by Terry Hughes. Part 1 written by Dave Jesser and Matthew Silverman. Story by David Lewman and Joe Liss. Part 2 written by David Goetsch and Jason Venokur. Story by Christine Zander.

The four-episode ending of this fantasy sitcom concludes with Mary (Jane Curtin) finally learning the true alien identities of the Solomons—Dick (John Lithgow), Sally (Kristen Johnston), Harry (French Stewart), and Tommy (Joseph Gordon-Levitt). Their mission leader, the Big Giant Head (William Shatner), summons them back to their planet because Dick turned Dr. Liam Neesam (John Cleese), a fellow alien, into a chimpanzee.

Mary decides to accompany them home and they throw a big farewell bash. At the last minute, she changes her mind and the Solomons are beamed back to their planet. Rick Bird reported in the *Cincinnati Post* that an alternative ending, which would have left the door open for the series to continue, was shot and has since aired in syndication and is included on the season 6 DVDs.

True Blood, "Thank You" (HBO, 8/24/14, 4.0 million viewers) Directed by Scott Winant. Written by Brian Buckner.

All of the season's major conflicts are resolved. The blood of the heinous Sarah Newlin (Anna Camp) is the antidote for the Hep V virus, but Bill Compton (Stephen Moyer) refuses to drink it. He asks Sookie Stackhouse (Anna Paquin) to use her Fae powers to kill him, which would turn her into a normal human. She refuses, explaining that they are a part of her. Bill, still intent on dying, attends the wedding of his "daughter" Jessica (Deborah Ann Woll) who marries Hoyt Fortenberry (Jim Parrack), who has no recollection of their past relationship. The newlyweds will be living in Bill's house after making an agreement with Andy Bellefleur (Chris Bauer), his last living descendant, who agrees to only charge the couple a $1 for rent. When Bill is ready to die, Sookie tells him she loves him. Lying in his coffin in his original grave, she helps Bill stake himself. The story jumps ahead four years. The cure for Hep V, manufactured from Sarah Newlin's blood, has made Eric Northman (Alexander Skarsgård) and Pam (Kristin Bauer van Straten) billionaires when they use it to create "New Blood." Everyone thinks Sarah has escaped, but she's actually being held captive in the basement of their club, Fangtasia, where she is haunted by the ghost of her former husband-turned-vampire, Steve (Michael McMillian). In the final scene, we see everyone (humans and vampires) gathered in Sookie's backyard for Thanksgiving dinner. Sookie is now married to an unidentified man and has a child.

Twin Peaks, "Beyond Life and Death" (ABC, 6/10/1991, 10.4 million viewers) Directed by David Lynch. Written by Mark Frost, Harley Peyton, and Robert Engels.

Special Agent Dale Cooper (Kyle MacLachlan) rescues Annie Blackburn (Heather Graham) from his former partner, rogue FBI agent Windom Earle (Kenneth Welsh), whose soul is then taken by Killer BOB (Frank Silva). The following morning, Cooper wakes up and goes to brush his teeth. He smashes his head against the bathroom mirror. A crazed expression comes over his face and he laughs maniacally as he looks in the mirror and sees Killer BOB looking back at him. Killer BOB is now inhabiting the body of Agent Cooper.

Two and a Half Men, "Of Course He's Dead, Parts 1 and 2" (CBS, 2/19/2015, 13.5 million) Directed by James Widdoes. Written by Chuck Lorre, Lee Aronsohn, Don Reo, and Jim Patterson.

The series finale is a long, extended joke about the feud between series co-creator Chuck Lorre had with the show's original star Charlie Sheen, who delivered a series of public rants against Lorre and then went on to star in his own sitcom, *Anger Management.*

The joke is that although his family was told he was hit by a train and died, Sheen's character, Charlie, is not dead. His brother, Alan (Jon Cryer), finds out that Charlie has songwriting royalties totaling $2.5 million, but to collect them he needs to present a death certificate, but no one has it. It turns out he was held prisoner in a dungeon all this time by stalker/wife Rose (Melanie Lynskey) until he managed to escape. Now Charlie is out for revenge on everyone because they have been going on with their lives without him. Walden (Ashton Kutcher), who bought Charlie's house after his death and, therefore, has never met him, gets a threatening phone call from Charlie that sounds more like one of Charlie Sheen's rants when he departed show. Using some of Sheen's favorite words and phrase, he refers to his "ninja awesomeness" and vows to "deploy an army of assassins to destroy you" and "carve my initials into your reptilian skull and cover you in tiger's blood." There are plenty more inside jokes until the climax, when "Charlie" (you only see him from behind, and it's not Sheen) comes up to the house and a piano falls on his head. The camera zooms out to reveal Chuck Lorre, who, borrowing one of Sheen's catchphrases, says, "Winning!" A piano then drops on Lorre. In one of his trademark vanity cards, Lorre confirmed that they invited Sheen to be on the season finale, but he didn't think their idea was funny:

> Our idea was to have him walk up to the front door in the last scene, ring the doorbell, then turn, look directly into the camera and go off on a maniacal rant about the dangers of drug abuse. He would then explain that these dangers only applied to average people. That he was far from average. He was a ninja warrior from Mars. He was invincible. And then we would drop a piano on him.

Ugly Betty, "Hello Goodbye" (ABC, 4/14/2010, 5.7 million viewers) Directed by Victor Nelli Jr. Written by Silvio Horta.

Betty Suarez (America Ferrara) accepts a job in London, which upsets her boss Daniel Mead (Eric Mabius), who realizes he has feelings for his former assistant and doesn't go to her farewell party. Daniel hands the editorship of *Mode* magazine to Wilhelmina (Vanessa Williams) and flies to London, where he runs into Betty, who is enjoying her new life and career. Daniel asks her out to dinner. As she leaves, the title "Ugly Betty" appears on the screen—and the word "Ugly" then disappears.

The Wonder Years, "Independence Day" (ABC, 5/12/1993, 21 million viewers) Directed by Michael Dinner. Written by Bob Brush.

In the summer of 1973, Kevin (Fred Savage) quits his job working for his father and goes to a resort where Winnie (Danica McKellar) is working as a lifeguard. When he sees her kissing another lifeguard, he becomes jealous and starts a fight. Winnie loses her job, Kevin loses his car in a poker game, and the two are abandoned on a desolate highway, where they take shelter in a barn. They promise to be together, always (and presumably have sex for the first time). The next day, July 4th, they walk hand-in-hand back into town as a parade goes by. The show's narrator (Daniel Stern) reveals the fate of the characters, including Kevin and Winnie, who do not marry, but stay friends.

The West Wing, "Tomorrow" (NBC, 5/14/2006, 10.1 million) Directed by Christopher Misiano. Written by John Wells.

On Inauguration Day, President Bartlet (Martin Sheen) and his staff prepare for the transition between administrations. Sam Seaborn (Rob Lowe) returns to the White House to work for incoming president, Matthew Santos (Jimmy Smits). President Bartlet decides to pardon Communications Director Toby Ziegler (Richard Schiff), who leaked classified information about the existence of a military space shuttle to the *New York Times*. The daughter of the late chief of staff, Leo McGarry (John Spencer), brings a gift to the White House that she found among her father's things—a framed napkin the president had given Leo, with "Bartlet for President" written on it by Leo at the beginning of his campaign. McGarry was President Santos's running mate, but he died of a heart attack on election night. President Santos is inaugurated, and President Bartlet and the former first lady, Abbie Bartlet (Stockard Channing), say their farewells.

Bibliography

Abele, Robert. "Adjust and Conquer: Acclaimed UK Comedy Require Tweaks to Hit US Funny Bones." *Variety*, May 14, 2009.

Adalian, Josef. ———. "*Buffy* Losing Star's Bite." *Variety*, February 26, 2003.

———. "*Dexter*'s to Die for: Showtime Skein Tops 1 Million Viewers." *Variety*, October 3, 2007.

———. "Laughs End Comedy Drought: Sitcom Pilots Bring Needed Life to Genre in Search of an Injection." *Variety*, August 29, 2005.

———. "*Lost* Hatches Exit Plan." *Variety*, May 7, 2007.

———. "NBC Longs for Must-see Buzz." *Variety*, October 26, 2006.

———. "Peacock on *Studio* Beat." *Variety*, October 17, 2005.

———. "Revamp Results." *Variety*, July 10, 2002.

———. "*Rock* Rolls to Full Order." *Variety*, December 4, 2006.

———. "Speed Demons: *Breaking Bad*." *LA Weekly*, January 16, 2008.

———. "UPN Sinks Teeth into WB's *Buffy*." *Variety*, April 23, 2001.

———. "WB Decides It's Time for *Angel* to Fly Away." *Variety*, February 16, 2004.

Adams, Val. "TV Heroes on the Run." *New York Times*, February 27, 1966.

Allan, Marc D. "*How I Met Your Mother* Creators Play Coy About Pair's Hookup as Season Draws to End." *Washington Post*, April 10, 2008.

Allen, Stewart. "The Occasional Viewer." *Arizona Republic*, August 30, 1967.

Alley, Robert S., and Irby B. Brown. *Love Is All Around: The Making of* The Mary Tyler Moore Show. New York: Delta, 1989.

All My Children. "Final Episode." Directed by Casey Childs. Written by Lorraine Broderick, Addie Walsh, Lisa Connor, Lucky Gold, Chip Hayes, and Jeff Beldner. ABC, September 23, 2011.

Alter, Ethan. "*Angel* Creator's Finale Post-Mortem." *TVGuide.com*, May 20, 2004. http://tvguide.com/news/joss-whedon-angel-40041/.

Andreeva, Nellie. "DONE: AMC & Sony TV Reach Deal for 16-Episode Final Order of *Breaking Bad*." *Deadline Hollywood*, August 14, 2011. http://deadline.com/2011/08/done-amc-sony-tv-reach-deal-for-16-episode-final-season-of-breaking-bad-157448/.

———. "It's Official: *Dexter*'s Eighth Season Will Be Its Last." *Deadline Hollywood*, April 18, 2013. http://deadline.com/2013/04/its-official-dexters-eighth-season-will-be-its-last-478253/.

——. "It's Official: *One Life to Live* and *All My Children* Won't Continue Online." *Deadline Hollywood*, November 23, 2011. http://deadline.com/2011/11/its-official-one-life-to-live-and-all-my-children-wont-continue-online-197987/.

Archerd, Army. "Just for Variety." *Variety*, August 25, 1967.

Armstrong, Jennifer Keishin. *Mary and Lou and Rhoda and Ted: And all the Brilliant Minds Who Made* The Mary Tyler Moore Show *a Classic*. New York: Simon & Schuster, 2013.

——. "Mary Richards' Best of Minneapolis." Minnesota.cbslocal.com, May 7, 2013.

——. "*Will & Grace*: Series Finale." *Entertainment Weekly*, June 2, 2006.

Associated Press. "*M*A*S*H* Stars Turn Out as Unit In Korea is Deactivated." *The Deseret News* (Salt Lake City, UT), June 11, 1997.

As the World Turns. "Episode no. 13,858. Directed by Christopher Goutman. Written by Leslie Nipkow, Josh Griffith, David Smilow, Penelope Koechi, and Susan Dansby. CBS, September 17, 2010.

Ausiello, Michael. "*The Office* Mystery: Is Steve Carell Returning for the Series Finale After All?" *TVLine*, April 17, 2013. http://tvline.com/2013/04/17/the-office-finale-steve-carell-returning-michael-scott/.

——. "Spoiler Alert: *Shield* Boss Answers Burning Finale Questions." *Entertainment Weekly*, January 17, 2015. http://www.ew.com/article/2008/11/26/shield-boss-ans.

Baker, Kathryn. "*St. Elsewhere* Just a Child's Fantasy." *Kokomo Tribune* (Kokomo, IN), May 26, 1988.

Barney, Chuck. "*How I Met Your Mother* Braces for Ambitious Finale." *Los Angeles Daily News*, March 28, 2014.

Bauder, David. "*How I Met Your Mother* Enjoying Best Year Ever." Associated Press, February 2, 2012.

——. "Michael C. Hall Ready to Say Goodbye to *Dexter*." Associated Press, September 18, 2013.

——. "Ross, Rachel Together on *Friends* Finale." Associated Press, May 7, 2004.

——. "TBS tries to attract viewers with a sanitized *Sex and the City*." Associated Press, June 13, 2004.

Bedell, Sally. "NBC Hopes *St. Elsewhere* Will Repeat *Hill Street Blues* Pattern." *Hutchinson News* (Hutchinson, KS), January 2, 1983.

Bellisario, Donald P., Interview with Shelly Jenkins. Archive of American Television, April 28, 2008.

Berg, Steve. "Minneapolis Keeps Hearth Warm for Mary." *Los Angeles Times*, February 3, 1977.

Bernstein, David. "Cast Away." *Chicago Magazine*, July 23, 2007.

Bianco, Robert. "*Lost* Finale: Redemption as 'The End' Justifies the Journey." *USA Today*, May 25, 2010.

———. "Rachel Stays, So *Friends* Are Able To Leave Together." *USA Today*, May 6, 2004.

Bianculli, David. "Far from Final." *New York Post*, May 3, 1988.

———. "*Magnum P.I.*" *Evening Independent*, June 24, 1986.

Biden, Joseph. "Transcript: David Gregory Interview with Joseph Biden." *Meet the Press* transcript. MSNBC.com, May 6, 2012. http://www.nbcnews .com/id/47311900/ns/meet_the_press-transcripts/t/may-joe-biden-kelly -ayotte-diane-swonk-tom-brokaw-chuck-todd/no.VUgU6UtiE3M.

Bierbaim, Tom. "World Series Keys NBC's First Neilsen Win in More Than Year." *Variety*, October 20, 1982.

Blanco, Robert. "*Newhart*—Series Ends After 8 Years." *The Intelligencer/Record*," May 21, 1990.

Biskind, Peter. "An American Family." *Vanity Fair*, April 2007.

Braxton, Greg. "Roseanne's Kiss: And Now the Aftermath." *Los Angeles Times*, March 3, 1994.

Brooks, James L. Interview by Karen Herman. Archive of American Television, January 17, 2003; February 12, 2003. http://www.emmytvlegends.org/ interviews/people/james-l-brooks.

Brownfield, Paul. "101 Best Written TV Series." Writers Guild of America, West, June 2013. http://www.wga.org/101tv.html.

Buck, Jerry. "Going Home, Showing Scars." *Winchester Star* (Winchester, VA), February 28, 1983.

Burrows, James. Interview by Gary Rutkowski. Archive of American Television. December 17, 2003. http://emmytvlegends.org/interviews/people/ james-burrows.

Cagle, Jess. "As Gay as It Gets." *Entertainment Weekly*, May 8, 1998.

Cardozo, Erica K., and Bruce Fretts. "The Best Closers and Cliff-Hangers of All Time." *Entertainment Weekly*, May 12, 1995.

Carman, John. "*Creek* Runs Hot / Hormone-Fueled Teen Drama Looks Like a Hit for WB." *San Francisco Chronicle*, January 20, 1998.

Carroll, Joseph. "The Iraq-Vietnam Comparison." *Gallup.com*, June 15, 2004. http://www.gallup.com/poll/11998/iraqvietnam-comparison.aspx.

Carsey, Marcy, and Tom Werner. Interview by Karen Herman. Archive of American Television, March 10, 2003. http://www.emmytvlegends.org/ interviews/people/marcy-carsey.

Carter, Bill. "*Friends* Cast Bands Together To Demand a Salary Increase." *New York Times*, July 16, 1996.

———. "*Friends* Finale's Audience Is the Fourth Biggest Ever." *New York Times*, May 8, 2004.

———. "Jay Leno Takes Final Bow on *Tonight Show*." *New York Times*, May 30, 2009.

———. "NBC Close to a Deal to Keep *Friends* for Another Season." *New York Times*, December 21, 2002.

———. "One Last Cringe for *The Office* Finale." *New York Times*, May 1, 2013.

———. "Seinfeld Says It's All Over, And It's No Joke for NBC." *New York Times*, December 26, 1997.

———. *The War for Late Night: When Leno Went Early and Television Went Crazy.* New York: Viking, 2010.

Carter, Bill, and Brian Stelter. "CBS Cancels *As the World Turns*, Proctor & Gamble's Last Soap Opera." *New York Times*, December 8, 2009.

"CBS-NBC Washing Up 2 TV Soapers." *Variety*, September 6, 1962.

Cerone, Daniel. "*Seinfeld* is Suddenly Something: Sitcom That's 'About Nothing' Finding More Fans in New Time Slot." *Los Angeles Times*, March 4, 1993.

Chaney, Jen. "Talking *Lost* with Damon Lindelof and Carlton Cuse." *Washington Post*, May 20, 2010.

Charles, Glen and Les Charles. Interview by Gary Rutkowski. Archive of American Television, December 8, 2003. http://emmytvlegends.org/interviews/les-charles.

Chase, David. Interview with Karen Herman. Archive of American Television, April 29, 2009. http://www.emmytvlegends.org/interviews/people/david-chase.

Clehane, Diane. "Gotham's Fashion Elite Dress Up for *Sex*: Film Incarnation of HBO Hit a Magnet for Top-tier Designers." *Variety*, April 23, 2008.

Collins, Monica. "A Hit in the Making—HBO's New *Sopranos* is One Mobster Story That Really Sings." *Boston Herald*, January 7, 1999.

———. "*St. Elsewhere*: A Critical Cliffhanger." *USA Today*, May 27, 1987.

Collins, Scott. "*The Tonight Show* Experiences Dark Days." *Los Angeles Times*, August 27, 2012.

Colucci, Jim. Will & Grace: *Fabulously Uncensored.* New York: Roundtable Press, 2004.

Corkery, Paul. *Carson: The Unauthorized Biography.* Ketchum, Idaho, 1986.

"*Coronet* & *Saint* Looking Good in Premiere Ratings." *Variety*, June 16, 1967.

"Correction." *Variety*, December 9, 1992.

Coyle, Jake. "*The Sopranos* Writer David Chase Talks HBO Series Finale." *Huffington Post*, December 17, 2012. http://www.huffingtonpost.com/2012/12/17/sopranos-david-chase_n_2317801.html.

"*Dallas* Goes Through the Roof." *Variety*, November 26, 1980.

Dark Shadows. "Episode no. 1245." Directed by Lela Swift. Written by Sam Hall. ABC, April 2, 1971.

Dark, Stephen. "Bellisario." *Primetime Magazine* (1984).

Day, Patrick Kevin. "*Dexter* Finale: Fans Unhappy With How It All Ended." *Los Angeles Times*, September 23, 2013.

Day-Preston, Becca. "*Dexter* Finale: A Betrayal of the Characters We Knew." The Guardian.com, September 30, 2013. http://www.theguardian.com/profile/becca-day-preston.

De Moraes, Lisa. "*Friends* Finale Hoopla Snags 52 Million Fans." *Washington Post*, May 8, 2004.

———. "Jay Leno's *Tonight Show* Exit: Carefully Orchestrated Do-Over." Deadline.com, February 5, 2014. http://deadline.com/2014/02/jay-leno-tonight-show-exit-jimmy-fallon-677093/.

———. "Oprah Keeps On Going and Going and . . ." *Washington Post*, May 25, 2011.

———. "Oprah to Wrap Up the Daytime Conversation." *Washington Post*, November 20, 2009.

———. "Sex and Death: HBO's Sunday Recipe Pays Off." *Washington Post*, June 6, 2001.

Deane, Bill. *Following* The Fugitive: *An Episode Guide and Handbook to the 1960s Television Series*. Jefferson, NC: McFarland, 1996.

Deggans, Eric. "So, Is That All We Get?" *Tampa Bay Times*, June 11, 2007.

———. "For Oprah, Saying Goodbye is Nothing Short of 'Spectacular.'" *Washington Post*, May 24, 2011.

Dempsey, John. "Fox Harvests Record Prices for *MASH*." *Variety*, February 23, 1983.

———. "*Wire* Solid for HBO." *Variety*, June 5, 2002.

Dempsey, John, and Rick Kissell. "*Sex* Finale is Tops for Series." *Variety*, February 25, 2004.

"*Doctors* and *Texas* Fading from NBC Lineup." *Variety*, November 24, 1982.

Donahue, Phil. "Oprah Winfrey: 2010 Time 100." *Time*, April 29, 2010.

Dow, Bonnie J. "How Will You Make It On Your Own?: Television and Feminism Since 1970." In *A Companion to Television*, edited by Janet Wasko, 379–394. Malden, MA: Blackwell, 2005.

Dratch, Rachel. *Girls Walks into a Bar . . . Comedy Calamities, Dating Disasters, and a Midlife Miracle*. New York: Gotham Books, 2012.

Du Brow, Rick. "*Cosby* Finale: Not All Drama Was in the Streets." *Los Angeles Times*, May 2, 1992.

Edelstein, David. "Give It to Me One More Time: *Sex and the City* is the Finale the Show Should've Had." *New York Magazine*, June, 2, 2008.

"*Edge of Night* Cancelled After 28 Yrs. on Air." *Variety*, October 29, 1984.

Edgerton, Gary R., and Jeffrey P. Jones. *The Essential HBO Reader*. Lexington: University of Kentucky Press, 2008.

Editorial: "High *Wire* Act." *Los Angeles Times*, September 2, 2006.

Elbert, Lynn. "*Friends* Finale Gives NBC Ratings Boost." Associated Press, May 11, 2004.

Elfman, Doug. "Ready for Crime-Time; CBS Devotes Two-Thirds of Prime-Time Programming to Whodunits." *Chicago Sun-Times*, May 17, 2007.

"*Elsewhere* Renewed." *Variety*, May 8, 1987.

Eng, Joyce. "Ratings: *30 Rock* Rises for Finale; *Big Bang* Beats *Idol; Do No Harm* Bombs." *TVGuide.com*, February 1, 2013. http://www.tvguide.com/index .php/news/ratings-30-rock-do-no-harm-1060239/.

Entertainment Weekly Staff. "The Art of Saying Goodbye." *Entertainment Weekly*, April 10, 2014.

"Famed *Fugitive* to Stop Running." *Hutchinson News* (Hutchinson, KS), August 19, 1967.

Fernandez, Maria Elena. "*All My Children* Finale: Interview with Agnes Nixon, Susan Lucci," *Newsweek*, September 11, 2011.

———. "The Set Mom on *How I Met Your Mother*." *Los Angeles Times*, October 19, 2008. http://articles.latimes.com/2008/oct/19/entertainment/ca-mother19.

Ferretti, Fred. "C.B.S. Shuffles Its Fall Line." *New York Times*, July 22, 1970.

Finke, Nikki. "HELL NO! Conan Refusing to Delay *Tonight Show*; What Does NBC Do Now?" Deadline.com, January 12, 2010. http://deadline. com/2010/01/conan-obrien-resigning-tonight-show-22196/.

———. "It's Not One Big Happy Family on Set of *Roseanne*." *Los Angeles Times*, January 31, 1989.

———. "THAAAT'S What We Were All Waiting For? Angry *Sopranos* Fans Crash HBO Website." *Deadline Hollywood*, June 10, 2007. http://deadline.com /2007/06/thats-what-we-were-waiting-for-angry-fans-crash-hbo-website-2519/.

Finn, Natalie. "*Will & Grace* Move On." E! Online News, May 17, 2006.http:// www.eonline.com/news/52362/will-grace-move-on.

Flint, Joe. "Jay Leno's New Time Slot Wreaks Havoc for NBC Affiliates." *Los Angeles Times*, October 19, 2009.

Flynn, Gillian. "*The Office*." *Entertainment Weekly*, March 15, 2005.

Fontana, Tom. Interview by Karen Herman. Archive of American Television, June 30, 2009. http://www.emmytvlegends.org/interviews/people/tom-fontana.

Fretts, Bruce. "The One Where They Say Goodbye." *TV Guide*, May 2, 2004.

Frey, Jennifer. "*Sex and the City*, Groaningly fulfilled." *Washington Post*, February 23, 2004.

"*Friends* Creators Share Show's Beginnings." *Dateline NBC*. NBC. New York: NBC New York: May 5, 2004.

"*Fugitive* Reaches Peak in Finale," *Variety*, September 6, 1967.

Gardner, Paul. "Man on the Run—*The Fugitive* Emerges as Season's Cross-Country Winner." *New York Times*, June 21, 1964.

Garron, Barry. "Top 10 TV Series of the Decade." *The Hollywood Reporter*, November 24, 2009.

Gay, Verne. "OMG, LOL, XOXO: The *Gossip Girl* Is a Guy: Dan Humphrey." *Newsday*, December 18, 2012. http://www.newsday.com/entertainment/tv/omg-lol-xoxo-the-gossip-girl-is-a-guy-dan-humphrey-1.4347377.

Gelbart, Larry. *Laughing Matters.* New York: Random House, 1998.

Genovese, John Kelly. "And Suddenly They Lived Happily Ever After . . ." *Soap Opera Digest*, September 24, 1985.

Gent, George. "A.B.C. Programs for Fall Listed." *New York Times*, April 3, 1967.

———. "TV Show to Take Secret to Grave." *New York Times*, July 15, 1967.

Genzlinger, Neil. "A Gritty Drug World, From All Sides." *New York Times*, May 31, 2002.

Gervais, Ricky. "As *The Office* Ends, Ricky Gervais Spills Secrets From the Show's Start." *Wall Street Journal*, September 6, 2012.

Gilatto, Tom. "To Be Continued?" *People*, December 23, 2002.

Gilbert, Matthew. "*Dawson's Creek*: A Flood of Hormones." *Boston Globe*, January 20, 1998.

———. "In Brainy *Studio 60*, Aaron Sorkin Reviles and Reveres TV." *Boston Globe*, September 18, 2006.

———. "*Lost* Finds Its Way to Adventure." *Boston Globe*, September 22, 2004.

———. "Series Finale Had Plenty of Will, Lacked Grace." *Boston Globe*, May 19, 2006.

———. "Stylishly Graphic *Dexter* Pleases with a Killer Twist." *Boston Globe*, September 30, 2006.

Giles, Matt. "Breaking Down the Multi-Billion Dollar *Seinfeld* Economy." *Vulture*, June 29, 2014. http://www.vulture.com/2014/06/breaking-down-the-seinfeld-economy.html.

Girard, Tom. "*Magnum*: The Hero in MCA Third Quarter." *Variety*, October 17, 1986.

Gitlin, Todd. "*Hill Street Blues*: 'Make It Look Messy.'" *Inside Prime-time*, New York: Pantheon, 1985.

Gliatto, Tom. "*30 Rock* Finale Makes People TV Critic 'Deliriously Happy.'" *People*, January 31, 2013.

Goldstein, Meredith. "Why More *Sex*? Why now?" *Boston Globe*, May 25, 2008.

Goodman, Tim. "Aaron Sorkin Makes Dazzling Comeback on *West Wing*–like Sophistication." *San Francisco Gate*, September 18, 2006.

———. "*Breaking Bad* Deconstruction: Ep. 9: 'Blood Money'." *The Hollywood Reporter*, August 11, 2013.

———. "Trouble on the Island Makes for Terrific TV." *San Francisco Chronicle*, September 22, 2004.

"*Gossip Girl* on CW." Parents Television Council, November 19, 2007. http://www.parentstv.org/ptc/publications/bw/2007/1119worst.asp.

Gould, Jack. "TV: Now It's Johnny Carson vs. Sleep." *New York Times*, October 3, 1962.

Gowran, Clay. "Fugitive Finds He Chases Wrong Man." *Chicago Tribune*, August 24, 1967.

Graham, Jefferson. *Frasier.* New York: Pocket Books, 1996.

Graham, Renee. "*Cosby Show* Comedy Had a Serious Impact: Sitcom Gently Delivered Star's Message." *Boston Globe*, August 2, 2005.

Grahnke, Lon. "*Cosby* Bows Out as NBC's Top Finale." *Chicago Sun-Times*, May 2, 1992.

———. "Roseanne's Farewell Party." *Chicago Sun-Times*, May 20, 1997.

Gray, Timothy. "Review: *Roseanne.*" *Variety*, October 20, 1988.

Greco, Patti. "*Breathe Me*: The Oral History of the *Six Feet Under* Finale's Death Montage." *Vulture*, December 17, 2013. http://www.vulture.com/2013/12/six-feet-under-death-montage-oral-history.html.

Greenberg, James. "This Magic Moment." *DGA Quarterly* (Spring 2015). http://www.dga.org/Craft/DGAQ/All-Articles/1502-Spring-2015/Shot-to-Remember-The-Sopranos.aspx.

Greenhouse, Emily. "Farewell, *Gossip Girl.*" *The New Yorker*, December 21, 2012.

———. "*Friends* Stunt Helps NBC Win Ratings Game." *Chicago Sun-Times*, January 31, 1996.

———. "Roseanne's Farewell Party." *Chicago Sun-Times*, May 20, 1997.

Greenberg, James. "This Magic Moment." *DGA Quarterly* (Spring 2015). http://www.dga.org/Craft/DGAQ/All-Articles/1502-Spring-2015/Shot-to-Remember-The-Sopranos.aspx.

Gritten, David. "He's Hawaii's *Magnum* Force, But Tom Selleck Is Far from Pacific." *People*, March 8, 1982.

Gysel, Dean. "A Significant Social Statement Was Lost." *Corpus Christi Caller-Times*, September 3, 1967.

Hale, Mike. "*The Office* Ends the Way It Began: Modestly." *New York Times*, May 17, 2013.

Haley, Kathy. "From Dayton to the World: A History of the *Donahue Show.*" *Broadcasting*, November 2, 1992.

———. "Talking with Phil." *Broadcasting*, November 2, 1992.

Hall, Sam. "Here's What Really Happened to Barnabas & Co." *TV Guide*, October 9, 1971.

Hamil, Denis. "Do We Look Dead?" *New York Daily News*, June 15, 2007.

Hano, Arnold. "David's Drooping . . . Success has left *Fugitive* Janssen Tired, Tense, and Physically Ailing." *TV Guide*, March 6–12, 1967.

Harper, Valerie. *I, Rhoda.* New York: Gallery Books, 2013.

"Hawaii's *Magnum, P. I.* Home Sold to Obama's Close Friend," *New York Times*, March 19, 2015.

Hernandez, Greg. "Cranston Has Reason to Be Cheerful." *Los Angeles Daily News*, January 17, 2008.

Hibberd, James. "*Gossip Girl* Finale Hits Season High." *Entertainment Weekly*, December 18, 2012.

———. "*How I Met Your Mother* Officially Renewed for Final Season." *Entertainment Weekly*, January 30, 2013. http://www.ew.com/article/2013/01/30/how-i-met-your-mother-final-season.

———. "*Mad Men* Finale Ratings Below Show's Peak." *Entertainment Weekly*, May 19, 2015. http://www.ew.com/article/2015/05/19/mad-men-finale-ratings?asw.

Hinckley, David. "*Dexter* Series Finale Draws in Record 2.8 Million Viewers." *New York Daily News*, September 23, 2013.

Hirschberg, Lynn. "Desperate to Seem 16." *New York Times*, September 5, 1999.

———. "Heeeere's . . . Conan!!!" *New York Times*, May 20, 2009.

Horowitz, Joy. "June Cleaver Without Pearls." *New York Times*, October 16, 1988.

Horowitz, Murray. "TV 'Season' An Outdated Concept: Short Cycle Series Not Far Off." *Weekly Variety*, August 2, 1967.

Huggins, Roy. Interview by Lee Goldberg. Archive of American Television, July 21, 1998. http://emmytvlegends.org/interviews/people/roy-huggins.

Hyatt, Wesley. *The Encyclopedia of Daytime Television*. New York: Billboard Books, 1997.

Iredale, Jessica. "*Sex and the City*: For Better and For Worse Dressed." *Women's Wear Daily*, May 23, 2008.

Itzkoff, Dave. "Jon Hamm Talks about the *Mad Men* Series Finale." *New York Times*, May 18, 2015. http://artsbeat.blogs.nytimes.com/2015/05/18/mad-men-finale-jonhamm-interview/?_r=4.

Jacobs, A. J. "Launching *Sex and the City*." *Entertainment Weekly*, June 5, 1998.

Jacobson, Murrey. "The Oprah Effect, by the Numbers." PBS.org, May 25, 2011.

James, Caryn. "Death and All the Stuff That Comes Before and After." *New York Times*, June 1, 2001.

———. "Goodbye Already! For *Seinfeld* and Others, Parting Is Such Sweet Sitcom." *New York Times*, May 12, 1998.

———. "*Seinfeld* Goes Out in Self-Referential Style." *New York Times*, May 15, 1998.

———. "Television Review; Young, Handsome and Clueless in *Peyton Place*." *New York Times*, January 20, 1998.

———. "TV Weekend: In Pursuit of Love, Romantically or Not." *New York Times*, June 5, 1998.

———. "TV Weekend; No Horse Heads, But Plenty of Prozac." *New York Times*, January 8, 1999.

Jicha, Tom. "They Leave As They Began: With a Buzz." *Baltimore Sun*, May 2, 2004.

Johnson, Kevin V. "Fans Sink Their Teeth into Bootlegged *Buffy*." *USA Today*, June 3, 1999.

Johnson, Steve. "HBO is Still Firmly on Top with *Six Feet Under*." *Chicago Tribune*, May 30, 2001.

———. "HBO's *The Wire* Gives New Twist to the Cop Show Genre." *Chicago Tribune*, May 31, 2002.

Johnson, Ted. "*Will & Grace* Creators Thrilled at Biden's Shout Out, No So Thrilled at Obama's 'Evolving' Stance." *Variety*, May 7, 2012.

Johnston, Robert. "'Goodbye, Farewell and Amen' Ratings Analysis." Mash4077TV.com. http://www.mash4077tv.com/articles/gfa_ratings/.

Kaiser, Charles. *The Gay Metropolis: The Landmark History of Gay Life in America*. New York: Grove Press, 2007.

Kaufman, Dave. "*Cheers* Star Shelley Long Cheery Despite Low Numbers." *Variety*, February 2, 1983.

Kemp, Barry. Interview by Nancy Harrington. Archive of American Television. June 13, 2011.http://www.emmytvlegends.org/interviews/people/barry -kemp.

Kerr, Peter. "NBC Comedy *Cheers* Turns into a Success." *New York Times*, November 29, 1983.

King, Susan. "A Last Round for *Cheers*." *Los Angeles Times*, May 16, 1993.

Kissell, Rick. "*Breaking Bad* Finale Soars to Series-Best 10.3 Million Viewers." *Variety*, September 30, 2013.

———. "*Buffy* Boffo in UPN Preem." *Variety*, October 4, 2001.

———. "*Lost* in Flight: ABC Debut Soars but Eye Wins Night." *Variety*, September 24, 2004.

———. "Peacock's Not Laffing." *Variety*, October 20, 2006.

———. "Peacock's *Rock* Solid in Premiere." *Variety*, October 13, 2006.

———. "Wrap Session a Hit: *Friends* Finale Draws TV's Top Aud in 6 Years." *Variety*, May 10, 2004.

———. "*Will* Has Its Way in Finale." *Daily Variety*, May 22, 2006.

Knight, Bob. "Something Clearly Out of the Ordinary." *Variety*, February 23, 1983.

Kolbert, Elizabeth. "A Sitcom Is Born: Only Time Will Tell the Road To Prime Time." *New York Times*, May 23, 1994.

———. "Birth of a TV Show: A Drama All Its Own." *New York Times*, March, 8, 1994.

———. "The Conception and Delivery of a Sitcom: Everyone's a Critic." *New York Times*, May 9, 1994.

——. "Finding the Absolutely Perfect Actor: The High Stress Business of Casting." *New York Times*, April 6, 1994.

Kraft, Scott. "From Coast to Coast: A Rash of *M-A-S-H* Bashes." *Galveston Daily*, February 28, 1983.

Kronke, David. "'Big' Satisfaction But Sugar Overdose End Popular *Sex*." *Los Angeles Daily News*, February 23, 2004.

——. "CBS Hopes Everybody Forgets Raymond." *Los Angeles Daily News*, September 19, 2005.

Kung, Michelle. "*Monk* Finale Breaks Basic Cable Ratings Record." *Wall Street Journal*, December 7, 2009.

Laxson, Joan. "Medicine and Health." In *American Decades*, 1980–1989, edited by Victor Bondi, 461–532. Detroit, MI: Gale Research Inc., 1996.

Learmonth, Michael. "*Rock, Lights* in the Stream with NBC." *Variety*, December 21, 2006.

Lee, Ashley. "*Mad Men* Creator Matthew Weiner Explains Series Finale, Character Surprises and What's Next." *The Hollywood Reporter*, May 20, 2015. http://www.hollywoodreporter.com/news/mad-men-series-finale -matthew-797302.

Lee, David. Interview by Jim McKairnes. Archive of American Television, July 9, 2010. http://emmytvlegends.org/interviews/people/david-lee.

"Left in the Dark as Fugitive Tells Secret." *Chicago Tribune*, August 30, 1967.

Leno Calls Telecast on *Cheers* 'a Mistake': Drunken Cast Members Ruined *Tonight* Broadcast from Boston Bar, He Says." *Los Angeles Times*, May 28, 1993.

Leon, Melissa. "Michael C. Hall on Where *Dexter* Went Wrong and His New Killer Role in *Cold in July*." *The Daily Beast*, May 23, 2014. http://thedaily-beast/articles/2014/05/23/michael-c-hall-on-where-dexter-went-wrong-and-his-new-killer-role-in-cold-of-july-html.

Levine, Ken. "A *Cheers* Writer's Memory of the Show's Emotional and Drunken Finale Night." *Vulture*, March 18, 2013. http://www.vulture .com/2013/03/cheers-writers-memory-of-finale-night.html.

——. ". . . by Ken Levine." January 3, 2014. http://kenlevine.blogspot.com/ search?updated-max=2014-01-18T06:00:00-08:00.

——. ". . . by Ken Levine." September 30, 2012. http://kenlevine.blogspot .com/2012_09_01_archive.html.

Lewin, Soshana. "Sitcoms on Vacation, Part 2" MousePlanet.com, September 16, 2003. http://www.mouseplanet.com/7184/Sitcoms_on_ Vacation_ Part_2.

Lindelof, Damon. "Damon Lindelof on Why *Breaking Bad*'s Finale Let Him Say Goodbye to *Lost*." *The Hollywood Reporter*, October 2, 2013.

Lipton, Michael A. "*Creek* God." *People*, March 23, 1998.

Littlefield, Warren. Interview by Dan Harrison. Archive of American Television, December 12, 2011. http://www.emmytvlegends.org/interviews/people/warren-littlefieldno.

Lloyd, Robert. "Sad and Disturbing Chemistry." *Los Angeles Times*, January 18, 2008.

Love Is a Many Splendored Thing. Episode no. 1430. Directed by Peter Levin and Portman Paget. Written by Jerry Adelman, Kenneth Hartman, and Ann Marcus. CBS. March 23, 1973.

Lowry, Brian. "*Cheers* is Toast: NBC Pulls Plug." *Variety*, December 8, 1992.

———. "*Cheers* Seals NBC's Sweeps Win." *Variety*, May 24, 1993.

———. "*Cheers* Up for Refill." *Variety*, November 10, 1992.

———. "Grammys' Ratings Off Key." *Variety*, March 3, 1994.

———. "More *Roseanne* for ABC, C-W." *Variety*, March 13, 1996.

———. "Review: *Dexter*." *Variety*, September 27, 2006.

———. "Review: *Gossip Girl*." *Variety*, September 14, 2007.

———. "Review: *How I Met Your Mother*." *Variety*, September 19, 2005.

———. "Review: *The Office* Finale." *Variety*, May 16, 2013.

———. "Review: *The Wire*." *Variety*, September 7, 2006.

Lowry, Cynthia. "*The Fugitive* Stops Running; Series End." *Biloxi-Gulfport Daily Herald*, August 30, 1967.

Lyons, Margaret. "The *How I Met Your Mother* Finale Bailed on the Entire Show." *Vulture*, April 1, 2014. http://www.vulture.com/2014/03/how-i-met-your-mother-finale-review.html.

Marder, Keith. "NBC Will Air *Seinfeld* Finale Again Wednesday." *Los Angeles Daily News*, May 16, 1998.

Martin, Brett. *Difficult Men: Behind the Scenes of a Creative Revolution: From* The Sopranos *to* The Wire *to* Mad Men *and* Breaking Bad. New York: Penguin Press, 2013.

———. The Sopranos: *The Complete Book.* New York: Time, Inc. Home Entertainment, 2007.

Martin, Denise. "*Dexter* Builds Case: Showtime Taps Michael C. Hall to Star in Television Series." *Variety*, August 8, 2005.

———. "*Dexter* Draws More Life." *Variety*, November 3, 2006.

———. "Showtime Spices Up: Pilot Slate Includes Serial Killer, Escort Dramas." *Variety*, June 13, 2005.

Martin, Dick. Interview by Karen Herman. Archive of American Television, September25, 2002. http://www.emmytvlegends.org/interviews/.

Martin, George R. R., "*Breaking Bad*," Not a Blog (blog), September 16, 2013, http://grrm.livejournal.com/2013/09/16/.

Maslin, Janet. "She's Hunting Vampires, and on a School Night." *New York Times*, July 31, 1992.

"Master List by Rank." Phi Phenomenon, n. d., Phi-phenomenon, org/buffy.

Maynard, John. "*Dexter*: He'd Kill to Solve This Case." *Washington Post*, September 30, 2006.

McCarthy, Todd. Review of *Buffy the Vampire Slayer*. *Variety*, July 31, 1992.

McFarland, Melanie. "On TV: NBC Shows Some Muscle This Fall with Ambitious, Entertaining Dramas." *Seattle Post-Intelligencer*, September 17, 2006.

McIntyre, Gina. "Michael C. Hall Slices and Dices the Departing *Dexter*." *Los Angeles Times*, September 20, 2013.

McNamara, Mary. "*Dexter* Finale: Please, Give Jennifer Carpenter an Emmy Nomination." *Los Angeles Times*, September 23, 2013.

———. "*Lost* Loves." *Los Angeles Times*, May 24, 2010.

———. "*Sopranos* Fans Chase After an Explanation." *Los Angeles Times*, June 13, 2007.

———. " *Sopranos*: What Was That All About?" *Los Angeles Times*. June 11, 2007.

McNary, Dave. "Foursome Set for more *Sex*." *Variety*, February 6, 2009.

Mendoza, N. F. "WITH AN EYE ON . . . : Meet David Hyde Pierce, an Actor Who 'Out-Pompouses' the Pompous One on *Frasier*." *Los Angeles Times*, December 12, 1993.

Miller, Liz Shannon. "It's Time to Forgive the *How I Met Your Mother* Series Finale." *Indiewire*, November 26, 2014. http://www.indiewire. com/article/its-time-to-forgive-the-how-i-met-your-mother-series-finale-20141126.

Moore, Frazier. "A New Carrie Glows in a *Sex and the City* Prequel." Associated Press, January 11, 2013.

———. "*Breaking Bad* Finale vs. Other Finales." Associated Press, October 2, 2013.

———. "Carrie Ends up with Big in *Sex* Finale." Associated Press, February 23, 2004.

———. "*Dexter* Finale Cuts Its Own Throat in Sappy Series Ending.Associated Press, September 23, 2013.

———. "*Friends* Finale Ties Up Major Loose Ends." Associated Press, May 7, 2004.

———. "Life after *The Oprah Winfrey Show*: It will go on." Associated Press, May 24, 2011.

———. "*Lost* Finale Stirs Much Debate the Day After." Associated Press, May 24, 2010.

———. "Paper Wrap: *The Office* ends its 8-year run." Associated Press, May 16, 2013.

Morse, Barry, Robert E. Wood, and Anthony Wynn. *Pulling Faces, Making Noises: A Life on Stage, Screen and Radio*. Lincoln, NE: iUniverse, Inc., 2004.

Murphy-Gill, Meghan. "Oprah's 'Farewell Spectacular': A night to celebrate, and bid adieu." *Entertainment Weekly*, May 18, 2011.

"My Concerns with *Chosen*," Phi Phenomenon, n. d., http://www.phi-phenomenon.org/rank/.

Neuwirth, Allan. *They'll Never Put That on the Air: The New Age of TV Comedy*. New York: Allworth Press, 2010.

Newhart, Bob. Interview by Dan Pasternack. Archive of American Television, May 29, 2001. http://www.emmytvlegends.org/interviews/people/bob-newhart.

———. *I Shouldn't Even Be Doing This!: And Other Things That Strike Me as Funny*. New York: Hachette Book Group, 2006.

"*Newhart* Calls It Quits." *Weekly Variety*, March 7, 1990.

"*Newhart* Ending Run on CBS-TV," *Variety*, March 5, 1990.

Ng, Philiana. "*Gossip Girl* Series Finale: Mysterious Blogger's Identity Finally Revealed." *The Hollywood Reporter*, December 17, 2012. http://www.hollywoodreporter.com/live-feed/gossip-girl-series-finale-recap-403408.

Nichols, John. "Phil Donahue's War." *The Nation*. April 28, 2008. http://www.thenation.com/article/phil-donahues-war.

Niedt, Bob. "*Roseanne* Funny, Believable." *Syracuse Herald-Journal*, October 18, 1988.

"Nielsen Issues Most Popular Lists for 2006." *PR Newswire*, December 20, 2006. http://www.prnewswire.com/news-releases/nielsen-issues-most-popular-lists-for-2006-72262467.html.

Nimmo, Dan D., and Chevelle Newsome. *Political Commentators in the United States in the 20th Century*. Westport, CT: Greenwood, 1997.

Nochimson, Martha P. "Did Tony Die at the end of *The Sopranos*?" *Vox*, August 27, 2014. http://www.vox.com/2014/8/27/6006139/did-tony-die-at-the-end-of-the-sopranos.

Nussbaum, Emily. "Difficult Women: How *Sex and the City* Lost Its Good Name." *The New Yorker*, June 29, 2013.

———. "High-Wire Act: Neil Patrick Harris." *New York Magazine*, September 13, 2009.

———. "My *Breaking Bad* Bender." *New York*, July 24, 2011.

Obama, Barack. "Transcript: Robin Roberts ABC News Interview with President Obama." ABC News. May 9, 2012. Accessed December 27, 2011. http://abcnews.go.com/Politics/transcript-robin-roberts-abc-news-interview-president-obama/story?id=16316043.

O'Connor, John J. "A *Cheers* Spinoff, Set in Seattle." *New York Times*, October 21, 1993.

———. "Ed Flanders as Dr. Westphall in *St. Elsewhere*." *New York Times*, May 25, 1988.

———. "*Cheers* is Dead, but There's Always the Wake . . ." *New York Times*, May 21, 1993.

———. "Last *Cosby* Episode Bring the Huxtables A Happy Ending." *New York Times*, April 30, 1992.

———. "Roseanne Smirks Through the Trials of Life." *New York Times*, October 18, 1988.

———. "TV: 2 Comedy Series Have Their Premieres." *New York Times*, September 30, 1982.

———. "TV Weekend." *New York Times*, March 18, 1977.

Oldenburg, Ann. "And Now, The One Where *Friends* Says Goodbye." *USA Today*, May 5, 2004.

"*Oprah Winfrey* finale seen by 16 million viewers." Associated Press, June 8, 2011.

Ostrow, Joanne. "*Sopranos* End Isn't Out of Whack." *Denver Post*, June 12, 2007.

Oswald, Brad. "Barr refreshes as 'real' TV mom." *Winnipeg Free Press*, October 17, 1988.

Owen, Rob. "*30 Rock* Rules." *Pittsburgh Post-Gazette*, October 8, 2006.

———. "*Will & Grace* Reaches Finale Already Having Left Its Mark." *Telegraph-Journal*, May 18, 2006.

Patten, Dominic. "Leno's *Tonight Show* Exit Gets 14.6M Viewers, Best Result Since *Seinfeld* Finale Visit in 1998." Deadline.com, February 7, 2014. http://deadline.com/2014/02/jay-lenos-tonight-show-farewell-ratings-jimmy-fallon-best-ever-result-678957/.

———. "Leno's *Tonight Show* Exit Gets 14.6M Viewers, Best Result Since *Seinfeld* Finale Visit in 1998." *Deadline.com*, February 7, 2014.

Penton, Edgar. "Don't Ask Carson What Show Will Be Like." *Bristol Daily Courier* (Bristol, PA), September 29, 1962.

Perigard, Mark A. "Can *Lost* Finale Satisfy Everyone?" *Boston Herald*, May 21, 2010.

Peyser, Marc. "Must See or Must Flee: The Fall TV Season is Upon Us." *Newsweek*, September 20, 2004.

Pleshette, Suzanne. Interview by Stephen J. Abramson. Archive of American Television. February 9, 2006. http://www.emmytvlegends.org/interviews/people/suzanne-pleshette.

Poll, Julie. *Another World.* New York: HarperEntertainment, 1999.

———. *As the World Turns.* Los Angeles: General Publishing Group, 1996.

Poniewozik, James. "All-*Time* 100 TV Shows." *Time*, September 6, 2007.

———. "*Breaking Bad*'s White-Hot Slow Burn." Time, March 19, 2010.

———. "*Breaking* Record: What Boosted Walter White's Ratings?" *Time*, August 13, 2013.

———. "Do Not Adjust Your Set." *Time*, September 18, 2006.

———. "*The Office* Watch: That's What She Said." *Time*, May 17, 2013.

———. "*30 Rock* Finale: I Lizzed, I Cried." *Time*, January 31, 2013.

Poston, Tom. Interview by Stephen J. Abramson. Archive of American Television. February 9, 2006. http://www.emmytvlegends.org/interviews/people/tom-poston.

Potts, Mark. "Humana Sues NBC Over Name; A Surgical Strike Against *St. Elsewhere*." *Washington Post*, October 1, 1987.

Powers, Lindsay. "Oprah Winfrey's Last Show: I Won't Say Goodbye." *The Hollywood Reporter*, May 25, 2011.

Pressler, Jessica, and Chris Rovzar. "The Genius of *Gossip Girl*." *New York Times*, April 21, 2008.

Proctor, Mel. *The Official Fan's Guide to* The Fugitive. Bloomington, IN: Authors Choice Press, 2009.

"Profile of Cast from Hit TV Sitcom *Friends*." CNN. New York: CNN, September 20, 2003.

Purnick, Joyce. "The Legacy of Mary Richards." *New York Times*, February 20, 1991.

Raftery, Brian. "The Best TV Show That's Ever Been." *GQ*, September, 2012.

Remnick, David. "Family Guy." *The New Yorker*, June 4, 2007.

"Review of "The Judgment," *The Fugitive*. *Variety*, August 31, 1967.

Reynolds, Gene. Interview with Henry Colman. Archive of American Television video, August 22, 2000. http://www.emmytvlegends.org/ interviews/people/gene-reynolds.

Rhodes, Joe. "Shattering All Vestiges of Innocence." *The New York Times*, July 15, 2011.

Rice, Lynette. "*As the World Turns*: Kathryn Hays, a.k.a. Kim Hughes, Reflects on Final Day of Taping." *Entertainment Weekly*, August 31, 2010.

———. "*Friends* Demand a Raise." *Entertainment Weekly*, April 21, 2000.

———. "The WB's *Buffy* is Still Negotiating Its Future." *Entertainment Weekly*, March 21, 2001.

Richmond, Ray. "*Mad* Baby Slays the Conners." *Variety*, May 22, 1997.

Robertson, Nan. "Donahue vs. Winfrey: A Clash of the Talk Titans." *New York Times*, February 1, 1988.

Robins, J. Max, and Jim Benson. "*Cheers* Begets Sitcom." *Variety*, January 27, 1993. http://www.emmytvlegends.org/interviews/people/david-lee.

Robinson, Tasha. "Joss Whedon (Interview)" The A.V. Club, September 5, 2001. http://www.avclub.com/article/joss-whedon-13730.

Rosen, Christopher. "What the Real Guy Behind that Coke Commercial Thought of *Mad Men*." *Entertainment Weekly*, May 18, 2015. http://www.ew.com/article/2015/05/18/bill-backer-coke-commercial-mad-men.

Rosenberg, Howard. "*Frasier* brings Cheer, *Sinbad* Warmth Series: The New Season: One of a Series." *Los Angeles Times*, September 16, 1993.

———. "*Providence* Is Flat But *Sopranos* Really Sings." *Los Angeles Times*, January 8, 1999.

———. "*Roseanne*: Rare, Rip-Roaring Everywoman." Los Angeles Times, October 18, 1988.

———. "TV Review: It's Jerry Seinfeld's Show—and It's a Winner." *Los Angeles Times*, May 31, 1990.

———. "TV Reviews: NBC's Strongest Evening of the Week Has Its Weak Spot." *Los Angeles Times*, September 22, 1994.

Rosenthal, Phil. "NBC's *Studio 60* Fails to Reveal Dramatic Ratings." *Chicago Tribune*, October 18, 2006.

———. "NBC Executive Stands Apart By Taking Stands." *Chicago Tribune*, August 21, 2005.

Rothenberg, Fred. "Cheers for *Cheers*." *Walla Walla Union Bulletin* (Walla, Walla, WA), September 30, 1982.

Rothman, Lily. "*Breaking Bad*: What Does That Phrase Actually Mean?" *Time*, September 23, 2013.

Roush, Matt. "Cheers to NBC's *Frasier*." *USA Today*, September 16, 1993.

Rucker, Philip. "Die-Hard *Sopranos* Fans Take In Finale: Was It a Hit?" *Washington Post*, June 11, 2007.

Ruditis, Paul. Buffy the Vampire Slayer: *The Watcher's Guide, Vol. 3*. New York: Simon Spotlight, 2004.

Ruth, Daniel. "A New Hit? Fat Chance. Barr Squashes *Roseanne*." *Chicago Sun-Times*, October 18, 1988.

———. "The Best and Worst Series Shown on Television in 1988." *Chicago Sun-Times*, October 18, 1988.

———. "TV Critic Takes a Pounding from Angry *Roseanne* Fans." *Chicago Sun-Times*, January 3, 1989.

Schemering, Christopher. *The Soap Opera Encyclopedia*. New York: Ballantine, 1987.

Schneider, Michael. "NBC Still *Friends* for $10 Mil Per Seg." *Variety*, December 21, 2002.

———. "Long-running *Light* Goes Dark at CBS." *Variety*, April 2, 2009.

———. "Dratch Latched to Multiple *Rock* Roles." *Variety*, August 15, 2006.

Schwarzbaum, Lisa. "*The Cosby Show* Comes to an End." *Entertainment Weekly*, May 1, 1992.

Scott, Tony. "Review: *Cheers*." *Variety*, September 30, 1982.

———. "Review: *Cheers*, One for the Road." *Variety*, May 24, 1993.

———. "Review: *Frasier*." *Variety*, September 16, 1993.

———. "Review: *Friends*." *Variety*, September 22, 1994.

Scott, Vernon. "End in Sight for TV's *MASH*." *Pittsburgh Press*, March 13, 1982.

Segal, David. "The Dark Art of *Breaking Bad*." *The New York Times*, July 6, 2011.

Seibel, Deborah Starr. "Closing Time at Cheers." *TV Guide*, May 15, 1993.

Seinfeld, Jerry, and David H. Kennerly. *Sein off: The Final Days of Seinfeld*. New York: Harper Entertainment, 1998.

Sepinwall, Alan. "*How I Met Your Mother*—Last Forever: How They Conned Us All." *Hitfix*, March 31, 2014. http://www.hitfix.com/whats-alan-watching/series-finale-review-how-i-met-your-mother-last-forever-how-they-conned-us-all.

———. "David Chase Speaks!" *Star-Ledger*, June 11, 2007.

———. "*The Wire*, "-30-": Farewell to Baltimore." *What's Alan Watching*, March 9. 2008. http://sepinwall.blogspot.com/2008/03/wire-30-farewell-to-baltimore.html

"76 Million Tune in to Final *Seinfeld*." *Chicago Sun-Times*, May 16, 1998.

"*Sex and the City* Gets Sanitized for TBS." *USA Today*, June 14, 2004.

Seymour, Gene. "Final Episode of *St. Elsewhere* Used Private Humor, Mind-Twist." *Sandusky Register* (Sandusky, OH), May 24, 1988.

Shales, Tom. "A Big Hug Goodbye to *Friends* and Maybe to the Sitcom." *The Washington Post*, May 7, 2004.

———. "Gift of the Goddess; Barr's *Roseanne*, a Sitcom Winner for ABC." *Washington Post*, October 18, 1988.

———. "*How I Met Your Mother*: A Sweet Introduction." *Washington Post*, September 19, 2005.

———. "Mary Tyler's No More." *Washington Post*, March 19, 1977.

———. "On HBO, Meaningless *Sex*." *Washington Post*, June 6, 1998.

———. "Supporting Actors Prop Up the Show in NBC's *30 Rock*." *Washington Post*, October 11, 2006.

———. "Television, At the Heart of the Story." *Washington Post*, May 2, 1992.

———. "There's a Meth to AMC's Madness in *Breaking Bad*." *Washington Post*, January 19, 2008.

———. "Three *Cheers* New Comedy Leads NBC's Big Night." *Washington Post*, September 30, 1982.

———. "The Morning After *Cheers*; No Hangovers, Just a Warm Glow." *Washington Post*, May 22, 1993.

———. "*The Office*: NBC's Passable Duplicate Of the Brit Hit." *The Washington Post*, March 24, 2005.

———. "*Six Feet Under*: HBO Provides a Death Benefit." *Washington Post*, June 3, 2001.

Shaw, Jessica. "*Gossip Girl*: A hit for the blog generation." *Entertainment Weekly*, November 20, 2007.

Sheffield, Rob. "Goodbye, Michael Scott: Steve Carell Has Left the Building." *Rolling Stone*, April 29, 2011.

Simmons, Bill. *The B.S. Report*. Podcast audio, Los Angeles, December 17, 2014.

Simmons, Bill, and Larry David. *The B.S. Report.* Podcast audio. Los Angeles, December 14, 2014.

Simonini, Ross. "The Sitcom Digresses." *New York Times,* November 23, 2008.

Snierson, Dan. "Bryan Cranston and Aaron Paul." *Entertainment Weekly,* September 30, 2013.

———. "*St. Elsewhere* Reunion: Cast Members Reflect on That Controversial Snow-Globe Ending." *Entertainment Weekly,* October 12, 2012.

Solomonson, Ed, and Mark O'Neill. *TV's* M*A*S*H: *The Ultimate Guide Book.* Albany, Georgia: BearManor Media, 2009.

"Spaniards' Fugue on Fugitive." *Weekly Variety,* November 15, 1967.

Spencer, Walter. "TV's Vast Grey Belt." *Television Magazine* (August 1967).

Stanley, Alessandra. "A Comedy's Final Twists Lead to Love and Ratings." *New York Times,* April 1, 2014.

———. "He Kills People and Cuts Them Up. But They Deserve It. Besides, He's Neat." *New York Times,* September 29, 2006.

———. "One Last Family Gathering." *New York Times,* June 11, 2007.

———. "So Many Characters, Yet So Little Resolution." *New York Times,* March 10, 2008.

———. "Tina Fey Signs Off, Broken Barriers Behind Her." *New York Times,* January 30, 2013.

———. "TV Antics: A Sitcom Mocks Its Milieu." *New York Times,* October 11, 2006.

Sternbergh, Adam. "A Killer Role." *New York Magazine,* October 2, 2006.

———. "The Anti-*Sopranos.*" *Vulture,* March 10, 2008. http://www.vulture .com /2008/03/ sternbergh_on_the_wire_finale.html.

Stuever, Hank. "*The Office* Finale: There's A Lot of Beauty in Ordinary Things." *Washington Post,* May 18, 2013.

Stewart, Anna. "Will Finds His Way." *Variety Plus,* April 7, 2005.

Stoddard, Sylvia. "*Magnum, P.I.*" *Television Chronicles* No. 9, 1997.

"Surprises in store of *Oprah* finales." *Chicago Sun-Times,* February 25, 2011.

Swanson, Dorothy Collins. *The Story of Viewers for Quality Television: From Grassroots to Prime Time.* Syracuse, NY: Syracuse University Press, 2000.

Sweeney, Don. *Backstage at* The Tonight Show. New York: Taylor, 2006.

Talbot, Margaret. "Stealing Life: The Crusader Behind *The Wire.*" *The New Yorker,* October 22, 2007.

Tanzer, Myles. "Oprah's Last Episode: Like a Last Lecture That Isn't Final at All." *The Village Voice,* May 25, 2011.

Taylor, Charles. "The WB's Big Daddy Condescension." *Salon,* May 26, 1999.

"Television: Edgeville: U.S.A. [Review of *The Edge of Night*]." *Time,* March 17, 1961.

"Tempus *Fugitive.*" *Variety*, September 6, 1967.

"10 Questions for . . . Joss Whedon." *New York Times*, May 16, 2003.

Terry, Clifford. "Snippy *Roseanne* Premieres Tonight." *Post-Standard*, October 18, 1988.

"The Oral History of *Friends*: Jennifer Aniston Almost Didn't Play Rachel Green." *Vanity Fair*, April 4, 2012.

"*The Sopranos*: Definitive Explanation of 'The End'," May 11, 2008. http://masterofsopranos.wordpress.com

Thomas, Bob. "McLean Stevenson's Alive and Working for NBC Now." *Televues*, May 11, 1975.

Thompson, David. *Altman on Altman.* New York: Faber & Faber, 2006.

Thompson, Robert. "Rx for Success." *Washington Post*, December 17, 2006.

———. *Television's Second Golden Age: From* Hill Street Blues *to* ER. Syracuse, NY: Syracuse University Press, 1997.

"Top 10 Best & Worst Family Shows on Network Television: 1998–1999 TV Season." *Parents Television Council*, n. d., http://www.parentstv.org/ptc/publications/reports/top10 bestandworst/98top/main.asp.

"Top 10 Unrealistic Soap Opera Plot Lines." Soap.com, July 11, 2012. http://soaps.sheknows.com/latestnews/id/26593/.

"Tour Boston's Top 5 Attractions." Travelchannel.com, n. d., http://www.travelchannel.com/destinations/us/ma/boston/articles/tour-bostons-top-5-attractions.

Townsend, Sylvia. "Introduction to Richard Sylbert." In *Designing Movies: Portrait of a Hollywood Artist*, edited by Richard Sylbert and Sylvia Townsend, 13–28. Westport, CT: Praeger, 2006.

Travers, Peter. "Review of *Buffy the Vampire Slayer.*" *Rolling Stone*, July 31, 1992.

Tucker, Ken. "*Seinfeld*: The Finale." *Entertainment Weekly*, May 29, 1998.

———. "*Sex and the City/Six Feet Under.*" *Entertainment Weekly*, June 21, 2001.

———. "Sunday Best?" *Entertainment Weekly*, June 1, 2001.

———. "TV Show Review: Winning *Friends.*" *Entertainment Weekly*, October 21, 1994.

"2011's Best Episodes: Oprah's Last Lesson in Gratitude." *TV Guide*, December 25, 2011.

VanDerWerff, Todd. "David Chase Responds to Our *Sopranos* Piece." *Vox*, August 27, 2014. http://www.vox.com/2014/8/27/6076621/david-chase-responds-to-our-sopranos-piece.

Vejnoska, Jill. "*Sopranos* Ends with Blast of Brilliance." *Atlanta Journal-Constitution*, June 12, 2007.

Wallenstein, Andrew. "ABC Scrubs Two Soaps." *Variety*, April 15, 2011.

Warren, Ellen, and James Warren. "*Hill Street* Creator Pays 1st Visit to Police Station He Made Famous." *Chicago Tribune*, August 28, 1996.

Wharton, Dennis. "Hatch Scores Drug Messages." *Variety*, January 26, 1996.

Whedon, Joss. "Director's Commentary." "The Chosen." DVD, Disc 6. *Buffy the Vampire Slayer, Season 7*. Los Angeles: Twentieth Century Fox, 2003.

Whitaker, Mark. *Cosby: His Life and Times*. New York: Simon & Schuster, 2014.

Whitney, Dwight. "The End of a Long Run." *TV Guide*, August 19–25, 1967.

Wild, David. "HBO Triumphs as *Eight is Enough* Meets the Mob." *Rolling Stone*, March 4, 1999.

Williams, Tony. *Larry Cohen: The Radical Allegories of An Independent Filmmaker*. Rev. Ed. Jefferson, North Carolina: McFarland & Co. 2014.

"Windup of *Fugitive* Kept Secret in Angry German to Oct.; Madrid Spills It." *Variety*, September 13, 1967.

Witchell, Alex. "The Son Who Created a Hit, *The Sopranos*." *The New York Times*, June 6, 1999.

Wolfe, Sheila. "Alas, Fugitive Now Runs Backwards." *Chicago Tribune*, April 19, 1967.

Wolk, Josh. "Headline-Making Salary Feuds." *Entertainment Weekly*, March 23, 2007.

Wollenberg, Skip. "*Seinfeld* Finale Advertisers Paid Record Prices." Associated Press, May 14, 1998.

Yahr, Emily. "As *Dexter* Signs Off, A Look Back at Why People Fell For Such a Gruesome Show." *Washington Post*, September 21, 2013.

Young, Susan. "Wrapping Up Series Could Take Another Season or Two . . . or Perhaps More *Lost* Found Again." *Oakland Tribune*, February 6, 2007.

———. "Far from the Mother of all Finales." *Washington Post*, April 2, 2014.

———. "*How I Met Your Mother*: Teaching Life Lessons Until the Very End." *Washington Post*, March 29, 2014.

Zeitchik, Steven. "AMC's High on Originals." *Variety*, May 24, 2007.

Zimmerman, Amy. "The Bloated *HIMYM* Finale Ends Exactly Where We Knew It Would." *The Daily Beast*, March 31, 2014. http://www.thedaily beast.com/articles/ 2014/03/31/the-bloated-himym-finale-ends-exactly -where-we-knew-it-would.html.

Zurawik, David. "A Buried Treasure, A Funereal Pleasure." *Baltimore Sun*, June 3, 2001.

———. "The World According to *Seinfeld*: No Hugging. No Learning. No Aging, Commitment or Obligation." *Baltimore Sun*, May 3, 1998.

Index

THE FAQ SERIES

AC/DC FAQ
by Susan Masino
Backbeat Books
978-1-4803-9450-6 .... $24.99

Armageddon Films FAQ
by Dale Sherman
Applause Books
978-1-61713-119-6 .... $24.99

Lucille Ball FAQ
*by James Sheridan
and Barry Monush*
Applause Books
978-1-61774-082-4 .... $19.99

The Beach Boys FAQ
by Jon Stebbins
Backbeat Books
978-0-87930-987-9 .... $22.99

The Beat Generation FAQ
by Rich Weidman
Backbeat Books
978-1-61713-601-6 .... $19.99

Black Sabbath FAQ
by Martin Popoff
Backbeat Books
978-0-87930-957-2 .... $19.99

Johnny Cash FAQ
by C. Eric Banister
Backbeat Books
978-1-4803-8540-5 .... $24.99

A Chorus Line FAQ
by Tom Rowan
Applause Books
978-1-4803-6754-8 .... $19.99

Eric Clapton FAQ
by David Bowling
Backbeat Books
978-1-61713-454-8 .... $22.99

Doctor Who FAQ
by Dave Thompson
Applause Books
978-1-55783-854-4 .... $22.99

The Doors FAQ
by Rich Weidman
Backbeat Books
978-1-61713-017-5 .... $24.99

Dracula FAQ
by Bruce Scivally
Backbeat Books
978-1-61713-600-9 .... $19.99

The Eagles FAQ
by Andrew Vaughan
Backbeat Books
978-1-4803-8541-2 .... $24.99

Fab Four FAQ
*by Stuart Shea and
Robert Rodriguez*
Hal Leonard Books
978-1-4234-2138-2 .... $19.99

Fab Four FAQ 2.0
by Robert Rodriguez
Backbeat Books
978-0-87930-968-8 .... $19.99

Film Noir FAQ
by David J. Hogan
Applause Books
978-1-55783-855-1 .... $22.99

Football FAQ
by Dave Thompson
Backbeat Books
978-1-4950-0748-4 .... $24.99

Prices, contents, and availability
subject to change without notice.

The Grateful Dead FAQ
by Tony Sclafani
Backbeat Books
978-1-61713-086-1 .... $24.99

Haunted America FAQ
by Dave Thompson
Backbeat Books
978-1-4803-9262-5 .... $19.99

Jimi Hendrix FAQ
by Gary J. Jucha
Backbeat Books
978-1-61713-095-3 .... $22.99

Horror Films FAQ
by John Kenneth Muir
Applause Books
978-1-55783-950-3 .... $22.99

James Bond FAQ
by Tom DeMichael
Applause Books
978-1-55783-856-8 .... $22.99

Stephen King Films FAQ
by Scott Von Doviak
Applause Books
978-1-4803-5551-4 .... $24.99

KISS FAQ
by Dale Sherman
Backbeat Books
978-1-61713-091-5 .... $22.99

Led Zeppelin FAQ
by George Case
Backbeat Books
978-1-61713-025-0 .... $19.99

Modern Sci-Fi Films FAQ
by Tom DeMichael
Applause Books
978-1-4803-5061-8 .... $24.99

Morrissey FAQ
by D. McKinney
Backbeat Books
978-1-4803-9448-3............ $24.99

Nirvana FAQ
by John D. Luerssen
Backbeat Books
978-1-61713-450-0.............. $24.99

Pink Floyd FAQ
by Stuart Shea
Backbeat Books
978-0-87930-950-3............$19.99

Elvis Films FAQ
by Paul Simpson
Applause Books
978-1-55783-858-2............. $24.99

Elvis Music FAQ
by Mike Eder
Backbeat Books
978-1-61713-049-6.............. $24.99

Prog Rock FAQ
by Will Romano
Backbeat Books
978-1-61713-587-3............... $24.99

Pro Wrestling FAQ
by Brian Solomon
Backbeat Books
978-1-61713-599-6.............. $29.99

Rush FAQ
by Max Mobley
Backbeat Books
978-1-61713-451-7................ $24.99

Saturday Night Live FAQ
by Stephen Tropiano
Applause Books
978-1-55783-951-0.............. $24.99

Prices, contents, and availability
subject to change without notice.

Seinfeld FAQ
by Nicholas Nigro
Applause Books
978-1-55783-857-5.............. $24.99

Sherlock Holmes FAQ
by Dave Thompson
Applause Books
978-1-4803-3149-5............. $24.99

The Smiths FAQ
by John D. Luerssen
Backbeat Books
978-1-4803-9449-0........... $24.99

Soccer FAQ
by Dave Thompson
Backbeat Books
978-1-61713-598-9.............. $24.99

The Sound of Music FAQ
by Barry Monush
Applause Books
978-1-4803-6043-3............ $27.99

South Park FAQ
by Dave Thompson
Applause Books
978-1-4803-5064-9........... $24.99

Bruce Springsteen FAQ
by John D. Luerssen
Backbeat Books
978-1-61713-093-9...............$22.99

Star Trek FAQ
(Unofficial and Unauthorized)
by Mark Clark
Applause Books
978-1-55783-792-9...............$19.99

Star Trek FAQ 2.0
(Unofficial and Unauthorized)
by Mark Clark
Applause Books
978-1-55783-793-6...............$22.99

Star Wars FAQ
by Mark Clark
Applause Books
978-1-4803-6018-1.............. $24.99

Quentin Tarantino FAQ
by Dale Sherman
Applause Books
978-1-4803-5588-0 .... $24.99

Three Stooges FAQ
by David J. Hogan
Applause Books
978-1-55783-788-2...............$22.99

The Who FAQ
by Mike Segretto
Backbeat Books
978-1-4803-6103-4 .... $24.99

The Wizard of Oz FAQ
by David J. Hogan
Applause Books
978-1-4803-5062-5............ $24.99

The X-Files FAQ
by John Kenneth Muir
Applause Books
978-1-4803-6974-0........... $24.99

Neil Young FAQ
by Glen Boyd
Backbeat Books
978-1-61713-037-3.................$19.99

HAL•LEONARD®
PERFORMING ARTS
PUBLISHING GROUP

FAQ.halleonardbooks.com

0815